Professional Visual C++ 6 MTS Programming

Dr Richard Grimes

D1606984

Wrox Press Ltd. ®

Professional Visual C++ 6
MTS Programming

Published by Wrox Press Ltd, Arden House, 1102 Warwick Road, Acocks Green,
Birmingham, B27 9BH, UK
Printed in Canada
ISBN 1-861002-3-94

Trademark Acknowledgements

Wrox has endeavored to provide trademark information about all the companies and products mentioned in this book by the appropriate use of capitals. However, Wrox cannot guarantee the accuracy of this information.

Credits

Author
Dr Richard Grimes

Technical Editors
Karli Watson
Daniel Squier

Technical Reviewers
Richard Anderson
Markus Bosshard
Claus Loud
Davide Marcato
Christian Nagel
Christophe Nasarre
Prakash K. Pati
Kenn Scribner
Marc H. Simpkin

Index
Andrew Criddle

Managing Editor
Chris Hindley

Development Editor
John Franklin

Project Manager
Sophie Edwards

Design/Layout
John McNulty
Tom Bartlett
Mark Burdett
William Fallon
Jonathan Jones

Cover
Chris Morris

About the Author

Richard Grimes started writing code in the days of 8-bit computers, and has had a keen interest in the industry ever since. He has been a semiconductor scientist, a computer trainer, and a distributed object developer. Now he spends his time writing, speaking, and advising about COM and ATL. He can be reached via email at mts.dev@grimes.demon.co.uk

Author Acknowledgements

My thanks go to the guys at Wrox who have made sure that the book that you are holding in your hands is a polished product. In particular, I would like to thank Karli Watson for the considerable work that he has done on the book, and John Franklin and Chris Hindley for the smooth management of the project. Finally, I would also like to thank the reviewers who have run a metaphorical fine-toothed comb through the text and code.

Table of Contents

Chapter 3: Programming Issues   75

Chapter 4: Packages and Deployment 121

Chapter 6: Security 193

Chapter 7: MTS Debugging   225

Chapter 8: The Way Forward   259

Introduction

Welcome to *Professional Visual C++ 6 MTS Programming*! This book is an in-depth guide to Microsoft Transaction Server, aimed at the experienced C++ COM programmer. This introduction will explain what is contained in this book, and where this information is located, giving a chapter by chapter account of the contents.

First off, though, we should consider why learning about MTS is useful. Assuming that you are a COM developer, what benefits will MTS give you?

Well, there are problems with plain COM development. Firstly, there is the administration problem – how do you manage all of your objects? If your client uses many objects on many servers across the network it can be quite a task on the client-side to keep a list of which object runs on which machine; and then on the server-side of making sure that each object server is configured to allow the client to access it. Then there are installation problems – you need to package your components so that they can be installed and registered correctly.

The next issue is scalability. COM servers can take advantage of COM's multithreading facilities to give better availability of objects (or better performance on multi processor machines). However, there are limits to how many threads you can use, depending on how many processors your machine has, how fast they are, and the amount of memory installed. There will be a finite number of threads you can create before your machine will crawl to a halt. So, load balancing – a facility where machines are chosen to run an object based on how heavy the machine's load is – is an important issue.

What are the criteria of load? Well, resources like the number of client connections are clearly important, but in addition there are issues such as the amount of memory – the state – that is used by the object. Clearly, the more state an object has, the more memory it will consume and the fewer of such objects that can exist. This doesn't mean that objects shouldn't have state, it just means that you have to be careful about how you use it.

Finally, even if you have solved all these problems, there is the issue of the programming model that you can use. Multithreading in COM gives clear advantages, because you can leave issues like the creation of threads and their scheduling to the operating system and to COM. However, you do have to be disciplined because components that are designed to be used in a multithreaded environment need to protect thread sensitive code and data from multithreaded access. Furthermore, if multiple objects are used on multiple machines there are the issues of propagating errors from each machine, and maintaining the distributed thread and distributed security issue.

Microsoft Transaction Server will provide a solution to most of these problems, and for those that it doesn't solve, writing code to alleviate the problem is made easier. In addition, MTS provides distributed transaction support. Your objects don't have to use transactions, but if they do then MTS will add them to your object without any additional code on your part. For example, you don't have to initialize transactions, and when you create another transactional object from your object the transaction will be passed to it automatically.

The addition of transactions to objects changes the programming model entirely, because objects can no longer be treated as single isolated entities. They become part of a wider picture that includes resources and other (local or remote) objects – a single transaction can apply to all of these. In addition, transactions mean that an action is an all-or-nothing affair, so that when a method fails in one object in the transaction, the entire transaction is aborted, and all the changes already made are rolled back to the state before the transaction started. Because of this behavior the developer needs to identify the resources that are durable and will be rolled back if the transaction aborts, and those that are transient and hence are merely discarded.

In this book I will explore MTS 2.0 and explain how to use it. More importantly, I will explain how to write your applications as transactional applications.

Why did I write this book?

Ever since MTS was first released it has been shrouded in mystique. The documentation largely told you how to write MTS applications but said very little about how MTS worked. Indeed, most of the books that you will find in your local bookstore also follow this lead; you are told a series of rules that you must follow, and then to run an admin tool, and to click here, click there, and... voila! you have a distributed application.

I can't really use a technology unless I fully understand how it works. Magic doesn't exist, everything can be explained (though you may not like or understand the explanation). So I decided that the only way to understand how to use MTS was to determine how it worked. This book is the result of my investigations. I have gone through all the major facilities that MTS gives you, and (as well as I can) I have worked out how it provides those facilities. Where possible I have described how a similar functionality can be provided with plain old COM.

So what are my conclusions about MTS?

Well, COM is essentially a DLL management technology: you say you want to run some code and COM finds and loads the DLL that contains that code. MTS builds upon COM, and has many more facilities to allow you to install and administrate those DLLs on remote machines. This isn't magic, you could have written a similar tool yourself using DCOM.

MTS provides access to distributed transactions. These transactions are actually provided by the Microsoft Distributed Transaction Coordinator (MS DTC), and there's no reason why you should have to use MTS to use them – the MS DTC API is straightforward to use.

MTS will perform role-based access checks on accesses to components or interfaces on those components. Again, this is nothing new, with plain COM you can get hold of an access token for the client that is accessing a component and perform access checks.

So what does MTS provide for you?

If you were to write these facilities yourself then you would have a fair amount of code to write. In addition, the security and transaction enlistment code will have to be called from your components, that is, your component will need to know that it requires (for example) access checks, and explicitly make them. The NT security API isn't particularly straightforward, and is very VB unfriendly.

It is perhaps this last point that is the main driving force behind MTS. MTS is very VB friendly. All of the facilities that it supplies can be accessed using VB. Indeed, in some areas (particularly the MTS catalog API) the bias towards VB seems so extreme as to make programming in C++ at best convoluted.

Does MTS provide anything that is new? Yes, it does. The biggest change is the provision of facilities such as auto-enlistment in transactions and role-base access checks. MTS uses interception on each of your components, and applies your component's runtime requirements in a context object. This means that MTS can apply code to your component *without* it having to initialize any libraries, or explicitly call code. Instead, you configure your component using the MTS Explorer as using particular facilities, and MTS will ensure that when the component is activated it will have those facilities available. The component needs to do little (if anything) to use those facilities.

However, MTS is built over COM, it isn't integrated with it. This means that there is the possibility of the two pulling in opposite directions, so you have to be aware of how MTS applies interception. Occasionally this means that your code needs to be changed to work according to the MTS paradigm, but these changes are usually trivial.

Book Outline

This book attempts to delve as deep as possible into how MTS works, to remove the mystique and myth that surrounds it, and hence allow you to use MTS to the full.

Chapter 1: Interception

This chapter starts by explaining what interception is and what it is used for. Interception requires that MTS produces a wrapper object that looks exactly like your component, and to do so it needs to know what interfaces your component implements. This means that there must be some description of your component – this is held in type information.

There are two ways of recording type information: type libraries and fast format strings. Both have their strengths and shortcomings. This chapter describes both, and explains how and when they are used.

The final part of the chapter has a detailed look at interception and does this by describing several ways that you can do it yourself. It starts by explaining the interception that COM will give you (and always has, even before MTS was released) in the form of interface remoting. It then explains how you can get a more flexible interception through Keith Brown's Universal Delegator, and finally leads on to a description of how MTS applies interception, and the facilities that it provides.

Chapter 2: MTS and COM

MTS is built upon COM, and all MTS components are COM components. This chapter starts with a general overview of COM with respect to the code modules that are used to package COM components and how these modules are loaded. This leads on to a general discussion about process launch permissions and access permissions, to code in processes, and to a discussion on COM surrogates. The chapter then applies this to MTS, using it to explain the MTS surrogate and contrast how this is launched with how COM surrogates are launched.

Although MTS components can be run as COM components, the opposite is not necessarily true. The main reason is that MTS components must be written in such a way as to allow interception to occur. These requirements, and the reasons for them, are explained in full.

The rest of the chapter explains how MTS extends the facilities of COM. It explains how MTS is used to give access to components distributed across the network in such a way as to make the component's location unimportant to both the component client and the client's developer.

MTS components are created with a context object. The remaining part of the chapter explains what MTS context is and the sort of information that this holds, as well as explaining how to obtain this information from the context. Interception requires the use of a context wrapper object, that actually does the interception, and this is important in Just In Time (JIT) activation. JIT activation is a requirement to keep the work performed in one transaction isolated from another transaction, and MTS does this by deactivating components between method calls while keeping the context wrapper object alive.

Finally, the chapter takes a detailed look at how MTS actually activates a component, peeking under the covers to look at the low level objects that are used.

Chapter 3: Programming Issues

To use MTS components effectively you have to change how you program. Part of the reason is that clients must access the context wrapper object, so you must not allow the client to get direct access to the component. This chapter starts by looking into JIT in more depth, explaining how you should program components to use JIT to your advantage.

One of the main reasons that you will want to use MTS is because of the excellent facilities it gives you to write distributed applications. However, distribution comes at a cost, and this chapter explains what these issues are – and how to avoid writing components that suffer performance degradation due to excessive network usage. A further issue is how to marshal data in an efficient manner, and I present some results to guide you in deciding how to design your interfaces.

Transactions are used to group together actions into one unit of work. If a transaction aborts, then all the work performed under it will be undone. One of the reasons for a transaction to abort is if an error occurs, this chapter explains how to manage errors, both in terms of operating system exceptions and error objects. Transactions must be kept isolated from one another – this is one of the so-called ACID criteria. One area that you can break isolation is by using COM callbacks, commonly known as events. Events are useful and therefore there must be some way to allow them to be generated without compromising your transaction. Another area where isolation can be compromised is in how components manage state, and this leads to an explanation of the Shared Property Manager. Both of these issues are investigated in this chapter.

Visual C++ gives you some facilities to develop MTS components, but because MTS components are merely COM components these facilities are fairly thin. Indeed, the ATL MTS Component Object Wizard type removes some important facilities from you. I present a new Object Wizard type that returns those facilities to you. This section of the chapter also describes the little documented (and rarely discussed) Component Registrar (which is *not* the same thing as the ATL Registrar). This appears to have been designed for MTS, but has never been used. I explain how it works and suggest ways that you can use it.

Chapter 4: Packages and Deployment

Packages group together components that will run in the same process. They are defined in the MTS catalog, and this chapter explains how to administer the catalog both through the MTS explorer and by using the catalog API.

It starts by explaining where the catalog is saved, the various pieces of information that it contains, and how these interrelate. It then explains packages in detail, how to create them, and export them so that they can be installed on other machines. Server packages are run using the MTS surrogate, which will appear as mtx.exe in the task manager – with no indication as to the package ID. The chapter explains how to use the MTS API to determine which packages are running.

As I indicated earlier, the MTS Explorer is a facility that allows you to deploy components on remote machines. MTS calls this 'pulling' and 'pushing' components, which essentially means that an administrator, from a single machine, can install components on another machine, or install the necessary marshaling code and registry entries to allow machines to access components remote to them.

Finally, the chapter describes in detail the various components and libraries that are installed on your machine with MTS. Most of these libraries are used to manipulate the catalog, and I explain how to use them. The chapter concludes with an example that allows you to refresh components and to selectively shut down packages.

Chapter 5: Distributed Transaction Coordinator

The MS DTC is the service that creates and manages transactions. It is the MS DTC that distributes transactions across the network and performs 2-phase commit. MTS acts merely as client code that obtains transactions from the MS DTC, auto-enlists components, and initiates committal.

The MS DTC will give access to both its native OLE transactions and to XA transactions. OLE transactions are a COM-based wrapper around transactions, but can't be marshaled. To distribute transactions to another machine they have to be exported so that the other machine can import them. This is carried out using the MS DTC, which records which machines a transaction is exported to (and conversely where it is imported from) to build up a commit tree. This means that when a transaction completes, the commit message can be sent to all machines involved in the transaction, and each machine will inform the appropriate processes that have work performed under the transaction. The chapter explains these objects in detail, and explains how they participate in the workings of a transaction.

These 'appropriate processes' are called resource managers. Resource managers are written specifically to work with the MS DTC, and provide various callback objects that the MS DTC can use to inform them of transaction outcomes. Resource managers maintain durable, transactional state, which means that if transactions commit then they *must* make their work persistent. This chapter explains how this is performed, and how resource managers handle network and machine failures.

MTS provides auto-enlistment, that is, when a component that is configured to use a transaction is activated, MTS ensures that a transaction exists, and that the component is enlisted in it. It does this using code called resource dispensers that run in-process to the component. A resource dispenser actually has two roles. It acts as an in-process 'proxy' to a resource manager (providing a simple API to access the resource manager's facilities under a transaction), and is also used to provide pools of non-transactional resources. Both aspects are covered in this chapter.

Chapter 6: Security

Distributed applications mean that you'll access components on remote machines, which may mean that new processes will be started. This brings up two important considerations: does the caller account have the permission to start the package (process) that contains the component, and does the caller have permission to access the component? One of the most frequent problems encountered when people write straight DCOM–based distributed applications is making sure that the correct security is applied. MTS simplifies security by defining roles, and applying access checks to callers against these roles through interception.

This chapter starts by explaining how security is applied using COM, it explains the meager (and quirky) tools that are supplied with NT. It then explains how to apply access checks programmatically using ATL to make access checks on a per-process, per-component, per-interface and per-method call basis.

The chapter then explains how MTS does the same thing. What is apparent from the discussion is that most of the security administration is performed in the MTS explorer, and to a large extent the component developer doesn't need to write any security code. If the programmer does need to make programmatic access checks then these are done using an MTS provided API. The use of this API is remarkably simple.

This chapter concludes by explaining the security required for MTS administration, principally for importing and exporting components and administrating remote machines.

Chapter 7: MTS Debugging

Distributing components across many machines presents problems to a developer when they come to debug applications. How does the developer gather information from all machines in a manner that makes it useful? This chapter explains the various tools available to debug distributed applications.

MTS will generate connection point based events and the MTS SDK provides a tool called the MTSSpy that can be used to monitor these events on a single machine. I show you the types of events that are generated and how to generate your own custom events.

NT also provides generic tools to monitor processes, one such tool being the performance monitor. However, this doesn't have the facility to monitor MTS – at least it didn't until now. I show you how to write a performance monitor DLL, which uses statistics obtained by catching MTS events.

The event log is another NT tool. This is used by MTS to log information when something exceptional happens (the full list of MTS events is given in Appendix A). This is more useful than many people expect, because it can be used to monitor the NT event log events generated on remote machines. This means that the developer can trace a transaction failure through various components across the network and determine where the failure originated. However, although this facility is offered to the developer it isn't presented in a way that is easily used.

The solution is to use the Visual Studio Analyzer. This tool is provided with the Enterprise Edition of Visual Studio, and takes advantage of special (and largely undocumented) statistics generated by operating system libraries. VSA comes in two parts, the first sits on client machines, gathers these messages, and sends them to the other part: the server that collects and collates these messages. VSA can then be used to filter and analyze this data to determine which components (on which machines) take part in a method call.

Chapter 8: The Way Forward

MTS lays the foundation for COM+. COM+ is the runtime that is present on every Windows 2000 machine and is clearly intended to be the future of COM development. COM+ represents the integration of COM and MTS. Indeed, you no longer have to worry about whether the interface pointer you are about to marshal is a raw interface pointer, or whether you have given MTS the opportunity to apply a context wrapper. You don't have this worry because COM now knows about context, and will automatically determine if an object is a COM+ component. If it is, then it will apply context to it.

Windows 2000 also integrates MSMQ within the operating system, and provides a new event system. Both of these facilities are available to COM+ components. Following the lead of MTS these, and other services of COM+, are applied to components using interception, leaving the component requiring only the bare minimum of code to use them. COM+ also changes the way that components are activated and managed, in that it provides object pooling, synchronization, a new threading model, and compensating resource managers. COM+ has an expanded catalog and new tools to administer it, including new administration objects.

In this chapter I outline all of the new facilities of COM+, and explain how this will change your programming life.

Software Requirements

This book was written using MTS 2.01 supplied on the NT 4 option pack. It was installed on NT4 service pack 5 (where most of the tests were performed) and Windows 98. The code was developed using Visual C++ 6.0 service pack 3 using ATL 3.0. Chapter 7 uses the Visual Studio Analyser provided with the Enterprise Edition of Visual Studio 6.0. The final chapter was written using Release Candidate 2 of Windows 2000 and the beta Platform SDK.

Conventions and Terminology Used

We use a number of different styles of text and layout in the book to help differentiate between the different kinds of information. Here are examples of the styles we use and an explanation of what they mean:

> **These boxes hold important, not-to-be forgotten, mission-critical details that are directly relevant to the surrounding text.**

Background information, asides, references and extra details appear in text like this. For example,

> *'Click' or 'left-click' means click once with the primary mouse button,*
> *'Double-click' means double-click with the primary mouse button*
> *and 'right-click' means click once with the secondary mouse button.*

❑ **Important Words** are in a bold type font.

❑ Words that appear on the screen, such as menu options, are in a similar font to the one used on screen, for example the File | New... menu. The levels of a cascading menu are separated by a pipe character (|).

❑ Keys that you press on the keyboard, like *Ctrl* and *Enter*, are in italics.

❑ All filenames are in this style: mtx.exe.

❑ Function names look like this: sizeof().

❑ Template classes look like this: CComObject<>.

❑ Code that is new, important or relevant to the current discussion will be presented like this:

```
int main()
{
    cout << "Professional Visual C++ 6 MTS Programming";
    return 0;
}
```

❑ Whereas code you've seen before, or which has little to do with the matter at hand, looks like this:

```
void main()
{
    cout << "Professional Visual C++ 6 MTS Programming";
    return 0;
}
```

Tell Us What You Think

We have tried to make this book as accurate and enjoyable for you as possible, but what really matters is what the book actually does for you. Please let us know your views, whether positive or negative, either by returning the reply card in the back of the book or by contacting us at Wrox Press at feedback@wrox.com.

Source Code and Keeping Up-to-date

We try to keep the prices of our books reasonable, and so to replace an accompanying disc we make the source code for the book available on our web site at http://www.wrox.com. One-time registration there entitles you to code downloads, errata sheets, and lifetime support for all Wrox Press titles.

If you don't have access to the Internet, we can provide a disk for a nominal fee to cover postage and packing.

Errata & Updates

We've made every effort to make sure there are no errors in the text or the code. However, to err is human and as such we recognize the need to keep you, the reader, informed of any mistakes as they're spotted and corrected.

While you're visiting our web site, please make use of our errata page, which is dedicated to fixing any small errors in the book, or offering new ways around a problem and its solution. Errata sheets are available for all our books – please download them, or take part in the continuous improvement of our tutorials and upload a 'fix' or a pointer to the solution.

For those without access to the Net, we'll gladly send errata sheets by return of mail if you send a letter to:

Wrox Press Inc.,   Wrox Press Ltd,
29 South LaSalle Street,   Arden House,
Suite 520,   1102 Warwick Road,
Chicago,   Acock's Green,
IL 60603   Birmingham B27 6BH
USA   UK

1

Interception

Introduction

The **Component Object Model** (**COM**) allows you to implement components that have known **interfaces** of methods. This enforces **interface programming** on client programmers, in that they can only access components through well-defined interfaces. It also enforces this on server programmers, since they know that the only code exposed to clients will be through these interfaces.

There are several advantages to this. Being forced to program using interfaces is a good thing because it separates implementation from interface. The interfaces of a component define its behavior, so a client can use a component as a 'black box' without regard to how its behavior is implemented. Interfaces are *immutable*, that is, once they are defined they cannot change. This leads to predictability in the relationship between a client and a component – once a client has the interface to a component, it can make assumptions regarding what that component can do.

One such user is the COM runtime, which can assume that a client only accesses the component through its interfaces. Since these interfaces are usually registered, COM can get between the client and the component, a process called **interception**. COM uses interception in several ways. For example, if the component lives in a different process (or on a different machine) to the client code that calls it, COM will ensure that the calls are transmitted (or **marshaled**) to the component. This intervention by COM allows client programmers to code as if the component is always implemented within the same process, a facility called **location transparency**. Interception can also be used to provide correct **synchronization**, that is, to ensure that code written for access by a single thread will only ever be accessed by single thread.

Another advantage of interface programming is that since COM interfaces are a binary standard, any language willing to comply with this standard can use or write COM components. A Visual Basic client can use a COM component written with Java because the implementation and interfaces are separated. In implementation terms, the component's interface allows the VB runtime to talk to the Java Virtual Machine, even though neither knows about the other's existence. In this way COM interfaces are the *lingua franca* of component-based computer software.

In this chapter I will explain more fully some of the terms I have introduced above, and describe how they relate to MTS. In addition, I will look more closely into interception and show several ways of achieving it. To make interception as generic as possible requires some knowledge of the interfaces that a component implements, so I will also describe how interfaces can be described.

COM and MTS

COM is implemented on every 32-bit Windows machine. It is used by many user applications as well as the operating system. COM is therefore an important technology, and will remain so as long as Windows is available. Anyone who shuts their eyes to COM is denying themselves a huge repository of ready-made components just waiting to be used.

Interface Programming

Possibly the most important interface is IUnknown. A client can use this to request other interfaces and correctly manage reference counts. Reference counts allow interfaces to ensure that resources are released when they are no longer required, including the memory taken up by the component. Clients can ask for an interface by calling IUnknown::QueryInterface() and passing the interface identifier (IID). The IID is the real name of an interface, and is language independent, being a 128-bit unique integer. 128-bit identifiers are used for other COM entities, like classes and applications.

Strictly speaking, any component that implements the IUnknown interface is a COM component. However, for a component to be *useful*, it must implement at least one other interface.

Interfaces are immutable, that is once they have been defined they cannot be changed. The server *must* implement the methods on the interface and the client *knows* that these methods will be implemented. Interfaces consist of function pointers, and if the rules of COM did not guarantee the implementation of an interface method, clients would have to check interface method pointers for validity or run the risk of calling methods through NULL pointers.

Interfaces represent behavior, and when correctly written a single interface will represent just one behavior. A component with more than one behavior can implement more than one interface, and when a client requests a component it specifies which interface (behavior) it needs. Although **ODL** (**Object Definition Language**, used to define automation object hierarchies) allows you to specify the interfaces that a component implements, you should not regard this as absolute. The only way to determine whether a component implements an interface is to ask for it.

The server can implement components in any way it likes. Popular languages include C++, VB and Microsoft Java (where the Microsoft virtual machine will provide the COM interfaces based on a Java object's Java interfaces – another form of interception). This means that the client code and component code can be written in totally different languages. Since the client only accesses the component through an interface, it makes no assumptions about the component's implementation. Thus, interface programming brings enormous benefits to both clients and components.

COM and Resources

Interface programming may be wonderful, but there are some problems that it cannot solve, so client and server programmers do have to follow some guidelines. The first is resource management. COM components consume resources. They will either take up space in your process, or will live in another process that will use up memory (which can be on your machine or another). Because of this, you have to tell a component when it is no longer needed, so that it can free up the resources it's been using. Remember, COM doesn't know when you have finished with a component, so it can't do this automatically. Other technologies (like Java) use garbage collection techniques, which, although they are generally quite successful, are never perfect. The current version of COM (and COM+) takes the safe option, and puts the onus on the developer to decide when they have finished with a component.

In addition, when data is passed between the client and component there are strict rules about who should allocate memory and who should release that memory. Because different languages have different ways of managing memory, COM defines a universal memory allocator that can be used.

COM and Threading

32-bit COM runs on multi-threaded operating systems, so COM also allows multi-threading. In fact COM goes a bit further – it allows components that don't care about which thread accesses them (or components that protect thread-sensitive code), to run in a multi-threaded environment. For code that *must* be accessed by the same thread, COM provides another environment, and will even provide the infrastructure to ensure that only one thread ever touches the component's code. These environments are called **apartments**, and these two types are called **multi-threaded apartment** (**MTA**) and **single-threaded apartment** (**STA**) respectively.

A COM component knows whether it is safe to run in an MTA or STA, and is registered as running in a particular apartment type (or both). COM will ensure that when a component is activated it is run in the right type of apartment. Component activation will never fail due to the apartment type of the component, because COM will create the apartment for a component if necessary. All calls across an apartment boundary require **marshaling**. This ensures that code is called on a component according to its threading requirements. If the caller has different threading requirements, then COM will ensure that the change is applied automatically. COM provides the marshaling layer using interception, and this is completely transparent to both the calling code and the component.

This is illustrated in the following diagram, which uses the standard COM notation for components and interfaces:

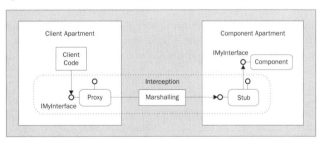

The component implements the `IMyInterface` interface, but has different threading requirements to the calling code. It therefore lives in a different apartment. COM allows the client to access the component through marshaling – the client gets a **proxy** object, which looks exactly like the component but lives in the same apartment as the calling code. This object knows how to make calls across apartments, which it will do to talk to another object (called a **stub**), which will call the component as if it were the original caller.

COM automatically loads these two objects, the proxy and stub, into the client and component apartments respectively. The client code sees a component just like the one it wants to access. This is interception – the proxy intercepts the client's calls and ensures that they are passed to the component.

COM and Context

Interception like that discussed above is not restricted to enforcing threading requirements. An interceptor gets between the client and component, which means that it can perform other work. For example, it can perform checks such as determining who is permitted to access a component, by testing the ID of callers and rejecting them if they are not authorized. Such code is provided by 'classic COM' when you make calls across process boundaries on an NT machine, but they usually appear to the developer when the processes are on different machines. This is because, without intervention, the security of the client and server will be different, so the security check fails.

Interception can also be used to check whether a component requires a transaction. In other words, the work being carried out by the component should complete in its entirety or not at all (as I'll explain later). In this case, the interceptor can check to see if the calling code is already running in a transaction, in which case it can enlist the component in it. Synchronization, security and transactions are all provided for you by MTS through interception. COM+ (only available on Windows 2000) provides more facilities, as you will see in the final chapter of this book.

The requirements of a component and the environment of the client are both **context**s. For plain COM, a context will simply equate to the apartment requirements, but for MTS it will also include the security and transaction requirements. The required context for a component must be stored somewhere, so that COM can read it before creating the component. This is necessary in order to compare this context with that of the calling code, and determine if a new context should be created for the component. For plain COM this information is stored in the registry (specifically the ThreadingModel registry entry for a component). For MTS (and COM+) the context requirements are stored in the **catalog**.

Entries are typically added to the catalog by an administrator using a tool called the MTS Explorer, but it is possible to change context requirements using code. However, context requirements are just that – a component runs in a specific context, and if this context is not available then the component won't run. The administrator should therefore know about a component's requirements. To alleviate this problem, the developer can configure the catalog to have the component's context requirement and **export** it, so that the administrator can **import** this rather than having to perform the actual configuration. This is always the safest option. We'll return to both the context and the catalog many times in this book.

Finally, it's important to point out that some components may not care about the context that they run in. These are known as context-neutral components, and they typically achieve this neutrality by using an object called the **free-threaded marshaler** (FTM). The name suggests that FTM is involved with apartment membership. Indeed, plain COM components can use it to allow any other code in the same process to access them without marshaling, regardless of the apartment they are in. However, the FTM goes further than this. A component that uses the FTM will be run in the context of the calling code (whatever that context is) as long as the calling code is in the same process.

COM and Component Activation

COM is essentially a DLL maintenance facility. When COM is asked to activate a component, it will locate the DLL that implements the component, load it, and ask the DLL to create an instance. COM will check the apartment of the caller and the apartment requirements of the component, and (if necessary) will create an apartment for the component. Some components may need to be run in an apartment in another process to the calling code (again, this is determined by a registry value). The marshaling layer will therefore need to perform **inter-process calls** so that code in one process can be accessed by code in another. Since this is applied through interception, neither the client code nor the component knows that this implementation is being used.

Extending this a step further, the component can be on a different machine to the client. In this case **remote procedure calls** (**RPC**) are made by the marshaling layer and applied by interception. Whatever distance there is between the client and component, the proxy will make the client code think that the component is in its apartment. Likewise, the stub object will make the component think that the client is in its apartment. As already mentioned, this is called location transparency.

Where does MTS fit in?

COM provides many facilities to activate components, but to use these facilities, components must be registered with the systems on which they will be run. The code used for interception must be registered on both the client and server machines. Furthermore, you have to deploy the components on the various machines that will run them, that is, physically copy their DLLs to the machines where they will run. MTS solves these problems, because you can remotely administer components as long as MTS is installed on the remote machine. In addition, MTS gives you better context management than plain COM, including both transaction and security in the context as well as synchronization.

This offers the possibility of developing distributed applications, where multiple components are run on several machines across the network. A scenario such as this is usually called a 3-tier application. The first tier is client code that uses COM to call business objects, which form the middle tier. Business objects implement interfaces that the client knows about, and also implement business logic, usually to access some data source (the third tier). It makes sense to have the business objects as close to the data as possible, and since data sources are typically large enterprise-level servers, the business objects will usually be on a different machine to the client.

MTS's administration and deployment facilities make managing such a distributed application far simpler than if you were to do it by hand, as well as providing other benefits. MTS allows components to enlist in distributed transactions. Data sources (for example SQL Server or Oracle) typically perform their work under a transaction, and if you are using several data sources when performing a task, then you need to make sure that the same transaction is used by all of them. Then, if an error occurs in one component, all the data sources will be informed to **roll back** the work they have done. Without a transaction, you would have to devise a list of all of the work carried out across the distributed application. You would need to find some way of indicating that this work needed to be undone, and all the components that perform the work would require code to undo it. Transactions, and the support for them that exists in applications like SQL Server, do all this work for you.

MTS applies all these facilities – transactions, synchronization and security – to components via interception. In this way, the component and client do not have to apply them. For example, when the component is configured in the catalog to have a particular transaction requirement if it is running, it can assume that its transaction requirement will have been fulfilled by MTS.

15

For MTS to intercept calls to your components, it needs a description of the interface being called (so that it can provide a copy for the client). COM provides a couple of ways to do this, as explained in the next section.

Interface Descriptions

Interception works because the interceptor looks like the component being accessed. The client code therefore calls the interceptor, thinking that it is the component it wants. The interceptor can perform its work when the client makes an interface call, and the client will be none the wiser. This implies that the interceptor knows about the interfaces it is to implement – there must therefore be some mechanism that describes interfaces.

Developers define interfaces using **Interface Definition Language** (**IDL**), based on **DCE RPC** (**Distributed Computing Environment RPC**) **IDL**. IDL uses a C-like syntax to describe the methods on an interface and their associated parameters. Additional information about interfaces and their methods and parameters is applied using IDL **attributes**. These are identified by square brackets, and are particularly important in supplying marshaling information, which is used when generating the code for proxy and stub objects.

> COM IDL & Interface Design *by Al Major (ISBN 1-861002-25-4) contains a thorough description of IDL, and is a handy resource for interface developers.*

IDL *completely* describes an interface, but there is only one facility written to interpret IDL – the **Microsoft IDL compiler** (**MIDL**). MIDL uses IDL to generate the code for the proxy and stub objects, but is not a runtime tool – proxy and stub objects don't call MIDL to determine what an interface looks like (in any case IDL files can be quite big). Instead, there are two other compiled interface description resources, type libraries and fast format strings. Both are generated by MIDL, which will perform all the parsing and error checking of user-supplied IDL.

Type Library Type Information

Interfaces can be described in two parts of an IDL file, either inside or outside the `library` section (which became part of IDL when Microsoft merged ODL with IDL). If an interface is declared outside the `library` section, then MIDL will generate proxy-stub code. However, if it is declared inside the `library` section (or is declared outside the `library` section but referenced within it), then the MIDL compiler will create a **type library**, a binary file containing type information. Type libraries can be distributed as stand alone files – typically with the extension `.tlb`, `.oca` or `.olb` – or can be bound into executable files as resources. (Visual Basic and the Visual C++ ATL AppWizard use the latter option.)

Type information is used for two things: syntax checking and marshaling. Tools like the VB IDE use type information to determine what components (described in the type library as **coclasses**) servers can instantiate, and what interfaces (and associated methods) are available on those coclasses. In addition, you can describe constants, global methods and structures. By describing these in type libraries, the VB IDE can check *as you type* that you are using the correct syntax, and can even offer you options of what methods and properties components can support.

Type information describes interfaces and their parameters, but doesn't cover all the attributes that you can use in IDL, nor all of the data types possible. Interfaces that do are called **oleautomation compatible**, because they use the `[oleautomation]` attribute (either explicitly, or implicitly when they use the `[dual]` attribute). The data types that can be used on oleautomation interfaces are those that can be placed in a `VARIANT` data type. This data type is used to pass method parameters through `IDispatch::Invoke()` and allows scripting languages to call them.

If your interface does use this restricted set of data types and attributes, then a marshaler can read the type library for the interface description and know exactly what data is being passed when a method is called. With this knowledge, the marshaler can determine what data needs to be transmitted to the component apartment. Such a marshaler is called the **type library marshaler** or (as it is available on all Windows machines) the **Universal Marshaler** (**UM**). Because it is used mainly with automation interfaces it is sometimes known as the **Automation Marshaler**. However, any interface (including those that are not derived from `IDispatch`) can use it.

Type Library Marshaling

If your interface can use type information for marshaling (it has the `[oleautomation]` or `[dual]` attributes), then the proxy and stub objects that will be used in the client and component apartments will use the UM. The interface must be registered to use an object called `PSOAInterface` with a CLSID of `{00020424-0000-0000-C000-000000000046}`. It must also indicate a registered type library that describes the interface.

For example, here are the registry entries for an interface called `IMyInterface`:

```
[HKEY_CLASSES_ROOT\Interface\{FC9D9F82-FF35-11D2-8828-0060973044A8}]
@-"IMyInterface"

[HKEY_CLASSES_ROOT\Interface\{FC9D9F82-FF35-11D2-8828-
0060973044A8}\ProxyStubClsid32]
@="{00020424-0000-0000-C000-000000000046}"

[HKEY_CLASSES_ROOT\Interface\{FC9D9F82-FF35-11D2-8828-0060973044A8}\TypeLib]
@="{C6832400-FF35-11D2-8828-0060973044A8}"
"Version"="1.0"
```

This indicates that any cross-apartment calls made on the `IMyInterface` interface will be marshaled using the Universal Marshaler. This uses information in the type library with the LIBID and version mentioned in the `TypeLib` key. Note that the version is a string of the form `%x.%x` — that is, the numbers are in *hex* (you usually don't see this because the major and minor versions are usually less than `0xA`).

Because the `TypeLib` key is added when the type library is registered, you have to be wary if you decide to use a proxy-stub with an ATL server. The reason for this is that the ATL-generated code will automatically register the type library and add this key. If you subsequently register a proxy-stub, the `ProxyStubClsid32` will be replaced, but the `TypeLib` key will remain. If you try to unregister the proxy-stub using the `regsvr32` utility, the operation will fail. The proxy-stub unregistration code will only remove registry entries originally written by the proxy-stub's registration code. If you decide to use proxy-stubs to marshal your interfaces, make sure that the module's type library is not registered.

Binding Type Libraries as Process Resources

Binding a type library into an executable file is a good idea in many cases, as the type information is held with the code that it describes. If you are using the component with the VB IDE this makes sense, because the information that describes the server then sits with the server. In addition, if the component is used across apartment boundaries and type library marshaling is used, then it makes sense for the type information used by the stub to be bound to the server.

However, there are cases where binding a type library to a server is *not* a good idea. If your component doesn't use type library marshaling, and it doesn't have dual or dispinterfaces implemented through a type library, then adding type information merely increases the size of the server. In addition, this demonstrates to the public *exactly* how to call your interfaces. ODL helps a bit by providing the [hidden] attribute, which indicates that type library browsers (like the one present in the VB IDE) do not show hidden items. However, this depends on the type library browser – OLEView, for example, will show everything in a type library. You may decide to use IDL to define an interface that only clients written by you can call (many of the Microsoft tools have such undocumented interfaces), so you must avoid providing type information for those interfaces.

Unfortunately, the ATL AppWizard in VC6 will always bind the type library to your server. If this isn't what you want then you have to remove the library by hand.

If your components are accessed remotely and do use type library marshaling, you will have to distribute the type information for the component's interfaces. In this case it makes more sense to distribute the type library to the remote client rather than the server with the bound-in type library. If you decide to distribute the type library then you must make sure it's registered – you have to ship the code to do this. When a type library is bound to a server, the server will typically contain this registration code, because COM servers should be self-registering. Clearly any deployment strategy you use should take these points into account.

Obtaining and registering a bound type library is straightforward enough (as will be explained later). However, there are some tools available to do it for you. The most popular is called RegTlib.exe and is distributed with Microsoft Office, but you can't guarantee that it will be available on every machine. When you add a DLL that has a bound type library to an MTS package, MTS will register the type library.

Obtaining Type Information

If a component is described by type information, getting hold of it is quite easy. There are essentially three ways to do this: you can ask a running component if it has type information; you can look in the resources of a server module; or you can look in the registry. If a component has the IDispatch interface then you can simply call IDispatch::GetTypeInfoCount() to see if type info is available (note: this specifies if type information is *available*, not *how much* type information is available). If this method returns 1 then you can call IDispatch::GetTypeInfo() to get an ITypeInfo interface for this implementation of IDispatch.

ITypeInfo has many methods that you can call to get a description of an entire interface. To get general information you can call GetDocumentation() and GetTypeAttr(). The first of these is used to obtain the human readable name and help string for the interface, the second gets you a pointer to a TYPEATTR structure containing information about the number of methods and properties and the IID of the interface. For every method you can call GetFuncDesc() (passing a number from zero up to, but not including, the total number of methods given in TYPEATTR) to get a FUNCDESC structure. Similarly, you can call GetVarDesc() to get a VARDESC structure for a property. Both of these structures have a memid member. This identifies the item you can pass to GetNames() to get an array of strings, which will include the name of the item (the first string in the array) and the parameters of the method or property. FUNCDESC contains both an array of ELEMDESC structures that describes the type of each parameter of the method, and another ELEMDESC member that describes the return type of the method. Similarly, VARDESC has a single ELEMDESC member that gives the type of the property.

So as you can see, the ITypeInfo interface gives you complete information about the members of an interface and their parameters. As I mentioned earlier, the interface obtained through IDispatch::GetTypeInfo() is applicable to one interface only. However, you can call ITypeInfo::GetContainingTypeLib() to get the ITypeLib interface on the type library, from which this type information is obtained. The type library may have type information for more than one interface – the number is obtained through ITypeLib::GetTypeInfoCount(). Individual type information can be obtained by calling GetTypeInfo().

Note that you can have type information in a type library for a coclass, but this lists only the interfaces mentioned in the coclass entry of the library statement. If your coclass implements other interfaces (which are not mentioned in the coclass entry) then these won't appear in the type information of the coclass – even if they have type information in the type library.

Type libraries can be bound into a module with the resource type TYPELIB, and a module can have more than one type library resource. To obtain this resource you can use the API function LoadTypeLibEx(), where the first parameter is the name of the file containing the resource, the second parameter is an enumeration that specifies whether you just want to load the type library (REGKIND_NONE) or register it as well (REGKIND_REGISTER), and the final parameter is an ITypeLib [out] parameter used to return the type library. If the module has more than one type library resource, the resource ID can be appended to the name of the module with a backslash:

```
ITypeLib* pTypeLib;
// get the resource with the ID of 2
LoadTypeLibEx(L"c:\\Test\\Test.dll\\2", REGKIND_NONE, &pTypeLib);
```

To get the resource IDs of the type library resources you can call EnumResourceNames(). This API will enumerate all the resources of a specific type in a module, by calling a callback function, which you implement. You pass the module handle, the type of resource and a function pointer to this method, as well as a user-defined LPARAM parameter. For each resource of the specified type, EnumResourceNames() calls the callback function, passing the resource identifier and the user-defined LPARAM parameter. When all of the resources have been enumerated, EnumResourceNames() will return, so typically your callback function will record the resources in a way that the calling code can use it.

To obtain all the type library resources in a module, you use "TYPELIB" as the resource type. For example, the following code will print out the IDs (or names) of TYPELIB resources for the module whose name is passed in strModule:

```
typedef std::vector<std::basic_string<TCHAR> > StrVector;

void PrintModuleTypeLibResources(LPCTSTR strModule)
{
    StrVector vec;
    HMODULE hModule;
    hModule = LoadLibrary(strModule);
    if (hModule)
    {
        EnumResourceNames(hModule, _T("TYPELIB"), CallbackResName,
            reinterpret_cast<LPARAM>(&vec));
        StrVector::iterator it;
        for (it = vec.begin(); it < vec.end(); it++)
            _tprintf(_T("%s\n"), (*it).c_str());
        FreeLibrary(hModule);
    }
}
```

The function to be called, CallbackResName(), is as follows:

```
BOOL CALLBACK CallbackResName(HINSTANCE, LPCTSTR, LPTSTR lpszName, LONG lParam)
{
    StrVector* pvec = reinterpret_cast<StrVector*>(lParam);
    if (HIWORD(lpszName) == 0)
    {
        TCHAR str[20];
        wsprintf(str, _T("%ld"), LOWORD(lpszName));
        pvec->push_back(str);
    }
    else
    {
        pvec->push_back(lpszName);
    }
    return TRUE;
}
```

Here the lpszName will either be a number (if the top 16-bits contain zero) or a string. The calling code passes the pointer to an STL vector of strings in the LPARAM parameter of EnumResourceNames(), which is passed to the callback function. This can then format the resource names and put them in the vector, so that PrintModuleTypeLibResources() can print them out.

Type Libraries and Registration

When you register a type library, COM will read all the interfaces described, and any that use the [oleautomation] or [dual] attributes, will be registered as using the Universal Marshaler.

Although type libraries have information about coclasses, this data is *not* added to the registry when the type library is registered. Tools like the ATL AppWizard will perform a separate registration step to register all the coclasses in the server. It will also add a key called `TypeLib` to the CLSID key of the coclass. The default value of this key is the LIBID of the type library. However, in addition to the LIBID, an application will need to have the version of the type library that describes the coclass. If you look in the registry you will see that most classes with a `TypeLib` key also have a `Version` key (note this is a *key* under the CLSID key of the coclass, rather than a value) that gives the type library version. Alas, the ATL AppWizard will not do this for you, so you have to edit the `.rgs` file by hand, for example:

```
NoRemove CLSID
{
    ForceRemove {CECB698D-C8FF-11D2-891F-00104BDC361E} = s 'MyObj'
    {
        ProgID = s 'Objects.MyObj.1'
        VersionIndependentProgID = s 'Objects.MyObj'
        ForceRemove 'Programmable'
        LocalServer32 = s '%MODULE%'
        val AppID = s '{CECB6981-C8FF-11D2-891F-00104BDC361E}'
        'TypeLib' = s '{CECB6980-C8FF-11D2-891F-00104BDC361E}'
        Version = s '1.0'
    }
}
```

Once you have the LIBID and version you can load the type library using:

```
LoadRegTypeLib(REFGUID rguid, WORD wVerMajor, WORD wVerMinor,
               LCID lcid, ITypeLib** pptlib);
```

but since type libraries contain information in strings, type libraries are localized, so you also need to pass a locale ID (`LCID`). If you want to load the actual registered type library file (whether it is a `.dll`, `.exe`, `.ocx`, `.oca` or `.tlb`) you can use the registry API and negotiate to the LIBID, version, locale ID, and system type (Win32, Win16 or the Mac, enumerated in `SYSKIND`) and finally get the path to the type library file. The automation API has a function, `QueryPathOfRegTypeLib()`, which will return this information, but only for the system type of the current machine.

The point of this discussion is to demonstrate that, if you have a file with a bound type library (or a separate type library file), you can get detailed information about all the coclasses in the server, the interfaces implemented on the server and the methods on those interfaces, and then use this information to create a proxy object.

Fast Format Strings

Type libraries are mainly used for OLE Automation, so that applications that use VBA (like the Microsoft Office applications, and the VB IDE) can get information about the coclasses and interfaces implemented in a code module. VB uses this information to check syntax in VBA code, and is therefore primarily concerned with the correct spellings of methods and coclasses. VB is not as concerned about the number, type and position of the parameters in a method (this is not too important in OLE Automation, because if a parameter's name is known then the component can match values to parameters, and if the type is wrong then the component can *coerce* it to the correct type).

In essence, the marshaler in an automation client just packages up as much information as it can obtain and passes this to the component, which then has the responsibility of deciphering it. OLE automation can do this because automation components use dispinterfaces – they implement just the `IDispatch` interface. The client calls `IDispatch::Invoke()` and passes information about the method it wants to call (and its parameters) in the parameters of `Invoke()`.

Clients that use interfaces other than dispinterfaces are not concerned with names. They are more concerned with the position of a method in an interface, and with the positions and types of the method's parameters. Type libraries do provide this (which is why oleautomation interfaces can be type library marshaled), but there is one big problem – type libraries can only contain information about a restricted range of data types and marshaling attributes.

To get round this, another sort of type information can be generated – **fast format strings**. These are undocumented, but as you'll see, with a bit of hunting you can get a good idea of what they represent. The MIDL compiler will add tables of fast format strings to the `_p.c` file it generates, and these will be added to the proxy-stub DLLs. Every DLL that has tables of fast format strings will export a function giving access to them, and to other information required by the marshaler – once you have navigated through all the various nested structures! The data in these tables allows you to determine the number of methods in an interface, their parameters, the types of those parameters, and any attributes that were applied to them.

MIDL and the /Oicf Switch

MIDL generated proxy-stub DLLs provide a much richer source of information if the proxy code is generated using the `/Oicf` MIDL flag. NT 3.51 introduced a new facility called the **marshaling interpreter**. This facility uses information added to proxies' DLLs when the IDL is compiled with the `/Oic` switch. NT4 supplies a richer range of features, and these can be added to the proxy DLL by compiling the IDL with `/Oicf`.

These proxies are poorly documented in the Platform SDK, and some headers refer to them as 'stubless proxies'. (For example, see the `USE_STUBLESS_PROXY` symbol referred to in `rpcproxy.h`, and `_MIDL_STUBLESS_PROXY_INFO` struct in `rpcndr.h`.) A more appropriate name is 'interpreted proxies', because they use standard marshaling – a stub object *will* be used, but MIDL will generate little code for the proxy or stub.

> *The platform SDK library also uses the term 'codeless proxies', a better description of their behavior than 'stubless proxies', since the code is provided by the system and not your DLL.*

Note that a proxy-stub is used to marshal an interface, which is not component-specific. This means that a proxy-stub file doesn't contain any information about components, just interfaces. This point will become significant in later chapters when the MTS Explorer is described, because the only way that the Explorer can determine the interfaces implemented by a component is through a type library.

Also note that the marshaling interpreter is not the same as the Universal Marshaler. The UM is a generic marshaler *object*, like the marshaler object that COM creates from your proxy-stub DLL. The marshaling interpreter, on the other hand, is called by your proxy object and (as it turns out) the Universal Marshaler. The UM creates an interpreted marshaler object from type information by calling the undocumented `CreateProxyFromTypeInfo()` function, which is exported from `rpcrt4.dll`:

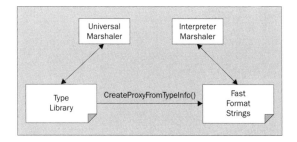

Interpreted proxies are essentially an optimization (which is why they are enabled with an /O switch), because you use system-provided code to marshal the interface. This means that proxy-stub files will be smaller and quicker to load. However, since type library marshaling ultimately uses the interpreted marshaler, once we account for the initial cost of loading the type library and converting type information to fast format strings, the performance of the two marshaling techniques works out roughly the same.

In the following table, I have used a high performance counter to time calls to a component. The 'time to load proxy' column shows how long it takes to perform a cross-apartment query for an interface on a proxy for the first time. This is an indication of any per-interface initialization that is occurring. The numbers in the table are proportions (in %) of the time taken to load the /Os proxy (non-interpreted marshaling). I actually took the average of 100 proxy loads, and ignored the first load (which included the time taken to load any EXEs or DLLs used by the server).

The 'time to call methods' column shows the time taken to make a call to the component (a simple call, passing a long to the component, which then returns it). Again the test was performed 100 times to get an average, and each value in the table is the percentage of the time it took the /Os proxy to make the call.

The results are given for three types of marshaling: type library marshaling, fast format strings (using the proxy generated with /Oicf), and non-interpreted marshaling (/Os) – which I call 'full code'.

Marshaling mechanism	Time to load proxy	Time to call methods
Type library	865	120
Fast format strings	98.8	108
Full code	100	100

The most striking thing is that the proxy takes almost 9 times longer to load using type library marshaling than with the other two mechanisms. This represents the time it has taken for the type library to be converted to fast format strings. The other two take about the same time to load the proxy. The other key thing to note is that the three mechanisms take almost the same amount of time to make the same method call.

Obtaining Fast Format Strings

The fast format strings are primarily used by the marshaling interpreter, but MIDL provides a back door for other code to read interface information. When you compile IDL, MIDL will add the following macros to the dlldata.c file:

```
EXTERN_PROXY_FILE(MyObjectIDL)

PROXYFILE_LIST_START
    REFERENCE_PROXY_FILE(MyObjectIDL),
PROXYFILE_LIST_END

DLLDATA_ROUTINES(aProxyFileList, GET_DLL_CLSID)
```

Note that this occurs whether you use /Oicf or /Os (the switch used to create non-interpreted code) so both types of proxies will contain fast format strings. In this example MyObjectIDL is the name of the IDL file used to generate this file. However, the entries in this table are *case sensitive*, and unfortunately MIDL does not overwrite dlldata.c between invocations (unlike the other files that it generates). Therefore, if you run MIDL twice like this:

```
MIDL MyObjectIDL.idl
MIDL mYoBJECTidl.idl
```

then *two* entries will appear in the proxy file list in dlldata.c, one for MyObjectIDL and another for mYoBJECTidl. However, since MIDL will recreate the other marshaling files (specifically the .h and _p.c files) they will only have code from the second invocation of MIDL. There will therefore be code missing, and your proxy-stub project will not compile. I guess this 'facility' exists to allow you to build proxy-stubs from multiple IDL files and combine them into one DLL, but the case sensitive aspect appears to be a bug.

EXTERN_PROXY_FILE() declares an extern variable of the ProxyFileInfo structure, and the PROXYFILE_LIST map defines an array of pointers to instances of this structure, declared in the _p.c file (also generated by MIDL). DLLDATA_ROUTINES() declares the DLL entry points:

Function	Ordinal
DllGetClassObject	1
DllCanUnloadNow	2
GetProxyDllInfo	3
DllRegisterServer	4
DllUnregisterServer	5

Most of these are familiar – they are just the usual exports for a COM in-proc server. However, notice the function `GetProxyDllInfo()`. This is defined in `rpcproxy.h`:

```
#define DLLDATA_GETPROXYDLLINFO(pPFList,pClsid) \
void RPC_ENTRY GetProxyDllInfo(const ProxyFileInfo*** pInfo, \
                               const CLSID** pId) \
   { \
      *pInfo = pPFList; \
      *pId   = pClsid;  \
   };
```

`pPFList` is the array of `ProxyFileInfo` structures defined in the proxy file list, and `pClsid` is by default the IID of the *first* entry in this array.

The `ProxyFileInfo` structure is interesting – here is the definition in `rpcproxy.h`:

```
typedef struct tagProxyFileInfo
{
    const PCInterfaceProxyVtblList* pProxyVtblList;
    const PCInterfaceStubVtblList*  pStubVtblList;
    const PCInterfaceName*          pNamesArray;
    const IID**                     pDelegatedIIDs;
    const PIIDLookup                pIIDLookupRtn;
    unsigned short                  TableSize;
    unsigned short                  TableVersion;
    const IID**                     pAsyncIIDLookup;
    unsigned long                   Filler2;
    unsigned long                   Filler3;
    unsigned long                   Filler4;
} ProxyFileInfo;
```

The first two members are arrays, which give information about the vtables for the proxy and stub objects for all the COM interfaces marshaled by this DLL. `TableSize` indicates the number of interfaces described by the structure. It also defines the size of `pNamesArray`, a pointer to an array of LPCSTR strings (yes, there is no UNICODE name).

> *Note that the other arrays use a value of zero in the last item to indicate the end of the array, rather than relying on* `TableSize`.

`pDelegatedIIDs` is used to identify dual interfaces, as it gives an alternative IID that can be used to call the interface (remember that dual interfaces suffer from this schizophrenia). `pIIDLookupRtn` is a pointer to a function that returns the index of an interface in the proxy vtable list.

Finally, `pAsyncIIDLookup` is a feature used only in Windows 2000, since it lists all the asynchronous interfaces associated with the other interfaces mentioned in the arrays. If an interface cannot be called asynchronously, then a value of 0 is used. If it can (it has the `[async_uuid()]` attribute) then the IID of its asynchronous version is given. The async interface also has an entry, which has a value of `-1`.

The pProxyVtblList and pStubVtblList tables of proxy and stub interface vtables contain the following structures:

```
typedef struct tagCInterfaceProxyHeader
{
#ifdef USE_STUBLESS_PROXY
    const void*    pStublessProxyInfo;
#endif
    const IID*    piid;
} CInterfaceProxyHeader;


typedef struct tagCInterfaceProxyVtbl
{
    CInterfaceProxyHeader header;
    void* Vtbl[];
} CInterfaceProxyVtbl;


typedef struct tagCInterfaceStubHeader
{
    const IID* piid;
    const MIDL_SERVER_INFO* pServerInfo;
    unsigned long DispatchTableCount;
    const PRPC_STUB_FUNCTION* pDispatchTable;
} CInterfaceStubHeader;


typedef struct tagCInterfaceStubVtbl
{
    CInterfaceStubHeader header;
    IRpcStubBufferVtbl Vtbl;
} CInterfaceStubVtbl;
```

The header information for the proxy points to a structure called MIDL_STUBLESS_PROXY_INFO (defined in rpcndr.h), which contains pointers to various useful tables of information:

```
typedef const unsigned char __RPC_FAR * PFORMAT_STRING;
typedef struct _MIDL_STUBLESS_PROXY_INFO
{
    PMIDL_STUB_DESC                    pStubDesc;
    PFORMAT_STRING                     ProcFormatString;
    const unsigned short __RPC_FAR *   FormatStringOffset;
    PFORMAT_STRING                     LocalFormatTypes;
    PFORMAT_STRING                     LocalProcString;
    const unsigned short __RPC_FAR *   LocalFmtStringOffset;
} MIDL_STUBLESS_PROXY_INFO;
```

pStubDesc points to a global structure, which contains general marshaling information, such as pointers to routines used to allocate and free memory, binding routines, and the version of NDR and MIDL used. This structure also contains a pointer to an array called __MIDL_TypeFormatString, which has the definition of all the types used by any interface in the proxy-stub.

Finally, `ProcFormatString` is an array that contains the actual interface method descriptions (it points to an array called `__MIDL_ProcFormatString`).

These format strings are not publicly documented, but presumably Microsoft developers will have access to the appropriate internal documentation. Thus they can write code that reads fast format strings and from this obtain an interface description. This is clearly how the MTS developers have been able to write a generic interceptor for components that don't use type library marshaling, but do use fast format strings.

The following diagram illustrates how to get fast format strings for an interface called `IMyItf`, in a proxy-stub file generated from an IDL file called `MySvr.idl`.

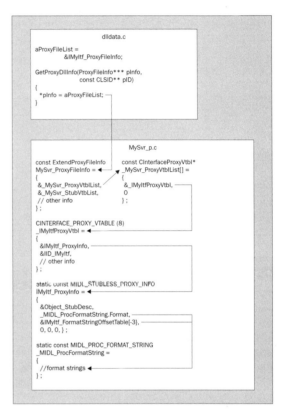

Fast Format String Descriptions

It is interesting to look at the tables of fast format strings generated for an interface, and since you can obtain them through code, it is possible to write your own interceptors (although there would be quite a lot of code).

Although the fast format strings are undocumented, MIDL does add enough comments in the files it generates to work out what the values mean. The fast format string tables (and the other tables returned by `GetProxyDllInfo()`) can be found in the `_p.c` file generated by MIDL.

The `__MIDL_ProcFormatString` table is global, and contains information for all the methods of all interfaces that the proxy-stub will marshal. `FormatStringOffset` is used to give the offset into this table of the format strings for a specified interface (it actually points to a table containing the offsets for all of the methods – curiously though, this pointer is 6 bytes before the table beginning).

Each parameter description in __MIDL_ProcFormatString has a flag that indicates the attributes used as well as an indication of the data type, held in a short. If it is one of the IDL primitive types, the data type is displayed with a simple value, as shown in the following table. This was obtained via two stages. The first was to dump symbol information from mtxih.lib (a static library, which must be linked to all proxy-stub DLLs for interfaces on MTS components – this will be explained more in the next chapter). The second was to compile various IDL files with interfaces that used all the IDL data types and constructs, then to examine the tables in the _p.c file.

Here I show the format strings that I have been able to determine. For most I have been able to indicate the IDL type or construct that the item refers to.

IDL Type	Table entry	Symbol
byte	0x01	FC_BYTE
char	0x02	FC_CHAR
boolean	0x03	FC_SMALL
	0x04	FC_USMALL
wchar_t	0x05	FC_WCHAR
short	0x06	FC_SHORT
unsigned short	0x07	FC_USHORT
long	0x08	FC_LONG
unsigned long	0x09	FC_ULONG
float	0x0a	FC_FLOAT
hyper	0x0b	FC_HYPER
double	0x0c	FC_DOUBLE
enum	0x0d	FC_ENUM16
[v1_enum]	0x0e	FC_ENUM32
[ignore]	0x0f	FC_IGNORE
error_status_t	0x10	FC_ERROR_STATUS_T
[ref]	0x11	FC_RP
[unique]	0x12	FC_UP
[ptr]	0x14	FC_FP
start of a struct	0x15	FC_STRUCT
union	0x1a	FC_BOGUS_STRUCT
[string]	0x22	FC_C_CSTRING
Interface pointer	0x2f	FC_IP

These are just a few of the possible values. The following table lists some more – their symbols give some indication as to what they do.

FC_ZERO	FC_BIND_GENERIC	FC_PP
FC_OP	FC_BIND_PRIMITIVE	FC_EMBEDDED_COMPLEX
FC_PSTRUCT	FC_AUTO_HANDLE	FC_IN_PARAM
FC_CSTRUCT	FC_CALLBACK_HANDLE	FC_IN_PARAM_BASETYPE
FC_CPSTRUCT	FC_UNUSED1	FC_IN_PARAM_NO_FREE_INST
FC_CVSTRUCT	FC_POINTER	FC_IN_OUT_PARAM
FC_CARRAY	FC_ALIGNM2	FC_OUT_PARAM
FC_CVARRAY	FC_ALIGNM4	FC_RETURN_PARAM
FC_SMFARRAY	FC_ALIGNM8	FC_RETURN_PARAM_BASETYPE
FC_LGFARRAY	FC_UNUSED2	FC_DEREFERENCE
FC_SMVARRAY	FC_UNUSED3	FC_DIV_2
FC_LGVARRAY	FC_UNUSED4	FC_MULT_2
FC_BOGUS_ARRAY	FC_STRUCTPAD1	FC_ADD_1
FC_C_BSTRING	FC_STRUCTPAD2	FC_SUB_1
FC_C_SSTRING	FC_STRUCTPAD3	FC_CALLBACK
FC_C_WSTRING	FC_STRUCTPAD4	FC_CONSTANT_IID
FC_CSTRING	FC_STRUCTPAD5	FC_END
FC_BSTRING	FC_STRUCTPAD6	FC_PAD
FC_SSTRING	FC_STRUCTPAD7	FC_HARD_STRUCT
FC_WSTRING	FC_STRING_SIZED	FC_TRANSMIT_AS_PTR
FC_ENCAPSULATED_UNION	FC_UNUSED5	FC_REPRESENT_AS_PTR
FC_NON_ENCAPSULATED_UNION	FC_NO_REPEAT	FC_USER_MARSHAL
FC_BYTE_COUNT_POINTER	FC_FIXED_REPEAT	FC_PIPE
FC_TRANSMIT_AS	FC_VARIABLE_REPEAT	FC_END_OF_UNIVERSE
FC_REPRESENT_AS	FC_FIXED_OFFSET	
FC_BIND_CONTEXT	FC_VARIABLE_OFFSET	

If the data type is more complex, like a structure (perhaps one you have defined in IDL, or a COM type like CY, BSTR or VARIANT), or an interface pointer, then the type member will be the offset in the __MIDL_TypeFormatString of the strings used to describe the type. The flags for the parameter indicate whether the data type is an offset or a description code.

Notice that only primitive data types have a type symbol – all other data types have to have a separate description. So if your interface uses a VARIANT, for example, then the description for VARIANT will be added to __MIDL_TypeFormatString. There is no centrally held description for known types. When a VARIANT is used in an interface method, it will add 922 bytes to the table. In addition, if any of these embedded types are user-marshaled (for example VARIANTs or BSTRs) then an additional table is added to the proxy-stub to contain pointers to the four user marshaling routines required.

Obtaining Proxy Data

So, the proxy-stub carries around with it all the information needed to describe and marshal the interface. Tools like MTS can read the proxy-stub format string, and know exactly what the methods' parameters are. For example, if you want to find the number of interfaces that have proxy-stub information in a DLL, you can use the following to get the DLL-marshaled interface names (assuming that the DLL is loaded by some code in LoadTheProxyStubDLL()):

```
// need to define this because proxy-stubs are C files
#define CINTERFACE
#include <objidl.h>
#include <rpcproxy.h>
#undef CINTERFACE

// define the function pointer
typedef void (__stdcall *GetProxyDllInfo_PROC)(const ProxyFileInfo*** pInfo,
                                               const CLSID** pId);

// obtain the proy-stub DLL from somewhere, for example load
// it using information from the registry
HMODULE hMod = LoadTheProxyStubDLL();
// now get the function
FARPROC fp = GetProcAddress(hMod, "GetProxyDllInfo");
GetProxyDllInfo_PROC proc;
proc = reinterpret_cast<GetProxyDllInfo_PROC>(fp);

const ProxyFileInfo** pInfo;
const CLSID * pId;
// call GetProxyDllInfo() to get the proxy information
proc(&pInfo, &pId);

// print the names of the interfaces that there are proxies for
unsigned short uTableSize = (*pInfo)->TableSize;
printf("In this DLL there are proxies for %ld interfaces\n",
       uTableSize);
for(unsigned short s = 0; s < uTableSize; s++)
{
    OLECHAR str[50];
    StringFromGUID2(pId[s], str, sizeof(str));
    printf("%S %s\n", str, (*pInfo)->pNamesArray[s]);
}
```

Problems with Fast Format Strings

Although fast format strings completely describe IDL (I suspect MIDL merely dumps out some intermediate language that it uses when processing IDL), there are problems. Firstly, you do not have the luxury of the type library interfaces to read the information. Secondly, although you can determine the number of methods in an interface, their parameters, the types of those parameters, and any attributes that were applied to them, you have neither method nor components names.

Method names aren't saved in the proxy-stub file, since the marshaler doesn't need them. All it needs is enough information to let it interpret the stack frame or construct one. As mentioned earlier, proxy-stub files are component independent so they don't contain component information.

This means that for the MTS Explorer to determine the components in a DLL, the interfaces implemented by them, and the methods on those interfaces, it needs to have a type library.

Interception

Type information, whether provided by a type library or fast format strings, means that a proxy object can implement interfaces that look *exactly* like those on the component it proxies for. Proxies, of course, are used to marshal interfaces across apartment boundaries, but this technique can be used by other components too.

Such components could accept your method calls, perform some method pre-invocation checking, invoke the method, and finally perform some post-invocation checking. This *interception* code must be able to decipher the parameters on the stack that your code constructs to invoke the method, which it can do if it has type information.

MTS performs interception for you, but to illustrate that this is not 'magic', I will explain some other ways to achieve the same thing.

> *In the following descriptions, I will ignore the issues of the component's* 'this' *pointer, which is implicit in every COM interface call. Interceptors, of course, make great efforts to preserve identity.*

Standard Marshaling Proxies

Interceptor code needs to intercept your method call in such a way that your client does not see it. Interface proxies do this, and are useful because they are part of standard marshaling, so COM will help you by creating a proxy whenever marshaling is needed. If you want to intercept standard marshaled interfaces, then you can use the /Os switch on MIDL to generate proxy-stub marshaling code. Be aware though, that you'll need to write some C code and hack around with the macros defined in rpcproxy.h. I have used this in the past to synthesize asynchronous COM calls, by making the proxy object create an extra thread. This then makes the actual call to the component, allowing the client thread to be unblocked. True asynchronous COM is available in Windows 2000, and this technique can be used to provide something similar on other operating systems.

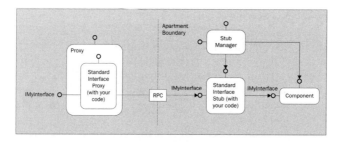

Since you are editing the MIDL-generated code, you can add interceptor code for both the proxy and stub object and leave it up to COM to load them. As I have already mentioned, MIDL will also add fast format strings for your interfaces to the proxy-stub file, as well as code to marshal all the methods in the interfaces, which can make your proxy-stub DLL quite large.

Custom Marshaling Proxies

The alternative is to use **custom marshaling**, where the component implements `IMarshal` and uses `GetUnmarshalClass()` to specify the CLSID of the custom proxy that COM will create in the client apartment. This proxy can unmarshal the interface using the standard proxy, after adding its own interceptor code. Although the client doesn't know that you are intercepting its calls, the component will – because it needs to implement `IMarshal`. Furthermore, the standard proxy object (which MIDL will generate for you) cannot be aggregated. The custom proxy will therefore need to give access to an implementation of *all* of the component's interfaces, even if it's only interested in intercepting one of them. The proxy, however, can create the standard proxy object and delegate calls to it.

In the following diagram, the implementation of `IMarshal` on the component has created the appropriate standard marshaling object by calling `CoGetStandardMarshal()`. This is passed back to the custom proxy in the custom marshaling packet, where the custom proxy can unmarshal and cache the standard interface proxy.

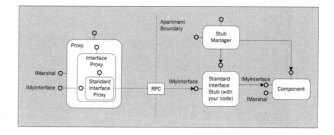

The Universal Delegator

Another option is to use a facility like Keith Brown's **Universal Delegator** (documented in MSJ January and February 1999). This object is generic, in that it can be applied to any component, irrespective of the interfaces it implements. It implements a 'one size fits all' thunking layer between your code and the proxy (or the stub and component). It therefore doesn't require type information, but does increase your code size. However, using the UD is a conscious decision, which will be made when you build your code. If you want to use it on the client-side, you must explicitly add it with the client code (although the server code will not be aware that it is being used). Similarly, if you want to use it on the server-side, you need to explicitly add it to your component. Again, the client will have no knowledge that it is being used. The UD cannot be applied to code that is already built.

Once you have applied the UD, its actions are largely transparent – it intercepts `QueryInterface()` and ensures that if other interfaces are queried for, then the UD will be applied to those too. Furthermore, the UD implements `IMarshal` in such a way that if it intercepts a proxy and this intercepted interface is marshaled to another apartment, then it can custom marshal itself to the other apartment. This ensures that the new apartment has the UD applied to a new proxy *to the component* rather than the creation of a proxy *to the UD* in your apartment.

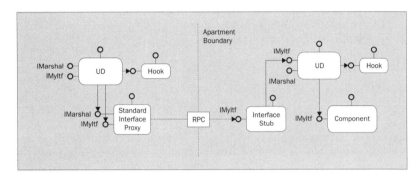

The UD works by providing an interface vtable with 1024 assembly code thunks (the maximum number of methods on an interface is 1024), much in the same way that ATL adds `_QIThunk` thunks for interface debugging when the `_ATL_DEBUG_INTERFACES` symbol is defined. These thunks have access to the stack frame from a client call, so they can make the actual method call without any knowledge about that method. Since it is the thunk code that is called, it can perform some action (like adjusting or checking security settings, or auditing method usage). It does this by using the services of a developer-supplied object called a **hook**.

The hook will be called when the intercepted interface is first queried, and can be accessed before and after each method is called. It gets access to the stack of the method call and the method `HRESULT`. It can therefore provide some parameter analysis, as long as it can determine what the parameters are from the stack frame. If this is what you want to do, then you will have to resort to type information to get a description of the stack.

Although the universal delegator is a very useful object, this does mean that the client (and/or server) developer needs to apply it, since it is not automatically applied for you. It would be nice to have interceptors as part of the operating system. In fact, COM+ (part of the Windows 2000 operating system) does have interceptors, which are called silently when you use the COM+ runtime (more details are given in Chapter 8). For earlier operating systems though, this is not an option. MTS is available for NT4 and Win9x, and provides a partial solution to the need for interceptors, but neither COM+ 1.0 nor MTS allows you to define your own interceptor code as you can with the UD.

Microsoft Transaction Server

In the previous sections, I have shown you several ways to intercept COM calls. Each has its advantages and disadvantages, but it should be clear that interception is not a black art, and anyone with some programming skill can do it. However, in all of the previous methods, the application of interception has been specific to a particular interface or component, and may require changes to the component source code. This is required because you perform interception to allow your code to be 'injected in'. Another, simpler method would be for the operating system to intercept COM calls for you and then run your pre- and post-invocation code.

Such a hypothetical mechanism would allow you to register a 'hook' with COM that can perform pre- and post-invocation actions for specific components or interfaces. However, current versions of COM do not support this.

MTS is designed to intercept calls to components 'configured' as MTS components. The MTS interception layer will perform checks on the method call, based on values for the component held in the MTS catalog. This means that rather than providing custom interception code, you are customizing MTS's interception code with values in the catalog. There are essentially three tasks that interception will perform using these values:

- ❑ Security access checks
- ❑ Automatic enlistment of transactions
- ❑ Concurrency management (synchronization)

These terms will be explained later in this chapter. First off, let's look at how MTS applies interception.

MTS Interception

MTS loads components that are implemented in DLLs, and DLLs must be loaded into a process. MTS groups together components in **packages**. If you put several components in a package, you can guarantee that they will run in the same process, so you will not get a performance hit from cross-process calls. There are two types of packages, **library packages** and **server packages**. The former means that the components will run in the client process, whereas the latter guarantees that they will run in some other process.

You create packages with the MTS Explorer, which you can also use to indicate the components that will run in the package. You have two options when adding components: you either add an already registered component, or add a DLL, which means that all the components in a DLL are added. In both cases, MTS Explorer will use a type library (either that registered for the registered component, or the one bound into the DLL) to get information about the interfaces implemented by the component. As mentioned earlier, fast format strings can't be used because component information isn't saved in proxy-stub files.

These interfaces are added to the catalog, and although MTS does not appear to use them, the Explorer will add all the methods on each interface into the catalog as well.

Server Packages

Components in a server package will run in the MTS surrogate process, mtx.exe. Each package defined on a machine will run in its own instance of mtx.exe. However, only one instance will be used per package.

When you add a component to a server package, the MTS explorer will adjust the COM registration for the component. It does this by changing the InprocServer32 key (to remove the path to the actual server), and adding a LocalServer32 key (to launch the MTS surrogate with the component's package). Since the explorer overwrites the component's InprocServer32 key, it needs to store the DLL path in the MTS catalog so that mtx.exe knows what DLL it should load. Since mtx.exe is now the 'server' of the component, it can perform any interception it wants.

The arrangement is shown in the following diagram:

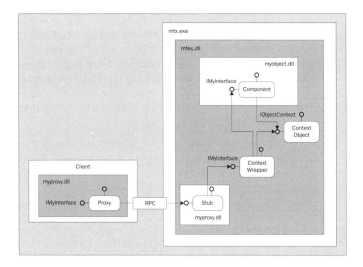

Interception is performed by an object called the **context wrapper**. This looks like the component, and implements all the interfaces that your component does. Information about the component is held in another object, called the **context object** – your component can always access its own context object.

The context wrapper object intercepts calls to `IUnknown::QueryInterface()` made on your component, so it can determine which interfaces are requested. It can then perform tests to see if, for example, the client is allowed to access the interface, and if so, it can delegate the call to the component. If this request succeeds, then the context wrapper knows it must implement this interface – it does this by obtaining a description of the interface from the type library or the fast format strings in the proxy stub file. This allows the context wrapper to create a vtable for the interface requested by the client. The client, of course just sees a standard marshaling proxy, so it has no knowledge that the call is being intercepted.

The component doesn't need to know that the method calls are being intercepted. Compare this with the other types of interception, shown before. Remember, to perform this magic, MTS doesn't need to *change* COM, but does need some extra help (in the form of type information) to make sure it can create vtables for the interfaces that it intercepts.

MTS has the advantage that during activation it can inject itself between the component and client – but there are problems with this. To enforce synchronization (so that components within a transaction cannot be accessed by more than one client thread) MTS has a concept called an **activity**, and each one of these has a lock. When `CoCreateInstanceEx()` is called, a new activity is created – if the component's package is not already running then MTS will start it, otherwise the new activity will be created in the running instance. Components within an activity will have free access to other ones in the same activity, but if they access components in another activity, they will need to obtain the lock for that activity. You do not need to do anything to obtain the lock to an activity, because MTS interception will do that, but you should be aware that a cross-activity call might result in the calling thread blocking while MTS obtains the activity lock.

To allow you to create components in the same activity you can use your component's context object. This implements an interface called `IObjectContext`, on which is a method called `CreateInstance()`. Components created by calling this method will be in the same activity as the caller.

Of greater concern however, is what happens if your component passes interface pointers as method parameters – either as [out] parameters (returned to a client) or as [in] parameters (when calling another component). If the method call is out of the activity then the interface pointer will be marshaled – but since MTS does not replace the marshaling layer (it uses standard marshaling) it won't be able to apply the interception code. Calls on this interface pointer will therefore not get the benefits of MTS interception. If your component does pass out interface pointers like this, it must first ask MTS for an interface pointer with the context wrapper applied to it, by calling SafeRef().

COM+ understands context wrappers and thus applies interception on calls to CoCreateInstanceEx() *and to interface pointers passed as method parameters.*

Library Packages

When a component is added to a library package it will be loaded into the client process (no separate surrogate is used), so some of the facilities applied through interception won't be available (specifically, security checks). When you add a component to a library package, MTS Explorer will alter the InprocServer32 registry key to point to the MTS executive, mtxex.dll. This is a free threaded component (ThreadingModel = Free), so it will be loaded into the client's multi-threaded apartment. The following diagram shows the simplest configuration, in which the client code is running in the MTA and the component is configured to run in the MTA. If the client code runs in an STA then clearly a proxy-stub will be used.

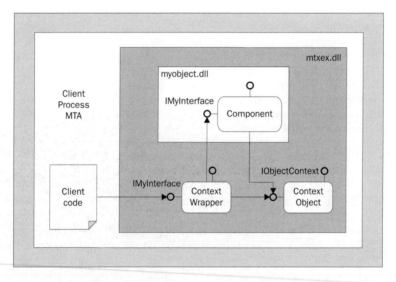

Since mtxex.dll is registered as the object server, it will be launched when an activation request is made for a component. The MTS executive can use the MTS catalog (maintained by MTS Explorer) to determine what DLL to load in order to create the component.

As in the server case, a component in a library package can access its context object. It does this by calling the API called GetObjectContext() to get the IObjectContext interface on the context object.

COM+ provides a richer context object, which is obtained through a call to CoGetObjectContext(), *available on Windows 2000.*

MTS Features

So what does MTS give you? Well, that is the subject of the rest of the book! There follows a brief list.

Deployment

One of the big problems with writing a distributed application is the management of all the different components that should be installed and the machines on which they will be installed. Typically, the application developer would determine the various machines that the application would use. He would then either hard-code the host name as the parameter to COSERVERINFO which is passed to CoCreateInstanceEx(), or use the RemoteServerName in the AppID of a server, and administer the intended remote server name with DCOMCnfg. (An intermediate solution is to use COSERVERINFO and get the machine name from some configurable, persistent store like the registry.)

If the application has many different servers spread across many different machines, you will have installation issues. You must: make sure that the correct server, type libraries (if any), and proxy-stub DLLs are installed on the server machines; that the correct type libraries and proxy-stubs are installed on the client machines; and that the AppID and CLSID for the remote components are also registered on the client machines.

This is clearly a problem, and MTS addresses the issue in two ways. Firstly, you *never* explicitly launch a component as a remote component (using CLSCTX_REMOTE_SERVER). Instead, you launch it locally with CLSCTX_LOCAL_SERVER (or with IObjectContext::CreateInstance() as explained in the next chapter), and let MTS determine the machine on which the component should run. This means that your client code (or the code in an MTS component that creates a new component) always treats the component as local, and doesn't need to hard-code any machine name.

Secondly, the MTS Explorer has facilities to allow you to administer MTS on several machines, which you can use to deploy both the client and server side of a component. MTS Explorer does this in two ways. Once you have installed a component into MTS, you can '**push**' this component to another machine. The proxy-stub and/or type library is therefore copied and installed on this client machine. In addition, the component is registered in the MTS catalog on the client machine as a remote component running on the machine that 'pushed' it. (Note that the actual component is not 'pushed', merely the ability to access it.) You can also '**pull**' a component from another machine, in which case the 'pulling' machine will be the client. In this case the proxy-stub and/or type library for the component will be installed, and the component is registered in the MTS catalog as being a remote component running on the machine from which it was 'pulled'.

This allows an administrator to specify which machines will have the correct files to act as clients to components, and to make sure that those machines know where these components are. However, it does not address the issue of how to install the server. To do this, the MTS Explorer allows the developer to '**export**' a package from the development machine, and allows an administrator to '**import**' it onto the machine where the components will actually run. MTS and deployment are covered in Chapter 4.

Concurrency Management

COM allows you to specify a component's concurrency requirements, by indicating which apartment type it will run in. Components in in-proc servers are registered with a `ThreadingModel` value (no value, `Apartment`, `Both` or `Free`), and COM will ensure that the component is created in the correct apartment type. If components running in an STA access others in the same apartment, you are guaranteed that the calls are serialized because there is only one thread. As you have seen, cross-apartment calls (from one STA to another, or between an STA and the MTA) are marshaled, and the marshaling layer will ensure that calls made into an STA will always be serialized.

COM does this by using a Windows message queue – all interface calls into the STA are held in the message queue as Windows messages. The single thread in the apartment 'pumps' the message queue, handling each message one by one.

MTS manages synchronization by running components in an activity. Each activity runs in an STA, so COM guarantees that only one thread will ever access the components therein, and that only one component in the activity will be running at a time. You can therefore write your component without regard to threading and synchronization issues. MTS implements activities like this to ensure that work in an activity is isolated from the work being performed by other code. Since every activity is in a STA (every component is therefore created in an STA) it means that access to components from other activities (or from the client) will be marshaled. The interception that is performed is provided by the standard marshaling mechanism, which ensures that calls into an STA are serialized.

However, activities are not a complete solution. An activity can contain components that run on multiple machines, so the STA-based solution, which uses a Windows message queue to serialize calls, will not work. This does mean that when remote components are used, developers are careful to ensure that other clients do not have access to those components to make concurrent calls. I will return to this issue later in this book.

Declarative Security

Different components in your application will want to perform different actions, some of which may require more privileged access than others. You can do this by programming with the NT security API to perform access checks. However, this is far from straightforward, and requires you to unify security policies across several machines.

MTS simplifies this with declarative security. Since every method call to a component is intercepted by MTS, the executive can make access checks on behalf of your component. The MTS administrator can use MTS Explorer to specify which accounts can access particular components (or specific interfaces on components) through **roles**. For a finer-grain access check, a developer can call methods on `IObjectContext` to determine if a client account is a member of a particular role. The important point is that roles will be exported with a package. When the package is installed on another machine, all the administrator needs to do is populate the role with the required NT accounts. (MTS Explorer even has a facility to export NT accounts if the package is to be installed on the same domain.)

> *COM+ adds a further level, where you can specify that particular roles have access to specific interface methods.*

Finally, in a distributed application, a call from the base client could involve a call stack extending across many components and many machines. MTS maintains the SID of the account that created the component and the originator of the call stack, as well as the account that makes the call. This forms part of the MTS context under which components run, and the component code has access to this information.

Roles and distributed security are covered in Chapter 6.

Distributed Transactions

MTS, of course, is the Microsoft *Transaction* Server. Transactions are applied declaratively through the MTS Explorer, and depending on the option you select, your component will use an existing transaction, create a new transaction, or not use one at all. If a component uses a transaction then it will be automatically enlisted in that transaction, and if it uses another component (or accesses a resource manager), the transaction will be automatically exported, so that the other component can also enlist.

The important thing about transactions is that if one component in a transaction aborts, the transaction finishes and all the other components are destroyed. Any work carried out by the components in the transaction will be rolled back. This is a great boon to developers of distributed applications, because they do not have to devise complex error handling schemes or maintain lists of the work carried out.

All this is distributed using the **Microsoft Distributed Transaction Coordinator (MS DTC)**, so the transaction can span several machines. Transactions are covered in Chapter 2, and the MS DTC is covered in Chapter 5.

Summary

This chapter has introduced you to the concept of interception, and explained how this can be used to provide runtime services at the server end (and in some cases at the client end). MTS was introduced as one way to provide interception services on the server side, in a way that is transparent to client.

An important part of MTS is that it is able to obtain type information about a component and the interfaces it implements. In the first part of this chapter we examined exactly what we mean by 'type information', and also looked at another way of describing interfaces – fast format strings. We saw how we can gain access to this information programmatically, and examined the interception and marshaling implications of this.

The rest of the chapter looked at the features of MTS in more detail, including how it can help us with the following:

- ❑ Deployment
- ❑ Concurrency
- ❑ Declarative security
- ❑ Distributed transactions

The next chapter will concentrate on MTS, the facilities it supplies, how it works, and how this affects the way in which you should write your programs.

2

MTS and COM

Introduction

In the last chapter I introduced the concept of interception, explained the kinds of things that you can do with it, and showed how these things can be achieved. MTS uses COM – its very existence is dependent upon it. Many clients use MTS components as plain COM components without realizing that MTS is involved. MTS does this through altering the registry and through interception. However, MTS extends COM and the facilities that it provides, and in some cases it changes the way that COM works.

Many of the things that MTS does appear as magic, indeed, this is the approach taken by many texts when they explain the facilities of MTS. However, there is no such thing as magic – everything can be explained with a little science! This is true of MTS. As you have seen in the last chapter, interception can be applied by making sure that MTS is always involved when a component reference is returned (by making sure that MTS is given as the 'server' for the component, and ensuring that the developer only passes around interface pointers that have been made safe with SafeRef()).

Other MTS facilities of role-based security, auto-enlistment in transactions and activities are applied through interception and some clever but straightforward COM code. This chapter will explain these facilities and present some information about how they work, along with their restrictions.

MTS and COM

MTS is designed to be used with COM components, and brings a new facet to COM programming. In this section I want to cover some of the aspects of MTS that extend COM, making it a 'better COM'. I will start by going over a few of the basics of COM, and then show you what MTS adds to it.

COM Servers

COM servers come in two forms – DLLs and EXEs. In-process servers are housed in DLLs, and are lightweight in code size and memory usage because they share the same resources as the client that loads them. Out of process servers are typically housed in a separate EXE, although a DLL-based component can be made to be an out of process component through a surrogate. They are more heavyweight, because in addition to the component server code, they contain code for the executable context (for example, code to initialize the C Runtime Library (CRT) and to create and manage threads). Furthermore, an out of process server will have its own memory address space, security token, and resources.

But why have EXE servers? To answer this you need to look at the processes that run on your machine. In most cases they are started by the interactive user and provide services just to that user. One such process could have services that would be useful to another application. For this application to access those services, it would require some **inter-process communication** mechanism – this can be provided by COM. For example, a word processing application, whose primary function is to allow an interactive user to create documents, could give other applications access to this capability via COM components. You can do this with Word, and indeed, since Word registers all loaded documents into the Running Object Table (ROT), it means that other processes running in the same Window Station can access these documents. Another example is a web server – in most cases it will be started by a system account and look for client requests on TCP port 80, but it could also provide administrative access to other users via COM components. In both cases the emphasis is on the fact that the application has a primary purpose and uses COM to give additional access to its functionality and data. To access these COM components the client could launch a new instance of the EXE server (for example, to print a Word document) or attach to a running instance (for example, if the code wants to access the document being edited).

It is true that, if an application wants to share functionality, it can do so by putting that functionality into a DLL that the application can load. Significantly, other clients can also load that functionality *without having to load the application.* Internet Explorer takes this approach – `iexplorer.exe` is a small container program that loads the `WebBrowser` control (`SHDOCW.dll`) to provide navigation, hyperlinks, favorites and history management. The `WebBrowser` control loads the `MSHTML` control (`MSHTML.dll`) to perform HTML parsing and rendering and to host scripting engines. If a client, say a VB form, wants to render a HTML page, or even just to view `GIF` or `JPG` files, it can use the `MSHTML` control without the need to load either the `WebBrowser` control or `iexplorer.exe`.

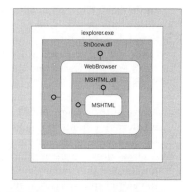

However, this is not always an option, especially with large applications that have a long heritage going back over many versions. In this case it may be impossible to factor out COM components from the legacy code (as appears to be the case with the applications in Office 2000). If it is possible to factor out the COM components, it makes sense to put them into one or more DLLs, since COM provides an effective DLL management system. So, are there any other reasons for COM EXE servers?

There are several. If your COM server needs to run as an NT service then it must be in an EXE. NT Services have two important facilities – the first is that they can be configured to start automatically, even before a user logs in. This means that the class factories of the COM components they serve will be available as soon as the host machine is available to accept client requests. The second facility derives from the fact that services are the way in which developers extend the NT operating system in user mode. As such, they are usually run under the `LocalSystem` account, which has `SeTcbPrivilege` – that is, it is part of the **T**rusted **C**omputing **B**ase and can thus create new logon sessions. Services running under this account will have access to any secured object that the system has access to, and are thus very privileged.

Furthermore, an EXE server is, of course, a process. This means that it can run on any Win32 machine (assuming the same processor and operating system version is used). Since DCOM leverages the facilities of RPC to allow interfaces to be remotely accessed, your components can be on remote machines. Of course, this represents a security problem to the server machine, because it must have control over who can launch processes. NT4 tackles the issues of NT process security token management and RPC authentication using a form of declarative security, typically administered through `DCOMCnfg`.

> *Win9x sidesteps this issue, because it requires the interactive user to launch any COM servers that will be accessed remotely. You don't have access to security APIs on an all Win9x network, although if there is a peer NT machine on the network this can be used to perform access checks when accessing components in an already launched server.*

COM also has a programmatic method of managing security (which is essential to enforce fine grain, component level, or method level security). However, users typically ignore this and allow COM to make access checks based on declarative security. If the component code does not have security code, then it closely resembles DLL component code. The reasons for implementing COM components in an EXE are thus diminished.

The other main security consideration is the security identity that the component will run under. If the component is in a DLL, then the component will run under the same identity as the client process that uses it.

It is unlikely that this client identity will have sufficient privileges to allow it to impersonate another user and access secured NT objects (files, processes, registry keys etc) under a false identity – although this is possible for any client account when accessing out of process COM components. If the component runs in an EXE, this process can be marked in the registry as running under a specified account, different to the client account.

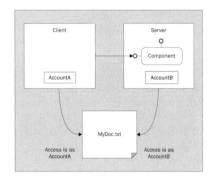

So in the diagram above, if the client accesses `MyDoc.txt` directly, access checks and auditing will be carried out on `AccountA`. However, if the client uses the component in the server that runs under the identity of `AccountB`, and that component accesses `MyDoc.txt`, then the access checks and auditing will be performed on `AccountB`.

Finally, since a process always runs in a protected memory space, whatever occurs in that process won't affect any other processes on the same machine. (Yet again, though, Win9x falls short, because to allow compatibility with Win16 it does allow some memory space sharing between processes. Win9x is not a good platform for COM servers.) If your component throws an exception your server will die, but the client will merely get an error status code when it tries to access the errant component. Your components, of course, will be well written and will never allow exceptions to go uncaught.

Surrogates

NT4 service pack 2 introduced COM surrogates. These allow you to launch a DLL-implemented component in a separate process to the client. This doesn't mean that anyone can launch the surrogate, because COM checks the declarative security attributes set via `DCOMCnfg` (Win9x, of course, requires that surrogates that will be remotely accessed are launched by the interactive user.) Similarly, this doesn't mean that the DLL-based components can be accessed by any user, because COM will apply the declaratively set access permissions (or if they do not exist, it will use default access permissions).

NT4 (and DCOM9x for Win9x) provides a generic surrogate called `DllHost`, but if you wish you can write your own. To use a surrogate you need to register your in-proc server with an `AppID` key that has the `DllSurrogate` value. This value can be empty, in which case `DllHost` will be used, or it can contain the path to the surrogate process. So that this key will be referenced by COM, the in-proc component's CLSID registration should have a value called `AppID` giving the AppID that mentions the surrogate. However, although the component will effectively be launched in a local server, it should not have a `LocalServer32` key, just the `InprocServer32` key giving the path to the DLL server. `OLEView` will do this registration for you (using the component's CLSID as the AppID).

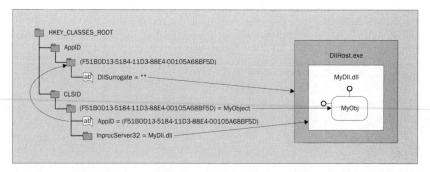

To make an activation request, the client should use the `CLSCTX_LOCAL_SERVER` activation context to create the component on the same machine, or `CLSCTX_REMOTE_SERVER` for a remote component. COM will start the surrogate process, tell it to load the DLL server and register the class factories in the DLL. This is similar to how an EXE server is used – COM starts the process and waits for the class factories to be registered before asking for a component instance. COM keeps a tally of all the interfaces that are marshaled out of the surrogate (presumably using some kind of interception), so when this falls to zero it can tell the surrogate process to close down.

The advantage of this type of activation is that the components are launched in a separate process to the client, so the client is protected from rogue or buggy components that may overwrite client memory or throw exceptions. It also means that the component can run under a different security identity to the client, which you can apply through DCOMCnfg. If your application has several components implemented in different DLLs, but you want them to run in the same process under the same identity, then you can do this with a surrogate by making sure that all the components' CLSID keys mention the same AppID.

In this way the server development is much simpler – rather than having the option of creating either an EXE server or a DLL server, the developer can have one choice – a DLL server. This is a great boon to, shall we say, the less sophisticated developer (OK, I admit it, I mean VB developers) who need all development to be as simple as possible. It also means that Microsoft can streamline their development tools by only offering developers a 'one size fits all' solution.

However, COM surrogates do not solve every problem, and indeed some people regarded them merely as a way to remote 'legacy' code implemented in DLLs. You can see their point – if you want to have fine grain control over which client account can access particular methods on your components (a facility that is crucial to distributed applications), then you have little option but to implement the component in an EXE. Only that way can you ensure that the component will run in a separate process to the client. As Chapter 6 will show, to determine the client account accessing the component, you must access the call context object with CoGetCallContext(). Even if you indicate that the DLL-based component should be used in a surrogate, you can't guarantee that this will be the case (the client could use the CLSCTX_INPROC_SERVER activation context). If this function is called by a component loaded in-proc it will fail with an error of RPC_E_CALL_COMPLETE.

MTS Surrogate

As you saw in the last chapter, MTS provides surrogate facilities and although it does it in a slightly different way to COM surrogates, the effects are the same. When you add components to a server package with MTS Explorer it will change the CLSID entry for the component to use mtx.exe as the server. However, MTS is not shy about this – it will all but obliterate your component's in-proc server registry settings and turn your component from an in-proc component to a local component.

This means that if, during the development cycle of your components, your component server gets reregistered after it has been added to the MTS catalog, then the MTS doctored registry values will be overwritten. However, the information added to the MTS catalog will be preserved (normal COM components know nothing about the catalog and won't touch its registry values). Because of this, MTS provides a command line tool, mtxrereg.exe. You can use this to refresh the COM registration values in HKEY_CLASSES_ROOT with the values stored in the MTS catalog and thus restore the component to being an MTS component. (This option is also offered by selecting Refresh All Components from the context menu of My Computer in MTS Explorer.)

Look at the parallels here between COM surrogates and MTS server processes. Both indicate that a DLL based component should be loaded into a process that is not associated with the server, and has no knowledge of the server's code. Both allow you to run more than one component in the same process – MTS allows you to add components to a package, so that the package ID groups together the components, and the DllSurrogate value allows you to run components in the same surrogate instance by giving them the same AppID. In both cases you can specify the identity of the process and you can apply declarative access permissions.

However, there are differences. In particular, MTS applies automatic transactions, and its declarative security can be applied to components and interfaces of those components. `DllSurrogate` launched processes however, have access permissions applied across the *entire* process.

MTS will allow only one instance of `mtx.exe` to run a specified package. This isn't usually a problem because the components in a package will be activated via COM, and COM will ensure that only one instance will serve those components. However, if you wish, you can start `mtx.exe` from the command line, passing the package ID as part of the `/p` switch, for example:

```
mtx.exe /p:{126B65CE-1A8D-11D3-898D-00104BDC35E0}
```

> **Just to confuse matters, COM+ uses `DllHost.exe` as the surrogate, and the command line switch is called `/ProcessID` (even though it takes the Application ID, which is the new name for the Package ID). More details on this are given in Chapter 8.**

You may decide to do this if the server package never unloads and you have decided that you want to pre-launch it to make it immediately available to clients. When a request comes from a client for one of the components in the package, COM will ensure that the running instance will be used. If, in error, you try to launch `mtx.exe` twice with the same package ID, then MTS will close down the second instance and give the following information message in the event log:

Source: Transaction Server
Severity: Warning
Category: Executive
Event: 4101
Description: An attempt was made to launch a server process for a package that was
               already actively supported by another server process on this computer.
               {126B65CE-1A8D-11D3-898D-00104BDC35E0}.

MTS Component Requirements

MTS extends the idea of the COM surrogate process as a 'container' to provide DLL based components as local components. Unlike COM surrogates, where the only requirement is that the class factories for the components in the DLL are accessible from `DllGetClassObject()`, MTS imposes more strict requirements, mainly to allow it to impose interception. The requirements are:

❑   The component must have a standard class factory implementing `IClassFactory` or `IClassFactory2`.

❑   The component must use standard marshaled interfaces, either through type library marshaling or through proxy-stubs generated using `/Oicf` and linked with `mtxih.lib`.

❑   The component coclasses should be described by a type library.

❑   The component's interfaces should be described in a type library.

❑   The DLL must be self-registering.

The proxy-stub DLLs have to be linked with `mtxih.lib` because it implements a class factory object and a stub object that works specifically with MTS – it needs some cooperation from the stub to implement interception. The stub object implements the undocumented `ITypeInfoStackHelper` interface (which one presumes is used to get information about methods, described by type information, from the stack frame of a method call). In addition, it provides methods that will allow MTS to interpret the parameters on the stack, which uses an undocumented interface called `IStackFrameWalker`.

Incidentally, the `ih` in this library name stands for Interface Helper. When the proxy-stub file is registered, it will add a value to each interface's key called `InterfaceHelper`, which has the CLSID of the interface helper object being used to interpret the interface. This CLSID is the same value given in the `ProxyStubClsid32` key, which is, of course, the stub object. The implication is that MTS will look in the registry for the interface helper for the requested interface, load it, and use it to determine how to intercept the method calls.

The MTS Explorer requires a description of the coclasses to be in a type library. If not, it will not be able to display the coclasses implemented in a DLL when you specify that you want to add a non-registered component. You can use a simple type library that lists just the coclasses and gives their `[default]` interface as `IUnknown`. However, there is little point – if you do, then MTS Explorer will complain that it cannot install the component. In fact it can and it does, but what it cannot do is add the interface information to the catalog. If you are building a type library that describes the coclasses in a server then you might as well add the interfaces too.

If you have no type library then the alternative is to register the component on the local machine and then use the Import component(s) that are already registered option in MTS Explorer. This will get information about components and the servers that implement them from `HKEY_CLASSES_ROOT`. Since this hive does not contain information about the interfaces that a component implements, MTS Explorer will not add interface information into the catalog (true even if the server has a bound or a registered type library – the reason for this is unknown).

If the component server has a bound type library, then when you install components with MTS Explorer using the Install new component(s) option, Explorer will load the type library and will use this to get coclass and interface descriptions.

The `/Oicf` MIDL option is required to allow MIDL to get information about the interfaces that the component implements. If you have a proxy-stub built from IDL compiled with `/Os`, then when you try to activate the component with this interface through the MTS surrogate, the client will get the `E_NOINTERFACE` error (even though the interface does exist and can be marshaled). The other option is to compile the IDL file with `/Oi`. However, this uses the NT3.51 interpreted marshaler, which is unlikely to be available on future versions of Windows. You therefore have no other option than to use `/Oicf` as the MIDL optimizer switch.

The component's class factory can implement `IClassFactory2`, since this derives from `IClassFactory`. In addition to either of these class factory interfaces, the `mtx.exe` surrogate will call `QueryInterface()`, querying for the two undocumented interfaces when it needs the class factory:

❑ {27F56410-6161-11D1-946E-00A0C90F26F1}
❑ {92F362C0-CF5A-11D1-A93C-0080C7C575C0}

It is unclear what these interfaces do.

The surrogate, of course, loads the MTS executive, which does the actual work of wrapping the component (and its class factory) with its own objects. The wrapper class factory object implements three interfaces in addition to IUnknown:

- ❑ IClassFactory
- ❑ IClassFactoryWithContext
- ❑ IClassFactoryWithContext2

These last two are used to create the component with a particular context.

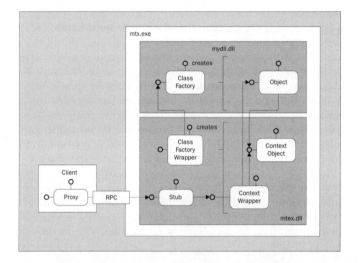

When the client makes a request to activate a new instance of the component, the MTS executive will create the class factory for the component, but will return a class factory wrapper object to COM. This wrapper object will then handle calls to create instances of the component by creating the context wrapper object and context object, and then asking your component's class factory to create the component. This is a crucial part of the interception process, because it makes sure that any calls from COM to create the MTS component will return the context wrapper object rather than the raw MTS component.

As you'll see later, your MTS class factory object is called upon many times, because **just in time** (**JIT**) **activation** will activate components when method calls are made, and deactivate them when the method returns.

MTS the Object Request Broker

There is an object middleware, popular with UNIX systems, which has ORB (Object Request Broker) as the three middle letters in its five letter acronym. When the client makes a request for an object, it is the ORB that will determine where the object resides, and return a reference to this object to the client. The client knows where the ORB is, but does not necessarily know the location of the objects that the ORB will return. This is clearly a useful facility because it puts the emphasis of physical object location on the ORB rather than on the client process.

Since the ORB has the responsibility of locating objects it can provide added features like load balancing and fault tolerance. Load balancing is a facility under which multiple objects can run on multiple machines. The ORB is able to calculate the number of clients accessing each object (and perhaps also the CPU usage of each machine) so that it can spread the load evenly across all machines. Fault tolerance works by replicating an object onto more than one machine – if the machine that the client is connected to dies, it can be connected to another object instance on a different machine.

The aforementioned (essentially) UNIX middleware has always used this mode of obtaining objects. COM, on the other hand, didn't until MTS. With MTS you can install MTS components as **remote components** on your local machine, or on another machine on the network that your account has been given access to. This means that when a client on a local machine makes a component activation request, and MTS on that machine has the component installed as a remote component, the component will be created on the specified remote machine.

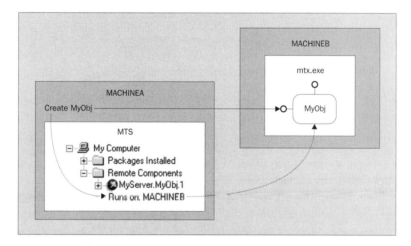

The client doesn't specify the server machine that the component should run on – instead the administrator determines this. Notice that the administration is performed on the machine local to the client. This is not quite the same as having a central ORB that determines where components run.

There is a variation to this – MTS allows you to export an **MTS Executable**. This is essentially all the information needed to launch the component on a remote machine. It includes the proxy-stub and type libraries needed to marshal the interfaces used by components in the package, and it will register the CLSID for these components. In addition, it will create an AppID for the package on the client machine and configure this to have the RemoteServerName point to the machine that has the server package.

By default this will be the machine that exported the package, but you can change this (more details will be given in a later chapter). This allows you to use components in a package remotely, from a client that *doesn't* have MTS installed:

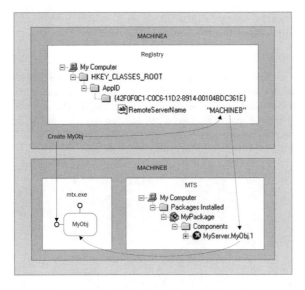

This works because MTS Explorer on the server machine adjusts the registry so that the appropriate package is launched and the client access to this package occurs through normal COM remote component activation. MTS 2.0 doesn't have the facility to dynamically determine which machine will be used to launch the package.

> *There is experimental code written by Tim Ewald of DevelopMentor that allows you to provide dynamic load balancing on MTS components (you can even supply the load balancing code). The neat thing about Tim's solution is that he solves the current restriction with* `CoCreateInstanceEx()`, *whereby a class factory can only return references to components created on the same machine (which stops class factory objects being able to perform dynamic load balancing).*
>
> *Tim does this with class factory objects that return a* custom marshaled *reference to the appropriate load balanced component. Effectively, it marshals by value the standard marshalling object reference to the component in the marshalling stream. This can be unmarshaled in the client apartment as a standard marshaled proxy by passing the restriction in* `CoCreateInstanceEx()`.
>
> *You can obtain the code from* www.develop.com/hp/ewald/lb/LB.ZIP.

In addition, you can't access the components in the Remote Components folder from a remote client. Since plain COM is used, the decision as to which machine will serve a component is made on the machine on which the client runs. It is possible to get round this problem by writing your own MTS based broker.

MTS doesn't provide fault tolerance on its own. However, you can get fault tolerance if you use it with Microsoft Cluster Server.

Object Context

As should be clear by now, MTS performs its magic through interception, but to do so it needs to maintain some information about the component. It does this through the object context. For every component that MTS creates it also creates an associated context object, which holds the information about the executable context of the component:

- ❑ Transaction information
- ❑ Activity
- ❑ Security information

The context is created when the component activation call is made from the client to MTS (thus it is not necessarily at the time that the MTS component is created).

The component has access to its own context by calling `GetObjectContext()`, which will return a pointer to the `IObjectContext` interface of the context object. In addition, resource dispensers will be able to access a component's context, to enable them to enlist the component within a transaction. The context object is *not* available when the component is being created or destroyed – that is, you cannot obtain it within a C++ component's constructor or destructor. However, you can obtain it when your object's interface methods are being called, and, if your object implements `IObjectControl`, within `Activate()` and `Deactivate()`.

Activity

A base client is the original client (process, non-MTS COM component) that called `CoCreateInstance()` to create an MTS component. The base client is the ultimate arbiter when it comes to deciding whether an MTS component should remain. True, it gets its component reference from the interception provided by MTS, and will therefore get the context wrapper object and not the requested MTS component. However, between method invocations MTS may keep the component alive (especially if the component isn't transactional). When the base client releases its reference on the context wrapper object, the MTS component and any other sub-objects will be released.

An MTS component may create other components, and this collection of components is known as an **activity**. The activity is part of the context, and once a component is part of a particular activity it always will be. MTS identifies each activity with an ID, which is a GUID. You can obtain this through the `IObjectContextActivity` interface that is implemented on the context object. This interface has a single method called `GetActivityId()`, the use of which is shown overleaf.

```
CComPtr<IObjectContext> pCont;
GetObjectContext(&pCont);
CComQIPtr<IObjectContextActivity> pAct;
pAct = pCont; // query for the interface
if (pAct)
{
   GUID guid;
   pAct->GetActivityId(&guid);
   WCHAR str[40];
   StringFromGUID2(guid, str, sizeof(str));
   ATLTRACE("activity: %S\n", str);
}
```

An activity can exist across multiple packages and hence across different processes on the same machine. MTS maintains concurrency through the activity in a server process and guarantees (within reason, see later) that calls to components in an activity are serialized. It does this to protect the state that the components in the activity use. Because of this, the activity can be viewed as a logical thread of execution. Components are added to the activity when they are created through calls to IObjectContext::CreateInstance(). Any component created through a call to CoCreateInstance() is created in a new activity and thus can be called concurrent to components in other activities.

> This is in stark contrast to COM+, where activity membership is an attribute of the component applied through the COM+ catalog. When a client calls CoCreateInstanceEx(), COM+ checks the synchronization attribute of the component. If the caller has an activity and the attribute is *Supports* or *Requires* synchronization, then the new component will be created in the caller's activity.

The base client can pass interface pointers to components in the activity to other client threads (clearly, COM rules of inter-apartment marshaling and MTS rules of safe references must be observed). In this case, if the components are within the same package (and hence the same server process) the calls into the activity are serialized, so that while one client is making a call, another client making a call will be blocked.

An activity can extend over several machines, but MTS does not guarantee that calls to components on different machines (within the same activity) are serialized. So if MACHINEA has PackageA, and MACHINEB has PackageB with components that are remote with respect to MACHINEA, then ClientA can call components in PackageA, while ClientB accesses components in PackageB, even if the components are in the same activity. Because the components are on different machines, concurrent access into the activity is possible.

However, if `ClientA` accesses components in `PackageB`, then these calls will be serialized with calls from `ClientB`, if the components involved are part of the same activity. This is because the components are in the same process.

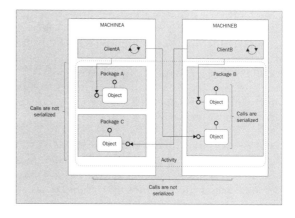

Indeed, it goes further than this. MTS will not guarantee that calls are serialized when components are created in multiple packages in the same activity on the same machine. So, clearly, if your design includes multiple clients and multiple packages, you need to take this into account. It is up to the components' resource managers (the processes that hold durable, transactional state, explained later) to ensure that locks are applied to protect the state that they maintain.

MTS takes the attitude that the cost of serializing activity calls across processes and machines outweighs the potential benefits of distributed serialization of calls.

Transactions

When an operation executes under a transaction, it is guaranteed to meet the ACID criteria: the operation is **A**tomic, either all of the action works or none at all; it is **C**onsistent, that is the operation does not violate any integrity rules; it acts in **I**solation from other transactions; and it is **D**urable, so its results are permanent.

MTS applies transactions automatically and you use the MTS Explorer to configure a component's transaction requirements. The component can either use a transaction or not, and if it does it can require that a new one is created. Note that even if a component needs a transaction, it does not necessarily need a *new* one – it can use another existing transaction. This is part of the magic of MTS – if such a component is created by another that is running under a transaction, then the new component can join the transaction of its creator.

> *You can indicate a component's preferred transactional requirements using a custom attribute, which is applied to a coclass in a type library. This is clearly the most logical way to apply attributes, because the type library describes what a component will do. Alas, it is only available for the transactional attribute, and the administrator is still able to change the transactional requirements through the MTS Explorer.*

MTS can create components across machines and these components can all run under the same transaction. This is managed by the Microsoft Distributed Transaction Coordinator (MS DTC) service. Each machine that runs the components must have the MS DTC running if it is to be able to use a distributed transaction, and there are versions of the MS DTC that can run on NT4 and on Win9x. The MS DTC will be covered in greater detail in Chapter 5.

Although MSDTC manages the distribution of transactions, the actual transactional work is carried out by a process called a **resource manager**, which **enlists** into the transaction. Resource managers maintain durable state (for example, a database), and ensure that actions on that state are done in a consistent way. Resource managers enlist into transactions, managed by the local machine's local transaction manager (implemented in the MS DTC), and the transaction ensures that the operation is atomic and isolated. MTS applies transactions automatically, so your component does not have to explicitly join a transaction. This is carried out through code called a **resource dispenser** (which is loaded in-process to the MTS component).

A resource dispenser (for example, the MTS ODBC connection manager) has access to a component's context, so when a component is running under a transaction it means that the resource dispenser will be able to access the transaction and enlist the appropriate resource manager into that transaction. A resource dispenser does *not* manage durable state.

Each transaction is unique. You can get the 'transaction ID' for your transaction from the dispenser manager using this code in an MTS component:

```
#include <mtxdm.h>
#pragma comment(lib, "mtxdm.lib")

CComPtr<IDispenserManager> pDM;
INSTID instID = 0;
TRANSID transID = 0;
GetDispenserManager(&pDM);
if (pDM)
{
    pDM->GetContext(&instID, &transID);
    ATLTRACE("INSTID = %x, TRANSID = %x\n", instID, transID);
}
```

The value returned for the 'transaction ID' is actually the `ITransaction*` pointer on an OLE transaction object, cast to a `DWORD`. (This will be explained in Chapter 5, but essentially it is a COM wrapper around an MS DTC transaction). It is safe to cast it back and then use this to get information about the transaction object:

```
if (transID)
{
    CComPtr<ITransaction> pTrans;
    pTrans = reinterpret_cast<ITransaction*>(transID);
    XACTTRANSINFO info;
    pTrans->GetTransactionInfo(&info);

    WCHAR ID[40];
    GUID guid;
    CopyMemory(&guid, info.uow.rgb, sizeof(info.uow.rgb));
    StringFromGUID2(guid, ID, sizeof(ID));
    ATLTRACE("Transaction ID %S\n", ID);
}
```

The uow member of XACTTRANSINFO stands for **unit of work**, a term that is synonymous with a transaction. As you can see from this code, uow is a 16-byte GUID. If you need a unique ID for a transaction, then uow is perhaps better than transID because a GUID is guaranteed to be unique, whereas the memory address of an interface may not be unique over time. When the transaction object is released, its memory will be recycled. It may therefore be possible that a future transaction object could use the same memory, and hence have the same address for the ITransaction interface. However, if you want to compare two transactions at the same point in time, then the value of transID is safe to use.

A **transaction stream** contains one or more components that share a single transaction – it is, if you like, the transactional aspect shared by those components. Transactions may or may not exist, depending on whether the components are still running under the transaction and whether the transaction has ended (committed or aborted). A transaction stream belongs to exactly one activity, but an activity can have more than one transaction stream, since there may be several components in the activity that require a new transaction.

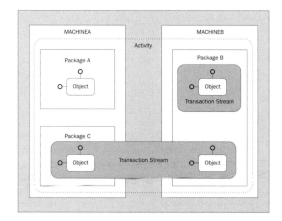

A transaction is created when a base component (the first component created by the base client) is created and is configured to require a transaction (or a new transaction). When any sub-components are created in the activity that require or use a transaction, they will join the transaction stream. However, if a sub-component in the activity requires a new transaction, then another transaction will be created and the component will be in another transaction stream.

A transaction ends when the base component in the transaction stream dies – that is, it is released, it commits or aborts, the transaction times out, or the component throws an exception. The context of a component contains information about whether the component is happy about the transaction and the component can use IObjectContext to change this information. If a component calls SetComplete() it means that it is happy about the transaction and that, as far as this component is concerned, the transaction can be committed. If the component calls SetAbort() then it means that the component is not happy about the work that it has done and it wants the transaction to be aborted. Calling either of these will not start the transaction committal mechanism unless the component is the base component.

MTS will take into account all of the components in the transaction stream when it decides whether to commit the transaction. If a single component is not happy (it called SetAbort()) then the transaction will be aborted and all resource managers that have enlisted in the transaction will be informed to roll back the work that they have done. If all components are happy then the work carried out by all the resource managers will be committed.

When `SetComplete()` is called the component is deactivated. The reason is that the component is indicating that it has completed its work. However, the component could have access to some transactional state and if the component lives beyond committing the transaction it could alter that state outside of the criteria of the transaction. This violates the isolation rule of transactions, and to prevent this from occurring, MTS deactivates and physically destroys the component. Typically components call `SetComplete()` at the end of each method on the component.

If a component must survive after each method call returns then it can call `DisableCommit()`. This indicates that the transactional work of the component has not been completed, so the transaction cannot be committed. Such a component can hold onto transactional state, but be aware that if the transaction is not completed within the timeout (the default is 60 seconds) then MTS will automatically abort it. In this situation, if the component is a sub-component, and the transactional component that created it calls `SetComplete()`, then the transaction can't be committed, so it will be aborted. This means that the method call on the base component will return `CONTEXT_E_ABORTED`.

However, if the base component in the transaction calls `DisableCommit()` and all the method calls made on the sub-components call `SetComplete()` then the transaction will survive the method return, as will the base component. However, since no attempt has been made to commit the transaction, the method call on the base component will not fail, and the base component will still survive. The base client is able to call another method on this component, and if this results in a call to `SetComplete()` then the transaction will be committed. If the base component is released without a call to `SetComplete()` then the transaction will be aborted. Bear in mind that this result isn't returned to the client because, of course, `IUnknown::Release()` does not return a `HRESULT`.

If a component decides that its transactional work has completed, but does not necessarily want to be deactivated, it can call `EnableCommit()`. This means that the component is happy with the transaction and that if the base component is released (and hence the transaction ends) then this component won't prevent the transaction from committing. However, unlike `SetComplete()`, this doesn't indicate that the component should be deactivated, so the component will still live until all references on it have been released. The programmer must be very careful to make sure that any state remaining in the component is not transactional, as it might violate the isolation criteria if it were.

Once a transaction has been committed, its results will be made durable by the resource managers that enlisted into the transaction (the **D** in ACID). However, if at a later stage the application decides that the changes should not be made (an order is cancelled, for example) then the application can perform a **compensating transaction**. As the name suggests, this is another transaction, and its purpose is to reverse the effect of a previous transaction. MTS doesn't provide compensating transactions because these are effectively part of the business logic of the application. It is up to the analyst to decide if compensating transactions are required, and if so the developer should add extra code to the component to perform them.

> **COM+ provides a facility called 'Compensating Resource Manager'. Despite this name, it is not used to provide compensating transactions, but is instead essentially a lightweight mechanism for providing resource manager-like behavior.**

Transactional programming like this works well, and as you can see it adds useful features to COM. However, you have to be careful about the assumptions that you make about the identity of an MTS component. As far as the client is concerned, the identity it sees is provided by the proxy object, and this identity will be the same over all method invocations. If the component is part of a transaction that ends when each method is called, then the MTS component is destroyed – even though the context wrapper remains. This means that the real COM identity of the component that the client holds (the IUnknown pointer) is lost, along with any other logical identity (some identification value cached as a data member).

The component could maintain its identity in some durable storage, but this begs the question of how the component knows which of the persisted identities is its own. One solution is for the client to maintain the identity and pass this as a parameter on each method call (for example, some row identifier in a database table). After all, this is what happens with calls to interface methods, because a 'this' pointer is passed with every method call. This just means that with MTS you have to do all this explicitly, rather than allowing COM to do it implicitly.

Transaction Boundaries

A component that runs under a transaction can create a new component in the same activity using IObjectContext::CreateInstance(). If that new component supports or requires a transaction (but not a *new* transaction) then it will be created under the transaction of the creator component. MTS applies transactions automatically – if a component requires a transaction (either an existing one or a new one) then MTS will ensure that there will be a transaction for the component. Although this makes programming simple, it doesn't follow the model used by other transactional systems (for example, transactional databases) where the code explicitly starts and ends the transaction. Furthermore, a base client can't create two components in the same transaction. This is because MTS doesn't support a mechanism (other then creation in the same activity with IObjectContext::CreateInstance()) to indicate that objects should run under the same transaction.

One possible way to do this is to create an MTS component that requires a new transaction and then implement an interface on it that mirrors IObjectContext. Thus, this interface can have a CreateInstance() method that allows clients to add new components into the transaction, and Commit() and Abort() methods to end the transaction on the base component.

You don't have to do this work, because MTS provides such an object for you called the TransactionContextEx object, which is installed as part of the Utilities library package. This object requires a new transaction, so it can behave as the base component in a transaction. However, there are some issues that you need to be aware of.

TransactionContextEx is implemented in a library package, which means that if the client is not an MTS server, you will not get role based security on the methods that you call. If a client uses components installed in MTS on another machine through DCOM, then it doesn't need to have MTS or MS DTC to be installed on the client machine, as long as transactional components only run on the server machine. This is a great facility because it cuts down on the administration of the clients (you don't have to install MTS and MS DTC), and the client machine doesn't need the extra resources (disk space and memory) needed for them.

However, if the client uses TransactionContextEx to create those remote components, then you have no option but to install MTS/MS DTC, and you have the extra network calls required by a distributed transaction. Whatever you do, you should always try to reduce the number of network calls to a minimum.

These issues don't mean that you shouldn't use the `TransactionContextEx` object, but they do mean that you should be careful how you use it. In general, it should be restricted to breaking transaction propagation on the server side within an MTS server package – and kept off client machines.

Security

When enabled through the MTS Explorer, security access checks are performed whenever a client accesses a method on one of the component's interfaces (except `IUnknown` – the client access here is handled by the context wrapper). The access checks are made against roles defined for the package in which the component is installed. The MTS administrator can specify that accounts in particular roles can access any method on any interface on the component. Alternatively, the administrator can be more precise, and specify that particular interfaces can only be accessed by specific roles.

You cannot deny access through declarative security – the MTS Explorer only allows you to give access to particular roles. You have, for example, an object called `Inventory`, with two interfaces called `IViewItems` and `IAdministerItems` (allowing you to list or delete items in an inventory, or add new ones). It clearly makes sense to allow the `InventoryAdministrator` role to have access to both interfaces while the `TeleSales` role has access only to the `IViewItems` role:

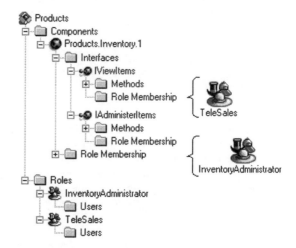

Here, `InventoryAdministrator` has been added to the Role Membership of the `Inventory` component, whereas `TeleSales` has been added to the Role Membership of the `IViewItems` interface.

Note that Role Membership indicates the *client accounts* that can access the component – it is only those client accounts that are members of the specified roles that have access to the component (or the specific interface on the component). The package identity is the account under which the package runs. Therefore, access checks will be made against and audited under this account when a component accesses a secured NT object (file, thread, process etc.).

The administrator can use the MTS Explorer to add NT accounts into the defined roles. When a client calls a method on a component, MTS makes the access checks against all the NT accounts in the role that have access to the component or interface. The caller account is the security token of the process that calls the component, and if this is a base client process then it is often the interactive user. If the caller is another package (or a COM server) then the account will be the identity of the server. In terms of an MTS server package this is defined through the Identity tab of the package's properties. By default this will be the interactive user, but administrators should use a named domain or local account, so that the package can run when there is no one logged on to the machine.

When you create a new package MTS Explorer will create an AppID with the Package ID and it will create a new CLSID that references this AppID (it has a value called `AppID` that mentions this GUID). It does this so that it can have an `AccessPermissions` value for the package. Whenever you add a new NT account to one of the package's roles, an access ACE (access control entry) for this account will be added to the ACL (access control list) held in this value. This AppID also has a `LaunchPermissions` value which gives launch permission to `EveryOne` and `SYSTEM`. There is no way that you can officially edit this value.

An MTS component can call `IObjectContext::IsCallerInRole()` to determine if the caller has been defined in a specific role. Since this method is called from an interface method, you can apply a more detailed approach to access checks – that is, you can perform method level access checks (or even finer) rather than the interface level access checks (the finest level possible with MTS 2.0).

> **COM+ allows method-level access checks to be declared in the catalog for a component.**

Note, though, that library packages run in-process in the base client, and therefore under the security of that client. Thus a call to `IsCallerInRole()` will always return `TRUE` in this case because security is not applied. The developer can call `IObjectContext::IsSecurityEnabled()` to determine whether the component is running within a library package.

When several components are installed as part of a package, they will be instantiated in the same process, regardless of whether they are physically implemented in different DLLs. Components in a package have access to other components in the same package, even if the administrator has configured the components to be accessed by different roles. For example, `PackageA` has two components, `Creator` and `ObjectOne`, where the former is used to return references to the latter:

```
STDMETHODIMP CCreator::CreateObject(IObjectOne** ppOut)
{
    CComPtr<IObjectContext> pCont;
    GetObjectContext(&pCont);
    return pCont->CreateInstance(__uuidof(ObjectOne), __uuidof(*ppOut),
                                (void**)ppOut);
}
```

`Creator` is configured to be accessed by the `CreationUsers` role and `ObjectOne` is configured to be accessed by `ObjectUsers` role. This means that the base client can have code like this:

```
CComPtr<ICreator> pCreate;
pCreate.CoCreateInstance(__uuidof(Creator));
CComPtr<IObjectOne> pObj;
pCreate->CreateObject(&pObj);
pObj->DoSomething();
```

This code will succeed even if the NT account of the base client is a member of the `CreationUsers` role but not the `ObjectUsers` role. However, if `ObjectOne` calls `IsCallerInRole()` then it will be able to check against the role membership of the caller, and thus make a check against the `ObjectUsers` role.

The MTS documentation recommends that the developer should define the package roles and program against this. The package can then be exported for deployment, and it is up to the administrator of the deployment machine to add users to the roles. However, note that a component can get hold of the roles using the MTSAdmin components, although it is hardly straightforward. As you'll see in Chapter 4, these components are written for scripting languages like VBScript, so with VC++ you have to jump through hoops before you can get them to do anything useful.

A library package means that the DLLs of the components are loaded in-process into the client that creates the components. If that client is a server package, this means that the component DLLs are loaded into the instance of mtx.exe that runs the server package. Consequently, the components in the library package can call IsCallerInRole(), but only for roles defined for the server package.

Just In Time Activation

One of the significant areas where MTS extends COM is in how components are activated. MTS uses **just in time** (**JIT**) activation. What this means is that when the client makes an activation call to create a component, the component is not returned – the context wrapper object is. This means that the component doesn't have to be there, and the client is happy because it still gets a reference to a real component.

When the client makes a call on a method other than one of the IUnknown methods, the context wrapper object has no choice but to pass it on to the MTS component – if the component doesn't exist then MTS must create it. If the component indicates that it will no longer do work in the transaction (for example, by calling SetComplete()) then MTS will deactivate the component – in other words it destroys the component. The client, of course, doesn't see this because it still has a reference to the context wrapper object. When the client makes another call to a method other than IUnknown, MTS once again activates the MTS component. In MTS 2.0 this will be a new instance of the component. There is no physical COM identity problem here because even for MTS components created in-process from a library package, the identity that the client sees is that of the context wrapper object. However, as mentioned earlier, there may be a logical identity problem.

A component can implement IObjectControl to manage per activation initialization. When the component is activated MTS calls Activate(), and when it is deactivated MTS calls Deactivate(). Unlike the constructor and destructor, the context object is available during these methods, so you are able to use it. Consider this pseudo code:

```
IMyObject* pObj;
CoCreateInstance(..., &pObj);
Obj->CallMethod()
Obj->CallMethod()
Obj->Release()
```

If the method `CallMethod()` calls `SetComplete()` before returning then the component will be deactivated and a new instance will be created on the second call. The actual calls to the component that occur are:

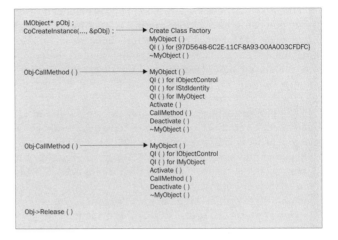

Notice that on the initial call to `CoCreateInstance()` an instance of the component is actually created and queried for `{979D5648-6C2E-11CF-8A93-00AA003CFDFC}` before the component is deactivated. This is MTS trying to detect if the component is a Java object or not. If it is a Java object, then MTS must do some special, one-time-only, initialization on the thread to accommodate the MS Java VM. It does this by querying for an undocumented Java interface. However, notice that this component is not cached, but is destroyed as soon as the `QueryInterface()` is called. (This behavior is removed from Windows 2000 – see Chapter 8.)

Imagine that your component performs some expensive initialization in the constructor (or the ATL method `FinalConstruct()`). Because of the extra activation, this initialization will occur during the construction of the first component (used to test for Java). Yet the initialized component will not be used, so the initialization will be wasted. This reinforces the fact that initialization should occur in `IObjectControl::Activate()` and cleanup in `IObjectControl::Deactivate()`. However, note that even if you do this you must ensure that this initialization will benefit the entire component. If the component has several methods and only one of these needs the initialization, then it makes sense to put the code there rather than in `Activate()`.

The context object survives as long as the context wrapper object. The context under which the component should run is therefore preserved, even though the MTS component may have been deactivated. Clearly, information such as the actual client making the method call could change, because once `ClientA` creates the base component it could pass the interface pointer to `ClientB` (which could be running under a different account to `ClientA`). Both clients can then make method calls on the MTS component. The context maintains the security account of the original creator as well as the more transient account of the caller of a method.

MTS and Threading

MTS components execute in an activity. This activity can span several server processes on the same machine, and it can span several machines. Each of these MTS server processes will have threads of execution that will be part of the activity, and conceptually the base client thread that created the base component can also be treated as part of the activity. There can be many threads, leading to the possibility of parallel execution.

Chapter 2

COM is synchronous – when a client makes a call on an interface method, the client thread blocks until the call returns. The situation is no different with MTS, since all COM calls are synchronous. However, MTS complicates matters, because components running in MTS can run under the influence of a transaction. This means that all the components in the transaction stream do their work in one atomic unit of action, and the transactional state that they use is isolated from any other component.

MTS components behave as if they are single threaded. MTS ensures that all components in an activity are serialized on the same thread (assuming a single machine and single server process). A server process may have many activities, and these will *usually* get individual threads. However, excessive numbers of threads are not good – contrary to popular belief, multithreading doesn't always give you better performance. If the threads are CPU-bound then creating extra threads will only improve performance on a multi-processor machine. It will give your clients a semblance of better availability, but switching between threads is an expensive task, and threads themselves take up system resources. Because of this, MTS restricts the number of threads that will run in a particular package.

This thread limit is a value held in the catalog entry for the package, which corresponds to the registry value:

```
HKLM\SOFTWARE\Microsoft\Transaction Server\Packages\{PackageID}\ThreadPoolMax
```

where {PackageID} is your Package ID. If the value is missing, then the default 100 thread limit is used. Once this limit is reached, MTS will start to reuse threads in the pool, so that multiple activities may run on the same thread.

My tests indicate that the algorithm used to distribute activities between threads in the pool does not appear to be evenly balanced. For example, I performed a test with a client that creates 200 threads synchronized by an event object. These threads call CoCreateInstanceEx() for the same MTS component, and then call the same method before ending. Once all the threads are created, the event is set to start the work of the threads. This means that 200 activities are created doing the same work and are (as near as possible) started at the same time. The component merely prints out the thread ID and activity ID to the debug stream, which I can monitor and thus determine which activity runs on which thread.

The package uses the default thread pool limit of 100, so I expected almost all the threads to have two activities. However, the results showed that MTS allocated many threads to run just one activity, while others had two, and a sizable number (20%) had three.

Note the previous warnings about activities. MTS only guarantees serialization between calls on components within the same package in an activity. So, for example, you might have two packages on the same machine, and run a component under each within the same activity. You could then create two clients on the same machine, and pass a reference to one of the components to each client. You'll find that only one of the clients will be able to access a component in a package – synchronization works within the package, but concurrent access to components in different packages is possible, even though the components are running in the same activity.

Each MTS thread is an STA thread. This means that your component should not be marked as `ThreadingModel=Free`. If it is, then MTS Explorer won't complain when you add it to a package, and `mtx.exe` won't complain when a client activates the component, but the component will *not* be created in the MTA because MTS only uses STA threads. Clearly, if you mark your component as `Free` there must be an important reason to do so, and this makes the component unsuitable to run under MTS. The usual reason to do this is because that component will access other threads in the MTA (an issue examined later), and by making the component `Free` you indicate that it will *always* be created in the process's MTA. A component that runs under MTS should be thread unaware, and therefore should not be marked as `Free`.

MTS components can be marked as `Apartment`, `Both` or have no `ThreadingModel` value (the single threading model). Single threaded model components will run on the main thread of the server process and should only be used with components that are not re-entrant. However, this has very limited scalability because access to instances of the component will always be through the same thread. At its worst, when the package has just this one component and many activities, all these activities will be on the same thread. The package will therefore be single threaded, and this thread will become a bottleneck. Only use the single threaded model when there is no alternative. Furthermore, if several single threaded components are used in a server process, there is a possibility of deadlocks.

Most MTS components should be `Apartment` or `Both`. The ATL Object Wizard, when asked to create a MTS Transaction Server Object, takes this second option in an inconsistent way – it registers the component as `Both` in the RGS file, but uses `CComSingleThreadModel` as the threading model template parameter of the `CComObjectRootEx<>` base class. The only reason I can see for this is that the author of the Object Wizard assumed that if the component will only run under MTS, then it won't need the thread locking provided by `CComMultiThreadModel`. This, however, leaves a risk of the component being used outside of MTS, within an MTA, while having thread sensitive code and data unprotected. It is best to change the RGS file so that the component will be marked as `Apartment`. Then, if there is a possibility that it will be used outside of MTS, there is no chance of multiple threads corrupting it.

MTS components have a context that defines the environment in which they should run. When a component's method is about to be executed, MTS will make its context the current one for the thread, remaining current as long as execution occurs in the component. However, if the component calls a method of another component (one with a different context), this causes a context switch. The caller's context is automatically restored on return from the method.

> *The code for the next chapter has an updated version of the MTS Object Wizard that fixes this, along with some other problems (principally that the supplied Object Wizard does not allow you to use error objects or connection points).*

Creating New threads

In general, creating a new thread from an MTS component isn't a good idea. The reason is that a worker thread will not inherit the context of your component, so it has no access to the context object and will not run under the transaction of the MTS component. This severely restricts what you can do in it. Even if you do have a good reason to use a thread that runs out of the context of your MTS component, there remains the issue of spawning threads from a DLL.

Normally, with COM DLL servers, you are advised to be careful of doing this because a client may call `CoFreeUnusedLibraries()`. If there are no components, most DLL implementations will return `S_OK` from `DllCanUnloadNow()`, thus allowing the DLL (and the code for the worker thread function) to be unloaded. However, this doesn't occur with `mtx.exe`, since the DLL will remain loaded as long as the package is loaded (whether there are extant components or not). You will still have to make sure though, that when the DLL is unloaded, any resources it holds are correctly released. You can prevent `mtx.exe` from unloading unexpectedly by the worker thread `AddRef()`ing a context wrapper object and maintaining this reference count until the worker thread decides that it is ready to die.

If you want to pass a reference to your MTS component to the worker thread, then you *must* make sure that you call `SafeRef()` to get a reference to the context wrapper. This should be marshaled to the worker thread using `CoMarshalInterface()` and `CoUnmarshalInterface()`. This is required because all MTS threads are STA and therefore any worker thread will always be in another apartment.

The fact that MTS components are run in STAs may bring about another problem. When a component in an STA makes an outbound call, it spins in a message queue waiting for the return from its call. Since inbound calls are serialized through this message queue, the component is re-entrant. Thus, the component must be written with this in mind. Alternatively, you can implement a message filter (with `IMessageFilter`) to handle the situation accordingly. MTS monitors access to transactional objects and if any calls are made concurrently on it, MTS will abort the transaction, since otherwise consistency will be violated.

Activation

MTS carefully monitors your component, and sometimes it does more work than you realize. MTS will intercept calls to your component's `IUnknown` methods and will monitor your response to them. The COM spec says that `AddRef()` and `Release()` should return the reference count, but clients should not rely on the returned value because it is only intended for debugging purposes. However, MTS does take some notice – it keeps a check on what the reference count should be (it knows this because it intercepts `AddRef()` and `Release()`) and if MTS thinks that the last reference count has been released it will check the return value from `Release()` to make sure that your component returns zero. If it doesn't, then MTS will figure that there is a problem, and will log a message to the event log.

Consider this code:

```
template <class Base>
class COddRefComObject : public CComObject<Base>
{
public:
    COddRefComObject(void* = NULL){}
    STDMETHOD_(ULONG, Release)()
    {
        ULONG l = InternalRelease();
        if (l == 0)
        {
            delete this;
            // MTS won't like this
            return 1;
        }
```

```
        return 1;
    }
};

class ATL_NO_VTABLE CMyOddObject :
    public CComObjectRootEx<CComSingleThreadModel>,
    public CComCoClass<CMyOddObject, &CLSID_MyOddObject>,
    public IDispatchImpl<IMyOddObject, &IID_IMyOddObject, &LIBID_ODDLib>
{
public:
    CMyOddObject(){ }
// replaces DECLARE_AGGREGATABLE()
    typedef CComCreator2<CComCreator<COddRefComObject<CMyOddObject> >,
                         CComCreator<CComAggObject<CMyOddObject> > >
        _CreatorClass;
//etc
};
```

This component is normal in all respects, except that the class factory creates it using
`COddRefComObject<>` rather than `CComObject<>`. The significant thing about this class is that it
returns the current reference count, *except when the value falls to zero*. In this case it will delete the
component as expected, but will return 1 rather then 0.

MTS notices this and will log the following to the event log:

Source:	Transaction Server
Severity:	Information
Category:	Executive
Event:	4098
Description:	Unexpected object reference count. The object still had references after the run-time environment released its last reference.
	Unbind (Package: Odd)
	(ProgId: Oddity.MyOddObject.1)
	(CLSID: {CBCEA4F4-0457-11D3-8971-00104BDC35E0})
	(Interface: IUnknown)
	(IID: {00000000-0000-0000-C000-000000000046})
	(Method: 2)
	(Microsoft Transaction Server Internals Information: File: d:\viper\src\runtime\context\ccontext.cpp, Line: 2807)

Clearly, this component is a bit strange, so why would you want to write code to do this?

One situation where you'll get this behavior is if you create an ATL singleton object, which
implements `IClassFactory::CreateInstance()` by returning a reference to a single instance
of your component created through `CComObjectGlobal<>`. This class implements `Release()` like
this:

```
STDMETHOD_(ULONG, Release)(){return _Module.Unlock();}
```

The return value from this will never be zero because the class factory objects will have bumped up the module lock count when asked for an interface. Thus MTS will get confused and log the message mentioned above.

Singletons are a controversial subject – some people swear by them, others swear at them. I don't want to add to the general debate here, but it should be clear that as far as MTS is concerned you shouldn't use singletons.

How MTS Activates Components

MTS is quite intimate with COM. Under NT4 and Win98, MTS is an extension to COM and as such it uses COM to activate components. However, as mentioned earlier, MTS does a little more than that. In this section I will show you some of the extra steps that MTS takes to activate a component. The following has been taken by monitoring calls to the registry and judicious application of `ATLTRACE()`.

In the following I have used a simple MTS component that runs in a server package on the same machine as the client. The calls to the registry come from several sources: the COM runtime in the client; the COM runtime in `mtx.exe`; the SCM (service control manager); the security provider and from MTS itself (`mtx.exe` and `mtxex.dll`). The striking thing is that the calls from MTS are both to the MTS catalog *and* to the COM registration in `HKEY_CLASSES_ROOT`. Indeed, MTS appears to cross check the values it has in the catalog against those in `HKEY_CLASSES_ROOT`, but it uses the former's values in preference to the latter's.

Creating the Class Factory Object

As mentioned earlier, because MTS activities run in STA threads, your component will be launched by MTS into an STA, whatever threading model it specifies in the registry (with the `ThreadingModel` value). However, having used MTS Explorer to add a component to a package, you'll find that although the correct threading model is added to the catalog, MTS Explorer will change the component's `HKEY_CLASSES_ROOT` registry entry to have a `ThreadingModel` of `Free`. This is to specify that the class factory object for the component should be launched in the process's MTA.

COM normally assumes that a DLL-based component's class factory object will be in the same apartment as the components it creates. However, this is not a requirement (though for an in-proc component, the marshaling from class factory object in one apartment to the actual component creator in another apartment *is* likely to become a performance issue). ATL uses this idea with the STA thread pool class factory (`CComClassFactoryAutoThread`) for EXE servers, where the class factory object is registered in one apartment (preferably the MTA) but uses component creator code in another apartment (one of a pool of STA threads).

MTS uses a similar approach. The class factory object that the client sees is the wrapper class factory object provided by the MTS executive. This is created in the MTA to take advantage of the greater availability that this offers. The actual class factory object of your coclass is created in the STA where the component is created. If you test for the thread ID that this class factory runs, and for its identity as you request several components of the same type, you will discover the startling fact that the *same* class factory object is moved from apartment to apartment to create these components:

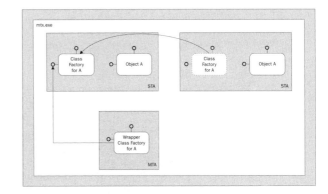

This contradicts COM's assertion that a component lives in exactly one apartment. MTS is able to do this because it knows the concurrency requirements that are needed.

Initializing MTS

When a client calls CoCreateInstance() to create an MTS component, the normal COM activation requests will be made. COM will check for security settings for the client (if the client doesn't call CoInitializeSecurity()), which is necessary if callbacks are likely to be made. COM will then read the registry to find the server name for the component. Since MTS Explorer will have altered the registry, this will result in COM reading mtx.exe as the server from the LocalServer32 key. COM will then read the AppID for the server to get the identity, launch permissions and start mtx.exe. This is a usual COM activation process – notice though that the identity will be the same as specified through the MTS Explorer, but the launch permissions will be set to EveryOne and SYSTEM. In other words, no fine grain access checks will be performed, the reason being that if access checks are enabled then role-based checks will be made.

MTS will then launch the MTS executive as an in-proc server within mtx.exe, and will determine if the MS DTC should trace calls (HKLM\Software\Microsoft\MSDTC\Trace) as well as obtaining other information about MS DTC (it will look for the undocumented CmCancelRpcAfter, CmMaxIdlePings and CmPingFreqSecs values in the MSDTC key).

At this point the client security is set, and the MS DTC has been initialized.

Initializing the Package

MTS then determines how long the package should remain in memory once loaded, so it reads the package's Latency and NeverShutdown values. At this point MTS loads a helper object called MTxRn.MTxRegNode.1 (it is not clear what this object does – the only registered interface it implements is IUnknown) and then checks to see if the package is a server or library package. Based on this, MTS determines the size of the threading pool that the package will use (the ThreadPoolMax value under the package in the catalog) and, if this value doesn't exist, uses the default value of 100.

Next, MTS does a lot of cross-checking. For example, it obtains the component's information from the catalog and checks the value for the ProgID against that registered for the component in HKEY_CLASSES_ROOT. It does the same for the LIBID of the component's type information. Note that the catalog does not contain the version of the type library, but it does contain the LIBID and the path to the type library. It uses these two pieces of information to enumerate all the entries in HKEY_CLASSES_ROOT\TypeLib for this LIBID. For each version it compares the path of the type library with the path in the catalog, and when the two agree it knows that it has the correct version.

In addition, COM will read the threading model registered for the component (which will be Free because MTS will have changed it to this when the component was added to the package), to specify which apartment type the (wrapper) class factory object should run (always in the MTA). MTS will then read the ThreadingModel value given in the catalog, which indicates the *actual* apartment type of the component and its class factory – this will be an STA, either Apartment, Both or none. MTS will also read the catalog to see if the component is enabled (the Enabled value under the component's entry in the catalog), and checks to see if the component is local.

At this point MTS can create the component, but it needs to make security checks. It checks to see if security is enabled for the package (SecurityEnabled), and determines the authentication level for the package (Authentication). It also does some security lookups for the MTS Impersonators alias, which certain accounts (like IWAM_computername in ASP) use.

MTS now needs to set up the environment for the component. It first creates a component with the CLSID of:

```
{0124efac-9e5a-11d0-8069-00c04fc2f9c1}
```

which is contained in mtxex.dll, and implements the IMainThreadHelper interface (the proxy stub is in mtxact.dll). MTS also accesses the IViperThread interface (proxy-stub in mtxact.dll) on one of its components, which presumably is used to manage MTS threads (Viper being the code name of MTS 1.0 when it was in beta testing).

MTS then sets up its event system by creating a CasperObj component (implemented in mtsevents.dll and presumably called that because of its ghost-like behavior) and searches for information about how MTS works by looking at the Extender key in the catalog for the undocumented ShutDownTimeOut and MaxQSize values. If you have Visual Studio Analyzer installed, MTS will load the MSVSA Inprocess Event Creator Class as well as the MTSEvents Class (Visual Studio Analyzer is used to monitor calls in a distributed application and is described in Chapter 7).

> *At this point MTS has determined how the package should run, the size of the thread pool, the threading model of the class factory object and the component. It also checks that the server can be launched and initializes the server threading and events.*

Initializing Transactions

Next, MTS needs to prepare itself to work with transactional databases. It checks for installed Oracle database libraries (the catalog keys OracleXaLib and OracleSqlLib), checks to see if tracing should occur (looking for the TRACE key in MTX.INI or the registry mapping in IniFileMapping\MTx.Ini), and then checks some more Oracle settings (MTxOciCPTimeout and OracleTraceFilePath).

It is interesting to see that these checks are only performed for Oracle — MTS checks for neither SQL Server nor any other database. I guess MTS has been optimized for SQL Server, which will account for the absence of checks for that. I expect that the specific checks for Oracle represent the fact that it is SQL Server's main competitor in situations where MTS will be used.

Now MTS can set up the transactional environment needed for components. MTS starts by obtaining information about the MS DTC from HKLM\SOFTWARE\Classes\CID, before reading the Transaction value in the component's catalog entry. Once MTS has determined the transaction it needs to determine the activity — it reads the ThreadingModel for the component from the catalog, and checks to see if it is 'wrapped' by looking for the Wrapped value in the component's entry. Some components have this value, which can be Y or N, but others don't. It is unclear as to what criteria are used to warrant this value or what wrapping means.

At this point MTS will have initialized Oracle, if it is used, and next it sets up the context for the component — its transaction requirements and activity membership.

Further Initialization

The next step is for MTS to set up the security infrastructure. When you add a package to MTS, MTS Explorer will add the PackageID into the HKEY_CLASSES_ROOT\CLSID key as a CLSID and create an AppID. It will also add an AppID for each component, and the SCM checks this AppID and reads the identity that MTS Explorer wrote there. Note that this AppID has an ACL in the LaunchPermission key, which includes all of the accounts that the administrator added to the roles of the package. (Chapter 6 will explain in more detail how role based security is managed in the registry.)

MTS then does some more administrative work by loading the MTS Catalog Class, MTS Catalog 1.0 Object (in mtxadmin.dll), and the AspTracker 1.0 Object. The first two are components used by MTS to access the catalog — the third one, however, is interesting. This component is loaded regardless of whether MTS is being used in an ASP application, and shows how intimate MTS and IIS are with each other.

At this point, MTS has checked for launch permissions and will have loaded the AspTracker object.

Handling the Component's Interface

MTS is about to marshal the component's interface back to the client, so it needs to get marshaling information — it also needs to set up the interception layer. To do this it needs to load the InterfaceHelper object, which I'll come back to in a moment.

MTS accesses the requested component's interface key in HKEY_CLASSES_ROOT and checks for the Forward key. This is undocumented, but from the interfaces that do have this key, it appears that it is used to indicate that the interface is marshaled using the proxy-stub of another interface. When MTS has the appropriate interface key, it checks how it is marshaled. In the case of type library marshaled interfaces, COM in MTS needs to load the type library using the information in the interface key (TypeLib key and Version value). If the interface is not type library marshaled, then it checks the interface key for the InterfaceHelper value. This will have a CLSID that corresponds to the InterfaceHelper object implemented in the proxy-stub file, and, as explained earlier, this gives information about the interface's methods.

After loading the proxy-stub for the interface (and any interface helper objects) the SCM loads the AspTracker 1.0 Object, which is in a package in MTS (again, regardless of whether ASP is being used).

At this point MTS will have loaded the InterfaceHelper *object for the requested component interface, along with any proxy-stub files needed to marshal the interface. It will also have loaded the* AspTracker *object again.*

Making the Method Call

Now the client makes the method call, and (for a type library marshaled interface) the SCM again loads the MTS Catalog 1.0 Object, and MTS accesses its ICatalogSession and ICatalogRead interfaces (the type information for these are in mtxcatex.dll). The first interface initializes the MTS Catalog component to read from the catalog, and the second one does the actual read (Chapter 4 will examine this component which is part of the MTS 2.0 Catalog Server library). These calls to the catalog will be used to get information about the MTS component, so that MTS can intercept the method call.

JIT activation requires the class factory object to be created – when this is done IClassFactory::CreateInstance() is called twice, the first time to perform the check to see if the component is a Java object. At this point there is an existing component. MTS adds the package name to the catalog Extender key. The default value of this key is the CLSID of the CasperObj, which suggests that this key is involved in managing the MTS events (see Chapter 4). The package entries in this key are DWORD values which always have a value of 0x10000. When a package finally shuts down, it removes itself from this key (this does not always happen, but it is unclear what prevents it). It then performs access checks on the package-level, the component-level and finally the interface-level to see that the client has permission to access the component.

If the access checks succeed then the method is called, and this ultimately leads to JIT deactivation. When the component is released, MTS gets catalog information again and then reads information about the package – it appears to read all the information, including the name and description. MTS then reads information about the IReceiveAspData interface (proxy-stub in mtxextps.dll) and the ITrackerAdmin interface (in mtxtrkps.dll).

The final actions are: the component's class factory is created, the component is checked to see if it is a Java object, and access checks are performed to see if the client can access it. The method call is then made and the object deactivated.

Activation Summary

These are the main steps that occur when a component is activated:

❑ The client calls CoCreateInstanceEx() for the MTS component.

❑ If the client does not initialize security then COM will do by calling CoInitializeSecurity(), using values held in the registry.

❑ COM looks for the server to load. The MTS Explorer will have altered the component's CLSID key to refer to either mtxex.dll (library package) or mtx.exe (server package) – in both cases the package ID is given as a command line.

❑ COM looks in the component's CLSID key for the AppID, which it uses to read the package identity and launch permissions. COM can then launch the package and (if it's a server package) start the process with the specified access token.

- ❏ If the package is a server then MTS loads the MTS executive, `mtxex.dll`.
- ❏ MTS initializes MS DTC.
- ❏ MTS initializes the package, determines how long it runs when idle and how large the thread pool should be.
- ❏ MTS obtains the type library that describes the component.
- ❏ MTS reads the threading model of the component to determine activity membership.
- ❏ MTS checks to see if the component is in-proc (in a library package), local (in a server package) or remote (if so checks `RemoteServerName` for the AppID for the component).
- ❏ MTS checks to see if role-based access checks are enabled and reads the authentication level used to access all components in the package.
- ❏ COM checks that the client account is able to access all components in the package.
- ❏ MTS initializes the thread using an object that implements `IMainThreadHelper` and `IViperThread`.
- ❏ MTS initializes the event system with the `CasperObj` component.
- ❏ MTS checks to see if Oracle libraries are installed, and if so it loads and initializes them.
- ❏ MS DTC is initialized
- ❏ MTS reads `LaunchPermissions` for the *component*.
- ❏ MTS reads the component's transactional requirements to see if a new transaction should be created, and then checks the activity membership.
- ❏ MTS loads the `AspTracker` object, regardless of whether ASP is used.
- ❏ MTS gets information about the requested interface by loading the `InterfaceHelper` object registered for the interface. (This is used both for components with a proxy-stub or a type library.)
- ❏ MTS loads the `MTS Catalog` object to get further information about the component.
- ❏ MTS creates the component class factory.
- ❏ MTS creates the component, destroys it (Java check), calls `IClassFactory::LockServer()`, and creates the component again.
- ❏ MTS adds the package name to the `Extender` key.
- ❏ MTS checks package-level ACL, component-level ACL checks, then interface-level ACL checks.
- ❏ The method is called.
- ❏ JIT deactivation occurs.

Summary

MTS is a better COM. It provides many facilities that were omitted from the original COM spec and others that make using COM child's play. In this chapter you have learned how MTS leverages COM to perform its magic, learned about the extra facilities that MTS offers, and gained a little insight into the secrets of how MTS works.

The chapter started by explaining the various server types that are possible with plain COM. It compared these to MTS's model, where components are always packaged in a DLL and it is the administrator that decides whether the component will be activated either:

❑   in-proc (library package)

❑   in a separate process on the same machine as the client (server package)

❑   on another machine (remote component)

The chapter then explained the requirements of a component to allow interception.

Next, the chapter explored three areas of the MTS object context: transaction requirements, role-based security, and activities. It looked into how you can get context information, including the transaction and activity identifiers. The discussion on transactions described what transaction streams are, and how transactions are created and ended – this led on to just in time activation, required to make isolated transactions.

The final section of the chapter was a blow-by-blow account of how MTS activates components. What was clear from this discussion was that MTS and IIS are intimately tied together, with MTS automatically loading ASP monitoring objects irrespective of whether the package is used by IIS.

In the next chapter you will see how to put MTS to work, and learn how the MTS model will change the way that you program.

3

Programming Issues

Introduction

COM is all about interface programming, and this imposes certain disciplines on a programmer. MTS adds transactions to this. These can be distributed over several machines, and may affect processes other than your server process (resource managers). Also, components configured to use transactions are automatically enlisted into them. This means that a programmer needs to look at the transactional aspect of the application and write components accordingly. Furthermore, although MTS is layered over COM, there are some rules that must be adhered to, in order to preserve the MTS context and maintain the transactional ACID criteria.

This chapter will start by explaining the programming issues, and will then explain MTS development with Visual C++ 6.0 and ATL 3.0. Along the way a new ATL Object Wizard component type that addresses some of the shortcomings of the default types will be introduced – it is included with the downloadable code for this chapter. Finally, this chapter includes a look at database access in MTS, including OLE DB usage in ATL.

Programming Issues

MTS changes the way that you program your COM components. There are several issues:

❑ Just In Time (JIT) activation

❑ Context

❑ Distributed Applications

❑ Transactions

❑ Errors

❑ Callbacks

❑ Marshalling

❑ Object state

This section will detail how to handle each of these.

Programming for JIT

Just in time (**JIT**) activation and deactivation are performed on MTS components to ensure that transactions are isolated. Without JIT (particularly the deactivation aspect) transactional data could exist beyond the end of the transaction, breaking the isolation criteria of the transaction. By deactivating a component when the transaction ends, there is no possibility of transactional data being accessed outside of a transaction.

JIT activation uses your component's `IObjectControl` interface. When your component is just about to be used (that is, the client has made a call on one of its interface methods), MTS will call `IObjectControl::Activate()`. When your component is about to die (because a method in a transactional component has called `IObjectContext::SetComplete()` or `IObjectContext::SetAbort()`, or alternatively because a non-transactional component is finally released), then MTS will call `IObjectControl::Deactivate()` followed by `IObjectControl::CanBePooled()`.

`CanBePooled()` was originally provided to enable an component to indicate whether it could be placed into an object pool after being deactivated. However, MTS doesn't support object pooling. COM+ does support object pooling (see Chapter 8), and you can use the Component Services MMC snap-in to specify the limits of this pool (the minimum and maximum number of objects that it can contain). You can use `CanBePooled()` to indicate that a component can't be uninitialized into a deactivated state. You must use this method because `Deactivate()` doesn't return a status code, so there's no way you can indicate that it has failed and that the component instance should be destroyed. With COM+, if you return `TRUE` from `CanBePooled()` then the uninitialized component will be put into the pool. So, to get yourself ready for COM+ you should monitor the actions of `Deactivate()` and use the results of its deactivation to determine the return value of `CanBePooled()`.

`Activate()` and `Deactivate()` are called as part of the normal course of a component's lifetime. `Activate()` is used to perform context sensitive initialization, and `Deactivate()` is used to do context sensitive clean up. Initialization and cleanup in ATL components is normally carried out in `FinalConstruct()` and `FinalRelease()`. (If the initialization code does not use any virtual method calls then it can occur in the constructor.) However, at this point the component won't have access to its context object.

Furthermore, when the MTS Executive first sees an activation request component in an instance of `mtx.exe`, it will create an instance merely to query for a Java COM-specific interface, as explained in the previous chapter. This will then be immediately destroyed – only when JIT activation occurs is the actual component created and activated. Because of this, if you have some lengthy initialization code it makes no sense to put it into the component constructor, as these efforts will be in vain. The best advice is to put this code in `Activate()`. Or is it?

If your component has several methods, then you have to be careful what initialization you put into `Activate()`. Remember, this method is called to allow you to do context specific initialization *for the entire component*. If your component is transactional, and uses `SetComplete()` and `SetAbort()` to indicate its view of the transaction's state, then the component will be deactivated immediately after a method call returns. Any initialization performed in `Activate()` will be called again when another method is invoked. Putting the initialization code in `Activate()` will make your code cleaner, because you don't need to replicate the same code throughout the interface methods. Strictly speaking, though, this isn't required. More importantly, if you have several methods on the interface, then the initialization in `Activate()` should be pertinent to all methods. Otherwise, a client could call a method and get initialization that it doesn't need.

JIT activation (and the associated, *as soon as possible* deactivation) are all about keeping transactions short, and making sure that those transactions are consistent and isolated – by ensuring that no transactional state is maintained between transactions. So, every time a client makes a call on a method of a transactional component, the component will most likely be activated and deactivated in the course of the method call. MTS, of course, maintains the context wrapper and context object between method invocations. So, where is the scalability? You have replaced each component (and the single class factory to create it) with *two* components (and the wrapper class factory and class factory) – thus $n + 1$ components maintained across method invocations without MTS are replaced with $2n + 2$ components when run under MTS. The purpose of JIT is not specifically to do with scalability, but to provide transaction isolation and consistency. I'll come back to this issue later in the chapter.

When the client releases the interface pointer to the MTS component, the context wrapper and context object will be released. The class factory (and its wrapper) will of course be released when the package shuts down, so we'll ignore that issue. This begs the question: should the client hold the MTS interface pointer for as short a time as possible, to ensure that the context wrapper is maintained for as short as possible?

There are pros and cons to this approach. If you release an interface pointer, it implies that you will need to create a new one to get the functionality of the component. This call means that a new activity will be created, and (depending on the timeout configured for the package and the time between activation requests) it may mean that a new instance of `mtx.exe` will be launched. On the plus side, if the component isn't written correctly to call `SetComplete()`/`SetAbort()` often, and thus relies on implicit transaction commit at context wrapper release, then releasing the interface pointer will often be required to keep the transaction short, and prevent excessive resource locking or transaction timeout.

However, holding onto interface pointers for a long time means that the connection/disconnection (and hence the setting up of the proxy and stub) is carried out just once. This reduces the time needed to create the appropriate marshaling components and associated network calls. The issue is clearly application dependent, so the solution can only be determined through application testing.

Use Your Context!

This should be second nature to you, but it needs to be reiterated here. Whenever you want to create a new component within an existing activity you must use `IObjectContext::CreateInstance()`. If you use `CoCreateInstanceEx()` then a new activity is created, and if the new component uses a transaction it won't have access to its creator's transaction. (Remember, a transaction stream belongs to only one activity, though each activity may have more than one transaction stream.)

If you want to return a pointer to your component as an `[out]` parameter then you must use `SafeRef()`. This is because neither your component nor the marshaling layer knows anything about the context wrapper object. The interface pointer you return will therefore be a raw pointer without the benefit of the context wrapper.

```
STDMETHODIMP CMyObject::GetMe(/*[out]*/ IMyObject** ppMe)
{
    CComPtr<IMyObject> spUnsafeMe;
    // ask the component for its IUnknown
    // this is the safe way to do it
    GetUnknown()->QueryInterface(&spUnsafeMe);

    // don't return spUnsafeMe
    *ppMe = reinterpret_cast<IMyObject*>(SafeRef(IID_IMyObject, spUnsafeMe));
    return S_OK;
}
```

`SafeRef()` will only return the context on the current component. Also be aware that an activity is only created for a component when you call `CoCreateInstanceEx()`. If you call `IObjectContext::CreateInstance()` then the sub-object will be created in the activity of the calling component – but (depending on its transactional requirements) it may be created in a different transaction stream. However, in both of these cases the new component will have its own context, so you don't need to call `SafeRef()` on such a pointer. Indeed, you will get a `NULL` pointer if you do so, because the call won't be on your own component.

If you generate non-creatable components (those that aren't created with a class factory) then these won't have their own context (because MTS will have no chance to intercept the creation) – you can't call `SafeRef()`. Don't be tempted to do this:

```
STDMETHODIMP CJobCenter::GetWorker(/*[out]*/ IUnknown** ppOut)
{
    CComPtr<IUnknown> spUnk;
    // use CComCoClass::CreateInstance() to create component
    CWorker::CreateInstance(&spUnk);
    // ERROR! will not return a context wrapper
    *ppOut = reinterpret_cast<IUnknown*>(SafeRef(IID_IUnknown, spUnk));
    return E_FAIL;
}
```

In this code, calling `SafeRef()` will return a `NULL` pointer. On the other hand, if you return the `spUnk` pointer, then the client will get a raw interface pointer, which means that MTS won't be able to intercept the method calls. The only way that you can return a component with a context is to call `CoCreateInstanceEx()` or `IObjectContext::CreateInstance()` and return that pointer (which one you call depends on whether you want a new activity to be created or not).

This presents a dilemma – code like `GetWorker()` is useful when you want to initialize a component to a specific value, because if your code creates the component rather than COM, it means that you get access to the `public` but non-COM methods. For example, with a class like this:

```
class CWorker :
    public CComCoClass<...>,
    public CComObjectRootEx<...>,
    public IWorker
{
public:
    // interface map and other stuff
    // IWorker
    STDMETHOD(DoWork)();
    // non-COM methods
    void Initialize(LPWSTR strName, double dPayRate);
};
```

In non-MTS code you can do this:

```
CComObject<CWorker>* pObj;
CComObject::CreateInstance(&pObj);
// call a non-COM method
pObj->Initialize(L"Karli", 10.00)
pObj->QueryInterface(IID_IWorker, reinterpret_cast<void**>(ppOut));
```

There are several problems here. The first is the lack of a context, which has already been mentioned. However, there are more serious problems. In particular, if this component is transactional and stateless, then the component activates and deactivates with each method call (and is therefore initialized afresh on each method call). In this case the initialization (performed through methods like `Initialize()`) will be lost.

If the component is stateful (and uses `DisableCommit()` to keep the component from being deactivated), then you could arrange to initialize it through an interface designed for that purpose, or even better use `IPersistStream`. This is because clients will not know the exact byte sequence required in the stream passed to `Load()`, so only your code will be able to initialize the component.

Distributed Applications

MTS is all about distributed applications – you can see this immediately in the deployment facilities in the MTS Explorer. However, although COM gives you location transparency (the client code accesses an interface pointer in the same way, whether the component is in-apartment, in a process on the same machine or on another), as an application architect you must still keep location in mind. The reason is clear – COM calls across the network are 10000 times slower than in-apartment calls, so a single call to a remote component can make any other calls in an MTS component's method insignificant. Furthermore, transactions must complete within the timeout defined by the commit coordinator in the transaction. This means that all efforts must be taken to keep the transaction short, so you must give particular attention to remote component calls.

Part of the problem is the VB mapping of COM components onto the method/properties model that it has always used for controls. This model allows you to change the properties of a control individually rather than as a batch, for example:

```
txtName.enabled = True
txtName.FontName = "Arial"
txtName.FontSize = 12
txtName.Text = "Richard"
```

Each change to a property is a method call. This is fine for a control, which is in-process (and ActiveX controls are in-apartment), because the only overhead in calling four `put_` methods over a possible single method alternative is the prolog and epilog calls of the `put_` methods to manage the stack. This code is only a few lines of assembler, and has little effect on the performance of the application. The VB programmer knows that intrinsic controls are in-process, and has known this for all the incarnations of VB since version 1. Thus it is ingrained in the VB psyche that property access like this is good.

To make life easier for VB programmers, Microsoft uses the same model for COM components:

```
Dim account as New Bank.Account
account.FirstName = "Richard"
account.LastName = "Grimes"
account.Balance = 1000000 ' in my dreams
account.ProcessAccount
```

However, COM has location transparency so the VB programmer *does not know* where the component is located, but due to the persistence of the property/method model they will treat the component as in-apartment. When the component is out of apartment (and particularly when the component is on another machine) the marshaling code and the inherent speed of the network both serve to impair performance

> *Note that some components available to scripting languages may use marshaling techniques to cache property changes in the proxy, and only write the data values to the actual component when some indicator method (`SaveChanges()`, for example) is called. You may choose to copy this technique yourself, but I still think it has its problems, because the component relies on the client developer remembering to call the indicator method.*

C++ programmers in general don't use this model, since it takes fewer keystrokes to bundle all the data into one method (and they are more concerned with efficiency, both in code and in the number of keystrokes they make):

```
CAccount* pAccount = new CAccount("Richard", "Grimes", 1000000);
pAccount->ProcessAccount();
```

or:

```
CAccount* pAccount = new CAccount;
pAccount->Initialize("Richard", "Grimes", 1000000);
pAccount->ProcessAccount();
```

When applied to COM, this C++ method of passing multiple values works much better for remote components. The point I'm making here is this: *Property access methods are evil, so don't use them!*

COM components don't have constructors, so only the last C++ example shown above can be applied to COM. This uses a separate initialization method, which is an extra network call for a remote component. However, for MTS components this sort of code should be avoided, because a transactional component would have to call `DisableCommit()` to prevent the component from being deactivated. The following pseudo code is much better:

```
CAccount* pAccount = new CAccount;
pAccount->ProcessAccount("Richard", "Grimes", 1000000);
```

This doesn't look alien to a C++ programmer.

There is another issue that you need to be aware of. COM allows you to pass data by value or by reference:

```
HRESULT PassPersonStruct([in] struct Person person);
HRESULT PassAnotherPerson([in] struct Person* pPerson);
```

In both of these calls a single `Person` structure is involved – if the calls are in-apartment, the data in the first method is passed by value, and therefore exists on the method's stack frame. In the second case, a pointer is passed, so the data exists in the caller. If the call is across apartment boundaries, the two methods are effectively the same, because the data in the structure is marshaled to the callee apartment. If the call is between machines, then the same amount of data is passed across the network in both cases (in one go). Although the component will treat the second method as having data passed by reference, because of the marshaling involved it is actually passed by value. In the following, the calls to pPerson do not involve network calls:

```
STDMETHODIMP CCustomers::PassAnotherPerson(struct Person* pPerson)
{
    DoSomethingWithAge(pPerson->Age);
    DoSomethingWithCountryCode(pPerson->Country);
    return S_OK;
}
```

You can pass a component reference as a parameter, but if you use standard marshaling the parameter *is* passed by reference. So in the following:

```
HRESULT PassPersonObject([in] IPerson* pPerson);
```

with the following implementation:

```
STDMETHODIMP CCustomers2::PassPersonObject(IPerson* pPerson)
{
    short sAge;
    pPerson->get_Age(&sAge);
    DoSomethingWithAge(sAge);
    short sCountry;
    pPerson->get_Country(&sCountry);
    DoSomethingWithCountryCode(sCountry);
    return S_OK;
}
```

The significant difference is that each call to pPerson involves a call to the actual component in the caller apartment. If the two components are on different machines this means that every access involves a network call.

The other option is to ensure that the data is passed by value. To do this you should make the component marshal by value (ADO disconnected recordsets do this, for example). Alternatively, you could put the data into some other entity that will be passed by value (like a struct), or even generate a byte stream, passing a byte array as the parameter. More details will be given later in this chapter.

So, to summarize, MTS applications are all about distribution, and during design and development you must keep this in mind every step of the way. Ensure that as few network calls are made as possible, and if necessary take steps to pass data by value.

Transaction Programming

Managing transactions correctly is the key to scalability in MTS applications. Components running under a transaction use resources – a transaction stream may contain many components, and these may use resources managed by several resource managers enlisted under the transaction. The important point is that the transaction determines how long these resources are held, so making the transaction as short as possible helps keep the usage of these resources efficient. MTS enforces this by automatically aborting the transaction in the event that it takes longer than the local machine's transaction timeout. (If several machines are involved, the timeout is taken from the transaction coordinator – the first machine enlisted in the transaction.)

This timeout is set by default to 60 seconds. If you find that your transactions are aborting due to timeout, you can change this, but first you should investigate why the timeout is occurring. It is more likely that you are doing work that is either non-transactional or can be split into several transactions.

Transactions are finished by one of four actions:

❑ Calling SetComplete() or SetAbort()

❑ Releasing the root component in the transaction

❑ The transaction timing out

❑ A component in the transaction throwing an exception

The first doesn't actually end the transaction, unless it occurs on the root component. If either of these two methods are called on a sub-object then, when the time comes to determine the transaction outcome, the transaction will be aborted if SetAbort() was called by any component in the transaction, or committed if *all* components in the transaction called SetComplete(). This decision time occurs when either of the methods is called from the root component.

Releasing the root component will always end the transaction, and depending on the opinions of the components therein (whether they called `SetComplete()` or `SetAbort()`) will commit or abort the transaction. However, the client gets no result from the transaction (`Release()` does not return a HRESULT). It is therefore far better to end the transaction by calling a method of the root component that calls `SetComplete()`, and returning the value from this method (which will reflect whether the transaction was committed or not).

The last two actions in the list will abort the transaction, because the work therein won't have finished, so the work that has already been done will have to be rolled back.

In fact, this behavior is extremely useful for distributed applications, because when a client requests an action to be performed, it may involve resources from several resource managers, which may be on several machines. If the action fails at all, then (without transactions) it would be very difficult to backtrack through all the successful changes in the resources to undo them. The client can retry the action by restarting the failed transaction from the beginning.

Rollback of work after a transaction fails is not the same as performing a compensating transaction. These transactions undo the effect of a *committed* transaction, and are used when the client realizes that a transaction was performed when it should not have been. Because the changes will affect state, they too occur under a transaction, but note that they don't undo the partial effects of an aborted transaction. (Such actions are performed automatically by the resource managers enlisted in the transaction.) Instead they are performed on the work of a committed transaction.

Non-transactional components gain little from using `SetComplete()` under NT4. However, under COM+ it will help if the components are pooled, because it means that the component will be deactivated and returned to the pool. This does assume, though, that the component will gain from pooling. Transactional components do gain by calling `SetComplete()`, and as often as possible, because it means that any potentially expensive resources (like database connections or transactional locks) can be freed and recycled for use by other components.

Errors

This behavior of transactions (that is, automatic transaction abort when an exception is not caught) enforces the atomic behavior of the transaction, and is called **failfast**. Transactional components should return an error HRESULT when they call `SetAbort()`, to allow the client to have an idea of what error occurred. If there isn't an appropriate code then the component can return CONTEXT_E_ABORTED. This code is also returned via the context if the transaction times out.

> *As a client, you'll need to know what state the server is in after the error. One of the beauties of MTS is that server state is managed explicitly, so you always know exactly where to restart.*

For example:

```
STDMETHODIMP CDuffObject::Naughty()
{
    CComPtr<IObjectContext> pCont;
    GetObjectContext(&pCont);
    int* pInt = 0;
    // cause an exception to be thrown
    *pInt = 0;
    // this next line is optimistic!
    pCont->SetComplete();
    return S_OK;
}
```

The client will be returned an error of E_OUTOFMEMORY, and the following entry will be generated in the event log:

Source:	Transaction Server
Severity:	Error
Category:	Context Wrapper
Event:	4104
Description:	An object call caused an exception.
	(Package: BadPackage)
	(ProgId: Application.DuffObject.1)
	(CLSID: {8B596F00-173F-11D3-8988-00104BDC35E0})
	(Interface: IDuffObject)
	(IID: {8B596EFF-173F-11D3-8988-00104BDC35E0})
	(Method: 7)
	(Microsoft Transaction Server Internals Information: File:
	d:\viper\src\runtime\cw\cwlib.cpp, Line: 935)
	(Exception: C0000005)
	(Address: 0x10007292)
	APPLIC~1 + 0x7292
	mtxex!ContextWrapper::OnCall(unsigned int,void * const,unsigned
	long * const) + 0x1C7
	mtxex!CWList::VbStopDebugging(void) + 0x281C
	RPCRT4!_NdrStubCall2@16 + 0x4E0
	RPCRT4!_CStdStubBuffer_Invoke@12_739erface@12_39_MESSAG
	E@@@Z_14_17EX@@@Z_76U_RPC_MESSAGE@@PAPAVWMS
	G_SBINDING@@IHHH@Z_1982379Z_55 + 0x1E
	OLEAUT32 + 0x18F2B
	ole32!StubInvoke(struct tagRPCOLEMESSAGE *,struct
	IRpcStubBuffer *,struct IRpcChannelBuffer *,unsigned long *) + 0x53

The description gives information about the exception that occurred: the name of the package; the component's ProgID and CLSID; the interface IID; and the method number (IDuffObject is dual, and Naughty() is the first method after those of IDispatch). The other piece of useful information is the exception, which is given as 0xc0000005 and is STATUS_ACCESS_VIOLATION as you would expect. The rest of the description gives the stack trace.

If a problem occurs, then in addition to returning an error code, MTS will clear all of the method's output parameters. If any [out] parameters are component references they will be released and the interface pointers will be set to NULL.

The error that caused the exception in `Naughty()` doesn't affect any other code or data – but MTS doesn't know this. Since the MTS component will be in a DLL running under the `mtx.exe` surrogate, it could have overwritten any memory within the process. This means that the only safe action is for MTS to close down the entire process. Think of the consequences of this. If there is more than one activity running in the package then all the other activities will be shut down as well, which means that their transactions will be aborted. This is desirable, because the rogue code could have modified some transactional data within those other activities. By aborting the transactions it ensures that this corrupted data is not made durable.

If a client uses code like this:

```
HRESULT hr;
CComPtr<IDuffObject> pDuff;
pDuff.CoCreateInstance(__uuidof(DuffObject));
hr = pDuff->Naughty();
hr = pDuff->Good();
```

The first call to `pDuff` will return `E_OUTOFMEMORY`, and the client should take the fact that an error has been returned to indicate that the actual server no longer exists. Methods that don't throw exceptions, like `Good()`, will return with the infamous code `RPC_S_SERVER_UNAVAILABLE` (`0x800706BA`) after a call to `Naughty()`, which means that the proxy is no longer valid. Thus, it's always prudent to check the returned status code with COM methods.

Remember that you should *never* allow a COM component to throw exceptions. Clearly *your* code is of the highest quality, so it will never be the source of exceptions, but you can't guarantee the same of third party code. One solution is to use C++ exception handling to catch any exceptions, call `SetAbort()` and return a suitable status code.

Note that (by default) ATL will turn off exception handling because this tends to increase the module size. You can turn it on again using Project | Settings – the option is found in the C++ Language Category on the C/C++ tab. An example of using C++ exceptions is shown here:

```
STDMETHODIMP CDuffObject::Naughty()
{
    CComPtr<IObjectContext> pCont;
    GetObjectContext(&pCont);
    try
    {
        int* pInt = 0;
        // throw an exception
        *pInt = 0;
        pCont->SetComplete();
        return S_OK;
    }
    catch(...)
    {
        pCont->SetAbort;
        return CONTEXT_E_ABORTED;
    }
}
```

If you don't want to use C++ exceptions, then you can use structured exception handling (SEH). However, note that SEH and C++ do not coexist very well – specifically SEH, will not correctly call destructors during the stack unwind (which does occur with C++ exception handling). This means that you have to make sure either that the code in the method doesn't use C++ objects, or that you don't rely on the cleanup in the destructors. CComPtr<> smart pointers are C++ objects, and will release the wrapped interface pointer when the destructor is called. Thus, if you use smart pointers in a SEH guarded block, you will have a resource leak:

```
__try
{
    CComPtr<IMyPointer> pObj;
    pObj->CoCreateInstance(CLSID_OBJ);
    pObj->DoSomethingNasty();
    return S_OK;
}
__except(EXCEPTION_EXECUTE_HANDLER)
{
    // how do you access pObj???
    return E_FAIL;
}
```

Error Objects

Every COM thread has an associated COM **error object** – so every activity will also have an error object. The client can access this, and can thus get detailed information about any errors that are generated. In fact, the concept of an error object introduced the idea of an 'activity' before MTS was released. This is because the 'thread' that an error object is associated with is a **logical** thread, which includes the physical client thread and any other physical threads involved in the call in the server:

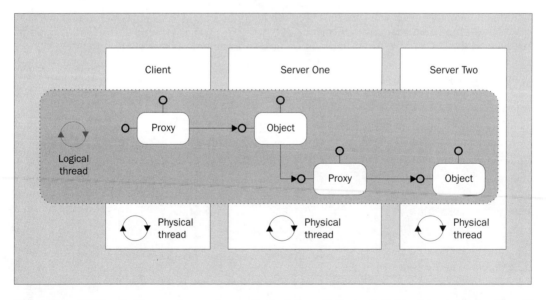

This is how MTS activities work – exchange 'logical thread' for 'activity' in this picture and you'll see what I mean.

Standard error objects are transmitted as out-of-band information, and as such you don't explicitly ask the component for the error object. Instead, client code calls an API method (GetErrorInfo()) to get the error object for the current thread. On the server side, standard error objects are created by the system, so rather than calling CoCreateInstanceEx() to create one, you call the API CreateErrorObject(). The error object that this creates should be initialized through its ICreateErrorInfo interface and then set as the current thread error object by passing its IErrorInfo interface to SetErrorInfo().

You can, if you wish, create your own error object. In this case, when you want to throw an error, you should create your own error object rather than calling CreateErrorInfo(). As long as your custom error object implements IErrorInfo, it can be made the current object for the thread, by calling SetErrorInfo(). However, although the interface pointer is passed out-of-band to the client, note that when you access the error object the call will be made to the server that generated the error. This will involve a cross-apartment (maybe even a cross-machine) call.

If there are several methods involved in the call stack, and code at the end of the stack generates an error, the information it adds to the error object will be available to the next method in the stack. If this method adds its own information, it will *replace* the previous information. This isn't the behavior that most developers want – they prefer to get a complete stack trace of the errors that occur, to determine exactly where the error occurred and the effect it has had on other methods. OLE DB uses **extended error objects** that have error records. These allow code to add its own information into an existing error object and thus provide more detailed information about the 'context' of the error. A client can access these error records individually, and obtain error information from the components that generated the error through a **lookup service**.

If you have OLE DB installed on your machine, then the error object that you obtain by calling GetErrorInfo() may be an extended error object – in the case that the error was generated by other code. If your code is at the head of the call chain, then you can create the extended error object explicitly (rather than calling CreateErrorInfo(), which will create the standard error object):

```
#include <MSDAGUID.H>
#include <OLEDB.H>


CComPtr<IErrorRecords> pErrorRecords;
// get rid of the standard error object
SetErrorInfo(0, NULL);
// create the extended error object
CoCreateInstance(CLSID_EXTENDEDERRORINFO, NULL, CLSCTX_SERVER,
                 IID_IErrorRecords, (void**)&pErrorRecords);
// add error records to the extended error object — see later
// get its IErrorInfo interface
CComQIPtr<IErrorInfo> pErrorInfo(pErrorRecords);
// now make it the thread error object
hr = SetErrorInfo(0, pErrorInfo);
```

Once you have done this, any code in the call chain that calls GetErrorInfo() will get the extended object you created. These methods can add their own error records to the error object, but note that they will still need to call SetErrorInfo(), even though this means replacing the thread error object with itself.

The extended error object implements two interfaces: IErrorRecords and IErrorInfo. The IErrorInfo interface is the interface that you are most familiar with. However, you can't query for ICreateErrorInfo, so it may not be clear where this object gets its information. The key is the IErrorRecords interface. This allows you to add and access records in the error object. The IErrorInfo interface on an extended error object gives access to the first record added to the object.

Each record is represented by the ERRORINFO structure:

```
typedef struct tagERRORINFO
{
   HRESULT   hrError;    // the error HRESULT
   DWORD     dwMinor;    // object defined error code
   CLSID     clsid;      // identifies the object class
   IID       iid;        // interface that caused the error
   DISPID    dispid;     // object usable code
} ERRORINFO;
```

Unlike the automation EXCEPINFO structure (which is the forerunner to the IErrorInfo interface), this doesn't have any strings describing the error or the help file that describes the error. The reason for this is that this information is *not* returned, but a lookup service is used instead. A lookup service is a COM component that constructs the description, source and help file strings, using information in an error record. Note though, that the lookup service is not used when the error is generated, only when the error is read from the error object, as you'll see in a moment.

The error record is added to the error object using IErrorRecords::AddErrorRecord():

```
HRESULT AddErrorRecord (ERRORINFO*    pErrorInfo,
                        DWORD         dwLookupID,
                        DISPPARAMS*   pdispparams,
                        IUnknown*     punkCustomError,
                        DWORD         dwDynamicErrorID);
```

The dwLookupID is used by the lookup service to determine the string properties of the IErrorInfo interface (description, help file etc.). This can be IDENTIFIER_SDK_ERROR, indicating that the error is defined by OLE DB and that the lookup service shouldn't be used. If you want to, you can even pass extra parameters that will be passed to the lookup service when the lookup is performed. These parameters are indicated in pdispparams, and are cached in the error object.

The punkCustomError parameter can be used to add a custom object into the error object. This is whatever object you feel the client should have access to (an example is SQL Server's ISQLErrorInfo).

When the client gets the error object by calling GetErrorInfo(), it can query the object for IErrorRecords and call GetRecordCount() to get the number of records in the object. The client can then call GetBasicErrorInfo() on this interface to obtain the ERRORINFO for the record, or GetErrorInfo() to get the IErrorInfo for the record. If the error record creator added a custom error object for a record, then the client can call GetCustomErrorObject() to obtain it. These three methods have a ULONG parameter that the client uses to pass the zero-based index of the record.

GetErrorInfo() returns an IErrorInfo interface, so where does the string information come from? That's the clever bit – when the client calls one of the string property methods (like IErrorInfo::GetDescription()), the error object calls the lookup service. The lookup service object implements IErrorLookup, with methods corresponding to the string properties of the error record. So, for the error description, the error object will call GetErrorDescription() and pass the error HRESULT, error code and any parameters provided for the record. The lookup service can then generate the description and source strings, which can be returned by the error object to the client.

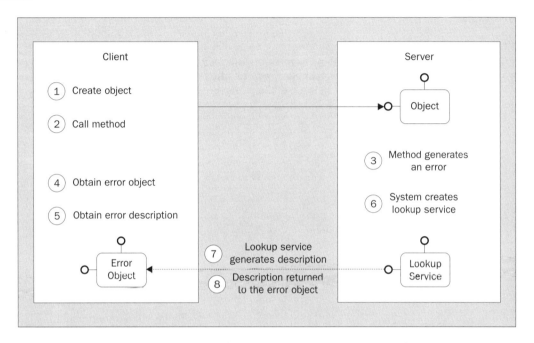

The lookup service could use some static data to map the dwLookupID and error record parameters to the description string – in this case the lookup service doesn't need to maintain any error object resources. On the other hand, the lookup service could maintain some dynamic resource for this particular error record. If this is the case, the source of the record should pass a cookie value for the last parameter of IErrorRecords::AddErrorRecord(). Typically, all records will use the same cookie value – but this is optional. The lookup service can then cache this resource, so that if the client calls IErrorInfo::GetDescription() several times, the cached resource can be used. When the error object is released, it calls IErrorLookup::ReleaseErrors(), passing the cookie values used when each error was added to the object. The lookup service can thus identify the resource and release it.

Why do extended error objects work like this? The reason is that if you have many components in a call chain each can return an error description. This is particularly useful for OLE DB providers, which can use many components in a single call, but you can use it too. If the client doesn't want to read the error information for all error records then they won't be all marshaled. Lookup services are based on the assumption that, if you want to get error information, you'll be willing to pay the price of another method call, which will most likely be out of apartment.

Developing Lookup Services

If you want to use extended objects then you'll need to create the error record and add it to the error object. You'll also need to register a lookup service.

The first is fairly easy – in order to use error objects, components should implement `ISupportErrorInfo` and provide checks in `InterfaceSupportsErrorInfo()` to see if specified interfaces can return error objects. This is standard support for error objects, and the ATL Object Wizard provides a check box that you can select to generate this code – *but not for MTS Components.*

> Because of this, the code for this chapter includes a new Object Wizard object type called **MTS Component** that will allow you to add error object and connection point support, as well as fixing some other minor bugs in the current Object Wizard version.

When a method generates an error it should create the error object and add the error record to it:

```
#include <MSDAGUID.H>
#include <OLEDB.H>

CComPtr<IErrorRecords> pErrorRecords;
// get rid of the standard error object
SetErrorInfo(0, NULL);
// create the extended error object
CoCreateInstance(CLSID_EXTENDEDERRORINFO, NULL, CLSCTX_SERVER,
                 IID_IErrorRecords, (void**)&pErrorRecords);

// initialize the extended error object
ERRORINFO errorInfo;
memset(&errorInfo, 0, sizeof(ERRORINFO));
errorInfo.hrError = E_INVALIDARG;
errorInfo.dwMinor = 1;
errorInfo.clsid = this->GetObjectCLSID();
errorInfo.iid  = IID_IMyInterface;
pErrorRecords->AddErrorRecord(&errorInfo, errorInfo.dwMinor, NULL, NULL, 0);

// get its IErrorInfo interface
CComQIPtr<IErrorInfo> pErrorInfo(pErrorRecords);
// now make it the thread error object
hr = SetErrorInfo(0, pErrorInfo);
```

To indicate that a particular component creates extended error objects that require a lookup service, the component should add the `ExtendedErrors` key to its CLSID key. Within this should be a key that has the CLSID of the error lookup object.

Error Objects and MTS

You can safely use error objects with MTS objects, because MTS will marshal the error object as out-of-band data, just like plain COM does. You can also use extended error objects, and if you use OLE DB to access a data source from your MTS component, it makes sense to add your error records onto those returned by the provider. Even if you don't use OLE DB, it makes sense to use extended error objects because it allows you to localize the strings returned from the error object (the methods of IErrorLookup have an LCID parameter). They also give you a way to add error records at stages in the call chain – particularly useful if you have several components in the activity.

Error objects are thread based, and in cases of high stress threads can be shared by activities. However, the way that activities work ensures that when a call is made into an activity no other call will be allowed to that thread (for the same activity or another activity sharing the thread) until the first call completes. This means that you will never get a situation in which one client calls into the activity and gets the error object for another activity.

ATL provides some client-side code for accessing extended error objects in atldbcli.h. CDBErrorInfo is a wrapper around IErrorRecords:

```
class CDBErrorInfo
{
public:
   HRESULT GetErrorRecords(IUnknown* pUnk, const IID& iid,
                           ULONG* pcRecords);
   HRESULT GetErrorRecords(ULONG* pcRecords);
   HRESULT GetAllErrorInfo(ULONG ulRecordNum, LCID lcid,
                           BSTR* pbstrDescription,
                           BSTR* pbstrSource = NULL,
                           GUID* pguid - NULL,
                           DWORD* pdwHelpContext = NULL,
                           BSTR* pbstrHelpFile = NULL) const;
   HRESULT GetBasicErrorInfo(ULONG ulRecordNum,
                           ERRORINFO* pErrorInfo) const;
   HRESULT GetCustomErrorObject(ULONG ulRecordNum, REFIID riid,
                           IUnknown** ppObject) const;
   HRESULT GetErrorInfo(ULONG ulRecordNum, LCID lcid,
                           IErrorInfo** ppErrorInfo) const;
   HRESULT GetErrorParameters(ULONG ulRecordNum,
                           DISPPARAMS* pdispparams) const;

   CComPtr<IErrorInfo>    m_spErrorInfo;
   CComPtr<IErrorRecords> m_spErrorRecords;
};
```

GetErrorRecords() is passed the interface that generated the error, and it will test to see if error objects are supported. If so, it will return the number of error records that the error object contains (and cache the IErrorRecords interface). The client can then call GetAllErrorInfo() to get information for a specified error record – GetBasicErrorInfo(), GetCustomErrorObject(), GetErrorInfo() and GetErrorParameters() are thin wrappers around the same named methods on IErrorRecords.

This class is used by AtlTraceErrorRecords(), which will access an error object and dump the information from each error record to the output debug stream (for debug builds only). If you are writing client code that accesses extended error objects, it is worth looking at the implementation of this method.

Callbacks

It is possible to make callbacks to clients and to other MTS components, for example, to indicate when some action has occurred. However, there are several issues that you need to be aware of. The 'standard' way to implement callbacks is to use connection points. The facility to do this via the ATL Object Wizard (and the fact that VB will do all of the advising and unadvising of sink interfaces) seems to make them attractive. However, connection points were designed for controls that are in-process, so they were not optimized to minimize interface calls. In particular, when the advise call is made (to tell the source of events about the client sink object), an IUnknown interface pointer is passed. This requires that the event source calls QueryInterface() to get the interface that it expects to call.

Connection points are also attractive in that they are very flexible. You can have one-to-many (one client gets events from several event interfaces) and many-to-one (many clients can get events from a single source object) topologies. ATL provides an implementation that allows both, but note that there are inherent problems.

The major problem is that if there are several clients connected to a single component, and that component sends an event to all of them, a performance problem arises. This is because COM calls are synchronous, and each client is sent the event in a serial way. This is how the ATL implementation generates events, and it means that the thread in the event source will be blocked when the event is generated. It is bad to do this in a transactional component, because you can't guarantee that all the calls will be completed within the transaction timeout, especially if some of the clients have died. One solution to this problem is to use an asynchronous callback mechanism like MSMQ, but that is beyond the scope of this book.

Another solution is to do the callbacks outside of the transaction, within a separate component. Such a component can use a dedicated thread to make the callbacks, but this does mean that this thread will be in a different apartment to the MTS component. Since the sink interface advising will be done on the MTS component, these interfaces will have to be marshaled to the event generation thread. There is no support in ATL's implementation of connection points for such an action.

Even if you have got the server-side components sorted out, there is the problem of security in the client. When a client is a sink for COM events, it will be a COM server. This means that the identity of the event source must have access permissions to call the client. This can cause problems, especially with VB clients that find it difficult to manage any rudimentary form of security. (In fact, it could be argued that Microsoft's main thrust for MTS role-based security is due to the fact that it allows VB servers to do security programming denied outside of MTS. However, a sink object in a VB client will not run under MTS, so role-based security doesn't solve this problem.)

Also, bear in mind that when a transactional component makes a callback to the client within the transaction, it's making an assertion to the client based on the current state of the component – not on the outcome of the transaction. A component doesn't know what the transaction outcome will be, because one of the other components (or the resource managers that they use) could abort the transaction. All in all, this violates the isolation aspect of the transaction (and it also implies that the transaction is not atomic, since the component can report on a partial action). In addition, transactional components are deactivated at the end of the transaction, which means that the client callback interfaces are also released. When the client makes another call on the component it therefore has to re-advise the connection point first.

These problems can be alleviated by using a non-transactional component – at the expense of slightly more complicated code. The idea is that the client talks to this extra component – telling it the callback interfaces. Since this component is non-transactional, it can survive between method calls and will therefore keep the references on the sink components. Furthermore, this non-transactional component knows the outcome of the transaction (from the return values of the methods it calls on the transactional component), and can use this to influence which event it generates. Indeed, since the non-transactional component can only call the transactional component in an atomic way, the isolation aspects of the transaction are preserved. (Remember, of course, that the pointer held by the non-transactional component actually points to the context wrapper object.)

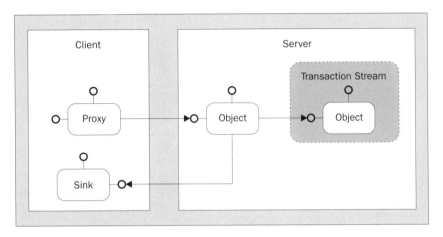

MTS components run in STAs. The COM implementation of a single threaded apartment means that when code in the STA is making an outgoing call (for example to generate an event), the STA thread spins in a message loop waiting for the reply. Unfortunately, incoming COM calls also appear as messages in the STA's message queue, which means that the component will accept any incoming calls. This means that the component must be re-entrant or implement `IMessageFilter` to take this into account.

Marshaling

All access to MTS components is via standard marshaling – either type library marshaling or through proxy-stub code created using the `/Oicf` MIDL switch. MTS components can't implement `IMarshal` because this implies that the components are custom marshaled, and for interception to work MTS components must be standard marshaled. This means that you can't take advantage of privileged knowledge of the component and its environment to custom marshal data. There are, however, ways around this.

Non-MTS components can implement `IMarshal`, and you are free to return a non-MTS component as an `[out]` parameter as long as this component is not treated as being part of the transaction. Components that are custom marshaled can optimize the way that data is passed over the wire. For example, a component that represents a list of items could be implemented so that rather than the proxy in the client obtaining each item as it is requested, it could read ahead, obtain items in blocks, and cache them. This way, calls to the component would be performed only when the cache is exhausted, reducing the number of network calls. The ultimate version of this is the marshal-by-value component, which marshals the entire component state when the proxy is created. With such a component, calls for the component state will never go beyond the proxy – the calls will always be in-apartment.

For example:

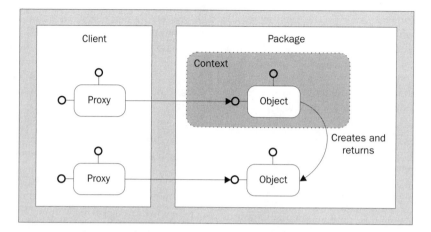

Since you can implement IMarshal on the non-transactional component (shown in the bottom right of the figure), you can provide a marshal-by-value component as described above. All access to this component will be to the proxy, and will therefore involve no cross-apartment calls.

Another option is to extract the non-transactional state and pass it back to the client in a stream, a raw byte array, or even using XML. This, in effect, is "freeze drying" the component, ready to be re-hydrated in the client. Of course, the client will need to create this uninitialized component and initialize it with the stream (perhaps via IPersistStreamInit) or the byte array. A marshal-by-value component performs this action automatically, so client code will be much cleaner, and the component can be used by COM-challenged languages that can't handle streams of any kind.

If you marshal the freeze-dried component via a stream, then you need to read the data out of the stream in the client apartment (into a client-allocated buffer), so that the client can interpret the byte stream. This means that there will be two allocations: the internally managed buffer in the stream and the client allocated buffer. If a raw byte array is marshaled, then the client has direct access to this buffer and can interpret the data directly without having to explicitly copy it into another buffer. For efficiency then, marshaling a raw byte array is the better option, and later in the current section I will return to this issue.

Proxy-Stub code

Proxy-stub code is required when you create an MTS component. Server packages are created in a separate process to the client that activates them. Even library packages require proxy-stubs, because when a client creates a component in a library package, it will be created in a new activity and therefore in a new STA. (Of course, if the library component is created within the activity of a server package, and no reference to the library component is passed out of the activity, then no proxy-stub will be required.)

If your components use type library marshaled interfaces, then all you need to do is ensure that a type library is generated and registered on each machine that will use a reference to the component. The ATL AppWizard and VB will bind the type library into the module, and, regardless of whether the type library is provided as a separate file, the MTS Explorer will ensure that it is deployed correctly.

Even so, the server file and the proxy-stub file need to be loaded into the surrogate process. You have to be careful to rebase proxy-stub files, so that they are loaded at a different load address to the other DLLs used in the process. If you don't do this then the DLL will be relocated in memory – although this relocation is a once-only affair, it still takes time and you should try to avoid it. Visual C++ and the Platform SDK are supplied with the REBASE tool, to change the load address of the DLL and hence prevent this relocation. (In the past, I have kept a list of all the DLLs that will be loaded in a process, along with their load addresses. This enabled me to ensure that new DLLs are loaded at different addresses.)

Another way to avoid this is to merge the proxy-stub code into the server DLL. You can do this with an AppWizard option when you create a project. However, even when you use this switch, you won't get the merged code. In fact, the project will refuse to compile. There are some other steps that you should carry out, and these are outlined in a later section.

If you decide to merge the proxy-stub into the server DLL, you still have the option of building a separate proxy-stub DLL for client machines. However, when you push or pull components to another machine, or export a package, MTS Explorer won't know that the proxy-stub file is in fact the server, so it will deploy the combined file to a client. Clearly, you are distributing code to the client that isn't needed.

Efficient Marshaling

Earlier in this chapter I talked about marshaling data in a distributed application. The message was clear and had two rules:

❑   Keep the number of network calls to a minimum

❑   Pass data by value

Going over the wire is like having to go to the local mall whenever you want a cup of coffee – it has its advantages and is needed sometimes, but is often unnecessary if you have a filter machine in your office. The same is true of distributed components – don't distribute components when you don't need to. Try to keep all your components in the same package, or at least on the same machine.

If you're going to marshal data then do it by value. If you marshal components then the data will be accessed by references – meaning more inter-apartment calls. There is a third issue that you need to address:

❑   Keep the data packets large

When you marshal data, it is better to marshal a few large packets rather then many small packets. DCOM takes up around 200 bytes of data of each packet, to hold RPC information and the DCOM extensions that allow component interfaces to be accessed remotely. A network call passing a char to a remote component is clearly inefficient.

In the following table, a component on a remote machine is used to marshal three buffers of 4K, 16K and 64K. The table shows average results over a series of tests, with the component installed into MTS and accessed from a remote client (the client machine didn't install the component as a remote component). Don't pay any attention to the absolute values, look instead at the relative values. Consider the difference between the times taken to marshal large buffers and that taken to marshal smaller ones, and also the differences between the various methods.

Note that I have chosen to show the time taken to get the data in a form that the client can access, and to clean up after using the data. In terms of passing a BYTE array, the [out] parameter can be used directly. Alternatively, if the server was passing an open array, the figures would represent the time taken to free the memory. With the IStream method, the figure includes the time taken to extract the data from the stream, and to free the stream when it's no longer needed. What isn't included is the time taken to interpret the data and make it into something useful, since that is an application issue.

Method	Time taken to marshal data (ms)		
	4K	16K	64K
Marshal By Value	30	40	100
IStream marshaled	20	30	80
Byte array	10	20	70

Clearly, marshalling the data as a BYTE array is more efficient because there is no pre- or post-processing. The MBV component takes much more time than the other two, because it is effectively the same as the IStream method, with the extra overhead of processing the IStream into a real component. In this example, this involves copying the data into a local buffer for the client to access. However, because this is hidden in the proxy I have included this in the figures, as it's an overhead over which the client has no control.

The table also shows that (whatever method you choose), marshalling 64K of data doesn't take 16 times the time that marshalling 4K of data does. Therefore, if you have the choice between calling a method 16 times to pass 4K buffers, or calling it once to pass a 64K buffer, then take the latter choice.

As an aside, wtypes.idl defines several 'BLOB' data types: BYTE_BLOB (essentially the same as BLOB), WORD_BLOB, DWORD_BLOB, BSTRBLOB, FLAGGED_BYTE_BLOB and FLAGGED_WORD_BLOB. These are essentially structs that contain a pointer to an array of the type (BYTE, WORD, DWORD) and a count of how large the array is. The 'FLAGGED' versions also have an extra member that takes a flag about the data being passed. This means that the following prototype:

```
HRESULT PassData([in] ULONG clSize, [in, size_is(clSize)] BYTE* abData);
```

can be replaced with:

```
HRESULT PassData([in] BLOB blob);
```

It's just a stylistic choice, but I think it makes the interface definitions more readable. The method will be called like this:

```
BLOB blob;
blob.clSize = 10;
blob.abData = (BYTE*)CoTaskMemAlloc(blob.clSize);
for (BYTE x = 0; x < 10; x++) blob.abData[x] = x;
pMyObj->PassData(blob);
CoTaskMemFree(blob.abData);
```

Object State

The transactional state in a component must be protected – if the state is available outside of the transaction, the isolation criteria of the transaction will be broken. This is why transactional components are deactivated at the end of the transaction – it ensures that all state is released so that there is no possibility of that state enduring until the next transaction. Note that this doesn't mean the component should be stateless, it can have state – it just means that transactional state should be protected. (However, in practice most of the state will be transactional, and this does mean that most transactional components should be stateless.) In addition, with a COM component the state is an implementation detail – the external view of a COM component is its interfaces, and these only define the behavior of the component, not the state it holds.

The stateless/stateful argument has raged ever since MTS 1.0 was released. Part of the reason was because the original documentation implied that MTS components should be stateless. There are many reasons that support this, but it is not a rule set in stone. Let's examine the issues.

There are several ways that you can manage a component's state. The component could be stateless, which means that the parameters passed from the client to the component contain information that determine the component's state. For example, a method such as this:

```
HRESULT Add([in] long operand1, [in] long operand2, [out] long* result);
```

uses the state passed in as parameters, and the component can therefore be stateless. More complicated methods may involve sending large amounts of data, and accordingly large numbers of parameters. The method signatures can be simplified using `struct`s or MBV components as parameters (*not* component references, because access will mean more cross-apartment calls).

The state in this case is maintained by the client. This is not as odd as it may appear. The state of an component is part of its logical identity – passing data like this as explicit parameters is no worse than a C++ object passing the `this` pointer as an implicit parameter, or indeed the `OBJREF` in a marshaled COM method call.

As mentioned earlier, making many remote calls passing small amounts of data is less efficient than few remote calls each passing large amounts. But assuming you have designed your application to minimize the number of network/cross-apartment calls, the data passed as parameters will affect the performance. The temptation then, is to cache some state in the component between method invocations.

Such **instance data** held in an MTS component doesn't require any locking when it is accessed, even if multiple clients try to access the same component. The reason for this is that components in activities are protected from concurrent access, because an activity is implemented in an STA and thus has just one thread of execution. However, such data only survives as long as the component – if the component is transactional this means as long as the transaction is active. This can be achieved at the end of the method by calling `EnableCommit()` or `DisableCommit()`, depending on whether the component needs to perform more work in the transaction.

The data preserved in such a component, delayed from deactivation, shouldn't be transactional. Another way to achieve this is to split the component into two separate components – one of which doesn't work under the transaction, holds the non-transactional state, and has a reference to the other (transactional) component, which will do the transactional work. This is a better solution than `EnableCommit()` or `DisableCommit()` as it ensures that the transaction is kept as short as possible.

If multiple components within an activity need access to shared state, then you can implement this in C++ with a global variable. This is safe because there will only be one thread with access to the data at any one time, but you must be careful about re-entrancy. If a method depends on the value of the global state and makes an out-of-activity call, it's possible that another incoming call could change the state before the outgoing call returns.

On the other hand, if the application design requires state to be shared across activities, then you can't use a global variable, because multiple activities mean multiple threads. (OK, if there are more activities than threads in the thread pool, then more than one activity can run on one thread, but you cannot guarantee which activities will co-exist like this.) Instead, you need to use some facility that provides locking – MTS offers two: shared transient state managed through a resource dispenser, and durable state managed through a resource manager. MTS provides the **shared property manager** (**SPM**) resource dispenser for transient state, and you can access your favorite database through resource managers to shared durable state.

If you store the component state in a database then you can identify the actual table row or view through a cookie value that the client can maintain. In this way the cookie acts as the logical component identity, even though the actual physical COM identity will change between method invocations (as the MTS component is activated and deactivated).

Shared Property Manager

The SPM is a resource dispenser, which means that the resources it manages aren't durable (the data doesn't survive machine crashes), and it is therefore non-transactional. However, the SPM is useful to maintain transient state across activities, because it uses lock management to make sure that only one activity has access to a property at any one time.

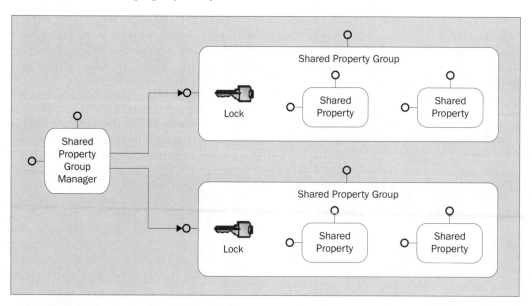

Locks are applied on a per-group basis – each group can have more than one shared property, which means that once a lock is obtained and held on a group, code can change multiple properties in an atomic way.

To create a property group, code should first access the **Shared Property Group Manager**, by creating an instance of the CLSID_SharedPropertyGroupManager class. The client can then use CreatePropertyGroup() to create a new named group, an interface of which is returned as an [out] parameter of the method:

```
HRESULT CreatePropertyGroup([in]BSTR name,
                            [in, out] LONG* plIsoMode,
                            [in, out] LONG* plRelMode,
                            [out] VARIANT_BOOL* pfExists,
                            [retval, out] ISharedPropertyGroup** ppGroup);
```

If the property group already exists, then a reference on this component is returned and pfExists returns VARIANT_TRUE. The other two parameters, plIsoMode and plRelMode are [in, out] parameters used to specify the lock and release modes. The values passed in for these modes are used when creating a new property group. If the group exists, then the values used for it are returned.

The plIsoMode parameter can be either:

Symbol	Description
LockGetSet	Lock is applied to the property group when a property is accessed, and released once the access has completed
LockMethod	Lock is applied to the property group when a property is accessed, but is maintained until the caller method returns

Potentially, LockGetSet implies better performance than LockMethod, because the lock is only applied while the property is accessed. However, if the code wishes to change several values in a property group in an atomic fashion (to ensure that no other activity can access any of the group properties until all changes are made), then LockMethod should be used.

plRelMode can be one of the following values:

Symbol	Description
Standard	The property group is released when all references to the group have been released
Process	The property group is released only when the process is terminated

If you use Standard, the group will exist in memory only as long as ISharedPropertyGroup interface pointers (which may be from multiple activities) remain. This is the standard COM behavior. If you use Process, then MTS will hold an additional reference to the property group. This means that when all the activities have released their references, the property group will remain. When another activity requests access to the property group, it will be returned with its values intact.

Once the client has an interface pointer on the property group, it can create a property either by name or position:

```
HRESULT CreateProperty([in] BSTR name,
                       [out] VARIANT_BOOL* pfExists,
                       [out] ISharedProperty** ppProp);
HRESULT CreatePropertyByPosition([in] INT index,
                       [out] VARIANT_BOOL* pfExists,
                       [out] ISharedProperty** ppProp);
```

Again, if the property exists, then a reference is returned and pfExists returns a value of VARIANT_TRUE. The property has the following interface:

```
[
    uuid(2A005C01-A5DE-11CF-9E66-00AA00A3F464),
    dual
]
interface ISharedProperty : IDispatch
{
    [id(DISPID_VALUE), propget] HRESULT Value([out, retval] VARIANT* pVal);
    [id(DISPID_VALUE), propput] HRESULT Value([in] VARIANT pVal);
};
```

Notice that the properties are VARIANT. This means that you can place any oleautomation compatible value in the property group, which also implies that you can save component references. However, you should restrain yourself from doing this, as the SPM will store the raw interface pointer, which another activity can access, and this violates COM's marshalling rules. If you do want to store interface pointers, then it is safer to put the interface into the Global Interface Table and store the GIT cookie in the SPM.

The SPM's interfaces should not be marshaled. An activity can access the SPM by creating an instance through CoCreateInstance() or IObjectControl::CreateInstance(). However, the values in the SPM are process specific, so you can't share the values across process boundaries.

MTS and Visual C++

Visual C++ provides facilities to develop MTS components, through the ATL AppWizard and the Object Wizard. The following section describes these two wizards, what they provide, and what is missing. The source code for this chapter has a new Object Wizard component type that corrects for these missing facilities.

AppWizard Supporting MTS Option

The Supports MTS option on the AppWizard adds the following:

- ❑ It adjusts the proxy-stub file to ensure that it is compatible with MTS
- ❑ It adds the mtx.lib and mtxguid.lib to your DLL's link line
- ❑ It delay loads the executive, mtxex.dll.
- ❑ It adds a comment in the custom build step, to remind you to refresh the catalog so that the component is run under the executive or mtx.exe

You can do all of these by hand, and perhaps the step that you are most likely to forget (because the project will compile fine without it) is the first one. The proxy-stub file must be linked to `mtxih.lib` to get the interface helper code and adjusted class factories. This must be the first library on the link line. It must also be linked with the `/MD` switch, so that it is linked with `msvcrt.lib` to use the CRT based in a DLL. Furthermore, it must link with the MTS libraries (`mtx.lib`, `mtxguid.lib`), and because they use registration and some of the COM runtime APIs (normally proxy-stubs use the RPC runtime APIs), it must also link with `ole32.lib` and `advapi32.lib`.

If you want to use a proxy-stub DLL with your interfaces, using the **Supports MTS** option makes sure that all of these changes are made. If you don't link with `mtxih.lib`, and you then try to access your component's interfaces, COM (on the instruction of MTS) will tell you that the interface does not exist and you will get the following message in the event log:

Source:	Transaction Server
Severity:	Error
Category:	Context Wrapper
Event:	4103
Description:	Microsoft Transaction Server does not support this interface because it is a custom interface built with MIDL and has not been linked with the type info helper library.
	(Package: BadPackage)
	(Interface: IDuffObject)
	(IID: {8B596EFF-173F-11D3-8988-00104BDC35E0})
	(Microsoft Transaction Server Internals Information: File: d:\viper\src\runtime\cw\cwhlpapi.cpp, Line: 318)

The other makefile changes are required to allow the proxy-stub to compile correctly.

The two other changes made by the AppWizard allow you to use the MTS API. You may decide not to use your component under MTS – if this is so then your components will still need to link with `mtx.lib` so that your code can call the MTS API (these calls will fail, of course, and such a failure will be handled by your code). However, in such a situation the executive will not have been automatically loaded (MTS does this when components that have been registered in the catalog are requested) – but you don't want `mtxex.dll` loaded when the component's DLL is first loaded, because you may not need it. The solution used by Visual C++ 6.0 is to use **delay loading**, which ensures that the DLL is only loaded when the first exported function is called.

The final action that this AppWizard option will undertake indicates a vital step for you to perform. When you build a server, it will be registered using a custom build step, but this registration will write over the information put in the registry by the MTS Explorer. You therefore need to refresh this registration using information in the catalog. To do this, you can run `mtxrereg` – hence the AppWizard added custom build step:

```
regsvr32 /s /c "$(TargetPath)"
echo regsvr32 exec. time > "$(OutDir)\regsvr32.trg"
echo Execute mtxrereg.exe before using MTS components in MTS
```

The .trg file is used to create an output to the build step. Notice that the build step *reminds* you to re-register the component's MTS settings rather than actually doing it. The reason is that, if you don't have the path to mtxrereg in the path environment variable, attempting to run it will cause the build to fail. However, it makes sense to edit the custom build step to actually run mtxrereg (assuming it can be found through path), to save you having to remember to do this manually:

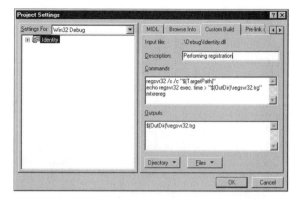

If you are debugging an MTS application, one thing you'll come across regularly is that when you detect a problem in your component and stop debugging the client, the component will still be running, because it is hosted by the surrogate, mtx.exe. Of course, if you're actually debugging the component code, you will have this process attached to the debugger, so when you stop debugging the process will stop. If your component is still running under mtx.exe when you try to rebuild the server, you will find that the link step will not work because write access is denied on the DLL.

If this is the case, before you can successfully perform the link step you need to stop the server – either by using MTS Explorer or by running the command line tool mtxstop.exe. The advantage of the former is that you can just stop the specified server process, whereas the latter will stop all server processes. However, the advantage of using mtxstop.exe is that you can add it as a pre-link step in the project settings:

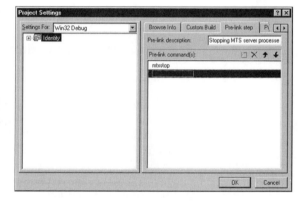

Note that mtxstop *will return immediately, so* nmake *will then attempt to link the project. However,* mtxstop *works by posting the message* WM_USER *to the channel window of each STA apartment in all instances of* mtx.exe. *Since the message is posted,* mtxstop *will return without checking that the instances of* mtx.exe *have stopped. The result is that the link step will still most likely fail. However, rebuilding the project a second time (once the server has had a chance to finish), will succeed. Incidentally, this posted message is not the result of a COM method because, as explained in* Professional DCOM Programming *(ISBN 1-861111-60-X), COM calls result in a message with a* WPARAM *of* 0xbabe, *and* mtxstop *does not use this value.*

The next chapter has a better solution to this problem – explicitly waiting for the process to stop.

AppWizard ATL Proxy-Stub Merging Option

The ATL AppWizard gives you the option of merging proxy-stub code into a DLL server. To do this you select **Allow merging of proxy/stub code** on the AppWizard dialog, and it will add an extra file, dlldatax.c, to your project along with extra code. The main file in the project (the .cpp file with the same name as the project) will have comments that indicate the steps that you must take to make the project compile. Since these are neither clear nor complete, I will describe the actual steps:

❑ The dlldatax.c file will be added to the **Source Files** folder in FileView. However, by default, it will not be included into the build. The solution is simple – select the file, then from the context menu in FileView select **Settings**, and from the **General** tab uncheck **Exclude file from build**.

❑ While you are editing the compile settings for this file from the **C/C++** tab, select the **Precompiled Headers** category, and check **Not using precompiled headers**, because it is a C file.

❑ Through **Project | Settings**, add _MERGE_PROXYSTUB to the project's preprocessor symbols.

❑ The project depends on the dlldata.c and _p.c file generated by MIDL from the IDL file, so you can adjust the project's dependencies by adding the MIDL step on the IDL file as a custom build (check **Always use custom build step** from the **General** tab). Then add these two C files and the type library to the **Outputs**. For the **Commands**, add the MIDL command line, but ensure that you use the /Oicf switch.

❑ Since you are providing proxy-stub code, you don't need type library marshaling. So, edit the wizard-generated DllRegisterServer() and DllUnregisterServer() so that the calls to _Module.RegisterServer() and _Module.UnregisterServer() have FALSE as the parameter. However, keep the type library bound as a resource, to keep the MTS Explorer happy when you install the components into a package.

Even if you check the **Supports MTS** option, the AppWizard is not clever enough to remember that you are using /Oicf marshalling with MTS. Thus, to keep MTS happy you have to do that yourself. Here is the additional step:

❑ From the project settings select the **Link** tab and add the following to the **Object/library modules**:

```
mtxih.lib mtx.lib mtxguid.lib advapi32.lib ole32.lib
```

Note that although you don't register the type library, you should still have it bound to the DLL (or provided as a separate .TLB) so that MTS Explorer will be able to get a list of all the coclasses in the DLL and get a (partial) description of the interfaces.

Object Wizard MTS Types

The ATL Object Wizard gives two object types related to MTS: the **MS Transaction Server Component** type and the **Component Registrar Object**.

As mentioned earlier, the ATL Object Wizard doesn't give you the option to support ISupportErrorInfo on your MTS components. This appears to be an oversight, and provided with this chapter is the code required for a new MTS Object Wizard that *does* supply this option. It is in the MTSComp directory for the code for this chapter. You may also need to RegRgs32 registration tool to install this Wizard – the source code for this is available from **www.worldofatl.com**.

MS Transaction Server Component

This type is essentially the same as the Object Wizard **Simple Object**, with only a few differences. This object type does not give you the familiar **Attributes** tab that you see with a simple object – instead it gives you a page that merely allows you to determine whether the component's first interface is dual or not. It also allows you to specify whether the component should support IObjectControl, and, if so, whether the component supports pooling. Selecting support for IObjectControl merely adds the interface to the class and map, implements Activate() by accessing the object context and caching it in an instance variable, and Deactivate() by releasing the interface.

However, note that you have no opportunity to specify the threading model of the component, nor its aggregation, connection point or error object support. This is a pity, because it implies that these facilities are not available to MTS components, which is *not* the case.

The Object Wizard will automatically mark the component as having a threading model of Both. While this value causes no problem when the component is run under MTS, it still should not have been used. The reason is that the Object Wizard will derive the ATL class from:

```
CComObjectRootEx<CComSingleThreadModel>
```

This means that no locking is used, which is as expected for a component run under MTS, because all access to components in an activity is serialized. However, if this component is *not* run under MTS, then (because Both is used) it can be created in the MTA, so multiple threads can access the component concurrently. In this situation, locking *must* be applied to thread sensitive code and data, otherwise data can be corrupted. Even if you decide that the component will only be run under MTS, it's *still* a good idea not to use this combination, as under COM+ a configured component marked as Both can be used in an MTA.

It is safer, therefore, to edit the .rgs file created by the Object Wizard and change the threading model to Apartment. While you are editing the .rgs file, it is also worth adding the type library version. As mentioned in Chapter 1, the wizard will add a TypeLib key (with the LIBID as its default value), but not the version key.

The object Wizard will also add the DECLARE_NOT_AGGREGATABLE() macro to your ATL class. This is presumably because the author argued that the component context is not available during component construction, nor during calls to QueryInterface(). Therefore it is not possible to aggregate another MTS component within the same activity. However, while correct, this action did not account for COM+ (see Chapter 8).

> *Incidentally, you are free to aggregate other components into your MTS component, as long as they aren't MTS components but are created in the same apartment.*

Component Registrar

The ATL component registrar is an interesting beast – it isn't documented anywhere. As far as I can tell, neither the MTS examples nor the NT/Win9x system files implement it. The only reference to it in MSDN is a small sentence describing the use of the DECLARE_OBJECT_DESCRIPTION() macro, which implements a function called GetObjectDescription():

"The `GetObjectDescription` *function is called by*
`IComponentRegistrar::GetComponents. IComponentRegistrar` *is an*
Automation interface that allows you to register and unregister individual components in a DLL.
When you create a Component Registrar object with the ATL Object Wizard, the wizard will
automatically implement the `IComponentRegistrar` *interface.*
`IComponentRegistrar` *is typically used by Microsoft Transaction Server."*

In fact, `IComponentRegistrar` is not used by MTS 2.0 – more is the pity, because as you'll see later the component registrar can help to selectively register and unregister components.

By the way, don't confuse the component registrar with the ATL registrar. The latter is present in
`atl.dll`, *and is used by ATL code to register and unregister your components.*

When you add the component registrar object with Object Wizard, your IDL will have a `coclass` and an interface added to the library section:

```
[
    uuid(a817e7a2-43fa-11d0-9e44-00aa00b6770a),
    dual, pointer_default(unique)
]
interface IComponentRegistrar : IDispatch
{
    [id(1)]  HRESULT Attach([in] BSTR bstrPath);
    [id(2)]  HRESULT RegisterAll();
    [id(3)]  HRESULT UnregisterAll();
    [id(4)]  HRESULT GetComponents([out] SAFEARRAY(BSTR)* pbstrCLSIDs,
                                   [out] SAFEARRAY(BSTR)* pbstrDescriptions);
    [id(5)]  HRESULT RegisterComponent([in] BSTR bstrCLSID);
    [id(6)]  HRESULT UnregisterComponent([in] BSTR bstrCLSID);
};
```

```
[
    uuid(a817e7a0-43fa-11d0-9e44-00aa00b6770a)
]
coclass MyRegistrar
{
    [default] interface IComponentRegistrar;
};
```

The very same GUIDs are used whenever you add the registrar. Think about this. If the same `CLSID` is given for the registrar in every server that implements it, doesn't this mean that when you register this server it will overwrite the registry entry for the registrar registered by another server?

The answer is no. The registrar is added to the object map, which means that it can be created by a class factory object. However, it uses the `DECLARE_NO_REGISTRY()` macro, so no entries are added to the registry. Indeed, no `.rgs` file is generated for the `coclass`. However, the registrar `coclass` is added to the type library, as well as the definition for `IComponentRegistrar`. So when the type library is registered, `IComponentRegistrar` will be registered as a type library marshaled interface (but again, the `coclass` is *not* registered).

This means that the registrar object can be created by a class factory, but not by using the COM API (as it isn't registered). If you want to create it, you must explicitly call `CoGetClassObject()` and ask for this `coclass`.

However, registering a type library that contains `IComponentRegistrar` is a little risky. Imagine you have several projects that use the registrar, and each of these has registered a type library. This means that `IComponentRegistrar` will be type library marshaled with the type library of the *last* server registered, because each time a type library is registered it will overwrite the `Interface` entry for this interface. Now imagine that you unregister this last server. This means that the entry for `IComponentRegistrar` will be removed, and that the registrar can't be used in another server, because there is no `Interface` entry.

If this is something that you are likely to do, you should put the definition of this interface into a separate IDL file and compile it into a `.tlb` and header. You will then be able to remove the interface from your project's IDL, and use the header to provide the interface definition for the registrar class so that its code will compile. You should then register the type library separately, so that it will not be unregistered when your server is removed. The example code for this chapter contains such an IDL file.

The registrar allows you to either register all components, unregister all components or to selectively register and unregister individual components. In addition, it has a method that will return the component's CLSIDs with a description string. The description is specified in ATL by adding the `DECLARE_OBJECT_DESCRIPTION()` macro to the ATL class of each component. The problem with using this macro is that it turns off registration through `DllRegisterServer()`, the reason being that by using this macro you indicate to ATL that registration will be carried out by the component registrar. The ATL function `AtlModuleRegisterServer()` tests to see if this macro has been used (and that it specifies a non-NULL string). If so, it will skip the component registration. Also note that because `AtlModuleRegisterServer()` behaves in this way, `RegisterAll()` and `UnregisterAll()` will ignore any class that has `DECLARE_OBJECT_DESCRIPTION()`. It seems to me that this isn't the intended behavior of these methods.

This odd behavior of ATL is a problem, because it can lead to registration problems. If you add an unregistered component to a package, MTS Explorer will call `DllRegisterServer()` on the server. It will then assume that the registered components should be added to the package, but any classes that use `DECLARE_OBJECT_DESCRIPTION()` won't be registered.

Contrary to the statement in MSDN, MTS doesn't look for the registrar, so it doesn't give you the opportunity to selectively register components (this is also true of the Windows2000 COM+ Component Services Explorer). Clearly, the only way to get your components selectively (un)registered is to write a process to do it yourself.

Let's look at the issues. If you add a new component into a package, you have two options. You can either insert already registered components, or suggest a DLL. If you use the second option (Install new component(s)), then MTS Explorer will look for type information (or you can suggest a type library) and will try to install *all* the components mentioned as MTS components. If some of these are components that you don't want to run under MTS, you do have the option of deleting them from the package. However, if you do this then MTS Explorer will remove some of the registry entries for that component. It will remove the `CLSID` entry for the component, but not the ProgID. If you want to use these removed components, you must re-register the DLL and refresh its MTS components, so that you have the correct CLSID values for both MTS and non-MTS components. This is where the component registrar becomes useful, as you can re-register a component *without* affecting the MTS settings of other components mentioned in the type library. This removes the need to refresh the MTS components.

If you use the option Import component(s) that are already registered when adding new components to a package, then just that component's registry entries will be changed by the MTS Explorer. If, at a later date, you decide to remove it from the package, then the component's CLSID entry will be removed (again, *not* its ProgID). You will therefore have some components in the server that you can use and some that you cannot. The registrar can be used to re-register these 'deleted' components without having to reregister the entire DLL.

Using the Component Registrar

The example code for this book has an example project called Registrar, which allows you to selectively register and unregister components. The code is a simple GUI application based on ATL's CDialogImpl<>. It allows you to select a DLL, loads it, and calls DllGetClassObject() to get the component registrar's class factory. If this call fails, then the DLL does not have a registrar and you cannot do anything with the DLL. The application can then call the class factory and ask for the registrar. Note that it doesn't simply call CoCreateInstance(), because the registrar is never registered by a server, so this is the only way to get this object.

Once it has the registrar, the code calls GetComponents() to get a safe array of the descriptions and CLSIDs of the components in the server. It puts these in a list box so that you can select a component, and the code will check to see if that component is registered. It then displays this status using two radio buttons, which you can click on to register or unregister the component (carried out by calling RegisterComponent() or UnregisterComponent()).

This code will work with the default Component Registrar code generated by the Object Wizard. However, as explained earlier, I think there is little point in using the logic of this code. Instead, in my projects, I change the generated code so that you don't have to use DECLARE_OBJECT_DESCRIPTION() for a component to be registered through the registrar. Here are the pertinent changes to the wizard-generated registrar code:

```
static const GUID CLSID_REGISTRAR =
    { 0xa817e7a0, 0x43fa, 0x11d0, { 0x9e, 0x44, 0x00, 0xaa, 0x00, 0xb6, 0x77,
    0x0a } };


STDMETHOD(GetComponents)(SAFEARRAY **ppCLSIDs, SAFEARRAY **ppDescriptions)
{
    _ATL_OBJMAP_ENTRY* pEntry = _Module.m_pObjMap;
    int nComponents = 0;
    while (pEntry->pclsid != NULL)
    {
        // count all objects except the Registrar
        if (!InlineIsEqualGUID(CLSID_REGISTRAR, *pEntry->pclsid))
            nComponents++;
        pEntry++;
    }
    SAFEARRAYBOUND rgBound[1];
    rgBound[0].lLbound = 0;
    rgBound[0].cElements = nComponents;
    *ppCLSIDs = SafeArrayCreate(VT_BSTR, 1, rgBound);
    *ppDescriptions = SafeArrayCreate(VT_BSTR, 1, rgBound);
    pEntry = _Module.m_pObjMap;
```

```
    for (long i=0; pEntry->pclsid != NULL; pEntry++)
    {
        if (InlineIsEqualGUID(CLSID_REGISTRAR, *pEntry->pclsid))
            continue;
        LPOLESTR pszCLSID;
        StringFromCLSID(*pEntry->pclsid, &pszCLSID);
        SafeArrayPutElement(*ppCLSIDs, &i, OLE2BSTR(pszCLSID));
        CoTaskMemFree(pszCLSID);

        HRESULT hr;
        LPOLESTR pszDesc;
        // use the ProgID or the stringified CLSID
        hr = ProgIDFromCLSID(*pEntry->pclsid, &pszDesc);
        if (FAILED(hr))
            StringFromCLSID(*pEntry->pclsid, &pszDesc);
        SafeArrayPutElement(*ppDescriptions, &i, W2BSTR(pszDesc));
        CoTaskMemFree(pszDesc);
        i++;
    }
    return S_OK;
}
```

It is a pity that a non-NULL value is treated by `AtlModuleRegisterServer()` as signifying that the component should be left alone (and is not registered or unregistered by this function), as MTS 2.0 will treat it as being unsuitable to be an MTS component. If ATL didn't work this way, then you could use `DECLARE_OBJECT_DESCRIPTION()` in the class to get a nice description of what the component does. Instead I have decided to resort to just showing the ProgID.

MTS Component

Since the ATL3 Object Wizard **MS Transaction Server Component** has some quirks and removes some facilities that you will want to use, I decided to write my own version, which shows up in the component list as **MTS Component**. This is provided as part of the code for this chapter, and is installed by copying the `MTSObj.*` files to the

```
Microsoft Visual Studio\Common\MSDev98\Template\ATL
```

folder. In addition, this new object type needs to be registered, so I have provided an ATL Registrar file called `register.rgs`, which includes the necessary changes. You can either consult this `.rgs` file and make the changes by hand (using `RegEdit`) or you can use the `RegRgs32` registration tool (available from www.worldofatl.com).

Essentially, I merged the code from `Object.*` files with `Msdtx.*` files in the `Template\ATL` folder. Details of the special directives in these files and the format of the `.ctl` script files can be found in *Professional ATL COM Programming* (ISBN 1-861001-40-1), so I won't cover them here. Instead I will just mention some of the more interesting points.

When you select the **MS Transaction Server Component**, you won't see the **Attributes** tab because it generates the tabbed dialog with the following code:

```
[!Dialog("Names98", "ViperDlg98")]
```

The first entry gives the first page, which asks you for the short name of the component. The second gives you the MTS page that asks you if you want dual or custom interfaces, and whether you want IObjectControl.

I have changed this to:

```
[!Dialog("Names98", "ObjDlg98", "ViperDlg98")]
```

ObjDlg98 is the familiar **Attributes** page. However, there are problems. First, both the **Attributes** and **MTS** pages allow you to specify whether the interface is dual or custom. Clearly you don't want this option given in two places, as conflicting values could be selected. Secondly, there are options on the **Attributes** page that are irrelevant to MTS components. This means that some of the options on this page should be disabled, and this is done using the following line before the call to Dialog():

```
[!set(Attributes, "00011100101")]
```

This indicates the items on the **Attributes** page that should be disabled. You should consult *Professional ATL COM Programming* to see which bit in the bitmap corresponds to which option. The **Attributes** page will look like this:

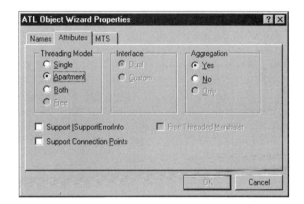

As you can see, I have disabled the <u>F</u>ree threading model and the <u>O</u>nly aggregation option. The reason for the first is that MTS components always run in an STA. The aggregation option is a bit more to do with personal taste – MTS components can aggregate other components, as long as these aren't other MTS components (since when the component is constructed it doesn't have access to its context, so it can't create another component in the same activity). The <u>O</u>nly option thus makes no sense. I have left the <u>Y</u>es option, because under COM+ activity membership is not determined by calling IObjectContext::CreateInstance() but from the component's attributes. I have also disabled the **Interface** frame – you should use the MTS page instead. Finally, the **Free Threaded Marshaler** option has been disabled, since under MTS this will allow cross-activity calls, bypassing MTS activity locking.

Debugging

There are two main problems with debugging MTS components. The first is that your component will most often be run within the mtx.exe surrogate, and is thus a separate process to the client. The second is that the MTS component will most likely want to access its context, so even if you aren't interested in debugging its transactional aspects, you must still involve MTS. The solution to these problems is to ensure that the component is launched under mtx.exe.

To do this, you should use the Project | Settings dialog for your MTS DLL. In the General category on the Debug tab put the full path to mtx.exe in the Executable for debug session edit box. (This is usually in the %systemroot%\System32 directory.) In addition, you need to add the following to the Program arguments edit box:

```
/p:{package guid}
```

where package guid is the package ID, which you can copy from the General page of the properties of the package. (Note that there is no space between the colon and the opening brace.) If, when you attempt to debug the package, you find that mtx.exe starts and immediately shuts down, there are three possible reasons:

- ❑ The package guid is invalid
- ❑ You may have a space between the colon and brace
- ❑ The package may already be running

Once the DLL is running under mtx.exe attached to the debugger you can set break points and wait for them to be hit. However, be aware that the package will be run under the identity of the interactive user and not the account specified in the package properties.

You can also attach a debugger to the instance of mtx.exe running your package. One way to do this is to right-click on the process in Task Manager and then select the Debug option. You can also do this through the Visual C++ IDE from the Build menu (Start Debug, Attach to process). The problem with either approach is that you may have several packages running (you will have at least two: yours and the system package). How do you decide which instance of mtx.exe to attach to?

The next chapter explains a technique for doing this – MTS provides a library that implements a component called MtsGrp, which allows you to access all the running packages. These are returned as components that implement the IMtsEvents, interface through which you can call GetProcessID(). With that, you can identify the process you want to attach to – the details will be given in the next chapter, but here is the code anyway:

```
// Type libs: MtsGrp, IMtsGrp are in mtxgrp.dll,
//            IMtsEvents is in mtsevents.dll

CComPtr<IMtsGrp> pMtsGrp;
pMtsGrp.CoCreateInstance(__uuidof(MtsGrp));

// determine how many running packages there are
long lPackages;
pMtsGrp->get_Count(&lPackages);

for (int i=0; i<lPackages; i++)
{
    CComPtr<IUnknown> pUnk;
    CComPtr<IMtsEvents> pEvents;

    // for each package get information, first get IUnknown
    pMtsGrp->Item(i, &pUnk);
```

```
    // query for IMtsEvents
    pUnk->QueryInterface(__uuidof(IMtsEvents),
                         (void **)&pEvents);

    // get the package name
    CComBSTR sName;
    pEvents->get_PackageName(&sName.m_str);

    // get the process ID
    long id;
    pEvents->GetProcessID(&id);
    ATLTRACE("%S process ID = %ld\n", sName, id);
}
```

You don't need to put this code in an MTS component, or even use MTS at all. As long as MTS is on the current machine (and `mtxgrp.dll` and `mtsevents.dll` are consequently present and registered) then this code will work.

One final point is that if you debug a transactional component, you must make sure that the time you spend single stepping in the component is less than the transaction timeout period (the default, machine-wide value is 60 seconds). If you take longer than this, the transaction will automatically abort. When you are debugging, you may find it useful to extend this timeout (from the MTS Explorer, My Computer properties, Options tab).

Database Programming

MTS comes with two resource dispensers. The first, the Shared Property Manager, has already been mentioned. The second is the ODBC Manager. This dispenser provides two facilities: connection pooling and auto-enlistment of transactions. The auto-enlistment is important, because it means that you don't need to communicate with the database to enlist the component into a transaction – the ODBC manager will do that. The connection pooling exists to efficiently handle the number of open database connections. The reason it exists is that database connections are expensive to create and maintain. They often involve network calls to a remote database, and usually involve some user – authentication to ensure that the database can determine who the client is (which often takes more network calls).

When an ODBC connection is requested for the first time (perhaps using ADO, or OLE DB using the ODBC provider, a connection is made. When the application releases the connection, the connection manager returns it to the pool. This means that when another application requests a connection with similar properties (the same data source and user), the pooled connection will be returned. This can be a huge performance boost to MTS components, which may open and close connections many times.

The actual pooling is carried out by ODBC, which means that you may have several components in a package, deployed in several DLLs. If they use ODBC connections then pooling will be used, even though the different servers know nothing about each other. There is no explicit initialization of the connection pool, other than to initialize the database library that you are using (ADO, OLE DB).

The pool is dynamic – connections are added to the pool when they are released by components, and they remain in the pool until the connection is inactive for a timeout period (the default is 60 seconds). The pool can be any size, limited only by the amount of free memory:

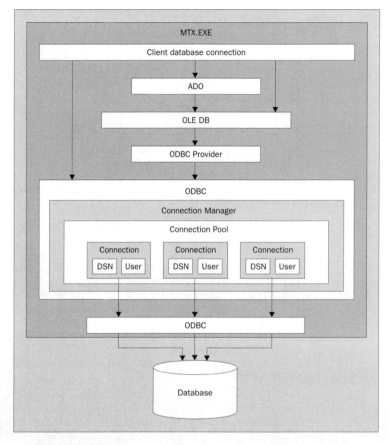

Notice that the connection pool is per server process (hence per package). If you have more than one package that uses database connections, then each will have a connection pool. Be aware that ODBC connection pooling is enabled whenever you use ODBC in an MTS component.

The connection pool timeout is specified in the registry under the following key:

```
HKEY_LOCAL_MACHINE\SOFTWARE\ODBC\ODBCINST.INI\Server Name
```

where *Server Name* is the name of the ODBC driver. This key will have a value called CPTimeout that has a string with the timeout value in seconds. If this value doesn't exist then connection pooling will not be used. You will rarely want to disable connection pooling, but one such occasion will be if the ODBC driver is not thread safe. The ODBC manager will make and close connections on different threads, so a non-thread safe driver will throw exceptions. These will be caught by the ODBC driver manager and logged as an event.

You can also turn off connection pooling through the ODBC Data Source Administrator in the control panel:

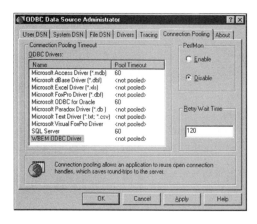

If you double-click on an entry in the list view, you get the option of specifying the connection pool timeout that will be used. As you can see in this screenshot, only Access, Oracle and SQL Server support ODBC connection pooling.

The Retry Wait time determines how long the pool is blocked if the server is not responding. If a database server does not respond to a connection request, ODBC will wait for this amount of time (in seconds) before retrying the connection. This is a global value and requires a machine reboot to change. The PerfMon setting allows you to monitor connection pooling using the performance monitor.

OLE DB

OLE DB abstracts all data source access to COM interface calls, much in the same way that ODBC abstracted database access to the ODBC API. The advantages are that the code uses a generic API, which isn't dependent on the actual provider used at runtime.

OLE DB extends this idea further, because OLE DB providers can be written to give access to a wide range of data sources (file systems, e-mail, and the event log for example) other than traditional relational databases. Indeed, any data that can be described in a table can be accessed through OLE DB, when the appropriate provider has been written. Since OLE DB uses COM interfaces, a wider range of languages can be used. This is in contrast to the C API of ODBC, which restricts its use to languages that can use pointers. Indeed, OLE DB is provided with an ODBC provider, which (as shown in the earlier diagram) is layered over ODBC. This means that if you have an ODBC driver for a data source, you can also access it through OLE DB.

VB, scripting languages, and other restrictive languages can use Active Data Objects (ADO) as a wrapper around OLE DB. You can also use ADO with C++ – the usual way to do this is to use `#import` to generate a C++ header from the type library. The advantage of using `#import` derives from the fact that ADO is designed to be used with scripting languages. This means that the type information in the type library will accurately describe the components and interfaces in the server, since the type library is usually bound to the server.

Like many wrapper libraries, ADO takes away some of the control from the database developer. OLE DB is the base line as far as data source providers go – all the functionality of the data source is provided through OLE DB. So if you want complete control, OLE DB is the way to go.

However, a certain amount of wrapping is always preferable, especially with code that you may wish to repeat many times. Thus, enter the ATL OLE DB consumer classes.

The ATL OLE DB consumer classes can be used within MFC code – they are merely C++ COM client code. However, make no mistake, the code is definitely ATL. In particular, these classes follow the ATL ethos of providing fully functional, efficient code.

These classes are usually, but not exclusively, accessed through the Object Wizard. The Object Wizard will generate header files, based on the information about a data source obtained through instantiating the `DataLinks` object. It will use code a little like this:

```
#include <msdasc.h>

CComPtr<IDBPromptInitialize> pPrompt;
CoCreateInstance(CLSID_DataLinks, NULL, CLSCTX_INPROC_SERVER,
                 IID_IDBPromptInitialize, (void**)&pPrompt);

CComPtr<IDBInitialize> pInit;
pPrompt->PromptDataSource(NULL, hWnd,
                 DBPROMPTOPTIONS_WIZARDSHEET, 0, NULL,
                 NULL, IID_IDBInitialize, (IUnknown**)&pInit);
```

The `hWnd` parameter here is the parent window of the property sheet dialog created by the `DataLinks` object. You can use `NULL` if you don't want to specify a parent window. The `DBPROMPTOPTIONS_WIZARDSHEET` option (or `DBPROMPTOPTIONS_PROPERTYSHEET` as they both appear to do the same thing) will create a property sheet dialog, with a **Next>>** button on the first property page to allow you to navigate to the next page. This is not a wizard, of course, because they have the **Next** and **Prev** buttons on the sheet dialog itself rather than on each page.

Note that since your program can invoke the `DataLinks` *object as indicated by the code above, you can write code completely generic to the data source eventually used, or edit the access properties of an OLE DB data source. This is the strength of OLE DB.*

If your code passes the name of an OLE DB provider as the sixth parameter (for example `SQLOLEDB.1` for the OLE DB SQL Server provider) then the `DataLinks` object will provide a **Connection** property page specific to the provider. Otherwise, a generic page will be used. The Object Wizard will take the latter approach, so the `DataLinks` object will fill the **Provider** page with the friendly names of all the OLE DB providers installed on the machine.

The ATL OLE DB Consumer Object Wizard uses the object returned by the `DataLinks` object to access the schema of the database. It can then present to the ATL developer the tables and stored procedures in the database. Once the user has specified a table from the Object Wizard, it will generate appropriate wrapper classes. Full details can be found elsewhere (*Visual C++ 6 Database Programming Tutorial* by Wendy Sarrett, ISBN 1-861002-41-6 is a good reference), but essentially ATL will generate the following two classes:

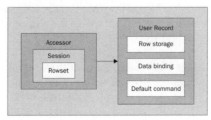

The accessor class has the name of the table or stored procedure that you selected in the wizard. It has a member variable for the current session, which holds a pointer to the current rowset. Transactions are applied to sessions, so any commands that you execute through the accessor on the same session object will be carried out under the scope of the same transaction.

The accessor class is derived from the user record class, which essentially has three types of data. The most immediate is the storage used for a row in the rowset. There will therefore be data members in this class for each column in the rowset. This is where the Object Wizard is most useful, because it will read the column types using the OLE DB provider, and add the appropriate storage to the class. (You can do this by hand, but this is tedious and error prone.) If the accessor is used to make parameterized queries on the database (passing data to OLE DB) then the user record data members are used to hold these parameters.

When you execute a command, OLE DB needs to know what storage it should associate with each column in the query. It does this using data binding, and the Object Wizard will create an **accessor binding map** for you. If your command is a parameterized query then you can use the user record to hold binding information for the parameters in the **parameter map**. Finally, a query must have a command of some kind to pass to the database. The Object Wizard will create a simple command and store this in the user record. If the command is parameterized then '?'s should be used as place holders. Clearly the parameter map, and/or accessor map should have entries that correspond to the parameters and columns in the command (if not, the command will fail).

When you use an accessor or parameter map you specify static binding information, but ATL allows you to provide dynamic binding information too. Similarly, the command that is specified in the user record is the default command, but you are free to provide a command at runtime.

Note that by default, ATL accesses the data source object for the OLE DB provider through code like this:

```
CoCreateInstance(clsid, NULL, CLSCTX_INPROC_SERVER,
                 IID_IDBInitialize, (void**)&pInit);
```

where `clsid` is the class of the OLE DB provider and a pointer to the data source object is returned in `pInit`, which ATL can use to create session object. This means that the OLE DB data services are not applied to the OLE DB provider, implying that resource pooling (explained later) will not be used.

OLE DB Providers

When OLE DB was released there were few OLE DB providers, so as an interim measure `MSDASQL` was supplied as an OLE DB provider built over ODBC. This provider used the existing ODBC driver manager to provide the OLE DB objects for the requested database. Because of this, developers could use OLE DB for databases that didn't have an OLE DB provider, but did have an ODBC driver. This relationship was illustrated in the figure earlier on in this chapter. Since this provider wrapped ODBC, it meant that ODBC connection pooling would be used.

More recently, native OLE DB providers have become available. In particular, SQL Server and Jet can be accessed through `SQLOLEDB.1` and `Microsoft.Jet.OLEDB.4.0` respectively. These provide significant performance improvements over ODBC, and, in addition, the SQL Server provider supplies **resource pooling**.

If you have MDAC 2.1 or later then resource pooling is available to any OLE DB provider that can be aggregated. The provider indicates whether it wants pooling by using the `OLEDB_SERVICES` value in its CLSID registry key. If this has a value of `0xffffffff`, resource pooling is enabled. When you install MDAC 2.1, the ODBC and SQL Server providers (`SQLOLEDB` and `MSDASQL`) will have this value, indicating that (by default) resource pooling will be used. If you want to use connection pooling in `MSDASQL` then you can change the value to `0xfffffffe` to disable resource pooling. Note that the Jet provider does not support resource pooling.

The term resource pooling is a little unfortunate, because it sounds more wide ranging than it actually is. When the OLE DB provider can use pooling, it is aggregated into the OLE DB Service Components – so when the client asks for an interface, the OLE DB Service Components get the first chance to provide the interface. If you request `IDBInitialize` to initialize the data source object, you'll get the version provided by the service components, rather than that provided by the OLE DB provider. There are two ways to get access to the Service Components: through the `DataLinks` object (`CLSID_DataLinks`), or through the Service Component Manager (`CLSID_MSDAINITIALIZE`). The data source object is created by calling `IDBPromptInitialize::PromptDataSource()` or `IDataInitialize::CreateDBInstance[Ex]()` – both will create an instance of the provider as part of an aggregate.

The object returned is known as the **Data source Proxy Object** (**DPO**), and it's instances of these objects that are pooled:

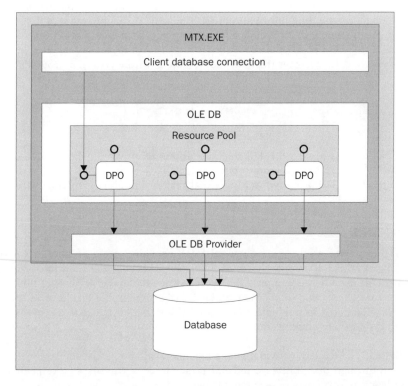

Like ODBC connection pooling, there are timeouts associated with resource pooling. The DPO objects will remain in the pool until the pool timeout is exceeded. This timeout is set to 60 seconds, and at present is non-configurable.

In MDAC 2.5 on Windows 2000, this timeout, the **session pool timeout***, will be configured through a value called* SPTimeout, *which will be under the provider's CLSID key.*

Resource pooling also has a **Retry Wait** timeout, but this works in a slightly different way to ODBC connection pooling. If the server is unavailable, the pool is initially blocked for a minute, at which point OLE DB will retry the connection. If that fails, the next retry will be after an additional two minutes and then every five minutes after that. Again, these values are not configurable in the current version, but will be in MDAC 2.5.

Resource Pooling with ATL

When the Object Wizard creates the wrapper classes for you it will add three methods to the accessor class:

Method	Description
OpenDataSource()	Accesses the data source object and creates a session object, which it caches
OpenRowset()	Executes the accessor command and caches the rowset
Open()	Calls OpenDataSource() and then OpenRowset()

By default, the first method will access the data source object by passing its CLSID to CoCreateInstance(). Developers typically use these methods like this:

```
CMyPersonDatabase db;
db.Open();
while (SUCCEEDED(hr = db.MoveNext()))
{
    if (hr == DB_S_ENDOFROWSET) break;
    ATLTRACE("Obtained %s, %s\n", db.Forename, db.Surname);
}
```

Since the OLE DB provider is used in the raw, you won't get the benefit of the Service Components. To use them you can replace the call to CDataSource::Open() (called in OpenDataSource()) with a call to one of the following methods in CDataSource:

Method	Description
OpenWithServiceComponents()	Obtains the data source object using the Service Component Manager
OpenFromInitializationString()	Obtains the data source object based on an initialization string
OpenFromFileName()	Obtains the data source object using an initialization string in a file
OpenWithPromptFileName()	Presents a browse dialog that you use to select a .udl file containing an initialization string, from which the data source object is initialized

117

Note that if you call `IDBInitialize::Uninitialize()`, the DPO is flushed from the pool and will no longer be available. Thus, when your code is finished with a database connection, it should instead release the `IDBInitialize` interface, making it available in the pool. However, for the pool to exist, there must be at least one reference extant on either `IDataInitialize` or `IDBPromptInitialize`. Once the last reference to either of these interfaces is released, the pool will be released.

The ATL code that uses Service Components does not hold on to the interface, because the `CDataSource` C++ object is only held briefly while the session object is created. To use the pool, your ATL code should query for, and hold on to, a separate reference to `IDataInitialize` or `IDBPromptInitialize`.

Transactions and ATL

If the OLE DB provider supports transactions, and if the MTS component runs under a transaction (requires, requires new, or supports a transaction and is created by a component that runs under a transaction), then the action of the OLE DB connection will work under that transaction. The session object (which under ATL is accessible through the wizard-generated accessor class as the data member m_session) gives access to a transaction through the following methods:

Method	Description
StartTransaction()	Starts a new transaction
Abort()	Aborts the previously started transaction
Commit()	Commits the previously started transaction
GetTransactionInfo()	Gets information about the previously started transaction

Note that these methods don't refer to the transaction created by MTS – instead they represent a **nested transaction**, and only work if your provider supports them. Indeed, these methods actually delegate to an OLE DB interface called `ITransactionLocal`. Essentially, nested transactions allow you to split up a transaction into smaller units of work, so if one of the nested transactions aborts, then so will the entire transaction.

If you call `Commit()` or `Abort()` without first calling `StartTransaction()`, you will get the error XACT_E_NOTRANSACTION, even if the MTS component is running under an MTS created transaction. Similarly, `GetTransactionInfo()` only returns information about the nested transaction. If you want information about the MTS-created transaction, then you need to obtain it through the resource dispenser, as shown in the last chapter.

Summary

MTS extends COM, but (in the version provided with MTS 2.0) is not integrated with COM. Because of this, you must change your programming habits to fit in with MTS. ATL 3.0 provides some facilities to develop COM components specifically for MTS, but these have some quirks. The facilities provided by the ATL AppWizard are hardly earth shattering – they can be added by hand if you forget to apply them and (with one exception) once compiled, the code will work fine without them. The exception concerns the changes that must be made to the proxy-stub makefile to ensure that the proxy-stub DLL is compatible with MTS.

ATL also provides some object types that you can use to create MTS classes. However, the MS Transaction Server Component type adds very little to the Object Wizard Simple Object – more disturbingly, it *removes* some useful facilities (particularly error object support). The other object type is the Component Registrar, which, although MTS 2.0 does not use it, can be useful if used with custom code. The chapter presented an updated Object Wizard object type, which redresses these problems.

Finally, the chapter concludes with a description of how to use OLE DB with ATL, the library of choice for COM and MTS development.

4

Packages and Deployment

Introduction

DCOM is all about distributed applications. It gives you the tools to access components remotely and to configure security so that only trusted accounts can access components. However, much of DCOM is 'developer friendly', not 'network administrator friendly'. That is, if you are happy identifying all the appropriate files that are needed, and manually copying these to the appropriate machines, then you are happy with deploying applications that use DCOM. If you are happy to start and stop your servers using existing NT tools, and test that they are working by monitoring them through their process IDs, then you are happy debugging and testing with DCOM. Finally, if you are happy to configure them and their environment with a collection of tools both GUI and command line based, then you will be happy installing servers with DCOM.

Network administrators are not happy with DCOM. They want just one tool, through which they can drag and drop files, configure components with property dialogs, stop them with a single mouse click and determine whether they are running by looking for a spinning ball. Yes, network administrators want life easy (and perhaps just a little bit boring!).

In fact, the MTS Explorer and the package administration API are more than just bells and whistles. A package is the base execution unit of an MTS application, and bounds the process that the MTS components will run in. The Explorer allows you to define what a package is and to define all the files it will use – it is trivial then to deploy the package on a different machine. The Explorer can also distinguish between client and server-side files. You can therefore create installation files to deploy on client machines, or even administer different MTS machines from a single administrator's machine.

The Catalog

MTS components are COM components, and as such they use the HKEY_CLASSES_ROOT hive (otherwise known as the HKEY_LOCAL_MACHINE\SOFTWARE\Classes key) to hold location and marshaling information. However, MTS introduced the concept of **declarative programming** – that is, a component is *declared* to have a particular transaction requirement. MTS needs to know this *before* it creates the component, so as to be able to set up the correct environment for it. Declaring transaction and security support means that this information needs to be stored somewhere external to the component. (This cannot be applied through an API, because that would imply that the component would have to be executed to set up its environment.) The registry may seem like an ideal place for this information, but that is flawed too.

The problem with the HKEY_CLASSES_ROOT hive is that the registry values used by COM were defined early on in its history. Since these are documented (indeed, the developer is encouraged to use them) they are kept fairly static. Furthermore, a component becomes an MTS component by being configured with the Explorer, which will store its magic information about the component. Non-MTS components are registered in HKEY_CLASSES_ROOT and the COM aspects of MTS components are stored there too. Both types of components should self-register their COM aspects. This means that if MTS only holds its information in the keys of HKEY_CLASSES_ROOT then, when a component is re-registered, the information will be overwritten. This can be overcome if the component knows its MTS properties and can self-register those too, but that results in a component that cannot be configured. This places the responsibility for the component's transactional and security aspects on the developer, and not the administrator. If administrators have this control then they can change those MTS aspects at deployment – a powerful technique.

The MTS designers decided to use the HKEY_CLASSES_ROOT hive to hold COM information, and to have their own private storage, the **catalog**, to hold MTS information. They had to use HKEY_CLASSES_ROOT for COM, because MTS 1.0 and 2.0 worked alongside COM and were not integrated with it. Thus, normal COM-isms like activation and marshaling had to be accommodated. With COM+, on Windows 2000, 'MTS' is integrated with COM, which means ultimately that the COM+ catalog will subsume the HKEY_CLASSES_ROOT hive.

The MTS catalog is stored in the registry under the

```
HKEY_LOCAL_MACHINE\SOFTWARE\Microsoft\Transaction Server
```

key, which isn't documented. The reason for this is clear – MTS provides an API to configure the catalog, which means that the actual implementation can save this information wherever it likes, in whatever form it chooses. The API merely abstracts this implementation detail.

Furthermore, the absence of documentation for the catalog's entries in the registry is a deliberate one, because it means that developers cannot depend on particular registry values. These values can be changed according to configuration demands without breaking the component code. This is the ethos behind 'configured' components.

However, understanding the values used by MTS in the registry leads to a better understanding of how MTS works, so in this section I will explain the various keys and values, and explain what they are used for.

The Catalog and the Registry

The catalog contains the following keys:

Key	Description
Components	Holds information about the components installed in all installed packages
Computers	Holds information about the computers that work with the local machine
Extender	Lists the packages that have recently run
Extenders	Gives the AppID of the "PackageExport"
Local Computer	Holds information about the local machine
Packages	Holds information about the packages installed on the local machine
Remote Components	Holds information about MTS components installed on remote machines that can be used in local packages
Setup(OCM)	Setup information

> **MTS on Windows 9x does not have the** Extenders **key.**

These keys are explained in the following sections.

Packages

The Packages key has a daughter key for every package installed on the local machine. Each of these has the package ID as its name, and contains two daughter keys of its own (Components and Roles), as well as values that are important for the security and activation of the package. Packages is arguably the most important key in the catalog, and contains most of the information that you see presented in MTS Explorer.

Each package key has the following values:

Value	Description
Activation	Determines whether the package is a server (Local) or a library (Inproc) package
Authentication	The authentication level used by default on components in the package
Authorization	Contains the SIDs of all the roles used in the package
Changeable	Corresponds to the value of the Disable Changes option

Value	Description
Deleteable	Corresponds to the value of the **Disable Deletion** option
Description	The package description
Latency	If the package shuts down when idle, this is the timeout in seconds
Name	The package name
NeverShutdown	Y if the package never shuts down, N if there is a timeout (in which case Latency gives the value)
SecurityEnabled	Determines if role checking is performed on component and interface access
System	Set to Y for System packages
UserId	The security identity of the package

Activation

A package can either be a **library** or a **server** package – this is configured using the **Activation** tab on a package's property page. This value is put into the catalog as the Activation value, which can be either Inproc (for a library package) or Local (for a server package). Library packages are run in-process and therefore don't use any security settings. However, a package will be created in the MTS Explorer without reference to whether it's a library or a server. Explorer assumes it will be a server and adds security values. When you configure a package to be a library the SecurityEnabled value will change to N, although the Authentication and Authorization values will remain intact.

Security

Server packages are used in conjunction with an AppID, which specifies the process's security settings. When you create a new package, the MTS Explorer will create a new key under the AppID key using the Package ID. This will contain the account that you specified for the identity of the package in the RunAs key, and will be used as the identity of mtx.exe when the package is run. Note that this identity is also saved in the package's UserId catalog key, so that it can be used to refresh HKEY_CLASSES_ROOT.

If you enable authorization checking on the package, then an access check is performed by checking the accounts in the Authorization key in the package's catalog entry, which will contain SYSTEM by default. If you have added accounts to the roles in the package, then the SIDs of these accounts are added to the Authorization key. This ensures that (using plain COM security) any account mentioned in any role can access any component in the server. Of course, MTS applies a finer grain access check through interception, but these coarse permissions must be applied to satisfy COM because it is COM that launches the mtx.exe process.

Within the package's key in the catalog, there will be keys called Components and Roles. The Roles key has keys for the roles defined for the package, each one of which has a value with the role name and description, as well as a value called SecurityDescriptor. This last value is an ACL that has the SIDs of the SYSTEM account and any accounts that the administrator has added as users to the role. In addition, the role key will have another key called Users, which will itself have a key for each account in the role (named in the form Domain\Account).

Components

When a new component is added to a package with the MTS Explorer, relevant information will be added to the Components key. It will create a key that has the component CLSID for its name. The package's Components key has an entry for every component installed in the package and each key has security information for the component. The other Components key (under Transaction Server and explained in the next section) has more detailed information about each component.

Within each component's key, there will be a key called Interfaces, listing all the interfaces that the type information specifies for the component. Within each of these will be a key called Methods, which will list all the methods on the interface, taken from the type information. In each of these keys there are various values giving the values that the administrator added through the MTS Explorer.

One interesting value is applied to interface methods: Lazy. *This is always set to* "Disabled", *and its use is unclear.*

Each component's key and each key under a component's Interfaces key has a RoleMembership key. This lists the GUID of each role that's given access to the component (or component's interface).

In addition, MTS Explorer will create an AppID for each newly added component, with the same GUID as the component. This AppID has the identity of the package in RunAs and has a LaunchPermission key, which is set to include the SYSTEM account. This means that the DLL will be loaded into mtx.exe (because the system will start mtx.exe). The MTS Explorer will also add a value to the component's key under the package's key in the catalog, called Authorization. This is an ACL that contains SYSTEM and the accounts defined for any roles that the component is a member of. Similarly, each interface that is a role member will have an Authorization value that is an ACL with the role accounts.

Interface, component and package entries within a package's catalog entry will also contain an Authentication value, giving the level of authentication that will be used when a client accesses the server process. As you can see, this offers far finer grained control than COM alone does.

> Note that Windows 98 doesn't have native security, so the security keys mentioned in this section will be missing.

Components

The top level Components key has a daughter key for each component installed in every current package. These contain the values entered via the component's properties and obtained from the server registration.

Value	Description
Description	Component description
DllServer	Full path to the DLL
Enabled	The component is enabled
Inproc	The component is used in a library package
Libid	LIBID of the type information for the component
Local	The component is used in a server package
Origin	Install if the component has been installed through MTS Explorer or an exported package
Package	Package ID of the package in which the component is installed
ProgID	Prog ID of the component
Remote	The component is remote
SupportsInternet	(not known, but is always N)
System	Y for system components
ThreadingModel	Threading model, as registered for the component in its CLSID
Transaction	String identifying the component's transaction support
Typelib	Full path to the type library (this is required because the type library version isn't saved)
Wrapped	(not known)

The Inproc, Local and Remote values are always present, and only one of the three will be Y. If the component is remote then the key will have no values (not even Remote!). Instead, it will have a key called Mtx, containing transaction support for the component and its description. Further details of the component are given in the Remote Components key.

Remote Components

The Remote Components key has a daughter key for each remote component. Within each of these is a key called Interfaces, containing a daughter key for each interface on the component. Each of these has values governing the description and name of the interface – this information is obtained from the remote machine.

When you install a remote component, MTS Explorer will register the component's ProgID, version independent ProgID and CLSID into the client machine's HKEY_CLASSES_ROOT. In the CLSID sub-key though, it won't give a path to a server (as it's on another machine). Instead, it will create an AppID (with the same GUID as the component) and place it as a value in the component's key. The AppID key will merely have a RemoteServerName key, containing the name of the server on which the component will run.

The message inherent in these registry values is that MTS isn't used for the component activation on the client-side – normal DCOM activation is involved. MTS *will* be involved on the server-side, because the component is installed in MTS, but on the client-side MTS is used merely for its deployment facilities (the MTS Explorer is required on the client in order to install the component as a remote component).

Local Computer

The Local Computer key has a daughter key called My Computer, which contains miscellaneous information about the computer. In particular, it holds the information present on the General and Options pages of the My Computer properties, and has information about extra DLLs needed for Oracle. Other values are:

Value	Description
Package Directory	Local directory where pre-built packages are installed
Remote Components	Local path where the proxy-stubs and type libraries for remote components are installed
RemoteServerName	When generating client files this is used as the name of the server
ReplicationShare	This gives the virtual server name when you use MTS with MS Cluster Server

Computers

This merely contains a daughter key for each computer installed in MTS Explorer, including My Computer.

Extender and Extenders

The Extender key is interesting – its default value is the following CLSID:

```
{6F9E4BD0-7970-11D0-B16C-00AA00BA3258}
```

which is the CasperObj class (MTST.CasperObj.1 in mtsevents.dll). This is *not* an MTS component (as you saw in Chapter 2), but is involved in the activation of MTS components. Its only registered interfaces are IUnknown and IMarshal, implying that it's involved in the marshaling of MTS.

Extender also has several named values with the name of a package, and each appears to be a DWORD value of 0x10000. The value doesn't represent whether the package is running, it just appears to be a list of the packages that have ever run on the local machine. Even if you remove a package, if it has run once or more, then it will have a value in Extender.

The Extenders key has a single named value called Package Export, which has the CLSID of an MTS component called MTS Client Export (MTS.ClientExport.1, in mtxclex.dll). This is part of the System package, and is used to export the client files, as explained later in the chapter.

Setup(OCM)

Contains the product version of MTS, the source path and the install path.

Package Deployment

Let's just consider COM for a moment. Because interfaces are accessed remotely, marshaling information must be supplied. This, in turn, means that the interfaces need to be registered on the client and server machines, and the proxy-stubs need to be deployed on all machines. Furthermore, COM allows for the remote launching of servers, thus requiring that the server be registered on the remote machine (to enable its SCM to locate it). Finally, the client code needs either to know the host machine of the component, or to have registration code that associates components of a particular class with a particular machine.

There is a lot of registration here, and several files that need to be deployed. With plain COM, the only administrative tool provided is DCOMCnfg (although users can install OLEView to get more facilities). The significant point is that the administration occurs on a *single* machine. This means that, with a distributed application, the administrator must tour all the machines, log on as a machine administrator, install the required components, and configure them with DCOMCnfg. If, when the administrator gets back to his or her own machine, the application fails to work because a component needs upgrading or a configuration is wrong, another tour around the machines will be necessary.

But isn't DCOM about distribution? You would *not* expect interface parameters to be transmitted by SneakerNet, so why should component deployment be done that way?

> *SneakerNet refers to a user copying code or data on to a floppy disk and actually walking to the machine that will use it.*

This is where the MTS Explorer comes in. The idea is that, once machines are added to the Explorer and correctly configured, all MTS package deployment can be done from a single machine. Components and their marshaling information are distributed via the network, and are registered and configured by MTS.

MTS Explorer

The Win9x version of MTS Explorer is different to the NT4 one – in more than just looks. Part of the reason for this is that Win9x doesn't have native security, so you can't configure this. The difference in appearance between the MTS Explorer on NT4 and Win9x is due to the fact that Explorer on NT4 is an MMC (Microsoft Management Console) snap-in, whereas on Win9x it is a separate application. This can be seen in the following two screen shots. The first is from NT4, where the various actions are installed into MMC as nodes, in a hierarchical manner. Each computer has a node under each of which there are nodes listing the installed packages, the remote components that the local machine can use, and details about the MS DTC.

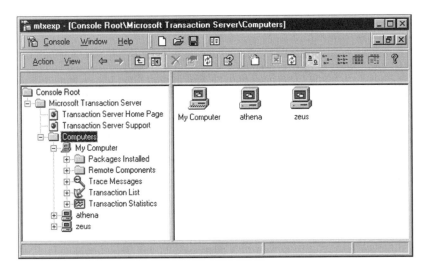

The actual information is given in the right hand pane. This typically has a listview control, but may have other window types. The whole idea of MMC is that it represents a common interface through which you administer your machine. In Windows 2000 this tool will almost replace the control panel with this capacity. I say 'almost' because Windows 2000 will still give a control panel view of the things that you can change, but instead of this being a classic shell extension it will be a web view.

Windows 9x has a totally different version of MTS Explorer:

When you run it you will get a single window containing a listview. You can either use that single window by double clicking on the icons to access the data they represent, or the New window menu item on the View menu to open additional windows (as I have done here). What is missing is the MMC treeview control, which can make the Win9x MTS Explorer confusing when you get deep down into the various folders.

In the following sections, I will show screenshots from NT4 as, by and large, the listview shown in MMC is the image that you will see in the Win9x version (except that there won't be any security settings). Indeed, the actual administration of the components is carried out through property sheets, which vary little between the two versions.

One very irritating thing about the MMC snap-in on NT4 is that when you shut down MMC you get a dialog asking whether you would like to save the console settings. You will get this whenever you navigate through the treeview, regardless of whether you make any changes. The reason is that the dialog comes from the console (not the snap-in), to see if you want to start up at a later stage at the same place in the snap-in. I find this irritating, and there doesn't seem to be a solution on NT4. (MMC on Windows 2000 has a switch, / s, that stops this behavior).

Computer Management

Of course a vital part of distribution is getting several computers to talk to each other. MTS enables this by allowing you to administer several machines from a single machine. When you install MTS from the option pack you will be given the following screen:

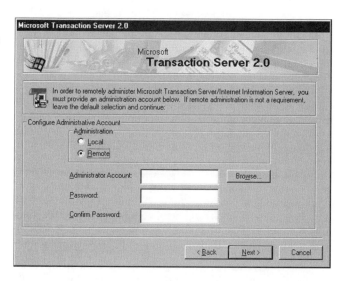

If you want to administer this copy of MTS from another (remote) machine (which will be the case for most machines that you'll use in a distributed application), then you need to specify an administrative account on this page. The account that you use should be one that's accessible from the remote machine, which means either a domain account (which is preferable), or the old DCOM trick of giving a local account (as long as the remote machine has an account with exactly the same name and password).

> *The danger with this trick is that one or other of the machines could change the password – access would then be denied. This is why a domain account is preferred. Both machines will then use the same account rather than two accounts that just look the same.*

If you opt to administer the machine locally then you can change this later because all this page does is add the account to the `Administrator`'s role of the `System` package. This package, as you'll see later in this chapter, is used to export packages and manipulate the catalog.

Once MTS is installed, your local copy will access remote instances using DCOM when requested by the user (through the MTS Explorer). The user will, of course, have to add the computer to the MTS Explorer, which is done simply by selecting and right-clicking on the Computers node, and choosing New | Computer.

Once you have a computer added to the Explorer view, you can use the icon as an indication of whether the MS DTC is running on the remote machine. In the screen shot given earlier, the local machine, My Computer, has the MS DTC running – consequently the computer symbol has a light green background. In the other two cases, Zeus and Athena do not have the MS DTC running, so the background is a darker shade of green. When the MS DTC is starting up the monitor background will be orange.

If you have the correct permissions on the remote machine, you will be able to start and stop the MS DTC from your administrator's machine. In addition, you'll be able to view the trace, transaction list and transaction statistics from the same machine. However, doing so will clearly put a burden on the network, so do this only when necessary.

Security and Remote Computer Management

The MTS Explorer gives you the ability to do quite powerful things to a remote computer. Indeed, if you have the appropriate permissions, you will have identical options to the local machine: start/stop the MS DTC; stop all server processes; stop a particular server process; install packages; install components into packages, and install remote components. This is very powerful from the administrator's point of view, but is also very risky from the perspective of the machines' owners. Therefore, each machine must give permission for the administrator's account to manipulate it (hence the option during set up). Furthermore, if files are moved between machines, then there must be shared folders with the appropriate access permissions given to the administrator's account.

The System package will be installed with two roles: the Administrator role and the Readers role – by default these will be empty. The package is also run under the interactive user identity, which means that the person who has logged on will be able to read and administer the catalog. To allow remote machines to view the catalog on your machine (view installed packages and remote components) you must add an appropriate account to the Readers role.

Similarly, you need to add an appropriate account to the Administrators role to allow remote machines to administrate your machine (to start and stop the MS DTC, view transactions, messages and transactions statistics, and to stop server processes). By default, the local Administrators NTLM group is added to this role. Curiously, an administrator's account on one machine, which isn't a member of the Administrators role on a remote machine, will appear to have permission to stop all server processes on another machine (the menu item will be enabled in the context menu of that remote machine in the Computers node):

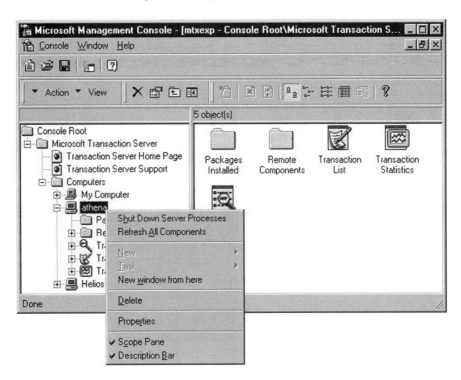

However, I say 'appear' because the menu item will have no effect until the user is actually added to the role. The MTS snap-in on NT4 has several such quirks.

In addition, if you want to add a remote component to your machine's **Remote Components**, then the account under which you are running must also be part of the `Administrators` role. The proxy-stub files or type libraries for these remote components will be installed in a directory with the name of the remote component package. This will be in a directory called `Remote`, itself within the MTS directory (usually in `\Program Files\Mts`).

Finally, since you are copying files across the network, you need to make sure that the appropriate folders are shared to the accounts that will be used. So, if you are setting up a remote component on the local machine ('pulling' files), you must get access to the component's proxy-stub/type library files. The folder that contains these files must thus be shared, and the account used to access them should have read access. If you are giving another computer access to a component in one of your packages ('pushing' files) then you need to share the folder containing those files with appropriate access permissions.

> *Note that MSDN talks about pulling and pushing components. This is not correct – you are pulling and pushing the proxy-stubs or type libraries. If you pulled or pushed a component, then it would mean that the component was not remote!*

Installing Packages

The **Packages Installed** node shows the packages installed on the local machine. MTS will install several packages for you during set up. These will include the **System Package** and **Utilities Package**, which contain components allowing you to install and configure packages and components via an API (and to provide components to scope transactions). However, the option pack will install MTS as part of IIS (Internet Information Server) and will thus install packages for ASP and IIS. These effectively give the ASP developer access to transactions.

You can add your own packages (it would be pretty useless if you couldn't) by selecting and right clicking on **Packages Installed**, and selecting **Package** from the **New** menu. This starts up a wizard that allows you to either create an empty package or install a pre-built one. I'll come to the second option later, but if you create an empty package, you'll have the option of giving it a name and an identity under which it will run.

> *At this stage you're not given the option of specifying whether the package is a library or a server. I find this odd, because if it is intended to be a library package, it will always be loaded in process – in which case it will take the identity of the client process.*

After the package has been created, it will be empty, and you'll have the option of adding components to it.

A package is the executable context for one or more components, so a component can only be installed into one package. This doesn't mean that one package can't use components in other packages (or non-MTS components) – it can. It just means that if a component is part of one package, it can't be installed in another.

Installing Unregistered Components

There are two ways to do this. You can either drag and drop DLLs, or use a wizard. Using the former, you drag a DLL from Windows Explorer, and drop it in the listview of a package's Components node. If the DLL has a bound type library (more about this later) then *all* components in the DLL will be added to the package.

If you choose to use the wizard, there are two more options. The wizard is invoked through the New | Component on the context menu of the Components node of a package. The first option is called Install new components, which allows you to select a file that implements components.

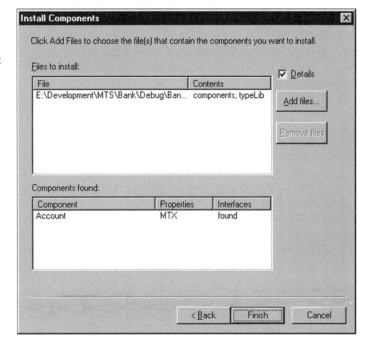

The Add Files button allows you to browse for the file. Notice in this screen shot that the DLL has type information bound as a resource. The Files to install box mentions that the DLL has components and a type library, and it uses the type information to determine the components in the server (it browses the type information for TKIND_COCLASS).

The names of these components are given in the lower box. The properties column for these components appears to always say MTX. This doesn't depend on whether you use the custom attributes defined in mtxattr.h – I guess it just indicates that any component with interfaces that can be marshaled can be an MTS component. The final column indicates whether the interfaces implemented by the component have been identified from the type information.

Take this with a pinch of salt. If your server doesn't have type information, no components will be placed in the lower box and the Finish button will be grayed (so you cannot add the component to the package this way). However, you can specify a separate .tlb file in the Files to install list.

To put a component's type information into a type library you must add a `coclass` section to the `library` section of the IDL. That `coclass` section *must* have a `[default] interface` statement, and, even if you just use `IUnknown` (which *every* COM component must implement) this Wizard will assume that it has found the component's interfaces. However, in this case, when you click on Finish you will get an error dialog:

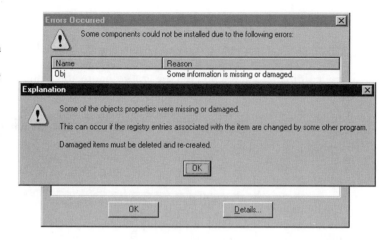

This means that the Wizard can't find any *meaningful* interfaces on the component. The solution is to make sure that if you install components via this method, you ensure that the `coclass` statement has all the interfaces that the component implements. If these interfaces are not oleautomation compatible, don't worry – this information will not be used to marshal the mentioned interfaces. The Wizard just uses this to read the type information. Don't be tempted to add the proxy-stub file in this case – it has no information about `coclasses`.

Make sure you remove the code that ATL puts in to register the type library!

When you add a DLL to the <u>F</u>iles to install list and the Wizard finds a `coclass` in the type information, it will ask the server DLL for the component's class factory by calling `DllGetClassObject()`, and ask for `IClassFactory`. If your class factory object doesn't support this interface then the install will fail. You should at least be aware that MTS Explorer does this. If this call succeeds, then the wizard will call `DllRegisterServer()` on the server to allow it to do its plain COM registration.

MTS Explorer will then install every component that it finds in the type library as an MTS component. If you don't want this, then you have two options:

❑ use a type library that doesn't include the unwanted components

❑ delete unwanted components after they have been installed into the package

The first is preferable, but it does mean that you should create a separate IDL file merely to contain the coclasses and their interfaces, for example:

```
[
    uuid(04387893-0CFA-11D3-897A-00104BDC35E0),
    version(1.0)
    helpstring("Type lib to describe the component")
]
library NoMarshalingLIB
{
    importlib("stdole32.tlb");
    importlib("stdole2.tlb");
    [
        uuid(0438789F-0CFA-11D3-897A-00104BDC35E0)
    ]
    interface ICustomItf : IUnknown
    {
        HRESULT DoSomething();
    };
    [
        uuid(043878A0-0CFA-11D3-897A-00104BDC35E0)
    ]
    coclass ObjWithCustomItf
    {
        [default] interface ICustomItf;
    };
};
```

This is effectively the `library` statement that the ATL AppWizard will add to the IDL file for you. You will no doubt remove it if you choose not to use type library marshaling.

> *If your intention is to use components that don't use type library marshaling, then by all means remove the* library *statement, but save the code and generate a type library that will keep the MTS Explorer happy.*

Remember that if the MTS Explorer can't determine the interfaces that the components implement, it will still install the components into the package. It won't, however, list any interfaces, so you won't be able to specify role-based security on the interfaces of the component.

If you decide instead to install all the components and then delete the ones you don't want, be aware that the MTS Explorer will remove the CLSID entries for these components in the registry, but not the ProgIDs.

When you click on the Finish button, the MTS Explorer will request the class factory again for each `coclass`, and will then call `DllRegisterServer()` for the whole server.

Installing Registered Components

The second option the wizard presents to install components is called Import component(s) that are already registered and this will present the following dialog:

The dialog contains all components that have been registered in the CLSID key *except* those that have already been installed into a package.

If you use this dialog, then you can choose individual components from a DLL (rather than having the MTS Explorer install them all, then deleting those you don't want).

Type Information

When you install components through the MTS Explorer, it will add the components registered in the type library. In addition, you can add the transaction support for the components to the type library, using the custom attributes mentioned in mtxattr.h. The MTS Explorer will then configure the installed component to have that support.

The attributes you can use may be any of the following:

```
TRANSACTION_SUPPORTED
TRANSACTION_NOT_SUPPORTED
TRANSACTION_REQUIRED
TRANSACTION_REQUIRES_NEW
```

This should be applied to the coclass attributes:

```
#include "mtxattr.h"
[
    uuid(04387900-0CFA-11D3-897A-00104BDC35E0),
    TRANSACTION_REQUIRED
]
coclass MyTransactionalObject
{
    [default] interface IMyInterface;
};
```

Note that this is the only MTS attribute that you can put in a type library. You cannot specify the roles to be used for particular components or interfaces. This is odd, because these attributes merely use the [custom()] IDL attribute that associates a VARIANT with a GUID. The designers of MTS could therefore have defined an InterfaceRoles GUID and a CoClassRoles GUID associated with a string that is a comma-separated list of role names. MTS Explorer could then have read the role names, checked them against those defined for the package, and made the appropriate catalog changes. There are no such GUIDs, and the MTS Explorer doesn't work this way, so you have no option but to apply roles by hand.

Exporting and Importing Components

Remote components run on another machine, of course, but in MTS terms this means that they are components installed in MTS on another machine. To access these remote components you need to have their interfaces registered on the local machine. This is the reason for the Remote Components node in the MTS Explorer.

The documentation says that you can **pull** or **push** files across the network. The difference depends on where components exist, and from where you want to access them. If a component is on a remote machine and you want to access it from your machine, then you must get the appropriate marshaling files from that remote machine – this is **pulling**. If the component is on your machine, and you want another machine to have access to it, then you have to **push** the files to that other machine.

MSDN (and, it has to be said, most other texts) talk about pulling or pushing *components*. As noted earlier, this is incorrect – it is the marshaling files (either proxy-stubs or type libraries) that are actually moved. However, if the type information is bound into the server file (or the proxy-stubs are merged with it) then the server file will be copied. If the server DLL is large, then there will be a once-only copying of that large file across the network. (In addition that file will take up disk space on the destination machine.) It may make sense to use a separate type library file (.tlb) or a separate proxy-stub, so that *only* the marshaling files are copied.

> *It does seem odd to copy the component's server file to the client, when the intention is to run the component on another machine (as a remote component). In actual fact, it would be relatively simple for MTS to extract the type library resource and transmit this to a remote machine, rather than the entire server file.*

These proxy-stub files or type libraries for the remote components will be installed in a directory with the name of the remote component package, in a directory called Remote in the MTS directory (usually in \Program Files\Mts). If you remove a remote component using the MTS Explorer, only the registration and catalog entries are removed. The package directory and the files will still remain. If these files are large, then you may consider periodically looking in this directory to see which files are being used, and deleting those that are not.

If you don't have a shared folder set up (as explained earlier), then you will get an error like the following, which is fairly self-explanatory:

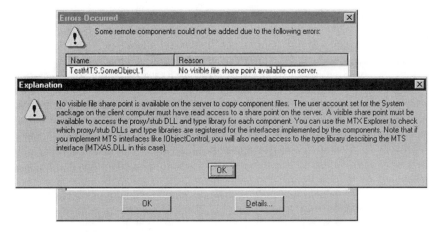

Actually performing the pulling or pushing is quite simple, once the correct security and sharing is set up. If you want to pull files, you must use MTS Explorer to open the **Remote Components** node for *your* machine (**My Computer**). Then, from the context menu select **New** | **Remote Component**, and you'll get the following dialog:

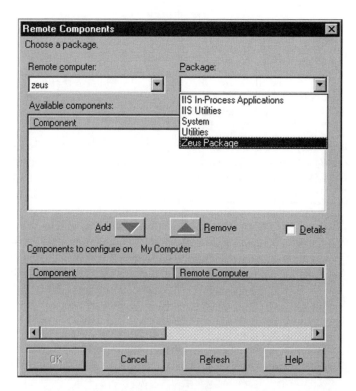

The Remote computer box will have the names of the computers that you have added to the Computers node. Note that the MTS Explorer doesn't check whether the computers are accessible, so if you select a computer that isn't turned on, or isn't connected to the network, the dialog will appear to hang – you can use the Cancel button to stop the access.

The dialog will list all installed packages in the Package box and, when you select one, it will add all the components installed in the package to the Available components list box. You should then select entries with the Add button to specify the components that you want to access, and click OK.

Note that once you have installed access to a remote component in this way, the MTS Explorer will register the ProgID and CLSID for the component in HKCR. The CLSID entry just has ProgID information, and it gives an AppID which lists the remote machine in RemoteServerName. The point of this is that there is enough information for both MTS components and ordinary (non-MTS) COM clients to access the component. Indeed, the access doesn't use MTS on the client machine – it uses simple DCOM activation and access. This highlights the point that you are *not* moving components around, but accessing them remotely.

Exporting Packages

Once you have finished developing your application, you'll want to package it up ready for deployment to the production environment. Before MTS this meant that you had to identify all the servers, all the proxy-stub files and/or type libraries, and all the associated DLLs. You would then have to create some kind of installation script that would register all these files. A lot of bother, but don't worry – MTS does all this for you.

To export a package, you select it from the **Packages Installed** node and from the context menu select **Export**. The MTS Explorer will ask you for a path to where the installation file will be created. The same directory will be used for the files that need to be distributed. You should select a new directory for these files, so as not to mix them with other files. The MTS Explorer will do three things:

❑ copy the server DLL, proxy-stub and type library files into the directory

❑ create an installation script with the extension `.pak`

❑ create a directory called `clients` that has an executable to install the client files

The `.pak` file is effectively a dump of the relevant entries in the registry. It has the following format, with the information getting more detailed from the bottom up:

```
component and interface details
role details
package details
package and MTS information
```

The file takes the same format as the old `.ini` files that were popular with 16-bit operating systems (including the hybrid Win9x). That is, there are sections denoted by square brackets, and within them are values in the form:

```
ValueName=value
```

This format has been bent to fit the problem. For example, each component (and role) description is in a section that has the package ID as the name. Because there may be several components, the names have been appended with an index. For example:

```
[{4DFBEE7E-2E35-11D3-899A-00104BDC35E0} - R1]
RoleID={043089A1-337C-11D3-89A0-00104BDC35E0}
    ... other stuff ...
[{4DFBEE7E-2E35-11D3-899A-00104BDC35E0} - R2]
RoleID={043089A4-337C-11D3-89A0-00104BDC35E0}
    ... other stuff ...
[{4DFBEE7E-2E35-11D3-899A-00104BDC35E0}]
Name=Products
    ... other stuff ...
[Packages]
Package1={4DFBEE7E-2E35-11D3-899A-00104BDC35E0}
    ... other stuff ...
```

Here you can see that the two role sections have `R1` and `R2` appended to the package ID.

The last section in the `.pak` file indicates how many packages it describes, and details about the version of MTS used. However, MTS Explorer doesn't allow you to add more than one package to the `.pak` file – if you try to reuse the same file Explorer will overwrite the existing values.

139

This section is preceded by the package details, which list the security settings, activation type and the number of roles and components described. For each role, the role ID, name and description are given. If you select the Save Windows NT user ids associated with roles option then the section will also contain the NTLM accounts that you entered in the role. You'll only want to do this if the package is to be used on the same network, and if they are domain accounts that the deployment machine has access to. In most cases you won't want to do this, instead allowing the local administrator to determine which accounts are in which roles.

> *Note that you get this option even if you export a* library *package.*

As a final warning, if you use custom utility DLLs in the servers in your package, they will not be exported, even though the package may depend on these DLLs. This is, in my opinion, an omission that could have been avoided – most DLLs are used through an export library (rather than dynamic linking using `LoadLibrary()` and `GetProcAddress()`), so MTS could have read the import table in the server, and prompted the user for any DLLs that it does not identify as system DLLs.

The only way for you to fix this problem is to copy the utility DLL to the export directory by hand. A longer-term solution would be to rewrite the utility DLL as a COM server, and add its components to the package.

Installing the Package

Once you have exported the package, you have all the information needed to import it onto another machine. Importing the package means that it will run on the specified machine. You can do this either from the actual importing machine, or via an administrator machine. In the first case, you will need to copy the `.pak` file and install files to the new machine, or give MTS Explorer on the importing machine access to the exported files directory on the exporting machine (though it doesn't need access to the `clients` directory). In the second case, the administrator's machine will need access to those package files.

You then need to select New | Package from the context menu of the Packages Installed node for the appropriate machine, and, from the Wizard, select Install pre-built packages. This allows you to select the `.pak` file, and it will then give you the option of determining the package identity. Finally, select a directory in which to install the package. This final dialog gives you the option of using the NTLM accounts specified for the roles (if these exist).

> *Note that the wizard doesn't appear to recognize when a package is a library package – it will still* ask you for the identity, and whether you want to use NT accounts for roles. Library *packages run under the client identity and do not have security.*

As mentioned earlier, if the package uses utility DLLs then you will need to copy these by hand, or rewrite them as COM DLLs.

Client Registration

If your clients are on a different machine to the package, then you need to have the correct marshaling information installed and registered. There are two options:

- ❑ 'push' or 'pull' all the marshaling files as explained for Remote Components above
- ❑ use the client installation file

There are two problems with the first option: it is tedious, and you have to do it from the machine that will be the final server. If there are many components in the package that will be accessed by clients, then it can be a big problem to pull or push all the data. Of greater concern is that (in both cases) the machine from which the files were pulled or pushed will be used in the RemoteServerName on the client. If the final server machine will be different, it entails using DCOMCnfg to change this name.

The advantage of the pull/push approach is that often a package will contain only a few components that clients will access. The other components are sub-components that should run in the same process, but aren't directly run by the client. In this case, it is better to pull/push the marshaling files for the few components that will be accessed, rather than allowing the client installation file to register *all* the components on the client.

The client installation file provides a single file means of installing the client end of a package on a machine. The file is an executable that will install and register the marshaling files of all the components in a package. It uses the Windows setup API, and has resources in it for customizing the dialogs and messages presented to the user. However, you have no access to this through MTS. The executable is quite large, containing as it does a .cab file as one of its resources. This holds the marshaling files for all of the interfaces used by the components in the package, as well as the following system DLLs:

- ❑ AdvPack.dll
- ❑ cfgmgr32.dll
- ❑ setupapi.dll
- ❑ w95inf16.dll
- ❑ w95inf32.dll

These are used by the program to install the package.

To indicate what files are installed and how the program should do it, there is also an .inf file. This will create the CLSID, ProgID and AppID registry entries for the components mentioned in the package. The CLSID entry simply has ProgID information and the AppID; the AppID entry just has RemoteServerName set to an appropriate value (either the exporting machine, or the one mentioned as the **Remote server name** on the **Options** tab of the **My Computer** property page). Setup will then create the interface marshaling keys and, if necessary, the type library keys.

.inf files are designed to be flexible, but since this one is embedded with a .cab file in a resource, you have to accept the values that MTS has decided for you. For example, at the end of the .inf file you'll get the section shown overleaf:

```
[Strings]
DiskName = "Installation Disk"
RemoteAppsDir = "Program Files\Remote Applications"
RemoteApp = "Remote Application"
Remove = " (remove only) "
pak = MyPackageName
pakid = {4DFBEE7E-2E35-11D3-899A-00104BDC35E0}
pakname = MyPackageName
computer = TheRemoteMachine
```

This indicates that the package will be installed in `Program Files\Remote Applications`. If this isn't what you want, then you can extract the cabinet and alter the files in it. The following command line program will extract the `CABINET` resource for you (error checking removed for brevity):

```c
#include <windows.h>
#include <stdio.h>
#include <tchar.h>
#include <Shlwapi.h> // for the file extension functions
#pragma comment(lib, "shlwapi.lib")

void main(int argc, char* argv[])
{
    if (argc != 2)
    {
        printf(_T("Please give the name of the ")
               _T("client install program\n"));
        return;
    }

    HMODULE hMod;
    hMod = (HMODULE)LoadLibrary(argv[1]);
    HRSRC hrsrc;
    hrsrc = FindResource(hMod, _T("CABINET"), RT_RCDATA);
    DWORD dwSize;
    HGLOBAL hGlobal;
    hGlobal = LoadResource(hMod, hrsrc);
    dwSize = SizeofResource(hMod, hrsrc);
    HANDLE hFile;
    TCHAR strFile[MAX_PATH];
    lstrcpy(strFile, argv[1]);
    PathRemoveExtension(strFile);
    PathAddExtension(strFile, _T(".cab"));

    hFile = CreateFile(strFile, GENERIC_WRITE, 0, 0,
                       CREATE_ALWAYS, 0, 0);
    DWORD dwWritten = 1;
    LPBYTE pv = (LPBYTE)GlobalLock(hGlobal);
    while (dwWritten > 0)
    {
        WriteFile(hFile, pv, dwSize, &dwWritten, 0);
        pv += dwWritten;
        dwSize -= dwWritten;
    }
    FreeLibrary(hMod);
    CloseHandle(hFile);
}
```

To edit an extracted cabinet you need to use the CAB SDK, which is supplied with MSDN. If you want to insert the edited cabinet back into the executable, you can use the `UpdateResource()` collection of APIs. First call `BeginUpdateResource()` to pass the file name and get an update handle. This is then passed to `UpdateResource()` along with the identifiers of the resource and its type, as well as an `LPVOID` pointer to the changed resource. Once the change has been made, it can be completed with a call to `EndUpdateResource()`.

Indeed, if you do this, then it's possible to change some of the other setup information and customize the installation. However, this is a book about MTS and not the Windows setup library, so you'll have to consult MSDN on how to do that.

Running Packages

Server packages have a Server Process Shutdown option (on the Advanced tab of their properties), which allows you to specify how long the server package will run when there are no longer any components running. You have the option of giving a shutdown timeout in minutes (so that machine resources are conserved), or specifying that the package should remain idle until a client needs a component. By specifying that a package is not shut down when idle, you greatly improve the availability of the components in the package (at the expense of having yet another process running on your machine).

You may decide that this approach (having packages running on your machine all the time) is a good idea. However, the MTS Explorer has no facility to start a package, so you have no option but to start `mtx.exe` from the command line, using the package ID as shown in the last chapter.

Note that if you attempt to run a library package like this, it will fail with the following error:

Source:	Transaction Server
Severity:	Error
Category:	Executive
Event:	4131
Description:	A server process failed during initialization. The most common cause is an invalid command line, which may indicate an inconsistent or corrupted catalog. This error caused the process to terminate. GetCLSIDsForPackage (Microsoft Transaction Server Internals Information: File: d:\viper\src\runtime\mtxex\cpackage.cpp, Line: 365)

This isn't as severe as it sounds! Clearly, MTS doesn't check that the package has been configured to be a library package, and blindly tries to launch it in `mtx.exe`.

MTS Explorer gives no indication of the fact that a package is running until a component is activated. Indeed, you will find that the context menu of each package (except system packages) will have the Shut down menu item enabled, *even for library packages*. This doesn't indicate that the package is running, and selecting it will do nothing unless it is.

Once a component is requested, the icon for the component in the MTS Explorer will start spinning. You can choose from several views of the components, the Status View is a particularly useful one:

This is obtained by selecting the Components node, and from the View menu selecting Status View. In the screen shot above, the icon is spinning because at least one component is activated (that's why you can't see the plane symbol). The Objects column gives the number of instances of the component that have been created. Activated gives the number of components that are activated, and of those the number that are currently in a call is given in the last column.

If the components are transactional, the details about the transactions created by MS DTC, as well as those that have been committed and aborted, are given in the Transaction Statistics node. Details of the transaction that are in doubt, and any messages generated by the MS DTC are given in the Transaction List and Trace Messages nodes respectively. I will defer a more detailed description of these until the next chapter.

Deployment API

The MTS Explorer will do a lot of work for you. However, this does mean that the creation and administration of packages is done through MMC (on Windows NT). Often you will want to do the same thing, but through your own process. For example, you may want to restrict the parts of the catalog that the administrator can access, either to prevent them from changing parts, or to prevent confusion (too much information can sometimes be a bad thing). To do this, you need to access MTS's deployment APIs programmatically. This section will explain the libraries available to you and what you can do with them.

MTS 2.0 Administrative Libraries

MTS 2.0 is provided with several administrative libraries, most of which are accessed through the MTS Explorer. However, since they are provided with type libraries, you are free to use them in your code.

Microsoft Transaction Server

This library (mtxas.dll) is provided as a convenience for VB programmers. It contains the [appobject] class called AppServer – this ODL attribute gives the VB programmer access to the classes' interface methods without explicitly instantiating a component, and in effect presents them as global functions. AppServer implements IMTxAS, which has SafeRef() and GetObjectContext().

The former is a VARIANT-based wrapper around SafeRef(), and the latter returns a reference to the context object through the interface ObjectContext (note that this interface doesn't have the standard I prefix). In addition to the methods of IObjectContext, this component has a Security property that implements SecurityProperty (a wrapper around ISecurityProperty) – a collection of properties giving access to the ASP objects. C++ programmers should have no use for this library.

Transaction Context

This library (txctx.dll) has two classes to perform the same actions, one for VB programmers (TransactionContext) with a dual interface, and another intended for C++ programmers (TransactionContextEx), which has a custom interface. Both components are wrappers around IObjectContext, and are installed in MTS in the Utilities package. Each requires a new transaction.

Essentially, these components exist to allow the programmer to use a declarative transaction programming technique in the client code. The client code declares the start of a transaction by creating an instance of the TransactionContext component, creating a component in its activity, and ending the transaction by calling Commit() or Abort():

```
Dim ctx as New TransactionContext
Dim acc as Account
Set acc = ctx.CreateInstance("Bank.Account") ' transaction starts
' use the Account object within a transaction
acc.Initialize(customerName)
Dim newBalance As Single
acc.DecreaseBalanceBy withdrawl
If newBalance < 0 Then
    Dim log as DebtorsLog
    ' do the work in the same transaction
    Set log = ctx.CreateInstance("Bank.DebtorsLog")
    log.AddDebtor customerName, newBalance
End If
ctx.Commit ' transaction ends
```

You don't have to use these components in C++, because it is trivial to write your own version. If you do choose to use them, take note of the warnings in the last chapter about their use in client applications.

MTS 2.0 Admin

This library is useful, and represents much of the functionality exposed through the MTS Explorer. It is implemented in mtxadmin.dll, and has the following classes (which implement like-named interfaces):

Class	Description
Catalog	Main entry into the MTS catalog
CatalogCollection	A collection of CatalogObjects
CatalogObject	An item within the catalog, the actual value depends on what sort of item you requested

Class	Description
ComponentUtil	Used to install components running on the local machine into a package
PackageUtil	Used to install, export, or shut down a package
RemoteComponentUtil	Used to install a remote component
RoleAssociationUtil	Used to add roles to a component or a component's interface

These components are designed to be used with VB and scripting languages, but they can also be used with C++. They are implemented with the Catalog Server library explained in the next section.

Even though the components are designed for scripting languages, they are a bit quirky to use. However, once you realize how they work, they are fairly straightforward. The following VB code illustrates how to fill a list box with all the installed packages:

```
Dim myCatalog As New Catalog
Dim myCatalogColl As CatalogCollection
' get a list of installed packages
Set myCatalogColl = myCatalog.GetCollection("Packages")
' no really, I do want them!
myCatalogColl.Populate

' now enumerate them
Dim p As CatalogObject
For Each p In myCatalogColl
    ' add them to a list box
    lstPackages.AddItem p.Name
Next
```

Notice that when you ask for a collection, it is not actually populated with the items that it contains. This means that before you can do things like getting the name of a collection or the number of items it will contain, you must explicitly fill it with items, using a call to Populate(). The reasoning behind this is that since you can connect to the catalog on a remote machine and collections may contain many items, the two-stage construction allows you the option of backing out if the collection is excessively large.

> *I don't really buy into this, because if I want a collection (say, of all the components installed into MTS on another machine), then I will be aware that this collection might be large.*

Let me reiterate – if you use these admin collection components, remember that you must call Populate() before you can access their items. I have had many irritating debug sessions where the code did not work, only to find that the problem was my forgetting to call this method.

So what are the collections that you can access? The following tables show the collections accessed on MTS 2.0:

Collection	Description
ComputerList	The computers that the local computer can access.
LocalComputer	The local computer – usually This Computer.
Packages	Installed packages. Also gives access to the ComponentsInPackage and RolesInPackage collections.
RemoteComponents	Components installed in MTS packages on remote machines, which local packages and other applications can access. Gives access to the InterfacesForRemoteComponent collection.

These collections can return components that can return collections themselves, as indicated in the preceding table.

Each package contains two collections:

Collection	Description
ComponentsInPackage	Collection of the components installed in a specified package
RolesInPackage	Collection of the roles in a specified package

To access these, you need to give the key of the package that you are accessing. For example, carrying on with the code from above:

```
Dim myCatalog As New Catalog
Dim myCatalogColl As CatalogCollection
' get a list of installed packages
Set myCatalogColl = myCatalog.GetCollection("Packages")
' no really, I do want them!
myCatalogColl.Populate
' now enumerate them
Dim p As CatalogObject
Dim packageItem As CatalogObject
For Each p In myCatalogColl
    ' add them to a list box
    lstPackages.AddItem p.Name
    ' find the System package
    If p.Name = "System" Then Set packageItem = p
Next


Dim components As CatalogCollection
' get a list of components in the System package
Set components = myCatalogColl.GetCollection("ComponentsInPackage", _
                                   packageItem.Key)
' reaffirm your desire (again)
components.Populate

' enumerate them
For Each p In components
    ' and add them to a list box
    lstComponents.AddItem p.Name
Next
```

This time, notice that the collection of components is obtained from the collection of `Packages`. You use the package ID, obtained by accessing the required package, and apply its `Key` value. (This is rather long winded, but you just have to accept it.) The package's roles can be accessed in a similar way. Once you have the role collection, you can select an individual role. Using its `Key`, you can obtain the `UsersInRole` collection from the `RolesInPackage` collection.

You can access each individual component from a collection, and then appropriate collections on that component:

Collection	Description
InterfacesForComponent	The interfaces implemented on the component
RolesForPackageComponent	The roles that this component is a member of

(Incidentally, if you get the `RemoteComponents` collection, you can access the `InterfacesForRemoteComponent` collection for each item. Clearly there is no equivalent of `RolesForPackageComponent`.)

The interfaces give access to two more collections:

Collection	Description
RolesForPackageComponentInterface	The roles that can access the interface
MethodsForInterface	The methods on the interface

If this object model looks complicated and tedious to program, then you're right. However, there is some salvation. Every collection will give access to a collection called `RelatedCollectionInfo`, which contains the names of all the collections obtainable from the current one. In addition, each item can be used to obtain a collection called `PropertyInfo`, which gives access to the names of all the properties that it supports. So, if you can't remember the properties of each item in the `Packages` collection, you can obtain the `PropertyInfo` collection and enumerate them.

If an error occurs when you access one of these components, you can get information about the error by accessing the `ErrorInfo` collection on that component. This will contain one or more error values to explain what caused the error – their names are self explanatory:

mtsErrObjectErrors	mtsErrNoRegistryCLSID	mtsErrBadForward
mtsErrObjectInvalid	mtsErrBadRegistryProgID	mtsErrBadIID
mtsErrKeyMissing	mtsErrAuthenticationLevel	mtsErrRegistrarFailed
mtsErrAlreadyInstalled	mtsErrUserPasswdNotValid	mtsErrCompFileDoesNotExist
mtsErrDownloadFailed	mtsErrNoRegistryRead	mtsErrCompFileLoadDLLFail
mtsErrPDFWriteFail	mtsErrNoRegistryWrite	mtsErrCompFileGetClassObj
mtsErrPDFReadFail	mtsErrNoRegistryRepair	mtsErrCompFileClassNotAvail
mtsErrPDFVersion	mtsErrCLSIDOrIIDMismatch	mtsErrCompFileBadTLB

mtsErrCoReqCompInstalled	mtsErrRemoteInterface	mtsErrCompFileNotInstallable
mtsErrBadPath	mtsErrDllRegisterServer	mtsErrNotChangeable
mtsErrPackageExists	mtsErrNoServerShare	mtsErrNotDeletable
mtsErrRoleExists	mtsErrNoAccessToUNC	mtsErrSession
mtsErrCantCopyFile	mtsErrDllLoadFailed	mtsErrCompFileNoRegistrar
mtsErrNoTypeLib	mtsErrBadRegistryLibID	
mtsErrNoUser	mtsErrPackDirNotFound	
mtsErrInvalidUserids	mtsErrTreatAs	

The components mentioned so far can be used to get information from the catalog. They cannot be used directly to change the catalog (with one exception), and instead an appropriate Util interface should be obtained by calling GetUtilInterface() on an appropriate collection:

Interface	Obtained through
IPackageUtil	Packages
IComponentUtil	ComponentsInPackage
IRemoteComponentUtil	RemoteComponents
IRoleAssociationUtil	RolesForPackageComponent or RolesForPackageComponentInterface

The obvious omission in this table is an interface to add roles to a package. In fact, this is carried out using the RolesInPackage collection, which also supports an Add() method. The reason is that the other interfaces allow you to *install* items.

For example, the IPackageUtil interface has two methods, called InstallPackage() and ExportPackage():

```
interface IPackageUtil : IDispatch
{
    HRESULT InstallPackage([in] BSTR bstrPackageFile,
             [in] BSTR bstrInstallPath, [in] long lOptions);
    HRESULT ExportPackage([in] BSTR bstrPackageID,
             [in] BSTR bstrPackageFile, [in] long lOptions);
    HRESULT ShutdownPackage([in] BSTR bstrPackageID);
};
```

InstallPackage() requires BSTRs to give the path to the package (.pak) file and the local path to where the components should be installed. ExportPackage() uses BSTRs for the package ID of the package to export and the for the path of the .pak file. In both cases, the long is a flag used to determine if the NT accounts in the roles are used (to be imported or exported respectively).

IPackageUtil's final method, ShutdownPackage(), is interesting. It takes a BSTR (which is the package ID) and does exactly what you'd expect it to do – it closes down the specified package, much in the same way as mtxstop does. Later in this chapter there is an example that uses this, although it uses the identically named ShutdownPackage() method on the IProcessControl interface.

`IComponentUtil` has methods that allow you to install the components in a server DLL:

```
interface IComponentUtil : IDispatch
{
    HRESULT InstallComponent([in] BSTR bstrDLLFile,
            [in] BSTR bstrTypelibFile,
            [in] BSTR bstrProxyStubDLLFile);
    HRESULT ImportComponent([in] BSTR bstrCLSID);
    HRESULT ImportComponentByName([in] BSTR bstrProgID);
    HRESULT GetCLSIDs([in] BSTR bstrDLLFile,
            [in] BSTR bstrTypelibFile, [out] SAFEARRAY** aCLSIDs);
};
```

You do this by specifying the names of the DLL, the type library and (if necessary) the proxy-stub file, as well as a method to import a component from information in the registry, using its CLSID or ProgID.

Note that you can only specify one type library and/or one proxy-stub file. If your server has components that use more than one type library or proxy-stub to marshal their interfaces, then you cannot install the server this way.

In addition, the interface has a method called `GetCLSIDs()`, which allows you to obtain the CLSIDs of all the components implemented in a DLL. The method takes two BSTRs with the name of the DLL, and a separate type library file (if needed), and returns a SAFEARRAY containing VARIANTs with the CLSIDs of the components.

MTS 2.0 Catalog Server

This library (implemented in `mtxcatex.dll`) represents the low level access to the MTS catalog. The library is described in a type library, and is arranged in an object model. However, because it uses [out] parameters (and not [in, out]) on returned SAFEARRAYs of data, VB will complain that such methods do not use an automation type. This means that the designers' efforts to use VARIANTs, BSTRs and SAFEARRAYs have been in vain, because VB programmers can't use these interfaces. The library should really have been written without VB in mind, because C++ programmers get annoyed that they have to use ugly VB-isms like these.

With that said, let's look at what the library contains. There is just one component, called `MTSCatalog`, and this is defined in the IDL as:

```
[
    uuid(182C40F0-32E4-11D0-818B-00A0C9231C29),
    helpstring("MTS Catalog Server Class")
]
coclass MTSCatalog
{
    [default] interface ICatalogRead;
    interface ICatalogUpdate;
    interface IComponentInstall;
    interface IPackageInstall;
    interface IPackageExport;
    interface IClientInstall;
    interface IGetClientEntries;
    interface IProcessControl;
    interface ICatalogSession;
};
```

The first point to make about this is that VB programmers will be instantly confused, because once they create the component it won't work! The reason for this is that the component needs to be initialized through ICatalogSession, and the VB programmer will get ICatalogRead. Of course, it is relatively easy to QI() for ICatalogSession, but this does not fit in with the VB programming style – but I digress. In any case, once the VB programmer initializes the library they can do little with it (because all interfaces except IProcessControl have [out] parameters).

Using the component is relatively easy, as long as you can get used to using SAFEARRAYs. First you must initialize the component:

```
#import "mtxcatex.dll" no_namespace

CComPtr<ICatalogSession> pSess;
pSess.CoCreateInstance(__uuidof(MTSCatalog));
float verSess;
pSess->InitializeSession(0, 3, 0, &verSess);
```

The first two parameters are the version in minor, major order (3.0), which is current for NT4sp5 at the time of writing. This was obtained by trial and error. The third parameter is a LCID, and the final parameter returns the current version of MTS – for my machine this returns a value of 2.01.

After that you can QI() for the various interfaces to perform various tasks:

Interface	Description
ICatalogRead	Read items in the catalog, replicate a package to another computer
ICatalogUpdate	Apply changes made to the catalog, refresh the catalog, verify the current user
IComponentInstall	Install components and get info about components in a package
IPackageInstall	Get information about a package, install packages
IPackageExport	Export packages
IClientInstall	Install marshaling files on a client
IGetClientEntries	Get information about client files
IProcessControl	Shut down a single package or all packages
ICatalogSession	Initialize the session component

The object model is a little like that for the `Catalog` components described earlier. For example, when you read values you use:

```
[id(1)] HRESULT GetCollection([in] LONG eType,
    [in] SAFEARRAY(BSTR) aParentKeys,
    [out] SAFEARRAY(BSTR)* aObjects,
    [out] SAFEARRAY(LONG)* aErrors);
```

where `eType` is the coarse description of the data that you want, `aParentKeys` identifies keys, and the data is returned in `aObjects` (with any errors in `aErrors`). This is similar to using `ICatalogCollection::GetCollection()`, which takes a string describing the collection (equivalent to `eType`) and a key to identify the component you want to get the collection on (equivalent to `aParentkeys`). This method returns a collection and (if errors occur) a collection of errors can be obtained.

The values to use for `eType` are undocumented (as is the rest of the library). However, here are the values that I have ascertained:

eType	Description
1	Computers
3	Packages
4	Components in a package
6	Remote components
7	Roles in a package
11	My Computer information
14	CLSID

Using a value of 14 will return a `SAFEARRAY` of the CLSIDs of all the components registered in `HKCR\CLSID`, and not just the MTS installed components. For types 4 and 7, you need to pass the package ID in the `aParentKeys`, for example:

```
SAFEARRAY* pKeys;
SAFEARRAY* pObjs;
SAFEARRAY* pErrs;
SAFEARRAYBOUND sab = {1, 0};
pKeys = SafeArrayCreate(VT_BSTR, 1, &sab);
BSTR* pBstr;
SafeArrayAccessData(pKeys, (void**)&pBstr);
// specify the System package
pBstr[0] = SysAllocString(L"{0C66DFD9-D523-11CF-A3EF-143AB8000000}");
SafeArrayUnaccessData(pKeys);

CComQIPtr<ICatalogRead> pRead = pSess;
pRead->GetCollection(7, pKeys, &pObjs, &pErrs);
```

```
for (ULONG i = 0; i < pObjs->rgsabound[0].cElements; i++)
{
   for (ULONG j = 0; j < pObjs->rgsabound[1].cElements; j++)
   {
      long pInds[2] = {i + pObjs->rgsabound[0].lLbound,
                       j + pObjs->rgsabound[1].lLbound};
      BSTR bstr = NULL;
      SafeArrayGetElement(pObjs, pInds, &bstr);
      printf(_T("[%ld, %ld] = \"%S\"\n"), pInds[0], pInds[1], bstr);
   }
}
SafeArrayDestroy(pObjs);
SafeArrayDestroy(pErrs);
SafeArrayDestroy(pKeys);
```

Of course, if the API used C arrays, the code would be simpler and easier to understand. The above code gives the following output:

```
[0, 0] = "Administrator"
[0, 1] = "{CB40671F-3F1E-11D0-ADA8-00A02463D6E7}"
[1, 0] = "Reader"
[1, 1] = "{CB406725-3F1E-11D0-ADA8-00A02463D6E7}"
[2, 0] = "(null)"
[2, 1] = "(null)"
```

Shutting down processes

The IProcessControl interface is quite useful, because it allows you to close down processes individually or en masse. ShutdownProcesses() stops all packages and is presumably the API used by mtxstop. ShutdownPackage() shuts down the package represented by its BSTR parameter (like the method of the same name on the IPackageUtil interface), so the following:

```
CComQIPtr<IProcessControl> pCtrl = pSess;
CComBSTR bstr = L"{0C66DFD9-D523-11CF-A3EF-143AB8000000}";
pCtrl->ShutdownPackage(bstr);
```

will stop the System package. As you can see, this will help with the problem identified in the previous chapter. To reiterate, the problem is that when you link a DLL project, you have to make sure that no packages are running that use the DLL, otherwise it will not be given access. mtxstop will stop all packages, which may take some time. However, this works by posting a message to all the threads in each instance of mtx, to tell them to shut down. Because the message is posted, mtxstop will return before the processes have shut down.

The best solution would be to get hold of a handle to the process, tell the package to shut down, and wait for the process handle to be signaled with WaitForSingleObject(). I'll explain how to do this later in the chapter.

MTS 2.0 Catalog Replication

This library is housed in `mtxrepl.dll`, and has a single component called `ReplicateCatalog`, which implements `IMTSReplicateCatalog`. This is used to replicate the catalog from one machine to another, and is applied when you are using Microsoft Cluster Server to provide fault tolerance. In this situation, many machines are used in a cluster, running identical software – when one machine dies, the cluster server will ensure that another server is used.

You can also do this using the `mtxrepl` command line tool.

MTS Client Export

This library (`mtxclex.dll`) has a single component called `Clex`, which implements `IExtenderPackageExport`. This has a single method:

```
[id(1)] HRESULT PackageExport([in] BSTR bstrPath, [in] BSTR bstrFileName);
```

in which the parameters indicate the path to, and the name of, the `.pak` file that the component will create. However, there's no obvious way to initialize the component with the package name to export (the only other interface that it implements is `ISupportErrorInfo`). The component is clearly intended to be used as part of another component (for example `IPackageUtil::ExportPackage()` through the `Catalog` component), so I guess it's of little use to the C++ programmer.

MtxGrp 1.0 and MTSEvents 1.0

These two libraries complement each other, which is why I'll describe them together. They are implemented in `mtxgrp.dll` and `mtsevents.dll` respectively.

`MtxGrp` implements a single component called `MtSGrp`, which gives access to information about the running MTS processes:

```
[
    uuid(4B2E958C-0393-11D1-B1AB-00AA00BA3258),
    helpstring("IMtsGrp Interface"),
    dual
]
interface IMtsGrp : IDispatch
{
    [id(1), propget, helpstring("property Count")]
    HRESULT Count([out, retval] LONG* pVal);
    [id(2), helpstring("method Item")]
    HRESULT Item([in] LONG lIndex, [out] LPUNKNOWN* ppUnkDispatcher);
    [id(3), helpstring("method Refresh")]
    HRESULT Refresh();
};
```

Note that although the Count property and the Refresh() method can be called by scripting clients, the most useful method, Item(), can't. This method gives access to the event component for each running MTS package. However, since this returns the component via an [out] LPUNKNOWN* parameter (and not a [out, retval] LPDISPATCH*), scripting languages like VBScript or JScript won't recognize the return value. This means that you can't write a script (on a web page for example) to monitor MTS packages using this component. It seems odd that the interface was designed this way, and the only explanation I can offer is that the designer goofed. However, if you want to expose this functionality in a scripting-friendly manner it is relatively easy to write a simple wrapper component.

An example of using this component was given in the last chapter:

```
CComPtr<IMtsGrp> pMtsGrp;
pMtsGrp.CoCreateInstance(__uuidof(MtsGrp));

long lPackages;
pMtsGrp->get_Count(&lPackages);

for (int i=0; i<lPackages; i++)
{
    CComPtr<IUnknown> pUnk;
    pMtsGrp->Item(i, &pUnk);
    ATLTRACE("object with IUnknown %x\n", pUnk.p);
}
```

The components that are returned from Item() implement IMtsEvents and IConnectionPointContainer. IMtsEvents looks like this:

```
[
    uuid(BACEDF4D-74AB-11D0-B162-00AA00BA3258),
    helpstring("IMTSEvents Interface"),
    dual
]
interface IMtsEvents : IDispatch
{
    [id(1), propget, helpstring("property PackageName")]
    HRESULT PackageName([out, retval] BSTR* pVal);
    [id(2), propget, helpstring("property PackageGuid")]
    HRESULT PackageGuid([out, retval] BSTR* pVal);
    [id(5), helpstring("method PostEvent")]
    HRESULT PostEvent([in] VARIANT* vEvent);
    [id(6), propget, helpstring("property FireEvents")]
    HRESULT FireEvents([out, retval] VARIANT_BOOL* pVal);
    [id(7), helpstring("method GetProcessID")]
    HRESULT GetProcessID([out, retval] LONG* id);
};
```

It is interesting to observe that this interface gives the package name, GUID, and process ID of the instance of mtx that is running the package. This is useful, particularly if you want to access a specific package.

The MTS SDK defines several event sink interfaces in `EventCpts.h` for various system events (see later in this section). These events are generated by MTS. Note that they are made using connection points, so there is the usual problem of multiple round trips to the server to make and break the connection. However, `MtxGrp` only gives access to the packages running on the local machines, so you don't have the problem of multiple *network* round trips.

You can define your own sink interfaces, but note the warnings given in the last chapter about events and transactional components. The event information must not be based on transactional data, because a transactional component won't know the transaction's outcome. It's much better to use a separate, non-transactional, component to generate events.

It isn't clear from the documentation how the events are dispatched – whether, for example, a separate thread is used. My tests show that this is indeed the case, because if I make the event handler take a long time (longer than the transaction timeout), it has no effect on a component's transaction. If the activity thread were used, then the long handling of the event would make the transaction abort due to a timeout.

To use custom events, the event sink object must implement `IMtsUserEvent`, which has a single method called `OnUserEvent()`. This is passed a `VARIANT`, which has information about the user event that has been generated.

The component that wants to generate the event must somehow access the list of connected components. To do this, it needs to create an instance of the `CoMTSLocater` component, which implements the `IMTSLocater` interface.

> **Note that the interface is `IMTSLocater` and not `IMTSLocator` — this can be confirmed by viewing the type library. However, MSDN calls the interface `IMtsLocator`.**

The `IMTSLocater` interface has the single method:

```
[id(1), helpstring("method GetEventDispatcher")]
HRESULT GetEventDispatcher([out, retval] LPUNKNOWN* pUnk);
```

This will return the event dispatcher for the current process. To use this you should `QI()` pUnk for the general purpose interface `IMtsEvents`, and generate the user event by calling `PostEvent()` using a `VARIANT` with the data of the custom event:

```
CComPtr<IMTSLocater> pLocator;
pLocator.CoCreateInstance(__uuidof(CoMTSLocater));
if (pLocator)
{
    CComPtr<IUnknown> pUnk;
    pLocator->GetEventDispatcher(&pUnk);
    if (pUnk)
    {
        CComQIPtr<IMtsEvents> pEventDispatcher = pUnk;
        CComBSTR bstr = L"Something important has happened";
        CComVariant var = bstr;
        pEventDispatcher->PostEvent(&var);
    }
}
```

Since a VARIANT is passed to PostEvent(), you can pass any item that correctly describes your event, but the sink object must of course know what the event means in order to be able to process it. It may be a string, as shown in the code above, or it may be a custom event object.

The MTS SDK defines the standard interface IMtsEventInfo that you can find documented in MSDN. This interface is an automation collection, that is, the Names() method returns an enumerator. It also has a Count property and the Value property, which returns a value for a specified key. In addition there are DisplayName and EventID properties, which identify the event (the EventID is a BSTR with a stringified GUID). The enumerator contains key-value pairs containing information about the event.

The MTS SDK has an example of such a custom event object. Note that although MSDN defines an interface to get information from the event object, it doesn't define an interface to initialize one. The example component, MtsUserEventData, has an interface called IMtsUserEventData, which allows you to set the event name and GUID and add one or more key-value pairs.

> *The* MtsUserEventData *component is part of the* MtsUserEventObj *project in the MTS SDK. It's interesting to see that this component returns an enumerator that implements* IEnumString. *This means that the component can't be used with VB, for which collection interfaces are the most useful. If you want to write your own custom component, then you should return an enumerator that implements* IEnumVARIANT.

The source interfaces that MTS knows about (defined in EventCpts.h) are:

Event Interface	Description
IMtsPackageEvents	Package activation and shutdown
IMtsInstanceEvents	Component creation and destruction
IMtsObjectEvents	Events associated with activation: activated, can deactivate, deactivated, and cannot be deactivated
IMtsThreadEvents	Thread interaction with activities: start, added to activity, removed from activity, and terminate
IMtsMethodEvents	Details about method calls: method called, method returned, and if an exception is thrown
IMtsSecurityEvents	Called when the user is authenticated
IMtsTransactionEvents	Phase one of transaction: start, prepare, and abort
IMtsUserEvent	Allows a MTS component to define its own events.

Each method on these interfaces has a 64-bit (LONGLONG) parameter that is an indication of the time when the event was queued for dispatch – you can use this to compare multiple events and put them in order.

> *Note that* IMtsPackageEvents *has a method called* OnPackageActivation(). *This can never be called! This is because the event model is based on sink objects connecting to the event object, obtained through* IMtsGrp::Item(). *The event object is only created when the package is activated.*

The documentation for IMtsUserEvents mentions that the MTS events aren't guaranteed to be dispatched. If they aren't then the events will be dispatched later using IMtsUserEvents.

Chapter 7 will explain how to use MtsSpy (described later) and the Visual Studio Analyzer to look at the events that occur during an application's execution, and use those to debug the package.

Example

The example code for this chapter has a project called MtsAdmin, which can be used for three things:

- ❏ refresh component registration from the catalog
- ❏ shut down all MTS processes
- ❏ shut down a specified package based on the package ID

The syntax is:

```
MTSAdmin -refresh|-kill [guid]
```

If you use the -kill switch with a GUID, then the specified package will be shut down – otherwise all packages will be shut down. For example, the following will shut down the System package (which isn't something that you'll want to do often):

```
MTSAdmin -kill {0C66DFD9-D523-11CF-A3EF-143AB8000000}
```

In this situation the code will wait for the package to shut down before finishing. This gets round the problem with mtxstop (identified in the last chapter), in which MTS will be told to shut down the packages, but mtxstop will not wait for them to finish. If this is added as a pre-link step the package may still be running when the link step is reached, causing a link failure.

The relevant code in MTSAdmin will be outlined here.

Firstly, the admin components are described in type libraries rather than headers, so in our C++ project they can be converted to a header file with the following:

```
#import "C:\WINNT\System32\Mts\mtxcatex.dll" no_namespace,
                     raw_interfaces_only, no_implementation
#import "C:\WINNT\System32\Mts\mtxgrp.dll" no_namespace,
                     raw_interfaces_only, no_implementation
#import "C:\WINNT\System32\mtsevents.dll" no_namespace,
                     raw_interfaces_only, no_implementation
```

Note that two of these libraries are in the `System32\Mts` folder.

The command line code checks to see if components are refreshed (in which case `bRefresh` will be set to `true`), or if packages should be killed (`bKill` will be set to `true`). In the latter case `strGuid` will point to the package ID or `NULL`.

Refreshing is simple:

```
CComPtr<ICatalogSession> pSess;
pSess.CoCreateInstance(__uuidof(MTSCatalog));
float fVer;
pSess->InitializeSession(0, 3, 0, &fVer);

if (bRefresh)
{
    CComQIPtr<ICatalogUpdate> pUp = pSess;
    hr = pUp->RefreshMtxComponents();
    if (FAILED(hr))
        printf("Failed to refresh components %08x\n", hr);
    else
        printf("All components have been refreshed\n");
    return 0;
}
```

Shutting down all processes is just as simple:

```
if (strGuid == NULL)
{
    // don't wait for all processes to end
    CComQIPtr<IProcessControl> pCtrl = pSess;
    hr = pCtrl->ShutdownProcesses();
    if (FAILED(hr))
        printf("Could not shutdown packages %08x\n", hr);
    else
        printf("All packages have been killed\n");
    return 0;
}
```

The bulk of the code lies in shutting down a single package. First the code needs to get the process ID, using the `MtsGrp` component:

```
CComPtr<IMtsGrp> pMtsGrp;
pMtsGrp.CoCreateInstance(__uuidof(MtsGrp));

long lPackages;
pMtsGrp->get_Count(&lPackages);
USES_CONVERSION;
CComBSTR bstrPackageGuid = A2W(strGuid);
CComBSTR bstrName;
DWORD dwProcessID = 0;
```

```
for (int i=0; i<lPackages; i++)
{
    CComPtr<IUnknown> pUnk;
    pMtsGrp->Item(i, &pUnk);
    CComQIPtr<IMtsEvents> pEvents = pUnk;

    CComBSTR bstrRunningGUID;
    pEvents->get_PackageGuid(&bstrRunningGUID.m_str);
    if (wcscmp(bstrRunningGUID.m_str, bstrPackageGuid.m_str) != 0)
        continue;

    pEvents->get_PackageName(&bstrName.m_str);
    pEvents->GetProcessID(reinterpret_cast<LONG*>(&dwProcessID));
}
```

This just iterates through all the running packages, checking the GUID of each until it finds the specified one.

```
HANDLE hProcess = NULL;
if (dwProcessID != 0)
    hProcess = OpenProcess(SYNCHRONIZE, FALSE, dwProcessID);
if (hProcess == NULL)
{
    printf("The package isn't running or doesn't exist!\n");
    return 0;
}

CComQIPtr<IProcessControl> pCtrl = pSess;
hr = pCtrl->ShutdownPackage(bstrPackageGuid);
if (FAILED(hr))
    printf("Error closing down package %08x\n", hr);
else
{
    printf("Waiting for the package %S to end\n",
            bstrName.m_str);
    WaitForSingleObject(hProcess, INFINITE);
}
CloseHandle(hProcess);
```

Once the process ID is known you can get a handle to that process, so that once the package is told to shut down you can wait on the process handle until the process has finished.

Now you can add calls to MTSAdmin in your pre-link, custom-build steps to shut down the package, and refresh the components therein.

MTS SDK Libraries

The MTS SDK is available from MSDN. This has examples of writing a resource manager and a resource dispenser. In addition it has examples of how to catch MTS events and generate custom events.

MtsSpy is an ATL UI project that hosts the MtsSpyCtl control. The actual work involved in connecting to the MTS connection points (and handling the generated events) is carried out by the control – MtsSpy is merely a container. Examining these projects gives you a good idea of how to generate and catch events. However, MtsSpy is very useful as a debugging tool, allowing you to see what is happening in your MTS-based application. Chapter 7 will describe this tool further.

Summary

The deployment features of MTS make DCOM a pleasure to use. Now you no longer need to worry about what files should be copied and registered on a client machine or a server machine – this is because (by and large) MTS Explorer will identify the correct files. Then it will transmit them to a remote machine (pulling and pushing marshaling files), or copy them to a installation directory with an install script (exporting a package), or embed them as a .cab resource within a setup executable (the client process when exporting a package).

Although MTS Explorer will do a lot of work for you, you may decide that you want more control, and you can get this by calling the MTS API directly. This functionality is provided through a series of DLLs, which are described by a type library. Although much of this is not documented, you do have sufficient information to use these DLLs. As an example, I have shown you how to use the MtxGrp and Catalog Server libraries to implement a simple command line tool to shut down specific packages.

5

The Distributed Transaction Coordinator

Introduction

Microsoft Transaction Server has the word 'transaction' in its title, so it's natural to assume that MTS is all about transactions. However, as you've already seen, MTS deals with more than just transactions – it brings a new programming paradigm to COM and makes DCOM more manageable in its deployment. This chapter will concentrate on transactions and the services that provide access to them, these being the MS DTC, resource dispensers, and resource managers.

In this chapter I will explain what OLE transactions are, and how they compare with the industry standard XA transactions. I will look at how they are distributed over a network, and the role that the MS DTC and the MTS Explorer play in this. Finally, I will show how a component in a package takes part ('enlists') in a transaction, how it expresses its opinion about the state of a transaction, and how this opinion is propagated around the network to commit or abort work. You don't need to be applying transactions to use it, but when you do you will discover a side of MTS that is remarkable.

MS DTC Architecture

First, some terminology. Resource managers are services that manage durable state – the most familiar variety are databases. Resource managers access and modify durable state under the influence of a transaction, so in order for changes to be made permanent, the transaction must commit. Resource managers may exist on multiple machines across a network, and a transaction can involve many such resource managers. If this is the case and the transactional work in one resource manager fails to complete, then all the other resource managers that have done work in the transaction must be informed. They can then identify the work that they have done and roll it back.

If the transaction is created on one machine but a resource manager is used on another machine, there needs to be some way of transmitting the transaction so that all work can be identified as being performed under the same transaction. This implies that some service should exist to distribute transactions and to initiate the commit mechanism – it does, and is called the **Microsoft Distributed Transaction Coordinator** (**MS DTC**). The MS DTC creates and coordinates transactions distributed across the network, as suggested by its name. More precisely, it manages resource managers distributed across the network, propagating transactions to them in such a way that the resource managers are informed of and can influence the transaction outcome.

MS DTC transactions are committed or aborted using an industry standard mechanism called **2-phase commit**.

The MS DTC and Transactions

When a client application uses a component that runs under the influence of a transaction (Requires, or Requires New), some code must obtain the transaction and ensure that all the work carried out on behalf of the component is done under it. When a transactional component requires work from a resource manager it must pass the transaction to the resource manager. The resource manager can then enlist in the transaction to define the boundary of its work. However, if this resource manager uses other resource managers then the transaction must be passed to them, so that they can enlist as well. The component is only ever aware of the resource manager that it uses. Nevertheless, the transaction can propagate over many machines throughout the network.

The MS DTC is the source of all transactions. When client code wants to use a new transaction it asks the MS DTC to create one for it. The new transaction can then be passed to a resource manager as a marshaled BLOB, a process called **exporting**. If the resource manager is on another machine then the MS DTC on that machine must know about the transaction (to allow the distributed 2-phase commit process to work). The resource manager therefore passes the exported BLOB to its local MS DTC, which returns the transaction. This process is called **importing**. This part of the MS DTC is known as the **transaction manager**. The MS DTC implements both an OLE transaction manager and an XA transaction manager, allowing it to import and export native OLE transactions and XA transactions.

> I will come back to this issue later in this chapter. Basically, OLE transactions are wrapper objects and are understood by the MS DTC, MTS and OLE DB. XA transactions are the industry standard. The MS DTC manages both and thus increases the number of resource managers that can be used.

MS DTC Components

Clearly, there is code in the client that needs to access the MS DTC. This code is in-process and is called the **resource manager proxy**.

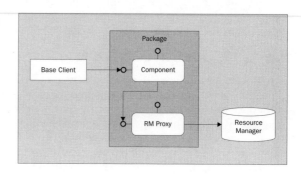

The RM proxy essentially provides the client side API to the resource manager. Typically, this is done through a COM interface, although this is not a requirement (for example, ODBC drivers for databases are RM proxies). In addition, the RM proxy is usually implemented as part of a **resource dispenser**, because it is the dispenser that gives access to the resource manager. Resource dispensers are always in-process (resource managers never are), and exist to give access to non-durable state. The RM proxy, which is a connection to a resource manager, is an example of non-durable state – if the package dies, the connection to the resource manager will be lost.

When the transaction finishes (the base object is released, calls `SetComplete()` or `SetAbort()`, or an exception is thrown), then all the resource managers enlisted in the transaction must be told about the transaction outcome. This allows them to make changes permanent, or rollback to a point before the transaction started. Furthermore, because transactions should be performed in isolation, resource managers will apply locks to those resources affected by the transaction, so that work being performed under other transactions can't access them. Thus, when the transaction ends these locks must be released.

Every system that needs to use transactions must have the MS DTC installed. The MS DTC contains a transaction manager that will, on request, dispense transactions. Clients (and resource managers) that need one can ask the transaction manager for a new transaction with a particular timeout, then pass this to the resource managers that will do the work.

MTS components don't explicitly obtain transactions – the resources they use are obtained through resource dispensers. These will be told by an MTS object called the **Resource Dispenser Manager**, DispMan, that a requested resource should be enlisted in a transaction. The resource dispenser won't create the transaction – that is the responsibility of DispMan (details are given later). The resource dispenser, however, has the responsibility of enlisting in the transaction – a mechanism called **auto-enlistment**. As you can see, MTS auto-enlistment in transactions requires a resource dispenser.

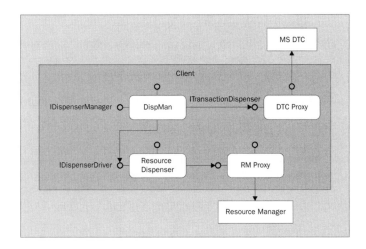

Commit Trees

The transaction manager that creates the transaction is called the **global commit coordinator**. This is the initiator of the commit process. There may be many machines and several resource managers involved in the transaction, and this builds up a commit tree of transaction managers and resource managers:

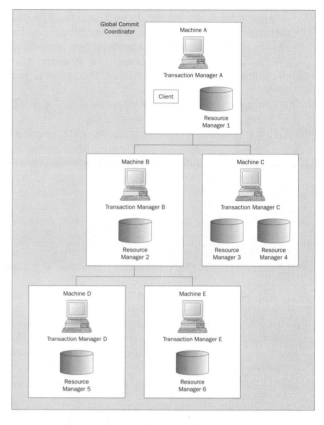

When one resource manager uses another resource manager on a different machine, the transaction manager of this new machine is regarded as **subordinate** to that of the first machine. These individual instances of the transaction manager must communicate with each other, and must therefore know each other's **whereabouts** (a GUID that identifies each transaction manager). When a transaction manager's whereabouts are known, a transaction can be exported to it. The remote resource manager can then import the transaction and enlist in it. This is done using the local transaction manager, which keeps a record of all active transactions.

When the transaction finishes, the commit mechanism must be propagated throughout the whole commit tree, moving from transaction manager to subordinate transaction manager. Each transaction manager is responsible for propagating the commit message to the managers enlisted below it in the transaction, which it knows from the records it maintains.

In addition, the transaction managers and resource managers maintain a durable log of the actions that *should* occur. In other words, the records in the log are made before the action happens. This is so that if an individual machine dies it can perform **recovery** when it restarts – that is, the actions can be carried out as expected.

There may be occasions when a transaction manager doesn't know the outcome of a transaction (for example when a subordinate transaction manager loses its connection to the transaction manager further up the tree), and in this case the transaction is said to be **in doubt**. To resolve this, the local transaction manager will query the transaction manager superior to it in the commit tree until it can get the outcome. As the global commit coordinator is always at the top of the tree, it is never in doubt.

Transactions will result in locks being applied to resources – these ensure that transactions are isolated and are maintained until the transaction ends. The purpose of a lock is to ensure that only one transaction can access the data. Clearly, the longer a lock is applied, the more the performance of the resource manager is compromised. A system operator can force an in doubt transaction to commit or abort, using the MTS Explorer.

MTS and the MS DTC maintain transactions as COM objects local to each machine. That is, although there will be just one transaction, each machine will have an individual object to represent it. A GUID is used to identify each transaction; these are created on the root of the commit tree, and then passed when a transaction is exported. You can therefore imagine a transaction as an all-encompassing blanket that covers the components that use it, wherever they happen to be on the network:

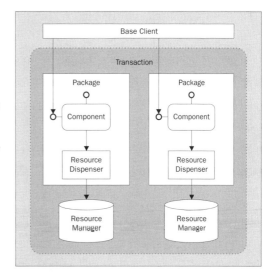

A component's context holds information about a transaction that it is part of, its identity, and the component's view of the transaction (whether it thinks that its work is finished, and, if so, whether it's happy that the transaction should commit). The component affects this 'opinion' of the transaction by calling `SetComplete()` or `SetAbort()`, but doesn't directly commit or abort transactions. MTS is responsible for that.

The MS DTC

The MS DTC is installed during the setup of MTS or SQL Server. Each MS DTC has a unique GUID (called `guidTM`), which is generated when it is installed. This is recorded in the registry in `HKEY_CLASSES_ROOT\CID`:

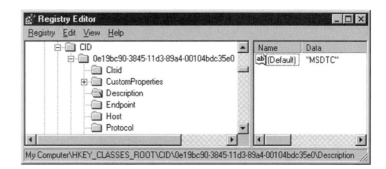

On my machine, shown in this screenshot, the GUID of the MS DTC is `0E19BC90-3845-11d3-89A4-00104BDC35E0`.

> You may have noticed
> `ITransactionExportFactory::GetRemoteClassId()` in the MSDN
> collection. This is rather badly named because it gives the CLSID of the local
> transaction manager — not a remote machine. You should also be aware that this is
> a *class* ID, and not the GUID of an instance. You can use this to compare the
> versions of DTC being used. The `Clsid` key in the screenshot above contains yet
> another GUID, this one being the CLSID of the DTC transaction manager
> component that is used within the MS DTC.

This component tracks incoming and outgoing transactions, and performs all the enlistment, prepare, commit, and abort calls (used for 2-phase commit) for local resource managers. In addition, the local transaction manager has to perform its responsibilities as part of a commit tree, propagating these prepare, commit, and abort messages to any subordinate transaction managers.

The MS DTC is an NT Service that you can start and stop using either the NT Services control panel applet or the MTS Explorer (or indeed via the SQL Server Service Manager). Applications and resource managers access the MS DTC through an object called the DTC Proxy:

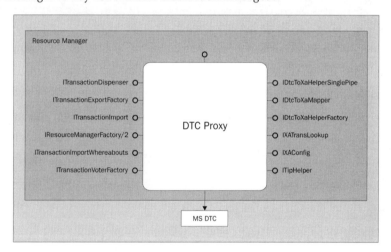

This proxy is obtained by calling `DtcGetTransactionManager()`. Note that I didn't say that the DTC Proxy is a *COM* object. Indeed, you don't have to call `CoInitializeEx()` before calling this function, or using the returned interfaces. The reason for this is that some non-COM code, like the ODBC connection manager, will access the transaction manager. For the remainder of this chapter it will be assumed that COM-aware code will use the MS DTC.

The figure shows the XA transaction and Transaction Internet Protocol (TIP) interfaces on the right hand side. I will come back to these later in this chapter, and in the final chapter of this book.

`DtcGetTransactionManager()` takes the name of the machine that the code wishes to access as the first parameter. If this is `NULL` then the transaction manager on the local machine will be used.

I have never been able to get this to work on NT4 sp5 other than by passing `NULL` as the machine name, despite the allusion in MSDN that it should work with a non-`NULL` machine name. The call fails with `E_FAIL`, which is documented with the unhelpful phrase "Failed to carry out the operation".

This function's other significant parameters allow you to specify the interface on the transaction manager and to provide an [out] parameter for the returned interface pointer. Of the possible interfaces implemented by the DTC Proxy, only ITransactionDispenser has marshaling code.

> *The* xolehlp.h *header file has a comment stating that you can access the transaction manager using* CoCreateInstance() *for the component with a CLSID of* CLSID_MSDtcTransactionManager. *However, this CLSID only appears to be registered on Windows 2000 machines.*

The proxy interfaces allow client code to create and start transactions. They also allow resource managers to import and export transactions, and to gain information about their locations. In addition, there are other COM objects associated with MS DTC that are used to allow resource managers to communicate with the transaction manager. These objects are given in the following table:

Object	Description
Transaction	Represents a transaction
Transaction Options	Used to specify the timeout and a descriptive string for a transaction when creating the transaction
Export	Used to export a transaction to a machine other than the one where it was created
Enlistment	Held by the DTC proxy to indicate which resource managers are enlisted in a transaction
Voter	Used to indicate the vote to determine the outcome of a transaction
Resource Manager	Object held by DTC proxy to represent the resource mangers that have been registered with DTC

These objects are described in the following sections.

Transaction Objects

MTS provides automatic enlistment into transactions, via transaction dispensers. If a component is marked as requiring a transaction, it will either be run under the current transaction (if one exists) or run under a new one. If it is specifically marked as requiring a new transaction then one will be created when it is activated.

> *It is interesting that MTS provides this action. COM always takes the attitude that a component should run if at all possible, and that COM shouldn't prevent a component from running because of the component's requirements. This action in MTS means that if the component must run under a transaction and one does not exist, then MTS will create one. Compare this with how COM creates an apartment to run an in-proc object if an apartment compatible with its* ThreadingModel *doesn't exist. In both cases, the environment for the component is created if it doesn't already exist.*

OLE transaction objects are a COM wrapper for a transaction. They can only be created by a local transaction manager, and shouldn't be marshaled across machine boundaries. This means that only a local transaction manager will be able to maintain a list of the current transactions and the resource managers enlisted in them.

A transaction object looks like this:

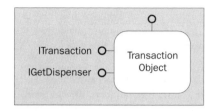

Again, I must reiterate that as far as an MTS object is concerned, the facilities of a transaction object are largely advisory. Thus, ITransaction can be used to obtain information about the transaction, and IGetDispenser is used to give access to the transaction manager that created it.

> *Transaction objects created on Windows 2000 machines give access to additional functionality, as explained in Chapter 8.*

The transaction object is created through a call to BeginTransaction(), on the ITransactionDispenser interface of a transaction manager. MTS objects and clients don't need to call this, because the MTS architecture guarantees that a component will be run under its configured transaction requirement.

When a component creates a resource, the resource dispenser will be requested to enlist in the transaction by the executive. The transaction will then be exported (by a resource dispenser) to the resource manager for which it is a proxy. The resource manager then imports the transaction and enlists in it – to do this, resource managers are passed the transaction using an opaque handle (that is, a blob of data that is meaningless to the resource manager) called a **transaction cookie**. This can be converted to a transaction object by calling Import() on the ITransactionImport interface (obtained from the DTC proxy object).

Transaction Options

Transaction objects are identified by GUIDs (which also identify units of work), which are generated by the transaction manager that creates the objects. When a transaction is exported, it is this GUID (along with other information) that is exported. The transaction object also contains a timeout period (in milliseconds) and descriptive text.

Transaction options are set using a transaction options object, obtained from the transaction manager by calling ITransactionDispenser::GetOptionsObject(). Client code can set the timeout and description by passing an XACTOPT structure to ITransactionOptions::SetOptions():

```
typedef struct XACTOPT
{
    ULONG         ulTimeout;
    unsigned char szDescription[MAX_TRAN_DESC];
} XACTOPT;
```

Objects created through MTS don't use this, of course, as MTS will create and initialize transaction objects. The timeout used by MTS objects is the global timeout value, set as a `My Computer` property (the default value is 60 seconds), and the `szDescription` is set to the ProgID of the base object in the transaction. For example:

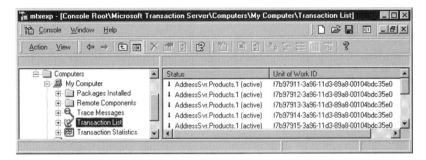

Here, five instances of `AddressSvr.Products.1` have been created, each requiring a transaction.

> *There is no mechanism in MTS 2.0 to change a transaction's timeout or description once it has been created, or any way to create a transaction object yourself and tell MTS to use it. However, Windows 2000 does allow you to associate a COM+ object with an external transaction object. This means that you can create the OLE transaction object with your own description and timeout, at the expense of relinquishing auto-enlistment.*

The transaction options object is passed to `ITransactionDispenser::BeginTransaction()`, to create the transaction:

```
HRESULT BeginTransaction([unique, in] IUnknown* punkOuter,
                         [in] ISOLEVEL isoLevel,
                         [in] ULONG isoFlags,
                         [unique, in] ITransactionOptions* pOptions,
                         [out] ITransaction** ppTransaction);
```

The first and third parameters are always zero. The second one is an isolation level – MTS objects are always created using `ISOLATIONLEVEL_SERIALIZABLE`, the highest level possible. This defines how changes to the data can be viewed, and is integral to the locking strategy used by a resource manager. This issue will be covered in a later section on resource managers.

`BeginTransaction()` will create a transaction object based on these parameters. Once it has been created its properties can't be changed, so you can't alter the transaction description or its timeout value. When the transaction is used on another machine, it has to be exported in a form that the resource manager can pass to its own local transaction manager, in order to import the transaction – it uses the transaction's GUID.

Resource Manager Object

The transaction manager maintains a resource manager object for each resource manager registered with it. This is done by obtaining the IResourceManagerFactory interface on the DTC proxy object and then calling its Create() method:

```
HRESULT Create([in] GUID* pguidRM,
               [in, string] CHAR* pszRMName,
               [in] IResourceManagerSink* pIResMgrSink,
               [out] IResourceManager** ppResMgr);
```

The first parameter is a GUID for this instance of the resource manager. The transaction manager uses this to ensure that an instance of the resource manager only connects to the transaction manager once. The second parameter is a string name that describes all instances of the resource manager.

> *Note that MSDN documents the type of* pszRMName *as* TCHAR* *– it is in fact* CHAR*. *A* TCHAR* *parameter of an interface method is always a bad idea – it indicates that there could be a different interface depending on the symbols used during the compile, invalidating COM's idea of an immutable interface.*

The DTC proxy will create a resource manager object and cache it for later use. A reference to this object is passed back in the last parameter, which the resource manager uses to enlist in transactions. The third parameter is interesting – this is an interface to a sink object implemented by the resource manager, and is used to allow the DTC proxy to inform the resource manager that it has lost connection with the MS DTC.

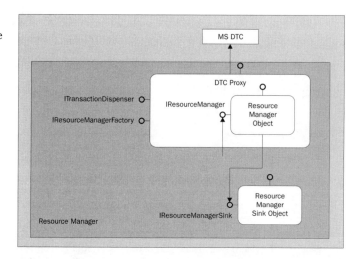

Typically, a resource manager only connects to one transaction manager, namely its local MS DTC transaction manager.

The sink object has one method, IResourceManagerSink::TMDown(), which the DTC proxy calls when the transaction manager fails. It does this to tell the resource manager to perform any recovery that isn't based on a transaction. The DTC proxy will also call ITransactionResourceAsync::TMDown() on the transaction resource sink object for each transaction that the resource manager is enlisted in. (I'll explain this object later.)

Export Object

Transactions need to be exported from the machine that creates them to the machines on which the resource manager resides. Exporting a transaction involves serializing the OLE transaction object into a byte stream. This stream is passed to the resource manager, which *imports* the transaction by initializing a locally created transaction object with the byte stream. Resource dispensers, in their role of resource manager proxies, export transactions.

Exporting a transaction involves using an export object. This is obtained by calling `Create()` on the `ITransactionExportFactory` interface of the DTC Proxy – only the transaction manager that created a transaction can export it. The resource manager proxy object can also query the transaction object for the `IGetDispenser` interface and then call `GetDispenser()` to obtain the export object.

The `Create()` method takes as a parameter a value that is used to specify the whereabouts of the transaction manager to which the transaction will be exported. Using this value, it returns an appropriate export object. The 'whereabouts' consists of some data identifying the remote transaction manager. The resource manager is responsible for obtaining this information, by calling `GetWhereabouts()` on the `ITransactionImportWhereabouts` interface on its local DTC proxy, then passing this information back to the resource manager proxy code on the other machine.

```
interface ITransactionImportWhereabouts : IUnknown
{
    HRESULT GetWhereaboutsSize([out] ULONG* pcbWhereabouts);

    [local] HRESULT GetWhereabouts([in] ULONG cbWhereabouts,
            [size_is(cbWhereabouts), out] BYTE* rgbWhereabouts,
            [out] ULONG* pcbUsed);
};
```

Although this method returns a `BYTE` array, if you examine the returned data you will find that it actually contains the `guidTM` of the transaction manager on the remote resource manager's machine.

The export object implements `ITransactionExport`, which has the following methods:

```
HRESULT Export([in] IUnknown* pITransaction,
  [out] ULONG* pcbTransactionCookie);

[local] HRESULT GetTransactionCookie(
  [in] IUnknown* pITransaction,
  [in] ULONG cbTransactionCookie,
  [size_is(cbTransactionCookie), out] BYTE* rgbTransactionCookie,
  [out] ULONG* pcbUsed);
```

Notice how `GetTransactionCookie()` *is* [local], *emphasizing the fact that only the local transaction manager can export a transaction.*

Exporting a transaction is a two-stage process. First, the resource manager proxy calls `Export()` to get the size of the byte stream that will be generated – in this process the local MS DTC will check to see if there is a connection with the MS DTC on the resource manager's machine. If there is no connection, it can access the whereabouts (cached from the call to create the export object) and make one. The local transaction manager will then pass the transaction GUID to the resource manager's transaction manager, which will create and initialize a new transaction object. This object will have the transaction GUID and an identifier of the client transaction manager.

The client DTC proxy then generates a byte stream from the transaction GUID (which the resource manager proxy can obtain by calling `GetTransactionCookie()`), passing an allocated buffer of an appropriate size. This byte stream uniquely identifies the transaction object on the resource manager's machine.

The byte stream is passed from the resource manager proxy (in the client) to the remote resource manager using some private resource manager API. This will query its local DTC proxy object for `ITransactionImport` and pass the byte stream to the `Import()` method, which locates the transaction object created earlier.

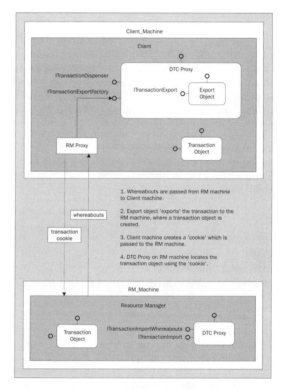

Enlistment Object

Before a resource manager can perform any work it needs to enlist in the transaction. It does this using the resource manager object, which the DTC proxy returns when the resource manager registers. The enlistment is performed by calling the `Enlist()` method on the `IResourceManager` interface, passing the transaction object and a transaction resource sink object (implementing `ITransactionResourceAsync`), which the DTC proxy will use to inform the resource manager of the various stages of the commit mechanism. In return, the DTC proxy returns a reference to an enlistment object. This implements the `ITransactionEnlistmentAsync` interface, the GUID of the transaction, and the isolation level that was originally requested by the client. The resource manager can use the GUID to check that the correct transaction is being used.

The transaction manager can then record the fact that the resource manager has enlisted in this particular transaction. These two objects (the enlistment object and the transaction resource sink object) are used in the communication between the DTC proxy object and the resource manager object to propagate the 2-phase commit messages.

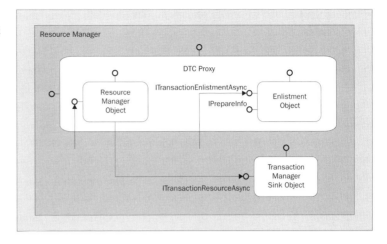

Once the resource manager has enlisted in the transaction it can perform its work.

Voter Object

The voter object is used to allow the application client to have a say over the first phase of the 2-phase commit. You don't use this with MTS because the executive takes the commit process out of your hands.

By default, when a client calls `ITransaction::Commit()` or `ITransaction::Abort()`, the call is made synchronously. That is, the client thread is blocked until MS DTC has determined the outcome of the first phase. However, both of these methods can be called asynchronously – the `Abort()` method has a `fAsync` parameter (that can be set to `TRUE`), and the `Commit()` method has a `grfTC` flags parameter (that can be set to `XACTTC_ASYNC`). In both cases, MS DTC will inform the client of the first phase of the transaction by calling its notify object:

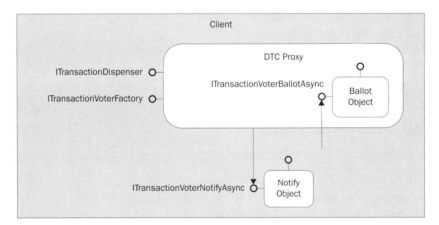

To register the notify object with the MS DTC, the client passes it, and a reference to the transaction object that it wants to influence, to `ITransactionVoterFactory::Create()`. This returns a reference to a ballot object, created in the DTC Proxy for the transaction. When some event concerning the transaction occurs, the DTC proxy calls the appropriate event method on the notify object, which handles the event and responds to the Ballot object by calling `VoteRequestDone()`.

`ITransactionVoterNotifyAsync` looks like this:

```
interface ITransactionOutcomeEvents : public IUnknown
{
    HRESULT Committed([in] BOOL fRetaining,
                      [in, unique] XACTUOW* pNewUOW,
                      [in] HRESULT hr);
    HRESULT Aborted([in, unique] BOID* pboidReason,
                    [in] BOOL fRetaining,
                    [in, unique] XACTUOW* pNewUOW,
                    [in] HRESULT hr);
    HRESULT HeuristicDecision([in] DWORD dwDecision,
                    [in, unique] BOID* pboidReason,
                    [in] HRESULT hr);
    HRESULT Indoubt();
};

interface ITransactionVoterNotifyAsync : public ITransactionOutcomeEvents
{
    HRESULT VoteRequest(
            [in] ITransactionVoterBallotAsync* pVoterBallot);
};
```

The MSDN documentation doesn't appear to have the same methods as present in the header files in the Platform SDK. Furthermore, the methods on these interfaces appear to vary according to the version of the SDK you have – so much for immutable interfaces.

When the first phase of the 2-phase commit starts, the `VoteRequest()` method is called. (The MTS SDK says that this takes a pointer to the ballot object, which is redundant. My tests have shown that this pointer is always `NULL` – later versions of the Platform SDK say that this method doesn't have a parameter.) The application gives its choice about the transaction outcome by calling `ITransactionVoterBallotAsync::VoteRequestDone()`.

The April 1999 MSDN documents this method as having the name `VoteReqDone()`.

The client can pass `S_OK` or `E_FAIL` as the first parameter of this method, to either allow the commit to proceed or abort the transaction. `Committed()` and `Aborted()` will be called depending on a known outcome of the transaction, `Indoubt()` otherwise. `HeuristicDecision()` is not called in the current version of MTS.

Distributed Transactions

The whole point about the MS DTC is that it can *distribute* transactions throughout the network, remote resource managers thus enlisting in transactions started on other machines. The previous section introduced you to some of the objects involved and the mechanisms used. This section will look at the finer details of the commit process. There are two other main issues to examine: firstly, when a transaction is completed, the result of the transaction should be propagated around all the resource managers enlisted in the transaction, so that they can commit or abort their work; secondly, there is the issue of handling the situation when a machine that has enlisted resource managers has died. The architecture of 2-phase commit allows for all of this.

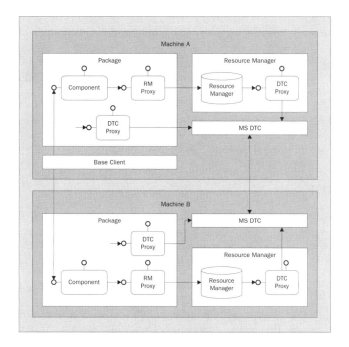

When client code uses a resource manager on a remote machine, both its local transaction manager and the remote transaction manager will be involved. The client tells the local transaction manager that there is an **outgoing relationship** with the remote transaction manager. The remote machine resource manager tells its local transaction manager that there is an **incoming relationship** with the other transaction manager. There may be several machines involved in the transaction, and any node in this tree can abort the transaction before the commit mechanism has started. If the resource managers enlisted in the transaction don't abort it, then it will be committed. These commit and abort messages have to be sent throughout the commit tree to allow the resource managers to commit or rollback their work.

If a machine dies while it has a resource manager enlisted in a transaction, then the possibility exists of that resource manager having performed some work, but not yet having committed it. This has immediate problems as far as the client is concerned, because the transaction is an all or nothing affair, so the transaction can't finish until the dead resource manager can complete the commit. Note that MTS applies a machine-wide transaction timeout of 60 seconds, and if the transaction takes longer than this it will automatically be aborted. There will be other consequences – if the resource manager on this failed machine used resources on other machines, those resources will be locked for the duration of the transaction, and remain so until the dead machine allows them to be released.

Imagine the situation of a distributed transaction being committed. All the work performed by all the resource managers should be committed, whatever happens to those machines. So, if a subordinate machine fails before it can commit its work, it must do so when it recovers. (If not, then the atomicity of the transaction will be violated.) To ensure this, resource managers must know what work they have performed for a transaction, and transaction managers must know which resource managers existing on the local machine are enlisted in a transaction. Therefore, both the MS DTC and resource managers must keep a durable log, and the resource manager should have a write-ahead log, so that if a failure occurs when it is only partly through its work, it will know what that work was when it recovers.

When the machine restarts, the MS DTC will restart and, as part of its startup process, will read its log to see what it was doing before it died – this log will list the transactions that were in force. It thus has an opportunity to get in touch with other transaction managers to determine the outcome of the transaction. (Transaction managers will respond to requests from other transaction managers about outgoing transactions that are in doubt.) The transaction manager can then check its log to see which resource managers are enlisted in the transaction, and inform them of the transaction outcome.

The net effect of this is that the transaction can be treated as atomic, because the MS DTC will ensure that all machines taking part in the transaction receive information about it and can affect its outcome. The transaction will also be isolated, since all resource managers will lock the affected resources for the duration of the transaction.

2-Phase Commit

The sending of commit or abort messages around the machines involved in a transaction is a vital part of a distributed system. The previous sections have explained how transactions are distributed, and have alluded to the 2-phase commit process. In this section I will look at the details of how 2-phase commit works.

The 2-Phase Commit Mechanism

In 2-phase commit, MS DTC issues two sets of messages – a **prepare** message and a **commit** message. (Their actual format, or how they are transmitted between machines, is unimportant.) The first tells a resource manager that the transaction has ended, so it should prepare to commit the transaction by writing the resource changes to a durable store. The resource manager doesn't commit the work, it just records what the changes are. At this stage, the resources involved in the transaction are still locked, because the transaction hasn't ended. Resource managers must do this to maintain the isolation aspect of the transaction.

Once the prepare messages have been sent to all resource managers in the transaction, it can be assumed that the transaction will have finished (in that no more work can be done). At this point, the MS DTC will issue a commit message, telling the resource managers to commit the changes they made and remove the locks that they maintain. If the resource manager can't prepare to commit (it finds out that it can't make the changes durable) it tells the transaction manager, which will abort the entire transaction. If all the resource managers have successfully prepared, then the transaction *must* commit.

If there are several enlisted resource managers on the single machine then they will be informed *in parallel*. If there are subordinate resource managers then they too will be informed in parallel. Parallel in this respect means 'as concurrent as possible', so although there may be only one network card in the machine (and the network cable by its nature serializes packets), the messages will be sent at the same time – the MS DTC will not wait for one machine to acknowledge the message before sending it to another machine.

Why Two Phases?

Two phases are used to allow for machine or system failure. The prepare message merely informs the resource managers to get ready to commit, allowing them a last chance to determine whether the commit will succeed. If the prepare phase didn't happen, then the situation could arise where a resource manager tries to commit the changes from the transaction, only to find that there is not enough disk space, for example. Such a situation would be determined in the prepare phase, which would indicate a problem to its transaction manager, ultimately aborting the entire transaction.

Once the prepare phase has completed and all resource managers are happy they can commit the changes, then the transaction *must* commit. Of course, this puts a responsibility on the resource managers, namely to ensure that after they have been prepared they *will* commit the changes – this may not be as simple as it appears.

The MS DTC and 2-Phase Commit

Let's take a look at how 2-phase commit works with the MS DTC. At the start of the mechanism, the transaction manager tells a resource manager to prepare by calling `ITransactionResourceAsync::PrepareRequest()` on the resource manager's transaction resource sink object. It replies by calling `ITransactionEnlistmentAsync::PrepareRequestDone()` on the enlistment object in the DTC proxy. The resource manager then queries the enlistment object for `IPrepareInfo`, and calls `GetPrepareInfo()` to get opaque prepare information (the information is meaningless to the resource manager), which is written by the resource manager to its log, along with the changes required to complete the transaction. The prepare information is saved to help in the recovery procedure, as you'll see in a moment. When all the resource managers on the system have completed the prepare phase, the local transaction manager will write a prepare record to its log, and inform the transaction manager immediately above it in the commit tree. This way, the completion of the prepare phase propagates back to the commit coordinator.

Once all the resource managers have prepared, the client transaction manager writes a commit record to its log, and tells all resource managers to commit or abort. This involves a similar parallel message, sent from a transaction manager to the resource managers and subordinate transaction managers. Once these messages have been sent, the transaction will have finished, so the original call to `ITransaction::Commit()` that started the commit mechanism (initiated by MTS) will return. Of course, the final work to commit the changes still won't have been carried out. The 2-phase commit mechanism guarantees that this work will be performed once the commit message has been sent – this is why the client is informed that the transaction has ended.

The commit message involves a `CommitRequest()` or `AbortRequest()` sent to the resource manager's transaction resource sink object. The resource manager replies by calling `CommitRequestDone()` or `AbortRequestDone()` on the enlistment object. It should then commit or abort the changes, and when all the resource managers have committed, the transaction manager will write a forget record to its log, indicating that the transaction has completed.

Recovery

In most cases, the commit work will start immediately. However, if the network fails then the commit phase won't occur, so the resource manager will be in doubt about the transaction. A resource manager in doubt will have data affected by the transaction, which will be locked. The problem is that code on the local machine may attempt to use that data. Write operations will therefore fail, and (depending on the isolation level chosen) so will most read operations.

> *Note that MTS creates transactions at an isolation level of* `ISOLATIONLEVEL_SERIALIZABLE` *– the highest possible. This means that when data is locked, all write and read operations originating from outside the transaction will fail.*

Clearly this situation must be resolved. If a resource manager (or the machine it runs on) dies, then all the partially completed transactions it is enlisted in will be aborted. However, if a transaction has been prepared before the resource manager dies, then the work of the transaction will have been completed so the final commit phase must be performed. Such a transaction is clearly in doubt.

179

When a resource manager starts up, it accesses the DTC proxy and registers itself by calling `IResourceManagerFactory::Create()` to obtain the `IResourceManager` interface on the resource manager object. At this point the resource manager will read its log to see if any transactions are in doubt – for each of these it will find the prepare information written there during the prepare phase. It will pass this information to the resource manager object by calling `IResourceManager::Reenlist()`, along with a timeout value that determines how long the resource manager will wait to learn about the transaction outcome.

The DTC Proxy passes this information to the transaction manager, which determines the transaction outcome and returns it to the DTC proxy. There are three possible outcomes. The transaction manager determines that the transaction should be committed or aborted (in which case the appropriate `CommitRequest()` or `AbortRequest()` message will be sent), or a timeout occurs. In this latter case, the `XACT_E_REENLISTTIMEOUT` error will be returned, prompting the resource manager to try again later. If the transaction outcome is returned then the resource manager will write a commit or abort record to its log and do the work. When the resource manager has learned of the outcome of all in doubt transactions it calls `IResourceManager::ReenlistmentComplete()`, so that the transaction manager can forget the transaction.

The MS DTC uses **presumed abort** with two optimizations. The first is called **read-only commit**, which means that the resource manager's work in the transaction has read data but not made any changes. In this case no changes need to be made. When the resource manager gets the prepare message, it can pass `XACT_S_READONLY` when it calls `PrepareRequestDone()` on the enlistment object, to indicate that it does not need the commit message. This increases performance, but reduces the isolation level.

The other optimization is **delegated commit**, which means that MTS allows the commit coordination to be performed by a transaction manager other then the root commit coordinator, or even by resource managers. This can only be done if there is just one subordinate transaction manager or resource manager enlisted in the transaction. In this case, the coordinating transaction manager sets `fSinglePhase` when calling `PrepareRequest()`. The resource manager can then pass `XACT_S_SINGLEPHASE` to `PrepareRequestDone()`.

Locking

Isolation levels are important for resource managers because they are intimately tied in with the locking policy that the resource manager will use. The locking policy, in turn, determines how clients can access data provided by the resource manager. The isolation level is specified when the transaction is created, with a call to `BeginTransaction()`. The following values are defined in the MTS SDK:

Isolation Level	Description
ISOLATIONLEVEL_READUNCOMMITTED	Data is read irrespective of applied locks
ISOLATIONLEVEL_READCOMMITTED	You cannot read the data until it is committed by the write transaction
ISOLATIONLEVEL_REPEATABLEREAD	Repeated reads on the data will not show changes in data that has already been read
ISOLATIONLEVEL_SERIALIZABLE	The highest level. Repeated reads in the same transaction will always yield the same result

Note that whatever isolations are used, the data is always locked for write access. The isolation level determines whether other code can *read* the data involved in the transaction.

The first isolation level, ISOLATIONLEVEL_READUNCOMMITTED, implies that clients can read data handled by the resource manager, irrespective of whether there is a current transaction updating the data. It may sound odd to allow clients to read data in such a state, but it is useful for some applications as a performance optimization. This isolation level will allow clients to read uncommitted data that may be rolled back, and thus be considered never to have existed. However, some applications may prefer to take this risk – if the changes in the values are small then the improved performance can be more important than the accuracy of the results.

For example, imagine that you have a database where a row contains the number of hits on a web page. The web server may place a lock on this row when it updates it, meaning that when an administrative tool tries to read the value to update a bar chart on screen, the isolation level could cause this read operation to fail. In this situation you may decide that the ISOLATIONLEVEL_READUNCOMMITTED level is acceptable, perhaps because the pixel resolution of a screen would mean that the least significant digit is unimportant (a bar on screen would show little difference in height for values of 1502 and 1503, for example). In this case it matters little that the actual value read will be slightly inaccurate.

The next level, ISOLATIONLEVEL_READCOMMITTED, applies read locks on the data until the present query has been completed – thus it only allows code to read data that has been committed. However, it doesn't prevent situations such as non-repeatable reads or phantoms. In the first case, a transaction could read a row twice while a second transaction has access to the same row. If the second transaction deletes the row before the first makes its second read, then the two reads will return different results. Alternatively, you could have two transactions, one of which makes a query twice while the other adds new rows. If the second transaction is performed before the first transaction's second query is carried out, an extra (phantom) row will appear.

ISOLATIONLEVEL_REPEATABLEREAD removes the problems of the non-repeatable read. When a transaction reads the same data twice it will always get the same value, regardless of other transactions that may be in force. This level of isolation will not prevent phantoms, because the resource manager will not maintain locks on indexes during the transaction. The final level, ISOLATIONLEVEL_SERIALIZABLE means that all concurrent transactions behave as though they were executed serially. This isolation level removes the possibility of phantoms.

> *MTS objects always have transactions created with* ISOLATIONLEVEL_SERIALIZABLE *to fulfill the ACID isolation criterion. Since Windows 2000 allows you to create a transaction and associate it with a COM+ object, you may use transactions at a lower isolation level (assuming, of course, that the resource managers you use support them).*

Resource Dispensers

Resource dispensers have two roles. Firstly, they act as resource manager proxies, presenting a friendly face of the resource manager to the client code. Secondly, they give access to resource pooling. Resources in this sense are non-transactional, transient resources. Resource dispensers are in-process, so the resource pools are per-process – a pool of resources used by one package is not accessible from another. Resource dispensers don't maintain any durable log of the resources, they don't perform actions under the influence of transactions, and they don't perform recovery on start up. Such actions are the domain of resource managers.

Although resource dispensers' resources are not accessed under transactions, they are used as part of MTS transaction auto-enlistment. What this means is that MTS knows whether the resource dispenser is being used to access a resource in a resource manager, and whether the component requires a transaction (or supports one where one is active). In this case, MTS will inform the resource dispenser that it needs to enlist the resource in the transaction. Note that this doesn't apply to the resource dispenser's resources, which are *never* accessed under a transaction.

Resource dispensers are typically accessed by components running in a package, and hence under the control of MTS. However, since they behave as resource manager proxies, they don't *need* MTS. A resource dispenser can therefore be used outside of MTS, but this will mean that auto-enlistment will not be performed, so the responsibility to do this will be put on the client code.

The various objects and their relationships are illustrated in the following diagram:

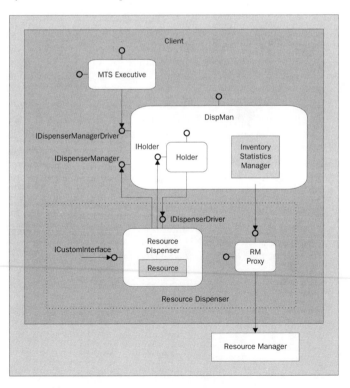

Resource dispensers are managed by the **Resource Dispenser Manager** (also known as DispMan, implemented in `mtxdm.dll`). DispMan manages the loading and unloading of resource dispensers and provides resource pooling, managing resources provided by the dispenser through a facility called the Inventory Statistics Manager. Furthermore, DispMan determines whether a resource provided by the dispenser should be enlisted in a transaction (by obtaining an object's context through the MTS executive), and reclaims resources to prevent leaks.

When the dispenser registers itself with the DispMan, an object called a holder is created, which gives access to the resource pool. DispMan polls each of the holders every 10 seconds, to tell them to re-adjust their resource inventories, ensuring that unused resources are released or that new resources are created. It does this by calling on the Inventory Statistics Manager to suggest the inventory levels for each type of resource. This may involve the holder asking the resource dispenser to create or destroy resources. In addition, the Inventory Statistics Manager will remove resources when they have not been used for a resource-specific timeout period.

The inventory holds existing resources, of which there are four distinct cases:

- ❑ **Unenlisted inventory** – the resource isn't in use or enlisted in a transaction. It is available for assignment to a component.

- ❑ **Enlisted inventory** – the resource isn't in use, but it is enlisted in a transaction. This means that the resource will be available to application code in same transaction. DispMan will move the resource to the unenlisted inventory when MTS executive tells it that the transaction has completed.

- ❑ **Unenlisted use** – the resource is being used, but isn't enlisted in a transaction.

- ❑ **Enlisted use** – the resource is being used, and is enlisted in a transaction.

DispMan can use auto-reclamation, by which the MTS executive tells DispMan when an object's lifetime has ended. DispMan can then tell each registered resource dispenser holder, to see if it has any resources held by the object – if so, the resource is freed. This facility is turned off by default, and it is not clear how to turn it on.

In addition, DispMan can track a resource that is not in the inventory, based on knowledge of the object's lifetime. Such a resource is said to be **tracked**. The resource dispenser creates it and calls `IHolder::TrackResource()`, indicating that DispMan should track the resource until either the resource dispenser calls `UntrackResource()` or the object is released, in which case DispMan frees the resource by calling `IDispenserDriver::DestroyResource()`, and the resource is not returned to inventory. This mode should be used for resources that don't need to be pooled, namely those that are inexpensive to create and destroy.

Resource Management

As you can see, resources are managed by two components: the DispMan (and its objects) and resource dispensers. The idea is that dispensers know how to create resources and free them – they can contain resources and know how to enlist an already created resource into a transaction if necessary. Dispensers don't know about the transactional aspect of client components, and they don't have any pooling responsibility – by and large they don't control resource lifetimes. DispMan has a generic pooling mechanism that works with opaque handles – it knows if a resource is being used, can determine if the resource should be used under a transaction, and can tell if the component using the resource is being released (and thus determine the resource's lifetime). DispMan can't know how to create and destroy resources, and it can't know how suitable a resource is to a given task.

Resources are created and managed by a resource dispenser, which knows about them and holds them. DispMan knows nothing about them and therefore cannot hold them – it only knows resources by an opaque RESID handle (declared as a DWORD). A resource dispenser can create resources of more than one type, and there may be more than one dispenser loaded into the process (each with its own holder object in DispMan). Therefore, to distinguish between each sort of resource, dispensers use a RESTYPID (again, declared as a DWORD).

The resource dispenser will have some API that the client code will understand (commonly a COM interface, but it could be a C API – in the previous diagram I called this ICustomInterface) and the client uses this API to ask for a resource. The dispenser asks its holder for the resource by calling IHolder::AllocResource(), passing the RESTYPID of the resource required. The holder checks its inventory of available resources, based on whether the resource should be used under a transaction, and then draws up a list of possible resources. However, it doesn't know how suitable these resources are for the task.

Therefore, for each of the candidates the holder calls IDispenserDriver::RateResource() on the dispenser, passing its RESID, RESTYPID, and whether the resource should be enlisted in the current transaction – it expects a rating between 0 and 100. 0 means that the resource is unsuitable for the task (if the resource is a section of memory, for example, this could be returned if the size of the memory is too small) and 100 means that the resource is a perfect fit. If 100 is returned then the resource will be used. If the rating is less than this, the holder will ask the dispenser to rate other resources and filter the list of possible candidates. The dispenser is told whether the resource should be enlisted, and since this may take some time, the dispenser may choose to rate an un-enlisted resource below that of an enlisted resource.

If all resources in the inventory have a rating of 0 (or if the inventory is empty), the holder will ask the dispenser to create a new resource by calling IDispenserDriver::CreateResource(), passing the RESTYPID of the resource to create. The dispenser should create the resource and return its RESID along with a timeout, which determines how long the resource can remain unused in the inventory before the holder asks the dispenser to destroy it.

Finally, if the client code has a transaction and the resource is not enlisted, DispMan calls IDispenserDriver::EnlistResource(), passing the RESID of the resource and the TRANSID of the transaction. A TRANSID is an ITransaction* cast to a DWORD, highlighting the fact that communication between DispMan and the resource dispenser doesn't use marshaling. (If the two were in different apartments, the TRANSID would be marshaled as a DWORD, not an interface pointer). If the holder passes 0 for the TRANSID, it means that the resource should be unenlisted in the transaction in which it was previously enlisted. Therefore, if you use transactional resources, you should keep a record of the transaction that each resource is enlisted in.

Resource dispensers don't manage transactional resources, which implies that a resource manager will be used. So, in response to EnlistResource(), the resource dispenser should export the transaction and use its private API as a resource manager proxy, to pass the transaction cookie to the resource manager.

Once the holder has obtained a resource (either from the pool or by requesting it be created anew), it can return the RESID of this resource back to the resource dispenser. This can determine what the RESID actually means and return the resource back to the client that requested it.

When the client has finished with the resource, it informs the resource dispenser via its API. The dispenser can then inform the holder that the resource is to be put back into the pool. It does this by calling `IHolder::FreeResource()`, passing the `RESID` the holder, then passing this back to the dispenser via `IDispenserDriver::ResetResource()`, which is used to initialize the resource. However, it may be enlisted in a transaction, so this shouldn't be changed.

Resource Dispenser Code

A resource dispenser is an in-proc component that implements `IDispenserDriver` and its own API. This API may be a COM interface or a C API. Indeed, the client should not have to call `CoInitializeEx()` before using the resource dispenser. Clearly, resource dispensers are COM objects, so some code must call `CoInitializeEx()` so that `IDispenserDriver` can be called and the resource dispenser can access the MS DTC interfaces to export transactions. You'll see how this is done in a moment.

On startup, the resource dispenser must register itself with DispMan, if it is available. It does this by calling `GetDispenserManager()` to get the `IDispenserManager` interface. If the interface is not returned it means that the resource dispenser is not being run under MTS, so there is no pool, and the dispenser will merely create resources on demand. If DispMan is available then the dispenser should call `RegisterDispenser()` passing its `IDispenserDriver` interface and its name. In return, it will be given the `IHolder` interface on its holder object.

When the resource dispenser shuts down, it calls `IHolder::Close()` to ensure that its resources are removed from the pool and destroyed (with calls to `DestroyResource()`).

The client that creates the resource dispenser can be running in an STA, an MTA, or (as mentioned at the beginning of this section) not in an apartment at all. To accommodate this, the in-proc resource dispenser should have a `ThreadingModel` of `Both`. This means that the dispenser must be aware that any proxies it holds to other objects may be accessed from a different thread to that which created the proxy. These proxies may therefore need to be marshaled, and this would advocate the use of the Global Interface Table.

In addition, there can only be one instance of a resource dispenser loaded in a process (otherwise DispMan would not know which dispenser to call to create resources), so it must be a singleton object. If there is just one instance in a process, it means that it can be accessed from code in different apartments, and to reduce thread context switches it should therefore aggregate the free threaded marshaler.

Administering the MS DTC

The MTS Explorer helps you to manage the MS DTC. As explained in the previous chapter, you can start and stop the MS DTC on the local machine, as well as on any remote machines you have administrative access to. The MTS Explorer uses colored icons to indicate the current status of the MS MTC – the monitor background is a light green when the MS DTC is running, dark green when it has stopped, and amber when it is starting up.

MTS explorer also has a node called **Trace Messages**. The MTS documentation suggests that this should give the event log messages specific to the MS DTC, but I have never seen this node contain any messages, even though I have managed to create lots of DTC event messages in the event log. There may be a filter that is only allowing certain messages to be shown, but I haven't been able to determine where that filter is set, nor what it is filtering out.

If you want to view event log messages for the MS DTC, I recommend that you run the NT event viewer (from the View menu select Filter Events) and then select MSDTC as the Source. (Or indeed, write your own MMC snap-in – which is relatively easy with ATL 3.0, and the data is straightforward to read from the event log. Windows 2000 has such an MMC snap-in.)

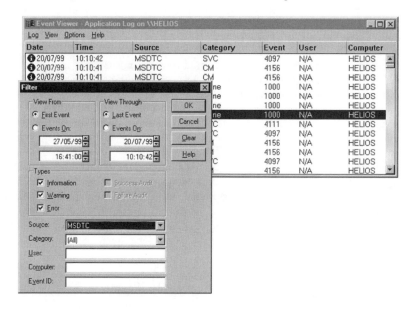

In addition, you can monitor the Transaction Statistics, which lists when the MS DTC started, along with information about current transactions as well as transactions since the MS DTC started. The Current pane gives the number of active transactions, the maximum number of transactions that have ever been active concurrently, and the number of current transactions that are in doubt. The Aggregate pane gives information about all the transactions that have been created, the total number, how many of those were committed or aborted naturally, and how many were forced to commit or abort. Finally, there is a pane called Response Times that lists the maximum, minimum and average response times.

Finally, you can obtain the list of current active transactions by looking at the Transaction List node. As explained earlier, this gives the transaction GUID and the text associated with the transaction. If it originated from MTS, this string will be the ProgID of the base object in the transaction. Note that often transactions are too short-lived to appear in the transaction list – to increase the refresh rate you must increase the Display Refresh of the DTC properties, as explained later. This view is particularly useful if there are transactions in doubt, because you can force the transaction outcome using the right-click context menu.

MS DTC can be administered using the MSDTC.UIS object. This object gives access to the following page:

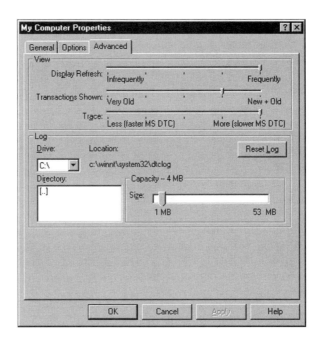

Note my statement that MSDTC.UIS is an object. Indeed, it appears to act as a coordinator object giving access to the MS DTC property page, the statistics page, trace messages and transaction list page. I say this because these pages can be accessed by MTS Explorer as well as the SQL Server MS DTC Admin Console. However, it doesn't appear to be implemented as a property page – MSDTC.UIS only seems to implement the IUnknown interface. If it implements any others, they are private interfaces that don't use marshaling.

At the bottom of the page are options to allow you to specify the location and size of the MS DTC log. If you have a machine with both FAT and NTFS partitions, it is beneficial (for performance) to put the log on the NTFS partition. The top part of the page allows you to alter how monitoring is carried out:

- ❑ Display Refresh – determines how often the transaction list is updated. Infrequently means approximately every 20 seconds, Frequently approximately every second.

- ❑ Transactions Shown – determines the minimum age of the transactions shown in the transaction list.

- ❑ Trace – determines which event messages are shown in the Trace Messages window.

The final facility for administering the MS DTC is a Control Panel applet. When you have several machines involved in a distributed transaction, the MS DTC installations on each machine must communicate with each other, in order to propagate transactions and their outcomes. You can specify the network protocol that the MS DTC will use with this applet:

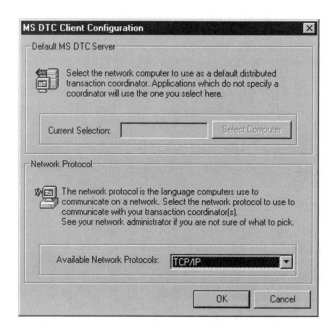

The Available Network Protocols will list all the protocols installed on your machine. You should clearly use a protocol common to all the machines that will take part in transactions. In these days of the internet, TCP/IP seems a good choice.

MS DTC Extensions

The MS DTC can be used for more than just OLE transactions. Some of the facilities that I mention in this section are only available on Windows 2000. However, you will find that although the facilities aren't available on NT4, the MS DTC will support the interfaces (this is certainly true on my NT4 test platform, with service pack 5 and SQL Server 7 installed). There have been no announcements as to how 'officially' MTS on NT4 and COM+ on Windows 2000 are expected to interoperate. (The official line appears to be that users only have the option to upgrade to Windows 2000.) The fact that some Windows 2000 interfaces are supported by MS DTC on NT4 appears to indicate one of two things: either Microsoft will allow NT4 access to XA transactions (and Transaction Internet Protocol transactions, explained in Chapter 8), or maybe there is merely a common code base for the MS DTC on both platforms.

XA Transactions

X/Open defines the **XA** protocol that a resource manager can use to talk to a transaction manager, join a transaction, perform 2-phase commitment, and recover in doubt transactions. XA is an alternative to OLE transactions, and is common in the Unix world. Clearly, for MTS to be used for truly distributed transactions it must be able to take part in XA transactions, otherwise it would restrict MTS to Windows machines.

The MS DTC contains an XA compliant transaction Manager that allows it to talk to XA resource managers and transaction managers. If you want to access data sources that use XA transactions you will need to use an ODBC driver. Such a driver must understand XA to be able to export the transaction to the resource manager. The DTC proxy uses an XA to OLE transaction mapper to allow it to communicate with such ODBC drivers:

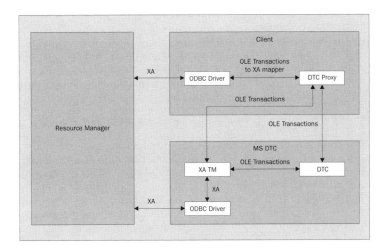

To do this, the DTC proxy implements the following interfaces:

Interface	Description
IDtcToXaHelperFactory	Used to create the XA mapper object which implements IDtcToXaHelper
IDtcToXaHelperSinglePipe	Used to map XA transactions to OLE transactions and to enlist in transactions for a single pipe connection
IDtcToXaMapper	Used to map XA transactions to OLE transactions and to enlist in transactions for a two pipe connection
IXATransLookup	Create a OLE transaction

Summary

One overlooked aspect of MTS is that the transactions used by components can be distributed. To do this involves a lot of effort from MTS, along with the co-operation of many other processes. Every machine with a resource manager must have an instance of the MS DTC installed, acting as a dispenser of transactions and coordinating the commit process.

The resource managers involved in the transaction must understand what that transaction is, so there must be some kind of standard. As it turns out, there are three. MS DTC understands OLE Transactions (its native transaction type), but can also act as a transaction manager for XA transactions and TIP transactions (under Windows 2000). By supporting the common transaction standards, the MS DTC can be used with as wide a range of resource managers as possible, which implies that MTS components can too.

When an MTS component needs a transaction, MTS must get hold of one and enlist the component in that transaction. Transactions are obtained from the MS DTC on the local machine, which has the responsibility of keeping a record of which transactions are active. If the component needs to access a resource manager under the transaction, then it does so using the MS DTC. The transaction is *exported* from MS DTC as an opaque blob of data that identifies the transaction and its commit coordinator. This is passed to a resource manager, which can then *import* the transaction from the local MS DTC in a form that the resource manager understands. This importing/exporting process means that even though many machines may be involved, the MS DTC on each one will know about any current transactions in the local resource managers.

This is important, because the MS DTC is crucial in the 2-phase commit process, where it acts as the coordinator. This (industry standard) mechanism informs all the players in a transaction of a transaction outcome. It does so in two phases, allowing a commit to occur atomically, even if machines involved in the transaction die in the process.

MTS performs auto-enlistment, that is, if a component should run under a transaction, MTS ensures that one is created and that enlistment occurs. In MTS, this is carried out by resource dispensers. These are components that have a dual role: they act as proxies for resource managers and can be used to pool resources. In its proxy role, a resource dispenser is informed by MTS (by the dispenser manager) that the work should be performed under a transaction. This gives the resource dispenser the opportunity to ensure that the transaction is exported to the resource manager for which it is a proxy.

All in all, MS DTC does a lot of work for you, much of which appears to happen as if by magic.

6

Security

Introduction

DCOM gives you a lot of facilities to enable you to build distributed applications. However, although you have the facilities you must work hard to use them. Chapter 4 explained how the MTS Explorer can be used to help deploy distributed applications on different machines across the network. The MTS Explorer can also be used to manage another difficult DCOM problem: security.

The problem is clear – any DCOM application (and I include MTS packages in this categorization) will involve a foreign user starting a process, which will be asked to access resources on behalf of that foreign user. This raises a lot of questions, principally whether you really want *anyone* to launch processes and change resources on your machine? If not, how can you specify which accounts can and can't access or modify resources? Furthermore, even if you have allowed a specific account to perform these actions, and such an account connects, how can you be sure that the account is being used legitimately? After all, some bad guy could pretend to be the trusted account.

Now look at this problem from the client's perspective. The client connects to the server process it requests – or does it? The client has to be sure that the server process it connects to is the one it wants, otherwise a rogue server could pretend to be the specified server to obtain information about the client. Furthermore, does the client want the server to access resources on behalf of the client (meaning that the changes are audited as being done *by the client*), or would the client prefer to restrict it so that the work is done under the server's own identity?

These problems can be described by the three terms **authorization**, **authentication** and **impersonation**, and this chapter will explain how MTS allows you to administer these and program security in code. By and large, everything that you can do with MTS security can be done with COM security, with a fair amount of coding. However, there are notable exceptions (things that you can do with MTS but can't do with COM security). For example, COM objects can determine their immediate caller, but MTS components can determine the account that *created* them, which in a distributed application is very useful. In this chapter I will explain the security aspects of MTS and present NT security code showing how you can do this without MTS.

COM Security

I will start by explaining how security is applied in COM, as a grounding for the discussion of MTS security later in this chapter.

COM, like other inter-process communication (IPC) mechanisms offered by NT, needs to authorize accesses to the code in a server and must authenticate the accounts that make those accesses. However, COM is unusual among IPC mechanisms because it allows remote launching of processes (COM servers or surrogates). It therefore needs to perform authorization checks to ensure that clients are allowed to launch processes.

DCOMCnfg

COM security is typically administered through the DCOMCnfg tool, which has two confusing aspects. Firstly, it gives access to both client-side and server-side security settings – novice users often confuse the two and apply unnecessary settings. Secondly, the settings applied through DCOMCnfg are applied to an entire COM server, and not to an individual component in that server. Granted, the main dialog of DCOMCnfg does explicitly say that the security settings are applied to *Applications*, as shown in the following screenshot:

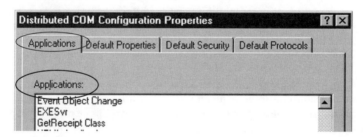

However, as you can also see from this, DCOMCnfg lists both servers (for example, EXESvr) and object classes (for example, GetReceipt Class). Don't be fooled by this! The changes you make to 'GetReceipt Class' will be made to the server of this class, and will therefore be applied to *all* components served by it. In this respect, the settings that you apply via DCOMCnfg can be viewed as the base security settings, upon which you can apply extra checks programmatically.

When DCOMCnfg populates the **Applications** listbox, it looks in the AppID key under HKEY_CLASSES_ROOT and adds an entry for each GUID it can find. If it can find a default value for an AppID, it will use that as the application name (that's where EXESvr came from). If it doesn't find a server name, it will trawl through the CLSID key looking for classes that give a GUID for their AppId value. If this matches the AppID that DCOMCfg is looking for, it will take the default value of the class, which is often the class name (for example, GetReceipt Class). If none of the classes have default values then DCOMCnfg uses the AppId GUID.

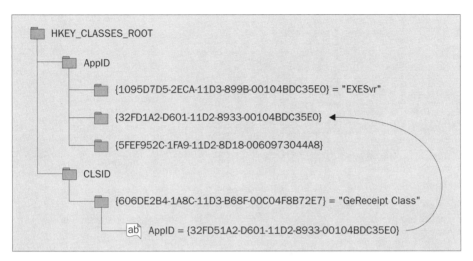

The previous figure shows how this process works. For the three values in AppID, DCOMCnfg will give the strings EXESvr, GetReceipt Class and {5FEF952C-1FA9-11D2-8D18-0060973044A8}.

> *Personally, I would prefer it if* DCOMCnfg *checked the default value of each* AppID *GUID. If it didn't find a server name then it would use the name of the server in* LocalServer32 *or* InprocServer32 *of the first class it found, rather than the class name. This would emphasize that the settings are applied* only *to servers. Alas, it is not so, and this means that novice users of* DCOMCnfg *must be instructed that the security settings are* not *applied to classes.*

If different objects in a server specify different AppIDs then the security settings of the first object, which caused the server to be launched, will be used. This will have odd effects as far as the client is concerned (as it could mean that the identity of a server would depend on the order in which components are activated), and should therefore be avoided.

AppID values can be applied to DLLs as well as EXEs, so long as the DLLs are run under a surrogate. This means either that the AppID has a DllSurrogate value, or that the LocalServer32 key of a class in the server gives the surrogate – MTS takes the second option.

The AppID key for a server has two named values: LaunchPermissions and AccessPermissions. These are self-relative ACLs (Access Control Lists), containing the accounts that are allowed or denied to launch the server and access components in the server.

For example, the following code shows how to obtain the ACLs associated with an AppID. The code assumes that the actual GUID (including curly braces) is passed as a command line parameter.

```
#include <atlbase.h>
#include <stdio.h>

void DumpSIDs(LPVOID pb);

int _tmain(int argc, _TCHAR* argv[])
{
   if (argc != 2)
   {
      _tprintf(_T("Error! Parameter must be ")
               _T("an AppID\n"));
      return 1;
   }

   CRegKey hKey;
   hKey.Open(HKEY_CLASSES_ROOT, _T("AppID"));
   if (hKey.Open(hKey, argv[1]) != ERROR_SUCCESS)
   {
      _tprintf(_T("Error! Cannot open %s\n"),
               argv[1]);
      return 1;
   }

   DWORD dwSize;
   if (RegQueryValueEx(hKey, _T("LaunchPermission"), 0, NULL, NULL, &dwSize)
      == ERROR_SUCCESS)
   {
      LPBYTE pbLaunch = new BYTE[dwSize];
      RegQueryValueEx(hKey, _T("LaunchPermission"), 0, NULL, pbLaunch, &dwSize);
      _tprintf(_T("Launch permissions: \n"));
      DumpSIDs(pbLaunch);
      delete [] pbLaunch;
   }

   dwSize = 0;
   if (RegQueryValueEx(hKey, _T("AccessPermission"), 0, NULL, NULL, &dwSize)
      == ERROR_SUCCESS)
   {
      LPBYTE pbAccess = new BYTE[dwSize];
      RegQueryValueEx(hKey, _T("AccessPermission"), 0, NULL, pbAccess, &dwSize);
      _tprintf(_T("Access permissions: \n"));
      DumpSIDs(pbAccess);
      delete [] pbAccess;
   }
   return 0;
}
```

The values obtained from the registry keys contain binary data, which is the ACL. The SIDs can be accessed with the usual NT security API:

```
void DumpSIDs(LPVOID pb)
{
    BOOL bPres = true;
    BOOL bDef;
PACL pacl = NULL;
    GetSecurityDescriptorDacl(pb, &bPres, &pacl, &bDef);
    if (bPres)
    {
        ACL_SIZE_INFORMATION aclSize;
        GetAclInformation(pacl, (LPVOID)&aclSize, sizeof(ACL_SIZE_INFORMATION),
                          AclSizeInformation);
        for (DWORD x = 0; x < aclSize.AceCount; x++)
        {
            ACCESS_ALLOWED_ACE* pace;
            GetAce(pacl, x, (void**)&pace);
            SID_NAME_USE snu;
            TCHAR strName[MAX_PATH];
            TCHAR strDomain[MAX_PATH];
            DWORD dwName = sizeof(strName);
            DWORD dwDomain = sizeof(strDomain);
            LookupAccountSid(NULL, (PSID)&pace->SidStart, strName, &dwName,
                             strDomain, &dwDomain, &snu);
            _tprintf(_T("%s\\%s"), strDomain, strName);
            if (pace->Header.AceType == ACCESS_ALLOWED_ACE_TYPE)
                _tprintf(_T(" allowed\n"));
            else
                _tprintf(_T(" denied\n"));
        }
    }
}
```

This simple code is useful to investigate the registry values that MTS uses to apply declarative security.

The LaunchPermissions value has the accounts that will be allowed (or expressly denied) permission to launch the server. These accounts need to have the "Log on as Batch Job" privilege, and DCOMCnfg will add this to the accounts that you specify. The AccessPermissions value has the accounts that are allowed (or expressly denied) permission to access *all* components in the COM server. COM does not give any finer grain declarative security than this – once an account is given access in AccessPermissions then it will have access to any component unless you write code to prevent it.

When a request comes in to activate an object, and that object is implemented by an out of process server that isn't already running, the COM **Service Control Manager** (**SCM**) will launch that server under the account specified as the **identity** of the server. By default this will be set to Launching User, which means that the client's account will be used. This is the default for legacy reasons – before DCOM was released, COM servers expected to be launched in the Window Station of the client that requested the object. You should never leave this default when administrating a DCOM server, for reasons given later (in the section on Window Stations). When the server starts, it will register its class factory objects and wait for a request to be made. This request will come from the COM SCM, which will impersonate the account specified as the identity.

COM Call Context

When an object is accessed by an out of process client, COM will create a call context object. This is different to the context object that MTS creates. The call context object implements `IServerSecurity`, which the server can call to get information about the client that made the activation call, allowing it to impersonate that client.

In the following sections I will use this to show how, *in an EXE server*, you can apply per-component, per-interface and per-method access checks.

> *On Windows 2000 the call context object also implements* `ISecurityCallContext`, *which serves the role of* `ISecurityProperty` *and the security methods of* `IObjectContext`.

Component Level Access Checks

If you want to restrict component creation to certain accounts (a subset of those listed in `AccessPermissions`) you can do so by altering the class factory for those objects.

For example, in an ATL class you can use this macro in the `public` section of a class to specify a class factory other than the default ATL class:

```
// note only use this in an EXE server
#if !(defined(_WINDLL) | defined(_USRDLL))
DECLARE_CLASSFACTORY_EX(CRestrictedClassFactory)
#endif
```

and define a class like this:

```
class CRestrictedClassFactory
    : public CComClassFactory
{
public:
BEGIN_COM_MAP(CRestrictedClassFactory)
    COM_INTERFACE_ENTRY(IClassFactory)
END_COM_MAP()

    STDMETHOD(CreateInstance)(LPUNKNOWN pUnkOuter, REFIID riid, void** ppvObj)
    {
        CComPtr<IServerSecurity> pSvr;
        CoGetCallContext(__uuidof(pSvr), (void**)&pSvr);
        LPWSTR strClient;
        pSvr->QueryBlanket(NULL, NULL, NULL, NULL, NULL, (void**)&strClient,
                           NULL);
        if (!CheckClient(strClient))
        {
            // need this to release the server
            if (_Module.GetLockCount() == 0)
            {
                _Module.bActivity = true;
                SetEvent(_Module.hEventShutdown);
            }
```

```
        return E_ACCESSDENIED;
    }
    return CComClassFactory::CreateInstance(pUnkOuter, riid, ppvObj);
  }
private:
  bool CheckClient(LPWSTR wcsClient);
};
```

Here, the CheckClient() method will check that the account name passed as the parameter is permitted to create the object. This method uses the string returned in the 6th parameter of QueryBlanket(), which identifies the immediate client. This is dependent upon the authentication package being used, which for all practical purposes means either NTLM (NT4 and Windows 2000) or Kerberos (Windows 2000). In both cases this string is in the form Domain\User and is allocated by the system, so you shouldn't make any attempt to free it. If the client machine is not in a domain then NT treats it as a domain of one, giving the machine name in place of the domain. Your implementation of CheckClient() can thus check for domain/machine membership as well as individual accounts. It could be as simple as:

```
bool CRestrictedClassFactory::CheckClient(LPWSTR wcsClient)
{
  if (wcscmp(wcsClient, L"HOSTNAME\\Account") == 0)
    return true;
  else
    return false;
}
```

or it might involve more complicated logic.

One interesting point is the requirement to set the Win32 event when the call to CreateInstance() fails and the server is an EXE. The reason is that an ATL EXE process will only shut down when the last module lock count is released – _Module.Unlock() will check to see if the lock count falls to zero and will start the unload process by setting the hEventShutdown event. However, if the requested component is the first requested from the server then the lock count won't have changed from the initial value of zero it has when the server starts. This means that _Module.Unlock() won't be called, so the server will remain in memory.

Note that this code makes a check when a client requests that a component is created, and after this no further checks are performed. Therefore, if the client that obtains the component reference passes it to another process, there will be no access check to see whether that new client can access the component. However, because MTS security uses interception this isn't an issue.

Interface Level Access Checks

What if you have several interfaces on an object and want one of them to be accessible only to certain users? Well, you can put code in the object's QueryInterface() to check the client account. In ATL you can do this by specifying that a query for an interface should be handled by a special method, called ItfCheckAccess() in the code overleaf:

```
BEGIN_COM_MAP(CMyObject)
   COM_INTERFACE_ENTRY(IDispatch)
   COM_INTERFACE_ENTRY_FUNC(__uuidof(IMyObject),
                          offsetofclass(IMyObject, _ComMapClass),
                          ItfCheckAccess)
END_COM_MAP()
```

The `COM_INTERFACE_ENTRY_FUNC()` indicates that when a query is made for `IMyObject` then the `static` method `ItfCheckAccess()` is called. Since this is `static` it means that the method will not have access to instance data (`static` members don't have implicit access to the C++ `this` pointer). However, ATL will make sure that the `this` pointer is passed as a parameter to `ItfCheckAccess()`, but you still need to indicate the interface that should be returned if the check succeeds. This is given as the second parameter to the macro, which has the offset of the interface within the object's vtable.

```
static bool ItfCheckClient(LPWSTR strClient);

static HRESULT WINAPI ItfCheckAccess(void* pv, REFIID iid, void** ppvObject,
                                   DWORD dw)
{
   *ppvObject = 0;

   CComPtr<IServerSecurity> pSvr;
   CoGetCallContext(__uuidof(pSvr), (void**)&pSvr);
   LPWSTR strClient;
   pSvr->QueryBlanket(NULL, NULL, NULL, NULL, NULL, (void**)&strClient, NULL);
   if (!ItfCheckClient(strClient))
       return E_ACCESSDENIED;
   IUnknown* pUnk = (IUnknown*)((int)pv + dw);
   pUnk->AddRef();
   *ppvObject = pUnk;
   return S_OK;
}
```

ATL will pass the object's `this` pointer in `pv` and the second parameter of the `COM_INTERFACE_ENTRY_FUNC()` macro in `dw`. The interface being queried for is passed in `iid`, and if the function determines that the query should succeed, the interface pointer should be returned in `ppvObject`.

`ItfCheckClient()` (the implementation of which isn't shown here) checks the string to see if it contains an account that's allowed to use the interface. If so, `ItfCheckAccess()` obtains the interface pointer by the brute force method of using the offset passed in `dw` and the object pointer passed in `pv`. The interface pointer and status code returned by `ItfCheckAccess()` are passed almost directly back to the client.

Note that this code makes a check when a client requests an interface on the component. After this check no further checks are performed, so if the client that obtains the interface passes it to another process, there will be no access check to see if that new client can access the interface. Again, as MTS security uses interception this isn't an issue.

Method Level Access Checks

What about a finer grain level of access control? You may decide that within a particular interface there are some methods that certain accounts can access. You may even decide that within an individual method certain actions are restricted to particular accounts.

In the previous sections, the access checks could be hidden in class factory or the component class code, or even better, as a base class of the component class. However, in this case you have no option but to add access control code to the method itself:

```
HRESULT CMyObject::FormatDisk(LPWSTR strDisc)
{
    CComPtr<IServerSecurity> pSvr;
    CoGetCallContext(__uuidof(pSvr), (void**)&pSvr);
    LPWSTR strClient;
    pSvr->QueryBlanket(NULL, NULL, NULL, NULL, NULL, (void**)&strClient, NULL);
    if (!MethodCheckClient(strClient))
        return E_ACCESSDENIED;

    // OK, clean up that disk...
    return S_OK;
}
```

As you can see in the case of access checks in methods, the call must be made explicitly. Even so, you can see that using the existing COM call context object, you can apply per-server, per-component, per-interface and per-method access checks.

Client Impersonation

Before I finish this section I should also point out that `IServerSecurity` has two methods called `ImpersonateClient()` and `RevertToSelf()` (I love the name of this method because it implies schizophrenic behavior, which, of course, happens during impersonation). The first of these methods makes the current thread impersonate the calling client and use the client's access token. Under the NT security model this means that any access check required to access a secured object will be made against the impersonated account. Furthermore, if auditing is enabled for that secured object, then the impersonated account will be put in the audit record.

When the server thread has finished impersonating the client, it can revert back to its own access token by calling `RevertToSelf()`. This impersonation process is so useful that COM even provides two wrapper APIs to do it:

```
HRESULT CoImpersonateClient();
HRESULT CoRevertToSelf();
```

Once your thread is impersonating the client, it can find out information about the client as well as doing things on the client's behalf. This latter option may look appealing, but it does have drawbacks.

If, for example, you impersonate the client and open files using its access token, you have the administrative problem of making sure that all possible client accounts have the required access to the file. Although you can put these accounts in an **NT local group** (also called an **alias**) you still need to maintain that group. If the file is on another machine then the security policy for accessing that file will be held in a location that is remote to the component. From a maintenance point of view it's far better to put this security policy within the component.

Furthermore, if you open database connections as this client then you will have a separate connection for every client, thus defeating the whole purpose of connection pooling. I will return to this issue later in this chapter.

Aliases

When a thread impersonates a client, you can obtain its access token with a call to
OpenThreadToken():

```
BOOL OpenThreadToken(HANDLE ThreadHandle, DWORD DesiredAccess, BOOL OpenAsSelf,
                     PHANDLE TokenHandle);
```

The first parameter is the impersonating thread, and the desired access should be at least
TOKEN_QUERY. OpenAsSelf should usually be TRUE, because this function should be used thus:

```
HANDLE hToken;
CoImpersonateClient();
OpenThreadToken(GetCurrentThread(), TOKEN_QUERY, TRUE, &hToken);
CoRevertToSelf();
// use hToken to get information about the client
CloseHandle(hToken);
```

In other words, impersonation is only used to get the access token, and if OpenAsSelf is FALSE, the
token handle will be invalid after the call to CoRevertToSelf().

The server can then call GetTokenInformation() to get a whole gamut of information about the
client (for example, the SID of the user account, its privileges and its group memberships). Again, you
can check the user SID against a list of SIDs that are allowed access.

Methods like CheckClient(), ItfCheckClient(), and MethodCheckClient() (shown in
previous sections) have the problem that they require you to maintain a list of accounts that have
access (or conversely, those accounts that are denied access). This means that you must make this list
persistent somewhere, and provide some mechanism to edit the list. Account editors like this are not
trivial to implement, especially if they provide a list of all possible accounts, like the ACL editor in
DCOMCnfg.

> With NT4 service pack 5 you can install the Access Control Editor, which allows you to use the
> NT editor with a COM interface. However, although this is very convenient, you cannot
> guarantee that the editor will be present on all NT4 machines where your code may be run. You
> can use the Access Control Editor API on any Windows 2000 machine.

There is a reasonable alternative. Since the client access token can give access to group membership,
you can define NT local groups for accounts that are allowed to perform particular actions. Adding
accounts to these groups is as simple as running User Manager on a machine and specifying that
particular accounts are members of the required groups. Note however, that local groups cannot
contain other local groups. If your client account is a member of a particular alias, then it can
perform the action.

There is a big issue that needs to be addressed. The methods described above to make per-
component, per-interface and per-method access checks (CheckClient(), ItfCheckClient()
and MethodCheckClient()) must be integrated, both with each other and with COM security.
There is no point in saying that MethodCheckClient() should allow members of the
FormatUsers alias to call the FormatDisc() method if the members of this alias haven't been
given access to its supporting interface, to the component that implements this interface, or to the
server of this component in AccessPermissions.

I will leave it up to the reader to determine the best way to do this, but clearly the ACL editor must have details regarding the use of the particular entity being edited. As you'll see later, this is a significant feature of the role editor in the MTS Explorer.

Authentication Levels

When a client accesses a server, the client must determine whether the server is the correct one, so as to prevent a rogue server pretending to be the one the client requires. Similarly, a server must be able to determine that a client isn't an imposter. These checks are known as **authentication** and are performed by the RPC transport layer. COM security provides 7 levels of authentication:

- ❑ RPC_C_AUTHN_LEVEL_DEFAULT
- ❑ RPC_C_AUTHN_LEVEL_NONE
- ❑ RPC_C_AUTHN_LEVEL_CONNECT
- ❑ RPC_C_AUTHN_LEVEL_CALL
- ❑ RPC_C_AUTHN_LEVEL_PKT
- ❑ RPC_C_AUTHN_LEVEL_PKT_INTEGRITY
- ❑ RPC_C_AUTHN_LEVEL_PKT_PRIVACY

As the name suggests, RPC_C_AUTHN_LEVEL_NONE indicates that no authentication is performed. The next level up (the level to which RPC_C_AUTHN_LEVEL_DEFAULT is mapped on NT4) is RPC_C_AUTHN_LEVEL_CONNECT , which indicates that authentication only occurs when the client first connects to the object. RPC_C_AUTHN_LEVEL_CALL is used to specify that authentication occurs on every method call, and with RPC_C_AUTHN LEVEL_PKT authentication occurs with every packet sent as part of the COM call. The last two levels are used to pass a message digest, so that the server-side of RPC can check that the packet has not been violated during transmission, and encrypt the entire packet to prevent eavesdropping.

Remember that both client and server require authentication, so both need to specify an authentication level. As with most security values used with COM, there is a declarative and a programmatic way to do this. The declarative way (available on NT4 service pack 4 and later) is to use the General page for the server in DCOMCnfg, which has a list box with the authentication values. The selected value will then be written in the AuthenticationLevel named value in the server's AppID registry key.

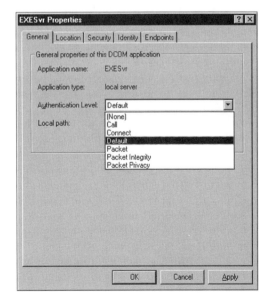

The client can also use a declarative authentication level by adding an `AuthenticationLevel` value to its `AppID` key. But a client is not a server, so how can it have an AppID?

If you have a remote client that doesn't use `COSERVERINFO` to specify a remote server name, it must use `RemoteServerName` in an AppID to indicate the remote machine's name or IP address. This is used by adding a CLSID key for each of the classes that the client will use. These keys will only contain an `AppID` named value with the AppID GUID. However, to use this AppID implies that the CLSID must be requested, implying in turn that COM is used – an authentication level must be set *before* COM is used, so how is the AppID specified? The clue is the name of the client process, which is added as a key to the `HKEY_CLASSES_ROOT\AppID` key. It has a named value called `AppID`, which specifies the AppID:

```
[HKEY_CLASSES_ROOT\AppID\MyClient.exe]
"AppID"="{1095D7D5-2ECA-11D3-899B-00104BDC35E0}"

[HKEY_CLASSES_ROOT\AppID\{1095D7D5-2ECA-11D3-899B-00104BDC35E0}]
@="My Server"
"RemoteServerName"="MyHost"
"AuthenticationLevel"=dword:00000005
```

The first entry indicates that all client code called `MyClient.exe` will have the *same* AppID as the server called `My Server` (which runs on `MyHost`). In fact, this AppID is only used on this machine (it isn't sent over the wire to `MyHost`), and on this machine it's used to group the 'components' in an application that have similar properties (in this case the authentication level and the remote host name). If another component is used by the same client, but runs on a different machine, it will need another AppID if declarative settings for the remote host name are used.

On the server machine, the server also needs an authentication level, which can be applied declaratively through `DCOMCnfg` (and ultimately in the registry) using two keys: one with the server name that resolves to the `AppID` key, the other with the `AppID` key. It is the `AppID` key that has the `AuthenticationLevel` named value.

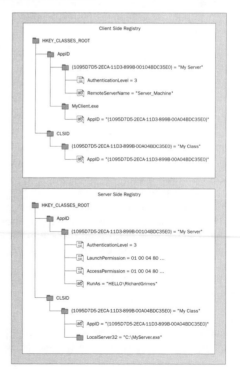

The server specifies the 'low water mark' level of authentication (that is, the lowest allowed level), and if the client specifies a different value this will only be used if it is higher than the server specified value. If either the client or the server doesn't specify an authentication level, the machine default will be used. This is specified using DCOMCnfg and is stored in the registry, with the default value RPC_C_AUTHN_LEVEL_CONNECT.

However, even if you specify an authentication level, you may find that COM will use a higher value. For example, with single machine calls the authentication level is always specified as RPC_C_AUTHN_LEVEL_PKT_PRIVACY. The reason for this is that all single machine COM calls are implicitly private, since calls will never go across the wire. However, this doesn't mean that a message digest or encryption will be used, as they aren't necessary.

Connectionless datagram protocols (like UDP) are promoted to at least RPC_C_AUTHN_LEVEL_PKT (except if the server and client specify RPC_C_AUTHN_LEVEL_NONE), because they are by their nature packet based. In addition, connection orientated protocols (like TCP) will promote RPC_C_AUTHN_LEVEL_CALL to RPC_C_AUTHN_LEVEL_PKT.

A further restriction that should be mentioned is that Win9x only uses TCP for DCOM calls (NT4 uses UDP by default, Windows 2000 uses TCP by default). A Win9x client can specify any authentication level, but a Win9x server can only use RPC_C_AUTHN_LEVEL_NONE or RPC_C_AUTHN_LEVEL_CONNECT.

As you can see, choosing an authentication level can seem complicated, but because COM will promote authentication levels where necessary you can be assured that the security of your calls will never be compromised. The only downside is that higher levels of authentication will reduce performance.

The client or server can specify an authentication level programmatically by calling CoInitializeSecurity() immediately after the first call to CoInitializeEx():

```
WINOLEAPI CoInitializeSecurity(
    PSECURITY_DESCRIPTOR pSecDesc,
    LONG cAuthSvc,
    SOLE_AUTHENTICATION_SERVICE* asAuthSvc,
    void* pReserved1,
    DWORD dwAuthnLevel,
    DWORD dwImpLevel,
    void* pAuthList,
    DWORD dwCapabilities,
    void* pReserved3);
```

The code can pass one of the authentication levels as the fifth parameter – it can also pass EOAC_APPID in the eighth (capabilities) parameter and pass a pointer to an AppID as the first parameter. Given that the declarative settings are used when CoInitializeSecurity() isn't called, it may seem strange to specify that CoInitializeSecurity() should use these settings. The reason is that this gives the code the option of using some predefined (and, I guess, tried and tested) settings. There is another reason, which has to do with surrogates, as you'll see in a later section.

The second and third parameters of CoInitializeSecurity() are used by servers to indicate which authentication services should be used. The third parameter gives the actual list, and the second parameter gives the number of items in the list. NT4 code typically uses -1 for this parameter, to indicate that COM should determine which service to use.

A server can determine the authentication level being used by calling
IServerSecurity::QueryBlanket() – it can use this to return an error if sensitive information is requested and the authentication level is too low. The client can also determine the authentication by querying the proxy for IClientSecurity and calling QueryBlanket(). If the authentication level being used isn't high enough, the client can increase it by calling SetBlanket() (or the wrapper function CoSetProxyBlanket()) on a proxy-by-proxy basis.

In a distributed application, the client and server can therefore indicate a low authentication level as the default, thus enabling low security objects to be accessed without the performance cost of high authentication. The client can access higher security objects by raising the authentication level that will be used on the particular proxy. The server, on the other hand, can check the authentication level being used on these higher security objects, and fail the call if the authentication level is not high enough. All in all, your distributed application can have as flexible an authentication policy as you want, as long as you're willing to write the necessary code.

Impersonation Levels

COM allows you to set the impersonation level that will be used. This is specified by the client because it indicates how much trust the client has in the server. The levels are:

❑   RPC_C_IMP_LEVEL_IDENTIFY

❑   RPC_C_IMP_LEVEL_IMPERSONATE

> *Windows 2000 also adds* RPC_C_IMP_LEVEL_DEFAULT *and*
> RPC_C_IMP_LEVEL_DELEGATE.

RPC_C_IMP_LEVEL_IDENTIFY indicates that the client is happy that the server can determine its identity by performing an access check. At this level the server can't impersonate the client to actually perform a task.

RPC_C_IMP_LEVEL_IMPERSONATE, on the other hand, indicates that the server can impersonate the client to carry out actions on the server's machine. This level of impersonation doesn't extend farther than the local machine, and is the highest level that can be used with NT LAN Man security. Kerberos, which is used by Windows 2000, is a truly distributed security provider, which means that (if the client account allows it and RPC_C_IMP_LEVEL_DELEGATE is specified) impersonation can extend to multiple machines.

It is perhaps best to use RPC_C_IMP_LEVEL_IDENTIFY, because this will mean that the server will have to perform actions under its own identity, so setting access control lists on secured objects will be a far simpler task. If your application uses RPC_C_IMP_LEVEL_IMPERSONATE and accesses a file (for example), then that file will have to have an ACL that has all possible client accounts, which may not be a trivial task.

If you want to specify the impersonation level then you should call `CoInitializeSecurity()` immediately after the first call to `CoInitializeEx()`, before you make any calls through COM (although it can be changed later on a per-proxy basis). If this isn't called then the machine default (usually set to `RPC_C_IMP_LEVEL_IDENTIFY`) is used. Impersonation levels cannot be applied declaratively on a per-client basis (unlike authentication level).

Anonymous Calls

You may decide that you want to allow anyone to access your objects. However, the default authentication level is at least `RPC_C_AUTHN_LEVEL_CONNECT`, so the security package being used will try to authenticate the user when the first connection is made. If this client account originates in a different domain (where no trust relationship is present), or isn't a member of a domain, authentication may not be possible and the call will fail. In this situation, both client and server should call `CoInitializeSecurity()`, specifying `RPC_C_AUTHN_LEVEL_NONE` to turn off security.

Identity and Window Stations

When a process accesses a secured resource (for example a file, a registry key, or another process) access checks are made to see if the process has the necessary rights. These access checks are carried out against the access token of the process. The question is, of course, where does this token come from?

The access token is derived from the logon session of the process that called `CreateProcess()`. A process can impersonate another account by calling `LogonUser()` before calling `CreateProcess()` if a different account is required. When you start a process through the Start menu, or through Windows Explorer, it's the shell (`Explorer.exe`) that makes the call to `CreateProcess()`. The shell uses the access token it was created with (just after the successful logon), which is created using the logon session created for the interactive user. In this situation, the access checks are made against *your* account (and group membership) as the interactive user.

What about COM servers though? When an EXE server (or a DLL launched in a surrogate) is started, it's the COM SCM that ultimately makes the call to `CreateProcess()`. The COM SCM is part of the operating system, and as such runs under the `LocalSystem` account. This account is very powerful on the local machine, but has no network privileges (on NT4) – both of these points are bad news for COM servers.

You don't want a COM server to be the 'super-user' on a machine, because these can be written by third parties, so you'll want to restrict what untrusted code can do. Similarly, you'll want the COM server to have network privileges so that it can access remote resources. Consequently, the COM SCM should start the COM server with another account, which has just enough privileges for what the server will do (including network privileges). Because the SCM knows neither what the server will want to do, nor the privileges that it requires, it is up to the administrator to determine what this account should be. This is the server's identity.

The identity is specified using `DCOMCnfg` and can take one of three values:

- ❑ The interactive user
- ❑ The launching user
- ❑ This user

(Or indeed, the LocalSystem account for a COM server that runs as an NT service.)

The launching user is the default, and as mentioned earlier, it should be avoided, since for each distinct user NT will have to create a logon session, which involves creating a **Window Station**.

A Window Station is a secured entity that ring-fences the desktop, mouse and keyboard, thus preventing a process running under a remote account from accessing the interactive desktop. If such access was not prevented then a remotely activated process could create or close down windows, pass messages to existing windows and generally be a pest. Instead, any windows action performed by the process will be performed in the Window Station for the remote account. Window Stations are expensive (about 500K), and by default NT4 restricts you to 16 (although this can be changed by tampering with the registry). Clearly, it is a priority to keep the number of Window Stations to a minimum, so make sure that you always choose an identity other than The launching user.

> *It is interesting to see that MTS, as you'll see later, only gives you the option of* The interactive user *and* This user *for the identity. You therefore don't have the potential disaster that* The launching user *presents. Note also that an MTS package can't run as the* LocalSystem *account.*

The This user option allows you to specify a local or domain account and a password. COM stores the password in a secure area of the registry, until the SCM needs it to impersonate the account to start the COM server. The advantage of using this option is that you can give the specified account just enough privileges to perform the actions that the server will do.

> *It is interesting to look at* HKEY_LOCAL_MACHINE\SECURITY\Policy\Secrets *key with* RegEdt32 *when logged on under an account that has Administrator's permissions. You will see a series of keys in the form* SCM:{AppID}, *where* AppID *is a GUID. These contain the password of the application's identity (which you can't view). The interesting aspect is that there are keys named* MTx:{AppID}, *where* AppID *is a package ID – these entries also have a corresponding SCM entry. It is not clear why MTX needs to cache security secrets, and why it can't use the SCM copy.*

When the server is created, it will remain in memory until the final reference on the last object it serves is released. If its class factory objects are registered with COM using REGCLS_MULTIPLEUSE, it means that when requests come in from other clients they will be handled by the same server instance, preventing new instances being launched (and more resources being used). The actions performed on behalf of these clients will be implemented by the identity account – if this involves connections to a database then just one connection will be made, which is a performance plus point.

The account used as the identity should have these properties:

❑ The user can't change the password

❑ The password doesn't expire

❑ It has the 'Logon as batch job' privilege

The first two are required because DCOMCnfg caches the password in the Secrets key mentioned earlier – if the password is changed externally, the cached value will become invalid. The third property is required because the COM SCM impersonates the account to do a batch logon.

As mentioned earlier, you should give this identity account just enough privileges. You shouldn't use the `Administrator` account as it will most likely have more privileges than required. In addition, you should regularly change the `Administrator`'s password since it's an obvious target for hackers.

Security and Surrogates

DLLs can only be used if they are loaded into a process. Any access checks performed on behalf of the DLL code will be performed using the host process's access token, and consequently DLL code doesn't have its own security settings. NT4 solved this problem by supplying a generic process, called `DllHost`, which acts as a surrogate for DLLs – that is, it will register the DLL's class factories as its own and behave as if the objects supplied by the DLLs are local server objects.

To specify that a DLL be loaded as part of a surrogate, the classes in the DLL must be registered with an `AppID` named value. In the corresponding `AppID` key there should be a named value called `DllSurrogate` – if this value is empty, the `DllHost` will be used, otherwise it gives a path to a process that will be used as the surrogate. Several DLLs can be loaded into the same instance of a surrogate, and to do so the `CLSID` keys of the classes should all have the same `AppID` value. This enables the DLLs to share common resources.

Once registered as using a surrogate, you can use `DCOMCnfg` to set declarative settings. COM will use the `LaunchPermissions` to determine whether the client account is allowed to launch the surrogate, and may also use the other settings (depending on the surrogate used). When a surrogate starts, it is passed the requested CLSID as a command line parameter. It can use this to determine the AppID that indicates the security settings to be used.

The system surrogate (`DllHost`) will call `CoInitializeSecurity()` when it starts, and pass a pointer to the AppID in the first parameter and `EOAC_APPID` in the capabilities parameter. This instructs COM to use the `AccessPermissions` and `AuthenticationLevel` values specified in the registry. If you want to specify values for `CoInitializeSecurity()` other than those in the registry, you will have to write your own surrogate.

COM Security Summary

COM provides two mechanisms with which to administer security: declarative and programmatic. The declarative way is fairly basic – you can specify an ACL, which determines the accounts that can launch (or conversely, those that are *not* allowed to launch) the server or surrogate, and you can specify an ACL of the accounts that are given (or denied) access to *all* components running in a server. Declarative access checks are very coarse grained. In addition, client and server code can specify the default authentication level used when accessing a component or receiving a call.

The programmatic methods are much richer. The basic, process level security settings can be set by calling `CoInitializeSecurity()`. This general-purpose function can be called by both the client and server, to specify the default authentication level used by the process. The client can also specify the impersonation level and indicate the identity of the client used when making out of process COM calls (if you don't want the client's access token to be used). The server can also use this to indicate the ACL for access to *all* components running in the server.

Furthermore, the client can query and change security settings on a per proxy basis, and a component can access the call context object associated with every call made into the process, to determine what the security settings are. The component is thus able to obtain information about the client account that made the call to the component. It can, if necessary, impersonate that client account to make access checks, or even to access secured resources as the client.

To get a finer grained control over security you have little choice but to write code. I have given an indication of the sort of code that you may write – as you can see, it is fairly straightforward to make per-component, per-interface, and per-method call access checks. The main problem occurs with ACL and account management, for which I didn't give a solution.

MTS Security

MTS security is based on COM security, but adds extra facilities that COM security doesn't support. As with COM security, this can be applied either declaratively or programmatically.

There are several aspects to MTS security:

❑   MTS makes access checks easy for VB.

❑   MTS simplifies access checks through MTS roles.

❑   The MTS Explorer makes administration simple and keeps ACLs consistent.

❑   Context objects retain information about the call chain.

The most obvious aspect is that you can apply per-package, per-component, and per-interface access checks without writing any code. I have shown that this is possible with non-MTS objects, but you've also seen that a fair amount of code is required. *It is significant that this code can't be written in Visual Basic.* MTS allows VB programmers to have a chance to perform fine grained access checks.

Rather than using the NT-specific concept of local groups, MTS uses **roles**. Roles define which users or local groups can perform particular tasks, and because they can contain NT local groups it offers one level of nesting (however, roles can't contain roles). Roles are defined by the developer, and when a package is exported the roles (and the component/interface role membership) are included in the .pak file (see Chapter 4). This means that, once installed on the deployment machine, the package only needs to have the roles filled with the appropriate accounts. If the package is developed on the same domain as that on which it will be deployed, then the accounts in the roles can also be exported, minimizing the work that the administrator needs to do.

Note that you can install MTS on Window 95 and Windows 98, but these operating systems have their roots in 16-bit Windows and are designed to run with as few resources as possible – consequently they don't have native security. DCOMCnfg gets round this problem for authentication and authorization checks on access to plain COM components (not *launch* permissions), by allowing you to nominate an NT peer machine, or a domain controller.

MTS on Win9x doesn't have *any* security. You don't specify an identity, because processes can't impersonate users – instead all packages are run under the 'interactive user' account, that is, the account you used to log on. Furthermore, there's no way to specify roles, so no authorization checks are made.

It seems odd to me that you can't use roles on Win9x, because COM servers can specify an ACL for AccessPermissions. *Consequently,* anyone *can access MTS components on a Win9x machine (subject to the default access permissions set for the machine). My opinion is that Win9x is pretty poor as a server of COM objects, and is next to useless for MTS components.*

The MTS Explorer

The MTS Explorer is used to manage roles through a straightforward user interface. Similar administration can be performed using the catalog API, so for completeness I will describe the Explorer's facilities and cross-reference them to the API (which you can access by #importing mtxadmin.dll).

Package Settings

Roles are defined as part of a package – you add new roles using the context menu of the **Roles** node under a package. Once you have created a new role, you will get a new node with the role name under the **Roles** node. To add accounts to the role you must open that node further to get the **Users** node. The context menu of this node will give you access to the NT ACL editor, which lists all the groups and accounts that you can add to the role. Roles have minimal properties – the property sheet merely gives the name, description and role ID (useful if you want to investigate the SecurityDescriptor of the role).

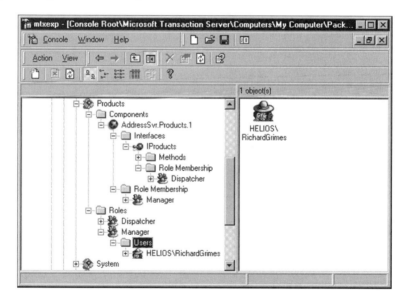

You can add roles to a package programmatically, by accessing the RolesInPackage collection and calling the Add() method. As I have mentioned before, the catalog API is a little odd in the way that it works. One such oddity is that when you call the Add() method, you don't pass any parameters about the item you want to add. Instead, the method returns an uninitialized object, which you should initialize with the properties that you want to set. Once you have finished adding items, you must tell the catalog to make the changes permanent by calling SaveChanges() on the collection.

As an example, here is some code to add a new role called `Clerks` to a package with the package ID of {9A950D6D-45C3-11D3-89B8-00104BDC35E0}, and then add the local group called `Clerks` to the role.

```
CComPtr<ICatalog> pCat;
pCat.CoCreateInstance(__uuidof(Catalog));

CComPtr<ICatalogCollection> pCol;
CComBSTR bstr = L"Packages";
pCat->GetCollection(bstr, reinterpret_cast<LPDISPATCH*>(&pCol));
pCol->Populate();
```

This first code gets access to the `Catalog` object – `CComPtr::CoCreateInstance()` takes a CLSID which is conveniently obtained using `__uuidof()` on the `Catalog` class generated by `#import`. The code then asks for the `Packages` collection and calls that pesky `Populate()` method, because we really do want to read the items in the collection.

```
// obtain the roles for this package
CComPtr<ICatalogCollection> pRoles;
bstr = L"RolesInPackage";
CComVariant var = L"{9A950D6D-45C3-11D3-89B8-00104BDC35E0}";
pCol->GetCollection(bstr, var, reinterpret_cast<LPDISPATCH*>(&pRoles));

// add an empty role
CComPtr<ICatalogObject> pRole;
pRoles->Add(reinterpret_cast<LPDISPATCH*>(&pRole));
// give the role a name of Clerks
bstr = L"Name";
var = L"Clerks";
pRole->put_Value(bstr, var);
long lNum;
pRoles->SaveChanges(&lNum);

// now add a group to the role
CComPtr<ICatalogCollection> pAccs;
bstr = L"UsersInRole";
// need to get the UsersInRole for this particular
// role, hence we need to specify a key
pRole->get_Key(&var);
pRoles->GetCollection(bstr, var, reinterpret_cast<LPDISPATCH*>(&pAccs));

// add the user by setting the User value
CComPtr<ICatalogObject> pAcc;
pAccs->Add(reinterpret_cast<LPDISPATCH*>(&pAcc));
bstr = L"User";
var = L"HELIOS\\Clerks";
pAcc->put_Value(bstr, var);
pAccs->SaveChanges(&lNum);
```

Each package has a Security property page with two items: a check box called Enable authorization checking and a dropdown list box called Authentication level for calls. If the check box isn't checked then no access checks are performed – this is the master switch for the entire package. The list box determines the authentication level used for access to all components. If you want a particular component to be accessed at a higher level, you have no choice but to programmatically check the security blanket through ISecverSecurity and reject calls at a lower level.

To enable authorization checking in a package you can access its SecurityEnabled property, and to change its authentication level you can change the value of the Authentication property. The following shows how to turn on authorization checking and use an authentication level of Connect:

```
// assume pCol is the Packages collection
CComPtr<IUnknown> pUnk;
pCol->get__NewEnum(&pUnk);
CComQIPtr<IEnumVARIANT> pEnum(pUnk);
CComVariant var;
// the only way to get the package is to
// search for it
while (pEnum->Next(1, &var, NULL) == S_OK)
{
    CComQIPtr<ICatalogObject> pObj(var.pdispVal);
    CComVariant varKey;
    pObj->get_Key(&varKey);
    // check to see if this is the package we want
    if (wcscmp(varKey.bstrVal, L"{9A950D6D-45C3-11D3-89B8-00104BDC35E0}") == 0)
    {
        // set the values
        CComBSTR bstr = L"SecurityEnabled";
        var = L"Y";
        pObj->put_Value(bstr, var);
        bstr = L"Authentication";
        var = 2L;
        pObj->put_Value(bstr, var);
        break;
    }
    var.Clear();
}
long lNum;
pCol->SaveChanges(&lNum);
```

Note that the Catalog API has the irritating property of only allowing you to access a package using the (arbitrary) package index in the collection, rather than accessing it via the package name or package ID. You have no choice but to iterate through all the items until you find the one that you require.

Component Settings

Components have a single property on their Security property page, a check box called <u>E</u>nable authorization checking, which determines whether access checks are performed when a client accesses a component.

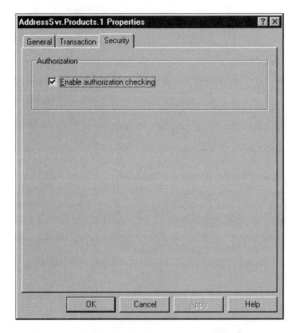

To set this programmatically, you need to access the component through the `ComponentsInPackage` collection and set its `SecurityEnabled` property to either "N" or "Y".

```
// Assume pCol is initialized to the
// Packages collection
CComPtr<ICatalogCollection> pComps;
CComBSTR bstr = L"ComponentsInPackage";
// Package to change
CComVariant var = L"{9A950D6D-45C3-11D3-89B8-00104BDC35E0}";
pCol->GetCollection(bstr, var, reinterpret_cast<LPDISPATCH*>(&pComps));
pComps->Populate();
```

This first code obtains the collection of components – you can then look for the component that you require:

```
CComPtr<IUnknown> pUnk;
pComps->get__NewEnum(&pUnk);
CComQIPtr<IEnumVARIANT> pEnum(pUnk);
var.Clear();
// enumerate all components
while (pEnum->Next(1, &var, NULL) == S_OK)
{
    CComQIPtr<ICatalogObject> pObj(var.pdispVal);
    CComVariant varKey;
    pObj->get_Key(&varKey);
    // component that we are interested in
    if (wcscmp(varKey.bstrVal, L"{1B5128F7-45B9-11D3-89B8-00104BDC35E0}") == 0)
    {
        // set the values
        CComBSTR bstr = L"SecurityEnabled";
        var = L"N";
        pObj->put_Value(bstr, var);
        var.Clear();
        break;
    }
}
long lNum;
pComps->SaveChanges(&lNum);
```

This code will turn off authorization checking on the component with CLSID {1B5128F7-45B9-11D3-89B8-00104BDC35E0} in the package {9A950D6D-45C3-11D3-89B8-00104BDC35E0} opened earlier.

Each component node under a package's **Components** node has a node called **Role Membership**. You can use the context menu of this node to add or remove roles. To add a new role via code you should query the RolesForPackageComponent collection for the IRoleAssociationUtil interface:

```
// Assume pCol is initialized to the
// Packages collection and pComps initialized to
// the ComponentsInPackage collection
CComPtr<ICatalogCollection> pComp;
bstr = L"RolesForPackageComponent";
var = L"{1B5128F7-45B9-11D3-89B8-00104BDC35E0}";
pComps->GetCollection(bstr, var, reinterpret_cast<LPDISPATCH*>(&pComp));
CComPtr<IRoleAssociationUtil> pUtil;
pComp->GetUtilInterface(reinterpret_cast<LPDISPATCH*>(&pUtil));
bstr = L"Clerks";
pUtil->AssociateRoleByName(bstr);
long lNum;
pComp->SaveChanges(&lNum);
```

This adds the Clerks role.

Interface Settings

Component interfaces do not have security properties. Once you indicate that authorization checks are made on a component, accesses to every interface are checked for role memberships.

The roles that can access the interface may be changed through the interface's **Role Membership** context menu. This allows you to add one of the package's roles to the interface role membership. It can also be carried out with the following code:

```
// assume pComps is initialized to the collection
// of components in a package
CComPtr<ICatalogCollection> pInts;
bstr = L"InterfacesForComponent";
// component to change
var = L"{1B5128F7-45B9-11D3-89B8-00104BDC35E0}";
pComps->GetCollection(bstr, var, reinterpret_cast<LPDISPATCH*>(&pInts));
pInts->Populate();

CComPtr<ICatalogCollection> pInt;
bstr = "RolesForPackageComponentInterface";
// the interface
var = L"{1B5128F6-45B9-11D3-89B8-00104BDC35E0}";
pInts->GetCollection(bstr, var, reinterpret_cast<LPDISPATCH*>(&pInt));
CComPtr<IRoleAssociationUtil> pUtil;
pInt->GetUtilInterface(reinterpret_cast<LPDISPATCH*>(&pUtil));
bstr = L"Clerks";
pUtil->AssociateRoleByName(bstr);
long lNum;
pInt->SaveChanges(&lNum);
```

Note that you have to get access to the collection for the component, then the collection of interfaces, then the roles for the interface before finally accessing the `IRoleAssociationUtil` interface.

Roles and ACLs

Roles simplify the security administration of an application, because the administrator is steered away from the less intuitive parts of NT security. Indeed, once a role has been populated with accounts and groups, the administrator doesn't see NT accounts at all, and all administration is performed using MTS roles. However, these are still based on NT security, so let's see how this is achieved.

When you create a package, MTS Explorer will also create an `AppID` entry for it. This won't have a default value, and so when you run `DCOMCnfg` you won't see it. Instead, the package will be present as one of the anonymous applications indicated only by their AppIDs. This is deliberate, because it is not intended that you administer the security aspects of a package through `DCOMCnfg`. MTS Explorer will also create a `CLSID` entry with the same GUID as the AppID. This exists to make sure that the AppID has at least one associated class (`DCOMCnfg` will complain otherwise).

When you add a component to a package, MTS Explorer will do its expected monkeying around with the `LocalServer32` and `InprocServer32` entries, to ensure that the `mtx.exe` surrogate is used to load the package. In addition, it adds an `AppID` entry for the component (using the same GUID as the CLSID of the component) and adds an `AppID` named value to the component's `CLSID` entry. Although the new AppID doesn't have a default value, the class that mentions it does, which means that the component is mentioned in `DCOMCnfg`.

Thus, you have an AppID for the package and an AppID for every component that you add to the package. MTS Explorer is trying to break COM's security rules by making security settings in the AppID registry key class-specific. However, this effort is in vain, because it isn't necessary.

The AppID created for the package merely has the identity of the package. However, the AppIDs created for the components have both the identity and a LaunchPermission value. This is logical, because when a client activates a component, COM uses the values in the component's CLSID key to launch the server. Since this CLSID key contains the component specific AppID, it indicates the identity and the ACL of accounts that can launch the surrogate. A package can contain many components, so the AppID entries for all components *must* be the same. If you administer the package through MTS Explorer then this will be the case.

The LaunchPermissions values are always set to SYSTEM and EveryOne, so anyone can launch the server. You should be aware of this if you are tempted to put some privileged or important code in the DllMain() of your component DLL, because you can't guarantee that a user launching a package is one that has been granted access to components in the package.

These AppIDs never have an AccessPermission value, implying that anyone granted permission through the default access permissions will have access to the components in the package. (By default, these default access permissions will be the interactive user and SYSTEM, but when IIS is installed it will add its accounts to the list.) The actual access checks are performed by the MTS Executive when the user makes the component activation request. If the user making the request is not in one of the specified roles then the MTS Executive will issue an access control failure.

As you have seen, roles are applied to two levels in a package: access to components and access to individual interfaces on a component. When the administrator adds an NT account to a role using the MTS Explorer, the account is added to an ACL maintained for that role, in a key in the catalog called SecurityDescriptor. Each role has a GUID, so when you specify that a component or an interface can be used by accounts in that role, the role's GUID is added as a key to the component's or interface's entry in the catalog. In addition, each component and interface has a named value called Authorization – an ACL containing all the accounts in those roles with access to the component or interface.

> *Note that roles* give *access – they don't* deny *access. This is in contrast to COM ACLs in AppIDs, where you can deny access to certain accounts. You must therefore be careful when adding local groups to roles. For example, if you add* EveryOne *to a role it means that everyone is included, unlike COM ACLs where you can exclude some accounts by denying access to them.*

Clearly, if a role has access to a component's interface, it also has access to the component itself (though not necessarily to other interfaces on this component). MTS Explorer takes account of this and will add the accounts in the role to the Authorization value for the component. As an aside, if you're going to apply role-based access checks on interfaces, it does imply that the components have more than one interface.

Interface role checking is an interesting concept, because the checks are done at the *interface* level, as opposed to the rest of the MTS attributes (for example transaction requirements), which are applied at the *component* level.

Roles and Distributed Applications

If your application involves multiple packages running on many different machines, you need to unify the security policy that you want to use across those machines. This is where roles really start to become useful. Clearly, if the packages are being run on machines on the same domain they could use domain accounts, so only one security authority would need to be used for authentication. Nevertheless, it is possible (though not desirable) to hard code domain accounts in the access checking code.

However, since roles are abstract, it is up to the administrator to determine what accounts are in which roles according to the roles' descriptions. A server can make a programmatic access check against a role and it won't matter what domain the caller is in. Contrast this to the plain COM situation, where `IServerSecurity::QueryBlanket()` will return a domain-account pair that the object will have to interpret and react to.

Note also that packages can pass component references to other packages, or indeed to the client. If these references are correctly created with `SafeRef()` or `IObjectContext::CreateInstance()` then the context object will be passed. This maintains security information about who created the object and who called it, which can be useful (as explained in a later section). However, remember that passing component references will increase the number of network round trips, which will have a detrimental affect on an application's performance.

Role Checking in Code

MTS will perform role checks when calls pass process boundaries, so when a client accesses a method of a component in a server package an access check will be performed. The implication is that if the component access is intra-process (package component to same-package component, or a call to a library package component), then *no* access checks will be performed automatically.

`IObjectContext` has two pertinent security methods, called `IsSecurityEnabled()` and `IsCallerInRole()`. `IsSecurityEnabled()` determines if the package is running in an environment that has security – in other words, it determines whether the package is running in a separate process to the client.

> *Note that* `IsSecurityEnabled()` *has nothing to do with the* `SecurityEnabled` *property of packages and components.* `SecurityEnabled` *determines if authorization checking is carried out, whereas* `IsSecurityEnabled()` *determines if authorization checking is possible at all.*

If a package is runs in a separate process to the client, the component can call `IsCallerInRole()` to see if the **direct caller** of the method is in the specified role. The direct caller will be discussed later.

Library Packages and Intra-Package calls

Since access checks are made when a process boundary is crossed, you must be especially careful about security with library packages – when these are used within a client, no access checks are made. Indeed, when you specify that a package is a library package, you won't be able to alter the package's `SecurityEnabled` property through the MTS Explorer.

However, this doesn't mean that you can't check role membership in your library code. An MTS server package can use components in a library package, so when a client makes a component method call, MTS will have determined the client's account – this will be available to the component code. Thus, if you know that your library package's components will be used in a server package, you can make role membership checks on the *server package's role*.

By the same token, when a component in a package accesses another component in the same package, no access checks will be made. This can be a problem, especially if one component performs some privileged operation, restricting it to particular roles, and a second component has access to the privileged component. If the second component allows access to different roles, and no access check is made when it calls the privileged component, low security roles may have access to the privileged component. For example:

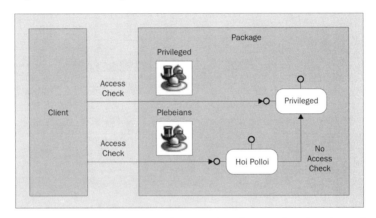

If you are likely to enconter this situation, make sure that the privileged code explicitly checks for role membership.

Other Security Issues

As mentioned earlier, if you want to allow anonymous access (or access from accounts in domains where you can't authenticate), then you must turn off security checks. To do this you should use the MTS Explorer (or the admin API) to set the authentication level *on a package* to **None**. When you do this, authorization checks will be disabled, so no role checking will be carried out. The client code should also turn off authentication.

MTS Security Properties

The context object for an MTS component implements ISecurityProperty – this interface allows you to obtain information about the caller and creator of the object:

```
interface ISecurityProperty : public IUnknown
{
    HRESULT GetDirectCreatorSID([out] PSID* pSID);
    HRESULT GetOriginalCreatorSID([out] PSID* pSID);
    HRESULT GetDirectCallerSID([out] PSID* pSID);
    HRESULT GetOriginalCallerSID([out] PSID* pSID);
    HRESULT ReleaseSID([in] PSID pSID);
};
```

The first four methods return a pointer to a SID, which is allocated by the context object. When you are finished with this SID you should tell the context object to release the resource by calling `ReleaseSID()`.

When you pass a component reference to another component, you actually pass a reference to the component's context object. (This is because you pass the reference returned from `SafeRef()` or `IObjectContext::CreateInstance()`.) The context keeps track of who created the component and who called it. The context does this when a process boundary is crossed – if `ObjectA` in server `PackageA` is created by a base client process `Client`, then calls `ObjectB` in the same package and `ObjectB` calls `GetDirectCallerSID()`, it will be returned the SID of the account used by `Client` and not the one used by `PackageA` (even though the direct call is from a component within the package).

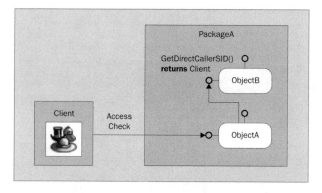

The original caller is the SID of the process that initiated the call chain. The original creator is usually the same as the original caller (because typically a process will create the reference and then make a call). However, if the process that creates the reference passes it to another process, which then makes a call on the object, the creator and caller will be different.

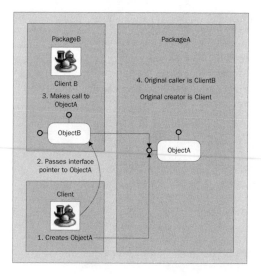

The direct caller and creator are the immediate process(es) that called (or created) the reference which caused the method to be called.

*MTS and COM security diverge with respect to the callers and creators, and also with the
original creator/caller SIDs. As you have seen, IS-erverSecurity::QueryBlanket()
will return the direct caller, but you can't get any other information about the call chain.*

You can use these methods to distinguish between various clients that may have references on the
same component, even when there may be several intermediate components in other packages that
have been used to give access to that component.

MTS and Identity

The identity of a package is important. As explained earlier, the identity determines the access token
used when accessing secured resources. Plain COM objects are allowed to run under the identity of
the launching user, but this isn't a good idea because of the large number of Window Stations that
could be created. MTS recognizes this and prevents you from using the option.

Another option is to make the identity a fixed account, but to actually access the resource while
impersonating the client. Impersonation is usually carried out using LogonUser() and
ImpersonateLoggedOnUser(). These require the calling account to have the **trusted computing
base** (**TCB**, or 'act as part of the operating system') privilege, which is generally too powerful for most
code. However, COM does allow you to impersonate the client account that called the object, by
calling CoImpersonateClient(). This is because the COM SCM has the required privileges and
knows who the client is. Both MTS and plain COM objects can do this to access secured resources. It
is not desirable that they do, though, as you will consequently need to configure the ACLs of those
secured resources with all possible client accounts, which may mean very large ACLs.

This problem can be alleviated by using NT local groups – a file, for example, could give access to a
group called FileAccessors, and add new users to it as they are created. This means that the
access check is performed at the resource rather than in the MTS component. If the resource is on a
remote machine this will involve a network call (which should, of course be avoided), and if the
access fails it's audited on that remote machine.

It's better to define an account that has the required privileges and use this for the identity. A plain
COM object can then impersonate the client to see if that client has been given permission to access
the resource, this being an object administration issue. MTS helps here with the
IsCallerInRole() context object method, which allows you to define roles that can access
resources and allocate the role membership with the MTS Explorer. So, for example, your package
could have a FileAccessors role and test for membership in this role before trying to access the
file.

The actual access to the resource is carried out using the account of the identity. This has the
advantage that you have just one account that you need to add to the secured resource's ACL, which
reduces administration. Since the access check is performed in the component, no unnecessary
network calls will be made, and the failure can be audited on the component's machine.

There is another good reason for using a single identity for accessing resources, which concerns
resource pooling. ODBC uses connection pooling and OLE DB uses resource pooling – the
difference between the two has been explained in Chapter 3. What the two have in common is that
the connections to a database are user-specific. If you make a connection to a database under UserA,
then use it and release it, the pooling mechanism will return the connection to the pool rather than
breaking the connection completely. If you ask for another connection to the database under UserA,
the pooled connection will be used. If you use another account, say UserB, then a new connection
will be made, thus defeating the purpose of pooling.

Finally, note that only one instance of a package can run at a time. If you have configured the identity to an account other then the interactive user and then wish to debug the package, you must first change the identity to the interactive user (and make sure that any running instances are shut down). Otherwise, the following error event will be generated:

Source:	Transaction Server
Severity:	Error
Category:	Executive
Event:	4155
Description:	The package could not be started under the debugger because it is configured to run as a different identity. CoRegisterClassObject (Package: MyPackage) (Microsoft Transaction Server Internals Information: File: d:\viper\src\runtime\mtxex\cpackage.cpp, Line: 1069)

Administrative Security Issues

The System package has two roles defined: Administrator and Reader. The former is required to change a package (or the configurations of any components in a package), while the latter is necessary to read information from a machine's catalog. By default, on a non-PDC machine, the System package doesn't have security enabled. This means that anyone can access MTS on your machine, and can read and alter its catalog – definitely not a good idea! The first thing you should do on a new machine is to add an appropriate account to the Administrator role (most likely the machine's administrator or members of the Administrators local group). After that, you should enable authorization checking on the System package. This is a risky thing to do, so MTS Explorer will warn you that there should be an appropriate account in the Administrators role. This will ensure that only privileged accounts can read or change the catalog, so you can then selectively add users to these roles, according to how that machine is used.

The MTS.ClientExport.1 and MTxCatEx.CatalogServer.1 components allow access to the Administrators role, which means that accounts in the Administrators role can call any interface on these objects. The Reader role is only given access to the following interfaces of the MTxCatEx.CatalogServer.1 component:

Interface	Description
ICatalogRead	Read catalog entries
ICatalogSession	Connect to the catalog
IGetClientEntries	Read information about a package

Furthermore, the System package has the identity of the interactive user, which means that if NT has booted up, but no user has logged on, you won't be able to access the catalog. The solution is simple – use the MTS Explorer to change the identity to an appropriate account.

Pulling and Pushing Components

As explained in an earlier chapter, when you pull or push components you don't actually *move* them. Instead, you move the required marshalling files (type libraries, proxy-stub DLLs) to a machine that is remote to the component. To be able to perform these actions, the account that you are using must be a member of the Administrators role of the System account on the remote machine. In addition, you must provide a share on the importing machine where the files will be copied. If you don't do this, the MTS Explorer will give you an error. Chapter 4 has more details.

MS DTC Security Issues

The MS DTC is designed to distribute transactions across the network, so the individual MS DTC instances must be able to communicate with each other. By default, MS DTCs run under the SYSTEM account (which doesn't have network privileges), and therefore use the Guest account to talk to other machines. The Guest account opens a security hole on an NT machine, so most machine administrators will disable it. This means that MS DTCs can no longer talk to each other, and transactions can't be distributed.

The solution to this problem is to use the NT Services control panel applet to change the account (through the MS DTC Startup options) to one that has network privileges.

Summary

Security, like many of MTS's functions, is often described as working by magic, being performed by MTS to prevent you from having to worry. In fact, much of the work that MTS does is plain NT and COM security programming. MTS intercepts calls, replaces your class factory with its own, and replaces the component with a context wrapper. I have illustrated that in this situation it's relatively simple to perform per-component and per-interface access checks.

When it comes to the management of ACLs, 'hand-rolled' access checks are found wanting. If an account is able to access the interface on a component, it stands to reason that it should be able to create the component. The ACL used to determine who can create a component should therefore contain the accounts that can access specified interfaces on the component.

MTS applies per-package, per-component and per-interface access checks through interception. This means that if interface pointers are passed between processes, the access checks can still be performed. The accounts that are given access are grouped together in roles – MTS manages the ACLs that these roles represent, to ensure that the role with access to an interface can make the original call to create the component.

Finally, COM allows a component to access the identity of the direct caller, whereas MTS can return the account of the original caller, as well as the direct and original creator.

7

MTS Debugging

Introduction

Debugging an MTS component isn't the same as debugging an in-proc COM component. When you debug an in-proc component you have to run a client EXE that uses the component. However, if the MTS component runs in a server package, it won't be loaded into your client process but into `mtx.exe`.

OK, so what about if you treat it as a local component, based in an EXE? Visual C++ gives you the option of RPC debugging. Once enabled, this means that when you activate a component and step into a component method then (usually) a second instance of Visual C++ will be created with the server – you can then step through the component code. The problem here is that the server is not your DLL, it's the MTX executive running under `mtx.exe`, so all you'll see is some machine code. Then there is the problem of security...

In fact, it's quite easy to debug MTS packages, as long as you make the correct changes to the package and load `mtx.exe` as the debugging executable.

The important point about MTS is that the components can be distributed around the network. This presents particular problems when you want to debug components and gather performance and trace information.

In this chapter I will explain how to utilize the tools provided by NT and Visual Studio to make debugging MTS applications easier.

Debugging MTS Packages

When you run a component installed in an MTS server package, you actually run it in an instance of `mtx.exe`. This means that you must debug `mtx.exe`, rather than your client application. Visual C++ gives you the option of using just-in-time debugging, enabled by going to the Tools | Options dialog and select the Debug tab. On this page you will find two check boxes: Just-in-time debugging and OLE RPC debugging. The first allows the debugger to be started if an error occurs in an application – if this isn't checked the second option won't be enabled.

When OLE RPC debugging is checked you'll be able to step into a COM method, even when the component is running in a different process on the same machine. This option was available with Visual C++ 5.0, but with that version you would find that when you stepped into a method the debugger in the new instance of VC would stop within the stub code – not in the method you wanted to debug. This wasn't too much of a problem, because all you had to do was step forward a few lines and you would get to your method.

Visual C++ 6.0 fixed that problem. Now when you debug a local server COM component (using just-in-time debugging) the new instance of the debugger will break at the start of the method that was stepped into, the behavior you would expect.

Unfortunately, this technique doesn't work when the COM component is on a different machine. The problem is that COM on the remote machine will start up Visual C++ with the following command line:

```
MSDEV.EXE -p %ld -e %ld
```

The first parameter here is the process ID for the debugger to attach to, the second is the handle of an event object (which the debugger should set to say that it has attached to the process being debugged). Both of these parameters are passed as decimals. If you try this with a remote object, `msdev.exe` will be launched on the remote machine, but you'll get the following dialog:

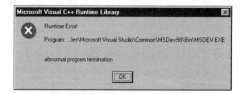

This doesn't appear to be a problem *per se* with `msdev.exe` as I've tried replacing it with a debugger I've written (using the `DebugActiveProcess()`/`WaitForDebugEvent()` API), and this also throws an exception (although it isn't consistent on which debug message that this occurs). Basically, this means that you can't perform just-in-time/OLE RPC debugging across machines.

Debugging MTX

If you use just-in-time debugging (as described above) to debug an MTS component running in a server package on the local machine, and the package uses the same identity as the interactive user, the debugger will be launched with `mtx.exe`. The debugger will stop in the executive – stepping through this to get to the component code is tedious. However, it's possible at this point to merely load the appropriate source file, set a breakpoint, and run to it.

Another way to do this is to debug the component *in situ*. In other words, start an instance mtx.exe with the component DLL and attach it to a debugger. If you do this in VC, you can set breakpoints in your component and start up mtx.exe under the debugger. MTS will register your component's 'class factory' with COM, so that when the client calls CoCreateInstance() (to ask COM to activate the component) the debugged version of mtx.exe will be used.

To do all of this, you need to use the Project | Settings dialog, specifying the full path to mtx.exe as the Executable for debug session, and the package ID for the Program arguments:

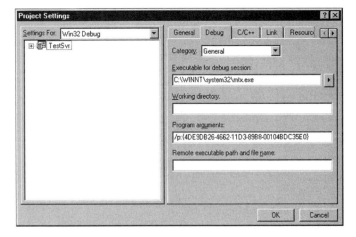

When you start a debug session, the IDE will start mtx.exe and pass the package ID. MTS will then register the 'class factories' of all the components.

> *In fact, MTS doesn't create your class factory objects and register them with a call to* CoRegisterClassObject() *like an EXE server would. Instead, it registers the wrapper class factory objects with COM, and on the first call to* IClassFactory::CreateInstance() mtx.exe *creates the appropriate class factory object in your DLL. That class factory object then survives as long as the package is loaded.*

If you find that when you start the debug session mtx.exe loads and then shuts down almost immediately, there are two possible problems:

❑   The command line could be invalid

❑   There may be an instance of the package already running

In the first case, check to make sure that the package ID is correct. In particular make sure that there are no spaces between the colon and the package ID.

You can use the package name instead of the package ID. However, I prefer to use the package ID as it's immutable. The package name is not so fixed, since you can change it using the package properties in MTS Explorer.

If the Program arguments you specify are invalid then you will get the error message 4131 in the event log. If there is already an instance of the package running, you will get the warning message 4101.

> *See Appendix A for a more detailed description of these (and other) messages.*

Remember that when you load `mtx.exe` in the VC IDE you must be running under the correct account. There are no problems if the package you are debugging has an identity of interactive user, but if it is configured to run under a specified account (which is most likely the case for production code) then your debugger will have to be running under that account. If this isn't the case then you will get error message 4155.

You can put trace messages in your code using `ATLTRACE()` and then monitor the output debug stream. I have found that the best tool to use is `DBMon`, which is supplied with the Platform SDK.

> *I have found that the otherwise excellent* `DebugView` *from* www.sysinternals.com *does not show* `ATLTRACE` *messages generated by processes running under accounts other than the interactive user. If I run* `DebugView` *under the package's Identity account (using Keith Brown's* `CmdAsUser` *from* www.develop.com/kbrown/security/samples.htm*) then the messages will be shown. However, this means that you have to know which account the package will run under, and different packages may run under different accounts.*

Another way to log messages is to use MTS custom events – `MtsSpy` can monitor such messages, as I'll show in the next section.

> *What about the NT event log? Don't use it for trace messages, as, by nature, trace messages are created in their hundreds and this will swamp the event log. Indeed, you may find that the capacity of the event log will be exceeded and earlier events will be over written – including important events logged by MTS and the rest of the system. The event log should be used to log diagnostic events during runtime, rather than trace messages at debug time.*

MtsSpy

The MTS Events API was introduced in Chapter 4. Basically there are two type libraries: `MtxGrp` and `MTSEvents`. The former gives access to all the running instances of `mtx.exe` through a component called `MtsGrp`, while the latter allows you to get information about running packages, access the event dispatcher and generate custom events. The `IMtsGrp` interface gives access to package components that implement `IConnectionPointContainer` and `IMtsEvents` (as well as `IDispatch` and `IUnknown`).

These components are event sources – the event interfaces (also described in Chapter 4) are in `EventCpts.h` installed by the MTS SDK. If you are interested in catching these events, you need to create a sink object and hook it up to the event source using `IConnectionPointContainer::FindConnectionPoint()` and `IConnectionPoint::Advise()`. I'll give an example of doing this later in the chapter.

If you are just interested in seeing what events are generated, you can use the `MtsSpy` utility. This is provided as a sample in the MTS SDK. In fact, the `MtsSpy` utility is a simple container for the `MtsSpyCtl` control, which has all of the required code to catch MTS events.

> *If you are interested,* `MtsSpy` *shows the basic code for writing a control container in ATL. The code appears to be an adapted ATL EXE server, but I wouldn't have written it like this. The reason is that it needs to provide container objects for the control handshake mechanism. These objects are only ever created in* `MtsSpy`*, but the code in the MTS SD registers these objects in the registry, which is overkill. Rather than creating this object with* `CoCreateInstance()`*, I would have used* `CComCoClass::CreateInstance()` *and made the* `CSpyCon` *class non-cocreatable.*

Since the main functionality is in the control, you can use it on a web page or VB form. Essentially, what the control does is provide sink objects for each of the event interfaces, and then allows you to choose which events you want to trace from a list of running packages.

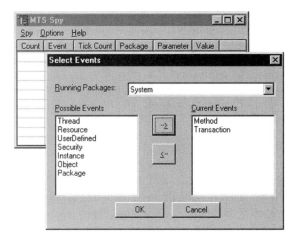

The screenshot shows a request for the method and transaction events on the System package, so two sink objects will be created – one will implement IMtsMethodEvents and another will implement IMtsTransactionEvents. If I then open the System node in an already running instance of the MTS Explorer I get the following events:

Event raised	Event Parameter
OnMethodCall	InitializeSession()
OnMethodReturn	InitializeSession()
OnMethodCall	GetServerInformation()
OnMethodReturn	GetServerInformation()
OnMethodCall	GetCollection()
OnMethodReturn	GetCollection()

The method calls are on ICatalogSession of the MTxCatEx.CatalogServer.1 component, except for the GetCollection() call which is on ICatalogRead.

Notice that calls that change the catalog aren't transactional under MTS 2.0. This is in contrast to Windows 2000, where changes to the catalog are transactional. To see this on Windows 2000, you must monitor the number of transactions in the Transaction Statistics rather then using MTSSpy. *Unlike NT4, where the* System *package is included in the list of packages returned by* MtsGrp, *under Windows 2000 it isn't. (Note that there is a different version of* MTSSpy *for use on Windows 2000, because these events are generated by the COM+ Event System and not connection points. More details are given in the next chapter.)*

The data presented in the grid can be saved to a file. However, no absolute times are given – the `perfCount` parameter (which every event method has) is effectively the value of `QueryPerformanceCounter()` (scaled to milliseconds using `QueryPerformanceFrequency()`). In other words, it's the number of milliseconds since the system started. This makes comparison of the MTS events with messages in the event log difficult to perform. However, if you're willing to write your own version of `MtsSpy`, you can use the time that the event was *received*, which should be close to the generation time (for an event on the same machine).

The other major problem with `MtsSpy` is that it only works on the local machine. This means that if you want to monitor the events in a distributed application, you must run a separate instance of `MtsSpy` on each machine. In this case, you should be aware that `QueryPerformanceCounter()` returns a figure that determines the time since each individual machine was started. The various machines used in a distributed application will have been started at different times, so you must determine the differences between values that are returned by those machines at exactly the same time in order to make timing comparisons. Also, you need to rush between machines to start the event logging. None of this is particularly convenient.

So, although `MtsSpy` is clearly useful on a local machine, it is of little use when several machines are involved. We can forgive the author of this tool, because it is, after all, just one example of how to sink MTS events. The solution to the problem of collecting events in a distributed environment is to use the **Visual Studio Analyzer**, as explained later in this chapter.

MTS Custom Events

To generate custom events you should create an instance of the `CoMTSLocater` component and call `GetEventDispatcher()` to get the event dispatcher for the current process.

> *Again, it is worth pointing out the spelling:* `CoMTSLocater` *and* `IMtsLocater`, *not* `CoMTSLocator` *and* `IMtsLocator`.

You can then query this for `IMtsEvents` and generate the user event by calling `PostEvent()`:

```
CComPtr<IMTSLocater> pLocator;
pLocator.CoCreateInstance(__uuidof(CoMTSLocater));
if (pLocator)
{
    CComPtr<IUnknown> pUnk;
    pLocator->GetEventDispatcher(&pUnk);
    if (pUnk)
    {
        CComQIPtr<IMtsEvents> pEventDispatcher = pUnk;
        CComBSTR bstr = L"CPingObj::DoSomething()";
        CComVariant var = bstr;
        pEventDispatcher->PostEvent(&var);
    }
}
```

This gives the following trace in `MtsSpy`:

Of course, your code will have much more descriptive messages, but you can see the mechanism.

Performance Monitor

Strange as it may seem, the option pack doesn't install a generic performance monitor DLL for MTS. Instead, you get performance monitor DLLs for ASP and IIS. The ASP performance monitor 'object' supports (amongst others) the following performance monitor counters:

❑ Transactions Aborted

❑ Transactions Committed

❑ Transactions Pending

❑ Transactions Total

❑ Transactions/Sec

So where is ASP getting this information from, and why can't we see the same information for MTS in general?

The first four counters are those shown in the transaction statistics node in MTS Explorer (called Aborted, Committed, Active, and Total respectively), but this information comes from the MS DTC. However, you can get similar information from MTS events. In terms of transactions you can do this by implementing an object to sink calls from `IMtsTransactionEvents`, and use the events to update five counters:

Counter	Incremented	Decremented
Transaction pending	OnTransactionStart	OnTransactionPrepared, OnTransactionAborted
Transaction committed	OnTransactionPrepared	
Transaction aborted	OnTransactionAborted	
Transaction total	OnTransactionStart	

The fifth counter, Transactions/Sec, could be updated by calculating the time between `OnTransactionStart()` and the associated call to `OnTransactionPrepared()` or `OnTransactionAborted()`, which is possible because these methods are passed the transaction GUID.

In this section I will show you how to develop a performance monitor DLL that shows the number of components and method calls in a package. First though, a few words about the performance monitor.

PerfMon Architecture

The Performance Monitor appeared in the first versions of NT, and as a consequence of this the API is rather arcane. The architects of PerfMon tried to make it extensible, and in the absence of COM they had to come up with a mechanism that allowed developers to write a DLL with performance monitoring code that PerfMon could load and call. If PerfMon were to be written afresh today it would call components that implemented some standard interface. Instead, it requires that you export a function from your DLL and register its name in the registry.

> *I do understand the situation that the PerfMon architects were in and shouldn't comment adversely on their solution – in pre-COM days, I designed and built a process that was extended with DLLs, using a similar mechanism to theirs.*

It works like this – each DLL that can provide performance data should export three functions. The names are not important, as they will be registered in the registry, so I will call then _Open(), _Close() and _Collect(). _Open() is called by PerfMon when it loads the DLL, and _Close() is called when it the DLL is unloaded. _Collect() is called to do two things: to get a list of the objects and counters for which performance data is available, and to get the actual performance data.

How does PerfMon know which DLLs to load? It trawls through every key in

```
HKEY_LOCAL_MACHINE\System\CurrentControlSet\Services
```

looking for a sub-key called Performance. If that is available, it will have a value called Library, which has the path to the performance data DLL. For example, if you look in

```
HKEY_LOCAL_MACHINE\System\CurrentControlSet\Services\Tcpip\Performance
```

you'll find the string value called Library with the value of PerfCtrs.dll.

> *Warning! Even though this is the path to the DLL, don't use an absolute path. The code that reads this value doesn't use a buffer of size MAX_PATH (as all conscientious developers do), so absolute paths more than a few folders deep will cause a buffer overrun and PerfMon will throw an exception. The convention is to place the DLL in a folder in the PATH environment variable, preferably in %systemroot%\System32. You should therefore register just the DLL name and PerfMon will use the PATH environment variable when attempting to locate it.*

PerfMon will need to know the names of the exported functions, so it looks in the Performance key for values called Open, Close and Collect containing names for those functions.

When you add a counter to a PerfMon trace you have to give three pieces of information: **object**, **instance**, and **counter**. For example, if you want to monitor processor counters, the instance is the particular processor that you are interested in (on uniprocessor machines there will only be one instance). If you are interested in performance data for a process, the instance is the process you are interested in. (Note that not every object will have an instance.)

The object is a category of counters, so if you are interested in processor statistics, Processor is the object. The actual statistics are called counters, so for processors this could be Interrupts/sec, % user Time, or one of many others. When you add a counter to a PerfMon trace you first select the object, and the instances that implement the object will then be shown (if available). Finally, you can select the counters in the object that you are interested in. For example, if you select Process, then RPCSS, and finally Handle Count, you will monitor the number of handles opened by the RPC subsystem.

The performance data DLL is loaded into PerfMon, but this DLL must be able to access performance data generated by your application, which will (usually) be a different process. This implies that some inter-process communication mechanism will be used – how you do this is up to you, but one solution is to place the data in a memory mapped file and control access to it with an event kernel object.

To read the data, PerfMon calls your process's _Collect() function:

```
DWORD WINAPI _Collect(LPWSTR lpwszValue, LPVOID* lppData, LPDWORD lpcbBytes,
                      LPDWORD lpcObjectTypes);
```

The first parameter is a string that indicates what objects PerfMon wants, the second is a buffer it has allocated, and the third is the size of that buffer. PerfMon expects _Collect() to fill the buffer with the performance data and increment the lppData pointer to point to the free space following where you have written the data. In addition, you must return the number of bytes written via lpcbBytes, and the number of objects through lpcObjectTypes. PerfMon works this way because it will call the _Collect() method successively for each performance DLL being used. Clearly, if the buffer passed by PerfMon is too small, you can indicate this to PerfMon.

PerfMon will also call _Collect() on your DLL the first time it is loaded, as it will want to know all the objects and instances that your DLL supports. At this stage, PerfMon isn't interested in actual performance data, but it does no harm to return it. Since PerfMon doesn't know the objects that your DLL supports, it will pass the string "Global" as the first parameter, telling you to return information about all objects.

The data you return is quite complicated, so I won't go into details here – it's documented in the MSDN and in the MSJ article that I reference in the example section below. Basically, your DLL determines (at runtime) the instances of the various objects that have been requested, as well as every object the instance supports, and every counter provided by each of the objects. In addition, this data also contains an indication of the names of the instances, objects, and counters.

The instance name depends on the type of performance data returned, so the actual name is returned to PerfMon. In the case of the objects and counters, the names (and descriptions) are saved in the registry, indexed by a number. It's this index that is returned to PerfMon. The management of these strings and indexes is a little complicated. The Performance key for the DLL usually has four more keys, in addition to those already mentioned (two each for the names and help strings): First Counter, Last Counter, First Help and Last Help. These list the first and last values that the DLL will use.

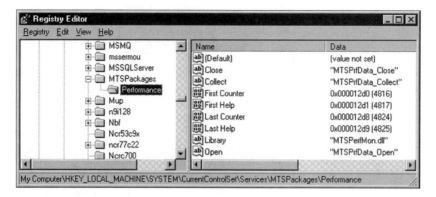

In addition, the actual strings are stored in a key called

```
HKEY_LOCAL_MACHINE\Software\Microsoft\Windows NT\CurrentVersion\PerfLib
```

This key contains Last Counter and Last Help values, which allow you to determine the last index used by *any* performance DLL on the system. It also has a daughter key for each locale supported on the local machine, named using the code page. Within these are two multi-string values called Counter and Help. This is where the object and counter names are held.

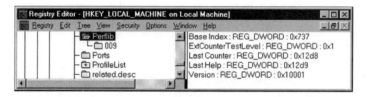

Note that in the previous screen shot I have used RegEdt32 and not RegEdit. The reason is that the latter will not show REG_MULTI_SZ values.

Despite its name, Counter has name-index pairs for both objects and counters, and PerfMon uses this key and the index returned from the _Collect() function to obtain the names it uses in the **Add to Chart** dialog.

Clearly you have quite a lot of registration to perform. At install time, you have to add the values for the exported methods and the library name. You must also read the current maximum counter and help indexes, increment this to reflect how many objects and counters you supply, and then update your own key. Finally, you need to update the Counter and Help keys with your strings.

There are two ways to do this. Either you can change all these registry keys yourself, or you can use the LoadPerf API (LoadPerf.h and LoadPerf.lib). This library has two methods called LoadPerfCounterTextStrings() and UnloadPerfCounterTextStrings(), which will make all of these changes based on a script that you supply. These methods are called by the lodctr and unlodctr utilities provided with NT. The Platform SDK has an example that uses an installation script with this API, and more details about using them can be found by doing a search in the Platform SDK Library.

Example

For this example I started writing the DLL from scratch. I developed my own facilities to call `LoadPerfCounterTextStrings()` and `UnloadPerfCounterTextStrings()` on scripts generated from module resources, and with object and counter names and help held in a map. That worked fine, but then I looked at the data returned from `_Collect()` and decided to give up. The problem was that there is a lot of buffer manipulation, calculations of sizes, and calculations of offsets that you have to do, and for a generic solution you must support many different counter types. While I could have developed a generic library to do all this, I decided that since this is an MTS book (not a performance monitor book), it would be better to use a prebuilt and freely available library. I decided to use the `PrfData` library written by Jeffrey Richter.

> *This library is described in the August 1998 MSJ and the code is available from the MSJ web site at* www.microsoft.com/msj.

I won't go into great details about this code – you can read it yourself. The DLL needs to do two things:

❏   It must provide the functions that `PerfMon` expects and register the required values.

❏   It should create sink objects and hook them up to the event generators in MTS.

The latter requirement implies that the DLL is a COM server. However, the objects will not be cocreatable, that is, they aren't created via `CoCreateInstance()` and are thus *not* registered. For convenience, though, I decided to use the ATL AppWizard to generate a DLL project. This is so that I can use the Object Wizard to create the sink component code.

Creating the Project

The starting point for the project is a DLL created by the ATL AppWizard, called `MTSPerfMon`. The generated code will need to be modified – a lot of the Wizard-generated code will need to be removed. First off, since the project will use standard interfaces, the IDL doesn't need to define any interfaces, indeed, it shouldn't be compiled at all. In FileView, select the IDL file and select the Settings context menu item. From the General page, click on Exclude file from build.

To use Jeff Richter's library you need to copy the following files to your project directory:

❏   `PrfData.h`
❏   `PrfData.cpp`
❏   `Optex.h`
❏   `Optex.cpp`
❏   `RegSettings.h`

and add them to the appropriate folders in FileView. For both of the `.cpp` files, use the Settings dialog to remove precompiled header support.

Next add a header file called `CmnHdr.h`. This is required by the `PrfData` code, but I have edited it slightly, so that only those macros actually used are provided:

```
// macros defined by Jeff Richter

// Assert in debug builds, but don't remove the code in retail builds.
#ifdef _DEBUG
#define chVERIFY(x) chASSERT(x)
#else
#define chVERIFY(x) (x)
#endif


// This macro returns TRUE if a number is between two others
#define chINRANGE(low, Num, High) \
    (((low) <= (Num)) && ((Num) <= (High)))
#define chFAIL(szMSG) { \
        MessageBox(GetActiveWindow(), szMSG, \
            __TEXT("Assertion Failed"), MB_OK | MB_ICONERROR); \
        DebugBreak(); \
    }

// Put up an assertion failure message box.
#define chASSERTFAIL(file,line,expr) { \
        TCHAR sz[128]; \
        wsprintf(sz, __TEXT("File %hs, line %d : %hs"), file, line, expr); \
        chFAIL(sz); \
    }


// Put up a message box if an assertion fails in a debug build.
#ifdef _DEBUG
#define chASSERT(x) \
    if (!(x)) chASSERTFAIL(__FILE__, __LINE__, #x)
#else
#define chASSERT(x)
#endif
```

Now add the following headers to `MTSPerfMon.cpp`:

```
#include <initguid.h>
#include "CmnHdr.h"
#include "PrfData.h"
```

You should also remove the `#includes` for `MTSPerfMon.h` and `MTSPerfMon_i.c`, because the IDL file is not compiled. As you'll see in a moment, the macros in `PrfData.h` used with the performance data maps that will be added to the project will define a global variable called `g_PrfData` (of type `CPrfData`). This gives access to the main code of Jeff's library.

The Application Wizard will also add `DllRegisterServer()` and `DllUnregisterServer()` to the project, but I don't want the code that performs object registration (because the objects won't be registered!) so delete that code. However, I will use these functions to do the performance DLL registration. The `PrfData` library has two static methods to do this (called `Install()` and `Uninstall()`, accessed through `g_PrfData`):

```
STDAPI DllRegisterServer(void)
{
    g_PrfData.Install(L"MTSPerfMon.dll");
    // adjust the registry to call our methods
    AdjustRegistry(L"MTSPackages");
    return S_OK;
}


STDAPI DllUnregisterServer(void)
{
    g_PrfData.Uninstall();
    return S_OK;
}
```

There are several comments that need to be made. Firstly, Install() is passed the path to the DLL, and since this should be as short as possible I assume that it is within the PATH environment variable. The other thing to notice is the call to AdjustRegistry(). There is a problem with PrfData in that it does too much work for you. In particular, I want to write my own version of the _Open(), _Close() and _Collect() functions to create the sink objects and do clean up. PrfData provides these as static members and registers them in Install().

On initial viewing, I thought I could derive a new class from CPrfData to call my versions of these exported functions, but this was a problem because the library works by providing object and counter data in a map. This map creates a single instance of the CPrfData class, so using my derived class would mean changing the map macros, which I was reluctant to do.

Instead, I decided it would be simpler to provide my own exported functions and change the registry to point to them, rather than using the functions that PrfData provides:

```
// Change the registry to call our methods...
void AdjustRegistry(LPCWSTR pszAppName)
{
    WCHAR szSubkey[100];
    CRegKey hKey;
    wsprintfW(szSubkey, L"SYSTEM\\CurrentControlSet\\Services\\"
              L"%s\\Performance", pszAppName);
    hKey.Open(HKEY_LOCAL_MACHINE, szSubkey);
    hKey.SetValue(L"MTSPrfData_Open", L"Open");
    hKey.SetValue(L"MTSPrfData_Close", L"Close");
    hKey.SetValue(L"MTSPrfData_Collect", L"Collect");
}


DWORD WINAPI MTSPrfData_Open(LPWSTR lpDevNames)
{
    return ERROR_SUCCESS;
}


DWORD WINAPI MTSPrfData_Close(void)
{
    return ERROR_SUCCESS;
}
```

```
DWORD WINAPI MTSPrfData_Collect(LPWSTR lpValueName,
   LPVOID* lppData, LPDWORD lpcbTotalBytes,
   LPDWORD lpNumObjectTypes)
{
   return CPrfData::Collect(lpValueName, (PBYTE*) lppData,
                            lpcbTotalBytes,
                            lpNumObjectTypes);
}
```

These need to be exported, and to ensure that the correct (unmangled) names are exported I have opted to mention them in the .def file, so edit MTSPerfMon.def to look like this:

```
LIBRARY        "MTSPerfMon.DLL"
EXPORTS
   MTSPrfData_Close    @1
   MTSPrfData_Collect  @2
   MTSPrfData_Open     @3
   DllRegisterServer   @4 PRIVATE
   DllUnregisterServer @5 PRIVATE
```

Notice that since this project is *not* a COM server, DllCanUnloadNow() and DllGetClassObject() aren't needed, so you can remove those functions from both the .def file and from MTSPerfMon.cpp. Additionally, remove the type library from the project – from the View menu, Resource Includes remove the 1 TYPELIB "MTSPerfMon.tlb" line from the Compile-time directives box. In addition, change DllMain() so that it does not use the LIBID:

```
BOOL WINAPI DllMain(HINSTANCE hInstance, DWORD dwReason, LPVOID /*lpReserved*/)
{
   if (dwReason == DLL_PROCESS_ATTACH)
   {
      _Module.Init(ObjectMap, hInstance);
      DisableThreadLibraryCalls(hInstance);
   }
   else if (dwReason == DLL_PROCESS_DETACH)
      _Module.Term();
   return TRUE;    // ok
}
```

The PrfData library assumes that your code is UNICODE, so through the Build | Configurations dialog you should remove the ANSI configurations.

Next, select the Project | Settings (for All Configurations) to define the following preprocessor symbol:

PRFDATA_COLLECT_SUPPORTED

This is needed to specify that this code will collect the performance data rather than generating it. While it is true that the DLL *generates* performance data, if this symbol isn't defined then the collection code will be compiled away by the preprocessor, and, of course, your DLL will do both. In addition, add the UNICODE symbol – the _UNICODE symbol will have already been defined by the ATL AppWizard, but isn't sufficient for the PrfData library.

While in the project settings dialog, remove the registration from the Custom Build step for the project (from the Custom Build tab, remove all entries from the Commands and Outputs boxes).

Sink Objects

The next step is to create three sink objects – these are Simple Objects with custom interfaces. Dual interfaces aren't used because you don't want to define any new interfaces, but instead use standard ones. You will therefore have to remove the Object Wizard-generated interfaces, and it's simpler to do this if they are custom. For each class, you must replace the Wizard-generated interface with an event interface from EventCpts.h. The short names and event interfaces are:

Short Name	Event Interface
MTSPackages	IMtsPackageEvents
MTSComponentInstances	IMtsInstanceEvents
MTSMethodCalls	IMtsMethodEvents

For example, CMTSPackages should be changed like so:

```
// MTSPackages.h : Declaration of the CMTSPackages

#ifndef __MTSPACKAGES_H_
#define __MTSPACKAGES_H_

#include <EventCpts.h>

/////////////////////////////////////////////////////////////////
// CMTSPackages
class ATL_NO_VTABLE CMTSPackages :
    public CComObjectRootEx<CComSingleThreadModel>,
    public IMtsPackageEvents
{
public:
    CMTSPackages()
    {
    }

DECLARE_NO_REGISTRY()
DECLARE_PROTECT_FINAL_CONSTRUCT()

BEGIN_COM_MAP(CMTSPackages)
    COM_INTERFACE_ENTRY(IMtsPackageEvents)
END_COM_MAP()

// IMtsPackageEvents
public:
    STDMETHOD(OnPackageActivation)(LONGLONG perfCount,
                                   REFGUID guidPackage,
                                   LPCOLESTR sPackageName);
    STDMETHOD(OnPackageShutdown)(LONGLONG perfCount,
                                 REFGUID guidPackage,
                                 LPCOLESTR sPackageName);
};
```

Notice how DECLARE_NO_REGISTRY() is used, the #include for resource.h is removed, and CComCoClass<> is no longer a base class (because the object is not cocreatable). Since no registration is performed, you can delete the Wizard-generated .rgs files by removing them from the **Resource Files** folder in FileView, and remove the associated resource from ResourceView. To be thorough, you can remove the coclass and interface from the IDL file, and the class entry from the object map (although both of these actions aren't strictly necessary, you must have at least an empty object map in the IDL file, because the Object Wizard will expect it to be there). Since the interface is a standard interface, you must copy the method prototypes from EventCpts.h.

The other two classes are similar, except that they have a public data member called m_inst, the purpose of which will be apparent later:

```
CPrfData::INSTID m_inst;
```

You must also copy the prototypes for the appropriate interfaces of the components from EventCpts.h.

The DLL will track performance data for two things: when components are created and destroyed, and when methods are called on those components. The MTSComponentInstances object tracks the creation and destruction of components in a particular package, and the MTSMethodCalls object tracks the methods that are currently being called.

For every package you select in the **Instance** box, an instance of these objects will be created in the PerfMon **Add to Chart** dialog. What happens though if one of these packages shuts down – what will the sink objects then be connected to? The answer is nothing, so to make sure that the appropriate sink object is destroyed when the package shuts down, the DLL creates an instance of MTSPackages. The OnPackageShutdown() method on this object is called when the package is about to go away, and the code can use this to break the connection.

Performance Data Code

Next you must set up PrfData to track our performance data. To do this you need to create a header file for the counter and object IDs. I have called this PerfCounters.h:

```
#include "PrfData.h"
#define PACKAGE_NAME_LEN    50
#define PACKAGE_MAX         20

PRFDATA_DEFINE_OBJECT(MTSPACKAGES, 100)
PRFDATA_DEFINE_COUNTER(TOTALCOMPS, 101)
PRFDATA_DEFINE_COUNTER(TOTALCALLS, 102)
PRFDATA_DEFINE_COUNTER(CURRENTCOMPS, 103)
PRFDATA_DEFINE_COUNTER(CURRENTCALLS, 104)
```

The macros merely define the symbols. The defines determine the maximum number of characters in a package name – remember that the instance name is passed back to PerfMon by _Collect, so space needs to be allocated for that string. The package name is used as an instance name.

One restriction on PrfData is that at compile time you must specify the maximum number of instances – this is the purpose of PACKAGE_MAX. (I am assuming that there will always be less than 20 packages running at a time.)

Add the header to `MtsPerfMon.cpp`:

```
#include "CmnHdr.h"
#include "PrfData.h"
#include "PerfCounters.h"
```

The information about the performance data is placed in a map, which I have put after the (empty) object map in `MTSPerfMon.cpp`:

```
BEGIN_OBJECT_MAP(ObjectMap)
END_OBJECT_MAP()

PRFDATA_MAP_BEGIN()
    PRFDATA_MAP_OBJ(MTSPACKAGES, L"MTS Packages",
        L"All currently running MTS packages",
        PERF_DETAIL_NOVICE, TOTALCALLS, PACKAGE_MAX,
        PACKAGE_NAME_LEN)
    PRFDATA_MAP_CTR(TOTALCOMPS,  L"Total Components",
        L"The total number of components in the package",
        PERF_DETAIL_NOVICE, 0, PERF_COUNTER_RAWCOUNT)
    PRFDATA_MAP_CTR(TOTALCALLS,  L"Total calls",
        L"The total number of calls made to package components",
        PERF_DETAIL_NOVICE, 0, PERF_COUNTER_RAWCOUNT)
    PRFDATA_MAP_CTR(CURRENTCOMPS,  L"Current Components",
        L"Current number of components in the package",
        PERF_DETAIL_NOVICE, 0, PERF_COUNTER_RAWCOUNT)
    PRFDATA_MAP_CTR(CURRENTCALLS,  L"Current calls",
        L"Current number of calls made to package components",
        PERF_DETAIL_NOVICE, 0, PERF_COUNTER_RAWCOUNT)
PRFDATA_MAP_END("MTSPackages")
```

There is just one object (called `MTS Packages`), and there are a maximum of `PACKAGE_MAX` instances (each with a name of `PACKAGE_NAME_LEN` or less characters). The default counter used is `Total Calls`.

Next I define the four counters associated with this object – they are all `PERF_COUNTER_RAWCOUNT`, which means they are 32-bit values. These counters give the total number of components ever created in the package, the number of active components, the total number of calls ever made in the package, and the count of calls currently active.

To keep track of all these counters, instances and sink objects, I also define some global variables in the main `.cpp` file after the performance data map:

```
CPrfData::INSTID g_Packs[PACKAGE_MAX];
IConnectionPoint* g_pCP[PACKAGE_MAX*3];
DWORD g_Cookies[PACKAGE_MAX*3];
GUID g_Guids[PACKAGE_MAX];
HANDLE g_hEvent = NULL;
HANDLE g_hThread = NULL;
DWORD g_dwThreadID = 0;
CComAutoCriticalSection g_arrCS;
```

g_Packs is an array of the current instances (running packages) and INSTID is an instance ID. g_pCP holds pointers to the connection point objects that the sink objects are connected to. (Since there are three sink objects for every package, the array is PACKAGE_MAX*3 in size.) g_Cookies is an array of the connection point cookies obtained through IConnectionPoint::Advise() and saved so that we can disconnect. Finally, g_Guids is an array of the package IDs of all current packages.

Because these are global variables, I use a critical section object called g_arrCS to protect access. The sink objects will be created in a single STA, so strictly speaking only one COM thread will have access to the arrays at any time. However, as you will see, this thread is created by our code, which means that any threads created by PerfMon accessing the DLL could access the global variables. In the current code there is no non-STA code that does this, but it may happen in the future, so to be prudent I protect all access. I'll explain the other variables in a moment.

Initializing the Performance DLL

Since we are serving components (the sink objects) we require an apartment. However, PerfMon does not know about COM (or at least the thread that calls your DLL is not in an apartment) so instead we must create one. Normally, you should not create threads in a COM DLL because you do not know when the DLL will be unloaded. However, we know when this will happen with performance DLLs because the _Close() function will be called. The _Open() function therefore looks like this:

```
// thread function
DWORD WINAPI CreateObjects(LPVOID)
{
    return 0;
}

DWORD WINAPI MTSPrfData_Open(LPWSTR lpDevNames)
{
    // Initialize arrays
    memset(g_pCP, 0, sizeof(g_pCP));
    memset(g_Cookies, 0, sizeof(g_Cookies));
    memset(g_Guids, 0, sizeof(g_Guids));
    for (int i = 0; i < PACKAGE_MAX; i++)
    {
        g_Packs[i] = (CPrfData::INSTID)-1;
    }

    // Create/open the shared memory containing the
    // performance info
    CPrfData::Activate();
    // Create thread to create the sink objects and manage them
    g_hEvent = CreateEvent(NULL, TRUE, FALSE, NULL);
    g_hThread = CreateThread(NULL, 0, CreateObjects, 0, 0, &g_dwThreadID);
    return ERROR_SUCCESS;
}
```

First the global arrays and PrfData are initialized, and then a new thread is created for the STA apartment we are going to use. The event object is created to prevent access to the performance data until the thread has created all the sink objects. It is used in the _Collect() function:

```
DWORD WINAPI MTSPrfData_Collect(LPWSTR lpValueName, LPVOID* lppData,
                                LPDWORD lpcbTotalBytes,
                                LPDWORD lpNumObjectTypes)
{
    // Call the class's static Collect() function to populate the
    // passed memory block with our performance info
    WaitForSingleObject(g_hEvent, INFINITE);
    return CPrfData::Collect(lpValueName, (PBYTE*) lppData,
                             lpcbTotalBytes, lpNumObjectTypes);
}
```

The thread function `CreateObjects()` has two purposes: firstly, it creates the sink objects and initializes the performance counters; secondly, it provides the message pump that *all* STA threads must provide. Let's look at this in detail.

```
DWORD WINAPI CreateObjects(LPVOID)
{
    HRESULT hr;
    hr = CoInitializeEx(NULL, COINIT_APARTMENTTHREADED);
    if (SUCCEEDED(hr))
    {
        CComPtr<IMtsGrp> pGrp;
        pGrp.CoCreateInstance(__uuidof(MtsGrp));

        long lPackages;
        pGrp->get_Count(&lPackages);

        g_arrCS.Lock();
        for (int i=0; i<lPackages && i<PACKAGE_MAX; i++)
        {
            // create sink objects
            // initialize counters
            // hook up to the connection points
        }
        g_arrCS.Unlock();
    }
    else
    {
        SetEvent(g_hEvent);
        return 0;
    }
    SetEvent(g_hEvent);

    MSG msg;
    while (true)
    {
        if (GetMessage(&msg, NULL, 0, 0) < 0 ||
            msg.message == WM_CLOSE) break;
        DispatchMessage(&msg);
    }

    // clean up
    CoUninitialize();
    return 0;
}
```

I will show the commented sections in a moment, but basically you can see that all that happens is as follows. First, COM is initialized, the current running packages, are enumerated and the sink objects are created. Next, for each sink object, the connection is made and the `PrfData` counters are initialized. After that, the event object is set to allow `_Collect()` to run, and the thread pumps the message pump. When the thread is told to end (in this case by posting a `WM_CLOSE` message), the thread should disconnect the sink objects and then release them. Finally, COM is uninitialized and the thread dies.

To determine the packages that are running, you need to use the `MtsGrp` component, so add these headers:

```
#include "MTSGrp.h"
#include "MTSEvents.h"
CComModule _Module;
```

The sink object creation code looks like this:

```
for (int i=0; i<lPackages && i<PACKAGE_MAX; i++)
{
    // create sink objects
    CComPtr<IUnknown> pUnk;
    pGrp->Item(i, &pUnk);

    CComQIPtr<IMtsEvents> pEvents = pUnk;
    CComBSTR bstrName;
    pEvents->get_PackageName(&bstrName.m_str);
    g_Packs[i] = g_PrfData.AddInstance(MTSPACKAGES, bstrName.m_str);
    bstrName.Empty();
    pEvents->get_PackageGuid(&bstrName.m_str);
    CLSIDFromString(bstrName.m_str, &g_Guids[i]);
    // initialize counters
    // hook up to the connection points
}
```

This code gets the name and GUID of the package, uses the name to create a new performance instance, and saves the GUID so that we can use it later.

```
for (int i=0; i<lPackages && i<PACKAGE_MAX; i++)
{
    // create sink objects
    ...
    // initialize counters
    g_PrfData.LockCtrs();
    g_PrfData.GetCtr32(TOTALCOMPS, g_Packs[i]) = 0;
    g_PrfData.GetCtr32(TOTALCALLS, g_Packs[i]) = 0;
    g_PrfData.GetCtr32(CURRENTCOMPS, g_Packs[i]) = 0;
    g_PrfData.GetCtr32(CURRENTCALLS, g_Packs[i]) = 0;
    g_PrfData.UnlockCtrs();
    // hook up to the connection points
}
```

This code initializes the counters to zero – there is no way to determine the number of components currently active, so the performance counter just shows how many components have been active since you started gathering performance data.

```
for (int i=0; i<lPackages && i<PACKAGE_MAX; i++)
{
    // create sink objects
    ...
    // initialize counters
    ...
    // hook up to the connection points
    CComObject<CMTSComponentInstances>* pInst;
    CComObject<CMTSComponentInstances>::CreateInstance(&pInst);
    pInst->m_inst = g_Packs[i];
    CComObject<CMTSMethodCalls>* pMeth;
    CComObject<CMTSMethodCalls>::CreateInstance(&pMeth);
    pMeth->m_inst = g_Packs[i];
    CComObject<CMTSPackages>* pPack;
    CComObject<CMTSPackages>::CreateInstance(&pPack);

    CComPtr<IMtsInstanceEvents> pInstEvts;
    pInst->QueryInterface(&pInstEvts);
    CComPtr<IMtsMethodEvents> pMethEvts;
    pMeth->QueryInterface(&pMethEvts);
    CComPtr<IMtsPackageEvents> pPackEvts;
    pPack->QueryInterface(&pPackEvts);
}
```

The `MTSComponentInstances` and `MTSMethodCalls` objects will need to record performance data for a particular package, so the object will need to have the instance ID. The `MTSPackages` object does not record performance data, so it does not require the instance ID.

```
for (int i=0; i<lPackages && i<PACKAGE_MAX; i++)
{
    // create sink objects
    ...
    // initialize counters
    ...
    // hook up to the connection points
    ...
    CComQIPtr<IConnectionPointContainer> pCont(pEvents);
    pCont->FindConnectionPoint(__uuidof(IMtsInstanceEvents), &g_pCP[i*3]);
    g_pCP[i*3]->Advise(pInstEvts, &g_Cookies[i*3]);
    pCont->FindConnectionPoint(__uuidof(IMtsMethodEvents),
                               &g_pCP[i*3 + 1]);
    g_pCP[i*3 + 1]->Advise(pMethEvts, &g_Cookies[i*3 + 1]);
    pCont->FindConnectionPoint(__uuidof(IMtsPackageEvents),
                               &g_pCP[i*3 + 2]);
    g_pCP[i*3 + 2]->Advise(pPackEvts, &g_Cookies[i*3 + 2]);
}
```

This final code connects the sink objects to the connection points, and stores the connection point pointers (not the sink object pointers) in the global array. This means that when the connection is broken, the last reference on the associated sink object will be released and die.

The clean up code appears just before the call to CoUninitialize():

```
    // clean up
    for (int i = 0; i < PACKAGE_MAX * 3; i++)
    {
        if (g_pCP[i])
        {
            g_pCP[i]->Unadvise(g_Cookies[i]);
            g_pCP[i]->Release();
        }
    }

    CoUninitialize();
    return 0;
}
```

The check to see that the connection point pointer is non-NULL is performed because the connection point interface may be released when the package is shut down, as you'll see in a moment.

The thread dies when the WM_CLOSE message is sent, and this is done in the _Close() function:

```
DWORD WINAPI MTSPrfData_Close(void)
{
    CloseHandle(g_hEvent);
    // tell the worker thread to die
    PostThreadMessage(g_dwThreadID, WM_CLOSE, 0, 0);
    // wait for half a second
    if (WaitForSingleObject(g_hThread, 500) == WAIT_TIMEOUT)
    {
        // it won't die, so kill it
        TerminateThread(g_hThread, 0);
    }
    CloseHandle(g_hThread);
    return ERROR_SUCCESS;
}
```

The first thing this code does is to clear up the event object, and it then posts the WM_CLOSE message. The DLL cannot unload until the thread has died, so it calls WaitForSingleObject() on the thread handle. If there is a problem this may make PerfMon hang, so the wait is restricted to half a second – if the thread is still active after this period it is forced to die.

Performance Logging

The performance logging is simple. This is the code for MTSComponentInstances.cpp:

```
#include "stdafx.h"
#include "CmnHdr.h"
#include "PrfData.h"
#include "MTSComponentInstances.h"
#include "PerfCounters.h"
extern CPrfData g_PrfData;
```

```
STDMETHODIMP CMTSComponentInstances::OnObjectCreate(
    LONGLONG perfCount, REFGUID guidActivity, REFCLSID clsid,
    REFGUID tsid, MTS_OBJID ObjectID)
{
    InterlockedIncrement(&g_PrfData.GetCtr32(TOTALCOMPS, m_inst));
    InterlockedIncrement(&g_PrfData.GetCtr32(CURRENTCOMPS, m_inst));
    return S_OK;
}

STDMETHODIMP CMTSComponentInstances::OnObjectRelease(
    LONGLONG perfCount, MTS_OBJID ObjectID)
{
    InterlockedDecrement(&g_PrfData.GetCtr32(CURRENTCOMPS, m_inst));
    return S_OK;
}
```

There is only one instance of CPrfData, and as you can see, a reference to the appropriate counter is obtained by calling GetCtr32() with the counter ID and instance value.

Package Shutdown

When a package shuts down, we no longer want to monitor the events from it (because there won't be any!) so we need to break the connection point. The MTSPackages object receives an event when a package is shut down, and we handle this by unhooking the connection point and zeroing the counters.

```
#include "stdafx.h"
#include "MTSPackages.h"
#include "CmnHdr.h"
#include "PrfData.h"
#include "PerfCounters.h"
extern CPrfData g_PrfData;
extern CPrfData::INSTID g_Packs[];
extern IConnectionPoint* g_pCP[];
extern DWORD g_Cookies[];
extern GUID g_Guids[];
extern CComAutoCriticalSection g_arrCS;

STDMETHODIMP CMTSPackages::OnPackageActivation(
    LONGLONG perfCount, REFGUID guidPackage,
    LPCOLESTR sPackageName)
{
    // should never be called
    return S_OK;
}
```

The OnPackageActivation() method will never be called, because the package has to be running for the event generator object to be created!

```
STDMETHODIMP CMTSPackages::OnPackageShutdown(
    LONGLONG perfCount, REFGUID guidPackage, LPCOLESTR sPackageName)
{
```

```
    int i;
    int iPackageID = -1;
    // get the index of the package
    for (i = 0; i < PACKAGE_MAX; i++)
    {
        if (g_Guids[i] == guidPackage)
        {
            iPackageID = i;
            break;
        }
    }

    if (iPackageID == -1)
        return S_OK;

    //need to stop the event generation
    for (i = 0; i < 3; i++)
    {
        g_pCP[iPackageID*3 + i]->Unadvise(g_Cookies[iPackageID*3 + i]);
        g_pCP[iPackageID*3 + i]->Release();
        g_pCP[iPackageID*3 + i] = NULL;
        g_Cookies[iPackageID*3 + i] = 0;
    }

    g_arrCS.Lock();
    if (g_Packs[iPackageID] != (CPrfData::INSTID)-1)
    {
        // make the counters zero, but keep the instance
        g_PrfData.LockCtrs();
        g_PrfData.GetCtr32(TOTALCOMPS, g_Packs[iPackageID]) = 0;
        g_PrfData.GetCtr32(TOTALCALLS, g_Packs[iPackageID]) = 0;
        g_PrfData.GetCtr32(CURRENTCOMPS, g_Packs[iPackageID]) = 0;
        g_PrfData.GetCtr32(CURRENTCALLS, g_Packs[iPackageID]) = 0;
        g_PrfData.UnlockCtrs();
        // we don't remove the instance, so that PerfMon sees
        // a zero value
    }
    g_arrCS.Unlock();
    g_Guids[iPackageID] = GUID_NULL;
    return S_OK;
}
```

First the code checks the GUID of the package being shut down against our list of GUIDs to get the index into the other arrays. It then breaks the connection and releases the connection point object, and in addition zeros out the members in the arrays to ensure that the thread shutdown doesn't try to access them.

Next, it zeros the counters, but doesn't remove the instance, as we want a zero value to be returned to PerfMon.

Method Call Statistics

Whenever a method is called on a package component, the MTSMethodCalls object will be called. The event methods merely increment or decrement the appropriate counters:

```
#include "stdafx.h"
#include "CmnHdr.h"
#include "PrfData.h"
#include "MTSMethodCalls.h"
#include "PerfCounters.h"
extern CPrfData g_PrfData;

STDMETHODIMP CMTSMethodCalls::OnMethodCall(
   LONGLONG perfCount, MTS_OBJID oid, REFCLSID guidCid, REFIID guidRid,
   ULONG iMeth)
{
   InterlockedIncrement(&g_PrfData.GetCtr32(TOTALCALLS, m_inst));
   InterlockedIncrement(&g_PrfData.GetCtr32(CURRENTCALLS, m_inst));
   return S_OK;
}

STDMETHODIMP CMTSMethodCalls::OnMethodReturn(
   LONGLONG perfCount, MTS_OBJID oid, REFCLSID guidCid,
   REFIID guidRid, ULONG iMeth, HRESULT hresult)
{
   InterlockedDecrement(&g_PrfData.GetCtr32(CURRENTCALLS, m_inst));
   return S_OK;
}

STDMETHODIMP CMTSMethodCalls::OnMethodException(
   LONGLONG perfCount, MTS_OBJID oid, REFCLSID guidCid,
   REFIID guidRid, ULONG iMeth)
{
   InterlockedDecrement(&g_PrfData.GetCtr32(CURRENTCALLS, m_inst));
   return S_OK;
}
```

Other Considerations

Note that since some of the code calls the CRT, you need to remove the _ATL_MIN_CRT symbol from the release build configurations.

Once you have entered all the code, you should compile it and copy the DLL to %systemroot%\system32 (my project does this in a post-build step). To install the DLL, you should call regsvr32 on it – on running PerfMon and opening the **Add to Chart** dialog you will then find **MTS Packages** in the **Object** box:

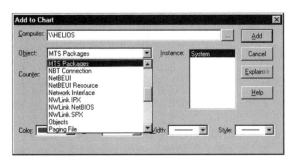

Having selected this, you will find the counters that you added to the map. As an example, select the `System` package as the instance and add all four counters. Then start MTS Explorer and open a few packages. You should see the counters in `PerfMon` change, as `System` components are created and released to access the catalog.

This code shows you how to gather performance information about the number of components and the method calls. Note that only performance data for packages with objects running when `PerfMon` is started will show up in the instances box. To see other packages, you'll have to restart `PerfMon`. As you can see though, it is straightforward to extend it to add performance data based on the other event interfaces.

Event Log

The event log is a useful repository for important events. Generating events is fairly simple, but (as with the performance monitor) the event log was designed in the old days of NT (indeed, it originates from the early days, when NT was actually the successor to OS/2). Consequently, it suffers from having an arcane and unwieldy API.

I won't go into the details of how to write event log code here because I have covered it elsewhere (*Professional ATL COM Programming*, ISBN 1-861001-40-1). One important point (that is often overlooked) is that the Event Log Viewer is a tool that can be used to view event logs on remote machines. To do so, you can choose the <u>Log</u> | <u>S</u>elect Computer menu item – if you are an administrator of the target machine you will then see the requested event log.

Beware when you do this, because if the event log is large, a lot of data will be passed over the network, slowing the display of the data and reducing the performance of the network. You can run more than one instance of the Event Log Viewer, so it is possible to read the events logged on several machines at a time. However, the viewer doesn't show events dynamically, so to view the latest events for a given machine you have to re-read its entire log.

If you would prefer to have event logs from several machines shown in one application and updated dynamically, you will have to write the code yourself. The API to read the Event Log is straightforward, so I'll leave it up to the reader to write a distributed event log reader. I wrote such an application several years ago, and the trick is to use `NotifyChangeEventLog()` to get notification of new events being added to the log. The only problem is in making sure that you read the right event, as event logs can 'roll-over' if they get full.

Visual Studio Analyzer

An earlier section explained the main problem with `MtsSpy`, namely the fact that it isn't network aware. However, Microsoft provides a tool that will capture MTS events (and others) from remote machines: the **Visual Studio Analyzer**. This is only available as part of the enterprise edition of Visual Studio, and requires NT4 Service Pack 4 to be installed.

Visual Studio Analyzer catches events generated by a variety of sources, but these events are not quite as you will understand them to be. Visual Studio Analyzer uses an event system called **VISTA**, which was designed specifically for its use. This system allows events to be broadcast across the network from a source machine to a specific target. The target machine initiates this, specifying that it will receive events from the source machine. After the target machine has done this, the source machine will start generating the events – note that without the initiation of the target machine, no events will be generated. Also note that although a target machine can receive events from many source machines, events from one source machine cannot be sent to multiple target machines.

> *The VISTA event system is only used by Visual Studio Analyzer, and there is no documentation on how it works, so you can't use it for your own devices. Although you can generate custom events to be captured by Visual Studio Analyzer, it is not documented how to write code to catch events. Furthermore, it is* not *based on the COM+ event system.*

As you'll see later, many system DLLs generate VISTA events, which means that they have been written specifically with Visual Studio Analyzer in mind.

To receive events from multiple machines, those machines must have the **Visual Studio Analyzer Server** components installed on the source machines (you can do this by running setup.exe from the va_ss directory on CD2 of the Visual Studio disks). The setup creates an account called VUSR_*MachineName* (where *MachineName* is the local machine name) and it configures the identity of the VSA server components (MSVSA Local Event Concentrator) to use this account.

> *Remember to add this account to the* Reader *role if you have security enabled on the* System *package. If you don't do this, your event log will fill up with warning messages that access cannot be gained on the* System *package.*

The machine that catches the events should have Visual Studio Analyzer installed via the Visual Studio setup.

The biggest problem with Visual Studio Analyzer concerns the sheer number of events that it will capture. These can often swamp you, and this raises the possibility of missing a vitally important event amongst other less important ones. Visual Analyzer allows you to define filters, and you are well advised to use these to remove events that you aren't interested in.

Most Microsoft technologies generate Visual Studio Analyzer (VSA) events. Notably for this discussion, all calls to MTS and COM objects generate events:

❑   **COM:** creation and release of COM objects, information about marshaled interfaces, method calls, COM class registration and revocation

❑   **MTS:** object context calls, transaction start, prepare, abort; object create, activate, deactivate, release; package activation and shutdown; resource create, allocate, recycle, destroy

If you look at the MTS VSA events available in Visual Studio Analyzer, you'll see that they correspond to the MtsSpy events, except that VSA does not support security and thread events (IMtsSecurity and IMtsThreadEvents). Indeed, VSA appears to get this information using the MTS event objects.

If you are interested in the thread generation, you can request **Performance Monitor Dynamic Source** events to be generated. This will provide events for some of the `PerfMon` DLLs provided by NT. In particular, you can get the `Process` object, and through this access the `Thread Count` counter. However, the `Process` object knows nothing about MTS, so the instance that you see will be `mtx.exe`. Since there is no way of distinguishing between the various instances running, you must view events from them all.

> *Visual Studio Analyzer is provided with an object that will obtain* `PerfMon` *events. However, it only appears to use the NT-provided performance DLLs. I can't determine how to get Visual Studio Analyzer to read custom performance data.*

To use Visual Analyzer, you must first create a VSA project. The simplest way to do this is to use the Project Wizard, which allows you to select which computers will generate events, as well as the event sources and events that you wish to view.

The list of event sources is:

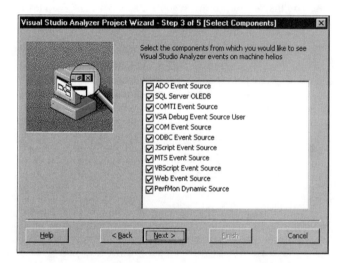

As you can see, this is very comprehensive and could generate many events. This may be an advantage, as it means you can compare the events generated by MTS with those generated by, for example, SQL Server or ODBC, and see which part of the application takes longest to perform a task. Visual Studio Analyzer is not a performance profile tool, but since there may be many components in a distributed application, which may involve several servers written in multiple languages (C++, VB, Script or even SQL stored procedures), it does give you an idea of which part of the application needs performance profiling.

> *Note that NT Event Log events are not caught by VSA. I think this is a pity, as it is useful to be able to compare the NT Event Logs of machines involved in a distributed application with the MTS calls being made.*

The next page in the Wizard allows you to select one or more of the predefined filters, so that you can restrict the generation of events:

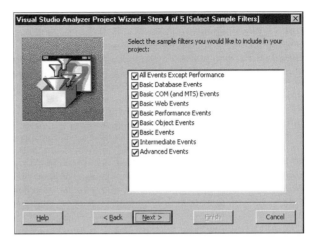

These filters are quite wide ranging, but, if you wish, you can view the data with a custom filter at a later stage. In fact, once you have defined a custom filter you can set this as the 'recording filter' to restrict the number of events generated. Once the computers, events and filters have been selected, you can start capturing events.

When enough events have been generated, you can stop capturing and view them as either a list or a chart. Be aware that even if you restrict your filter to only a few event types, you may still get a lot of events. You may therefore have to define an even more restrictive filter to view these events – indeed I have found it quite useful (and revealing) to export event data to a comma-separated file and use Microsoft Excel to manipulate the data.

For example, I have a simple MTS package called `TestPackage`, with an object called `TestSvr.PingObj.1`. The client, `TestClient`, creates several instances of the object and calls each one in turn. If I run Visual Analyzer as the client starts, I will get a flurry of events as the client initializes COM and then requests objects. The instance of `mtx.exe` is created, determines the DLL to load, creates the object, and returns the object reference. To determine the package properties, the `System` package is consulted to get information from the catalog.

Visual Studio Analyzer illustrates the various components and their connections in its **Process View**:

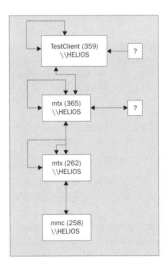

Here you can see that I have MTS Explorer open to view the package properties, and this is the process (ID = 258) called mmc at the bottom. Above that is the process 262, which is the System package. It is consulted by process 365 (TestPackage) to get information from the Catalog so that the MTS Executive can determine which DLL to load. The package is accessed by the client, which is shown as process 359 at the top.

The list of events is rather extensive (even when I use a fairly restrictive filter), so I will not show it here. You can view the values of each event though. For example, here is a typical one:

Field	Value
Arguments	
Binding	0x0800310037003200 2E00310030002E0031 00(
Category	COM Marshalling
Causality ID	{B4E61EE3-4E99-11D3-89C3-00104BDC35E0}
Correlation ID	{00136990-4128-77BB-0500-0000186FBC77}
Duration	0
Duration (ms)	0
Dynamic Event Data	0
Event	COM Marshall
Exception	
Full Category	All Regular Events::COM Marshalling
IID	{00000134-0000-0000-C000-000000000046}
Interface Name	IRundown
MOXID	{00000000-0000-0000-0100-0000BC8DE024}
Return Value	
Security Identity	RichardGrimes
Source	COM Event Source
Source Component	
Source Handle	{00000000-00D8-0000-2401-000000000000}
Source Machine	
Source Process	
Source Process ID	0
Source Session	
Source Thread	
Target Component	COM Event Source
Target Handle	
Target Machine	HELIOS
Target Process	TestClient
Target Process ID	216
Target Session	COM Runtime 216
Target Thread	124
Time	21:33:40.606 09/08/99
Type	Generic

Event - Event Log2 [11] - Unfiltered - Analyze14

As you can see, each COM event has a causality ID. Every COM call is provided with one of these, and it is used to group together interface calls on the many components that may have been caused by a single client call.

For example, imagine that a client can sink COM events. It makes a call to ObjectA, which makes a call to ObjectB, which in turn calls ObjectC, which makes a callback to the client. COM calls are synchronous, so when the callback returns (and the method calls to ObjectC, ObjectB, and ObjectA return) the client knows that the return value came from ObjectA. There is effectively a 'logical thread' that runs through the call train, from the client, through to the call on ObjectC, and back.

What about the callback? If the client can sink events, it means that it is waiting for COM calls to be made on the sink object – but this implies that *any* code with access to the sink object could generate an event, and it may not be desirable to handle this while the client is in an active call.

When your client initiates an outgoing call it is marked with a causality ID. This ID is attached to all COM calls to other components, and is effectively the 'logical thread' ID. Therefore, if a callback is made on the client, COM can check the causality ID to see if it is intended for the current active client call. Your object can supply a message filter (implementing IMessageFilter), which is called by COM when an incoming call is detected. It interprets (from the causality ID) whether the call is from the 'logical thread' of the outgoing call or a completely new call. Your message filter can thus determine if the call should be serviced, rejected, or delayed.

In terms of Visual Studio Analyzer, the causality ID is useful in tracing the effects of a single call from a client, and you can use this to ignore the other events being generated. Thus, I can manually filter out events (perhaps, as mentioned above, by using Excel).

```
CComPtr<IPingObj> pObj;
pObj.CoCreateInstance(__uuidof(PingObj));
long inVal = 0, outVal;
pObj->Ping(inVal, &outVal);
```

The sample above produces these events:

Event	Correlation	Interface/method	Source Process	Target Process
COM Marshall	{00136990-4128-77BB-0500-0000186FBC77}	IRundown		TestClient
COM Unmarshall	{00136990-4128-77BB-0500-0000186FBC77}	IDSCM	TestClient	
COM Client Call	12f7fc	IDSCM::4	TestClient	
COM Stub Enter	118fa44	IObjServer ::4		mtx
COM Client Return	12f7fc	IDSCM::4	TestClient	
COM Unmarshall	{00136990-4148-77BB-0500-0000186FBC77}	IPingObj	TestClient	
COM Client Call	12fc04	IPingObj:: Ping	TestClient	
COM Stub Enter	14efb18	IPingObj:: Ping		mtx
Object Activate	761750	–	mtx	
MTS Set Complete	761750	–	mtx	
Object Deactivate	761750	–	mtx	
COM Stub Leave	14efb18	IPingObj:: Ping		mtx
COM Client Return	12fc04	IPingObj:: Ping	TestClient	

In this table I have also given the correlation ID for each event – these allow you to associate a call with its return value. As you can see, some events use a GUID while others use a 32-bit value. Visual Studio Analyzer also mentions the source of the event (not shown here), which determines whether the event came from one of VSA's event objects or from some other object. In the table, the activation, deactivation and SetComplete calls originate from MTS event sources, whereas the rest come from the VSA COM event sources. It is perhaps for this reason that VSA doesn't record the interface and method called for those events. The IRundown, IObjServer and IDSCM interfaces aren't documented, but are clearly involved in server location and object activation.

If there are several machines involved, you'll get events from all of them. You can view the machines involved using the Machine Diagram, and event properties will have a source or target machine entry to indicate this.

As you can see, Visual Studio Analyzer is a superb tool for monitoring the calls being made in your distributed application. If you are careful with the filters you use, it is possible to gain interesting information about the COM and MTS calls made, and how these relate to transactions. Furthermore, timing information can give you an idea of which parts of the application are taking the longest and are therefore candidates for profiling.

Summary

MTS application debugging suffers from two main problems. The first is that MTS components (in a server package) are run in the mtx.exe surrogate process. You therefore have to make allowances for this by ensuring that you debug mtx.exe and indicate the package to use. You also have to make sure that you set up the correct security settings.

The other problem is that MTS applications are usually *distributed* applications, that is, packages can run on several machines. To get detailed information about errors or performance problems that may occur in the application, you must therefore monitor several machines. NT provides a number of tools that allow you to gather and view information about processes. Two in particular (the NT event log viewer and the performance monitor) have distribution built in. However, although you can gather information from several machines, it's problematic to actually analyze that data.

One major difficulty is that data will be generated with machine-specific time values, making it difficult to compare (and put in order) events that occur on different machines. Another problem is the sheer number of events that can be generated. The Visual Studio Analyzer solves these problems and adds more facilities. The COM and MTS DLLs have been built with VSA in mind, so they will generate VSA events (passed via a proprietary event system called VISTA), which indicate particular events not available for other sources. These are sent to the gather machine, which will store them in the order in which they were generated. You then have filter options that can weed out excessive events, allowing you to view those that are relevant to your debug session.

In this chapter I have indicated how you can use all of these tools to debug an MTS-distributed application. I have also shown how to use MTS events to write a performance monitor DLL.

8

The Way Forward

Introduction

The most important feature that MTS brought to COM was the context, which it added without knowledge of the client or the component. The MTS context holds extra information about the component, which turns it from an isolated, stand-alone object into one that can be part of a distributed application with distributed transactions and role-based security.

The context is clearly important, but it's quite fragile. As we have seen throughout this book, the context is applied to components created by MTS, but the usual COM APIs (like `CoCreateInstanceEx()`) know nothing about contexts and won't create them. Instead, the registry hacking that occurs when you configure a COM object to be an MTS component ensures that the object will be created in MTS, which *will* create the context and provide interception. Since the NT4 APIs don't understand contexts, sub-components created using `CoCreateInstanceEx()` can't be created based on their parent component's context. This is the reason for `IObjectContext::CreateInstance()` – it ensures that the newly created component's context matches that of the component that created it.

Furthermore, raw interface pointers from your component know nothing about the context. It is therefore an erroneous action to pass around raw pointers from an MTS component. Under MTS the solution is to use `SafeRef()`, but it is easy to forget to do this.

COM+ integrates MTS into the COM runtime – this means that all COM+ components will have a context. The COM APIs fully recognize this, not only from the point of view of creating a base component, but also when creating a sub-component within a transaction. This chapter will explain the ramifications of integrating MTS with COM, based on the version of COM+ supplied as part of Windows 2000 Beta 3 Release Candidate 2.

COM+ Concepts

Since COM+ integrates MTS, and MTS uses interception and contexts, it is reasonable to assume that COM+ will also use contexts and interception. However, as you'll see from this section, there is more to it than that.

In plain COM the base unit of execution is the apartment. This defines the concurrency requirement of components, and you design your component specifically for the apartment in which it will run. MTS introduced context to hold security, transaction and activity information about the component. MTS developers designed their components with the assumption that they would run in a single-threaded environment (using `ThreadingModel=Apartment`), so they no longer had to write synchronization code. Furthermore, MTS components could use transactions and security, but, crucially, they didn't have to implement the code to set up these environments. This was done for them, based on the configuration of the component. Transaction enlistment and committal, as well as cross-process access checks, are performed by the MTS runtime.

The context in MTS was fairly basic, but it changed the way that developers wrote their components. The context was an enclosing comfort blanket – the administrator chose what facilities the component could use, and this was recorded in the context. The component could then access these facilities, if it chose to do so.

Like MTS components, COM+ components have contexts, and these define the environment in which the component will run. However, COM+ has now subsumed more facilities into the runtime, so the administration of COM+ components has been expanded to support them. In addition to transaction and security support, COM+ components can be configured to use object pooling, just-in-time activation, concurrency and queuing. COM+ components can therefore be written to use a variety of features without having to initialize the appropriate runtime – COM+ will do this based on the context.

This first version of Windows 2000 is essentially a transitional operating system, marking the change from plain COM to COM+. Although COM+ is the preferred environment for components, you are still allowed to use COM components (essentially to provide backward compatibility). Just as in-proc COM objects can be used as MTS components, both plain COM and MTS components can be used as COM+ components, the only requirement being that there is an entry for the component in the COM+ catalog. Such components are referred to as **configured** components.

As with MTS, COM+ components can be run in the client's memory space or in a separate process. However, the terminology has now changed so that rather than using the term Package, COM+ refers to these deployment units as **Applications**.

> COM+ Application **is a new term introduced with COM+, and wherever I refer to it in the text I will capitalize it. This is to differentiate between it and the general term** application, **by which I mean something like Microsoft Word, for example.**

COM+ Applications can be server Applications (run in a separate process to the client), or library Applications (run in the same memory as the client). Configuration is still carried out through an MMC snap-in, but now it is referred to as **Component Services** rather than the MTS Explorer. The Component Services snap-in gives access to the catalog and also to snap-ins for the event log, security, and local services administration.

The COM concepts of apartment, activity, and context still exist in COM+. I'll use this section to explore their relationship, and the following sections to describe how components are configured.

Activation

Whenever you create a COM+ component the activation call will go through the COM+ runtime, which will check the (configured) component's required context, comparing it to the context of the client. The context is similar to MTS's idea – it describes the concurrency, transaction and security requirements of the component.

The component's context also indicates the **COM+ services** that it uses. A service is some facility in the environment in which the component will run. For example, if the component can generate COM+ events, then the appropriate libraries must be loaded at runtime and initialized – these libraries are COM+ services.

Traditionally, if a component needed some 'service' during runtime, the actual component code had to be linked with a static library that gave access to the 'service'. This was true even if the component used a DLL to get access to the 'service', because the component would usually use an imported static library to access the DLL's functions. Furthermore, the 'service' still had to be initialized before the component could use it. With COM+, the fact that a component uses a service is held in the COM+ catalog. The COM+ runtime can read this, and then load and initialize the required service, which means that component developers don't have to write this code themselves. The data entries in the catalog that describe the services a component uses are known as **COM+ attributes**.

The component doesn't specifically call the API of the services it uses – instead the COM+ runtime applies the services through interception (much as the MTS executive does when, for example, making security checks). When a COM+ component is accessed outside of its context (for example, from another apartment) then a proxy will be used. However, because the proxy really does represent the component (and therefore has the same COM+ services requirements), the proxy is also context–relative, and represents the difference between the contexts of the client and the component. This way the proxy adds only as much of the context as is needed. However, this does mean that when you have more than one client context, the proxy must be created in each of the different contexts. This isn't too much of a problem, since as a seasoned COM developer you will be used to marshaling component references between apartments – in COM+ the apartment is just one of the context attributes.

When the proxy has been created with the correct context, COM+ can apply its services through interception. If you decide that a component can run in the client context (in the in-proc case), you can aggregate the Free Threaded Marshaler (FTM). As in the old plain COM case, this component implements IMarshal in such a way as to decide whether to pass a raw interface pointer or to use standard marshaling. However, the focus of this component is now to marshal component references between contexts, rather than merely between apartments. Although the name persists, it's becoming inappropriate, because the FTM is used to make a component *context neutral*, not just *apartment neutral*.

One big change you'll notice with COM+ is that mtx.exe is no longer used. Instead DllHost.exe is the surrogate process used to house COM+ components. This illustrates further the integration of MTS and COM activation, because two surrogates are no longer needed. The only difference this makes to you is that when you debug a server Application, you must specify DllHost.exe as the executable to debug. Just as all components that you write for MTS are in-proc (DLL-based), COM+ components must also be based in DLLs. You can't use COM+ services as a component server in an EXE-based server.

Apartments

Apartments still exist in COM+, but they aren't the primary utility in call synchronization. As with plain COM, COM+ has MTAs and STAs. STAs ensure that the code will only ever be called by a single thread. This type of apartment must remain, as sections of the Windows operating system (and possibly your own code) have thread affinity, so they can only be accessed by the same thread. In particular, all UI COM *must* execute in an STA.

COM+ also adds the much discussed **Thread Neutral Apartment** (**TNA**). As the name suggests, this apartment doesn't have native threads, since threads live in STAs or MTAs. Like those other apartment types, a component can use the `ThreadingModel` registry key to specify that it wants to live in a TNA, and like plain COM, it can only be accessed from a thread within the apartment in which it lives. However, unlike with STAs, you aren't specifying that only a particular thread can access the component.

To perform this feat, a thread from an STA or MTA temporarily joins the TNA for the purpose of accessing the component. Because the TNA is thread neutral, when a thread runs code in it there is no *thread context* switch. There may be a *COM+ context* switch, which will involve marshaling across the context boundary. However, this marshaling is lightweight compared to thread context switches. Contrast this with the FTM, under which a component is context neutral, requires no context switches, and hence runs under the context of the calling code.

Since a TNA allows quicker access to a component's code, it is the preferred apartment type in COM+. However, since there are no native threads in a TNA, you still need to create threads to execute the code – this is why the other two apartments still exist. However, when creating a thread (or rather determining what apartment type a thread should be), your choice of which apartment to use depends on whether the thread will be used to service UI code. You shouldn't be influenced by synchronization issues. If your component runs in a server Application then you don't need to write any thread creation code – `DllHost.exe` will handle this for you.

Although apartments do still have synchronization requirements (and, by supplying a `ThreadingModel` value, a component can indicate the synchronization it supports), this is no longer the main way to ensure concurrency. Instead, COM+ provides a **synchronization attribute**, which indicates the synchronization that is applied through the more generalized concept of an activity.

Activities

An activity is a set of components running on behalf of a client with similar concurrency requirements. Every COM+ component belongs to an activity, and this is recorded in the component's context. Unlike MTS where `CoCreateInstanceEx()` will always create a new activity, under COM+ it will only create a new activity if the **synchronization attribute** of the component indicates that the component must always be created in a new activity. If the component is configured to use an existing activity, and `CoCreateInstanceEx()` is called from an existing activity, then that activity will be used, otherwise a new one will be created. Other attributes of the component (like supporting JIT activation, and transactions which require an activity) will constrain you as to which synchronization values you can use.

Transactions

COM+ transactions are managed through MS DTC, as with MTS, but you now have more access to the transaction via the context (explained in the next section).

Information about the transaction is part of a context, but it's just one part. There may be components that are part of the same transaction, but have different contexts because they use different COM+ services. This means that a transaction may involve several contexts. This association between the contexts involved in a transaction is, of course, the transaction stream. A COM+ transaction stream contains one or more contexts that are involved in the same transaction. When the root component in the transaction deactivates, it checks *all* of the contexts in the transaction stream to see if the transaction can commit.

Contexts

A context holds all the environmental information that components within it expect in order to run. A component's context object can be accessed through a call to `CoGetObjectContext()`. Unlike `GetObjectContext()` (which returns the single interface `IObjectContext`), this method will return one of several interfaces depending on the IID you pass. These are shown in the following table:

Interface	Description
IObjectContext	General access to the component's context
IContextState	Access to component deactivation and transaction voting
IObjectContextActivity	Access to the activity ID
IObjectContextInfo	Access to the transaction, its ID, the activity ID and context ID
IObjectContextTip	Access to a tip URL

In addition to these, you can access the as yet undocumented `IContextProperties` *and* `IObjectContextTransaction`.

`IContextState` gives access to the context state for a component. This contains two bits: the **doneness** and **consistent** bits. The doneness bit determines if the component should deactivate and is used on JIT components. You can retrieve this bit with `IContextState::GetDeactivateOnReturn()` (obtained from the root component of the transaction). As an added bonus, the HRESULT of this method can be used to determine if the component is running as a JIT component (if not, `CONTEXT_E_NOJIT` is returned). If this bit is false, the transaction will not finish until the client releases its references on the component. If it's true, the component will deactivate when there are no active method calls (which most likely means when this method returns, hence the name). If the client makes another call on an outstanding reference, COM+ will create a new instance of the JIT component to handle the call. You can set the bit to specify this behavior by calling `SetDeactivateOnReturn()`.

The consistent bit determines whether the transaction should commit or abort. When the root component deactivates, COM+ checks all the contexts in the transaction stream to see if the consistent bit is set to true. If any context checked has this bit set to false then the transaction is aborted. Note that this bit is checked when the root component deactivates, so changing it with a call to `IContextState::SetMyTransactionVote()` won't necessarily have an immediate effect. You can call `GetMyTransactionVote()` to see the current value of the consistent bit, and you can also monitor the return value to see if the component has a transaction (if not, `CONTEXT_E_NOTRANSACTION` is returned).

If you want to get access to the transaction, you can call `IObjectContextInfo::GetTransaction()` to get an `IUnknown` pointer, which you can query for the appropriate transaction interface. This is similar to calling `IDispenserManager::GetContext()`, but is more immediate.

In addition to the component's context, you can also access the call context with a call to `CoGetCallContext()`. With plain COM you can use this to get access to `IServerSecurity`. With COM+ though, it can access `ISecurityCallContext`, which can then be used to determine if the caller is in a role, or if security is enabled (mirroring the methods on `IObjectContext`).

In addition it supports security properties, obtained through an `Item` property:

```
ISecurityCallContext::get_Item([in] BSTR bstrName,
                               [out, retval] VARIANT* retval);
```

This interface, like many of the administrative interfaces on COM+, has been made VB-friendly by adding properties. In a C++ world, these values would have been returned in a structure, but COM+ is rapidly becoming the domain of VB developers.

The properties accessed through this interface are:

Property Name	Description
DirectCaller	The immediate caller of the component
OriginalCaller	The caller that originated the chain of calls that resulted in the component
MinAuthenticationLevel	The lowest authentication used in the chain of calls
NumCallers	The number of callers
Callers	The callers in the chain of calls

The first two are similar to MTS's `ISecurityProperty`, except that rather than returning a SID they return a component that implements `ISecurityIdentityColl`. This interface only has property methods, as shown in the following table. These represent the SID and account name, authentication level, impersonation level and authentication service used by the caller. Although you could do this with MTS, this method groups them in a more convenient form.

Property	Description
SID	The security ID of the caller
AccountName	The account name of the caller, a string
AuthenticationService	An integer that specifies the authentication service used (Kerberos by default)
ImpersonationLevel	An integer that gives the impersonation level specified by the client
AuthenticationLevel	An integer that gives the authentication level used to make the call

The Callers property retrieves all the callers used in the call of methods to get this current component. This information is returned in a component that implements another VB-friendly interface called ISecurityCallersColl. This interface has a collection of components that each implement the ISecurityIndentityColl interface.

Component Lifecycle

MTS allows a certain amount of component recycling (in fact the context component and stub are recycled from activation to activation). COM+ takes this a step further, recycling entire components in the object pool – the life cycle of a pooled component follows thus: when the COM+ Application starts, the pool is created along with the minimum number of components; if the component is configured to support component construction then the COM+ runtime will query each component it creates for the IObjectConstruct interface; if successful, Construct() will be called, passing a IDispatch pointer; your component can query this interface pointer for IObjectConstructString and access the ConstructString property; this construction string is used to indicate some initial state of the component that is common to all instances (for example, a data access component could be initialized with the name of the data source, whereas when *activated* individual instances would be initialized with the appropriate rowset); this string is set using Component Services MMC snap-in, and every component in the configured pool will have access to it.

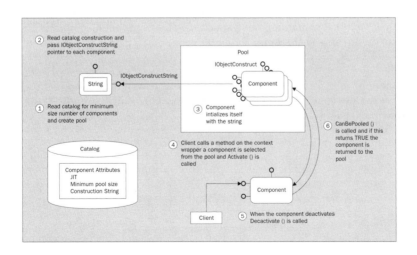

At this point, all the components are created and constructed, and will remain until the Application is shut down (or the component indicates that it can't be returned to the pool). When a client asks for a component instance, a context wrapper will be returned. When the client calls a method on the component, COM+ will select a component from the pool and activate it (there's no construction involved – this has already been done), so IObjectControl::Activate() is called.

When the method completes and the object is deactivated (the doneness bit is set) IObjectControl::Deactivate() is called (allowing you to release any instance–specific data or carry out instance–specific cleanup). The component should now be in the state that it was when it was originally put into the pool. The system will then call IObjectControl::CanBePooled() to see if the deactivation has been successful – Deactivate() doesn't have a return value. If CanBePooled() returns TRUE then the component is in its constructed state and will be returned back to the pool ready to be re-activated. (Contrast this with MTS, where no pool exists, so although CanBePooled() is called it has no effect on the component lifetime.)

COM+ Services

While the Microsoft team was integrating MTS into the COM runtime, they decided to add some more COM–related facilities to Windows 2000. These facilities are known as **COM+ services**, because they are provided by the system. By and large though, they are used by components with the application of COM+ attributes in the catalog. In this section I will outline these new services, and in the following sections show you how to administer them.

COM+ Events

There are several problems with connection point events. The major problem is that for a client to specify that it can handle events, and for a component to generate events, both the client and component server must be *running* and *connected*. For this reason it is said that the two are **tightly coupled**. Connection point events are merely the component that generates the event calling an interface method on the client. This is a normal COM call, so it's synchronous. This means that the component thread is blocked while the client handles the event. Although you can implement the event generation using multithreading to prevent the component thread being blocked, this requires you to write more code. In any case, this goes against the idea of an event, which is merely the component telling the client that something has happened – the component shouldn't be interested in the client's opinion of the event and therefore shouldn't care about the return value from the event method.

COM+ has solved these problems with **COM+ events**. These are **loosely coupled**, in that the COM+ event service sits between the component that generates the events (called a **publisher**) and the client that handles the events (called a **subscriber**).

The SENS Event System

Before explaining what COM+ events are, it's important to clear up one source of confusion. You may have noticed when you installed IE5 on NT4, that a server called COM+ Event System is installed, which serves an object called EventSystemTier2. In addition, there are several objects installed with names that begin with SENS:

❑   SENS Logon Events

❑   SENS Network Events

❑   SENS OnNow Events

❑   SENS Subscriber for EventSystem EventObjectChange events

On initial view this looks wonderful – IE5 has installed COM+ events for you on NT4! However, this is an early version of the COM+ event system used by IE5 to handle the System Event Notification System, which **publishes** network, logon, and power events for mobile machines. You don't get any other COM+ facilities, and you don't get the complete COM+ Event system.

A program can **subscribe** to these events using a subscription object. It does this by creating an instance of the system class CLSID_CEventSubscription. Using the methods on its IEventSubscription interface, the subscriber can initialize the subscription object to mention the CLSID of an **EventClass** (SENSGUID_EVENTCLASS_NETWORK, SENSGUID_EVENTCLASS_LOGON, or SENSGUID_EVENTCLASS_ONNOW), the CLSID of a **publisher** (which will always be SENSGUID_PUBLISHER for SENS), the IID of the event interface on the EventClass that you are interested in (ISensLogon, ISensNetwork or ISensOnNow), and the CLSID of a **subscriber** that will catch the events. These CLSIDs and IIDs can be found in EventSys.h, Sens.h and SensEvts.h in the Platform SDK (except for the subscriber, which is a component that you implement).

The object that generates the events is the SENS object. This will generate the event by creating an instance of the EventClass specified in the subscription, and call the appropriate event method on the event interface of the component catching the event. These interfaces and the SENS object are described in the type library in SENS.EXE. The EventClass uses the information added to the registry when the subscription is made. These values are held in

```
HKEY_LOCAL_MACHINE\Software\Microsoft\EventSystem
```

In this key you will find three other keys, EventClasses, Publishers and Subscriptions as shown in this screenshot (remember this is NT4, service pack 5 with IE5 installed):

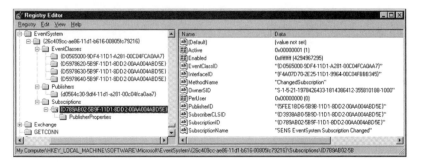

This is the NT4 **Event Store**.

The SENS system will use the values in the Subscriptions key to determine the component that will catch the event (SubscriberCLSID). It will then create an instance of the component and call the component according to the settings made in the subscription object. This means that the COM+ event system is *asynchronous,* in that no instance of the subscriber class has to be running to receive the event. Since the CLSID of the subscriber class is stored in the event store, the subscription will be a **persistent subscription**. Compare this to connection points, where the sink component must be running and connected to the event source.

You can also have **transient subscriptions**, where the subscribing application creates an instance of an component and passes the subscription interface to the CLSID_CEventSubscription component. In this situation, the subscription remains as long as the subscription component is alive, and because the subscriber class is already instantiated it means that the CLSID does not need to be recorded. This type of event catching is similar to connection points.

Once the subscription component is initialized, you record the subscription by adding it to the event store. This is done by creating an instance of the CLSID_CEventSystem system component and calling the IEventSystem::Store() method.

If you have IE5 installed on NT4, you can use all of these objects and make transient and persistent subscriptions. Windows 2000 extends this event generation by allowing you to write event classes as well as subscriber classes. In addition, it integrates the registration of events with the COM+ catalog, so you don't need to use the CLSID_CEventSubscription or CLSID_CEventSystem components, but can write to the catalog directly.

COM+ Events Architecture

The COM+ events system is a loosely coupled event (LCE) system. This means that the publisher, subscriber, and subscription are separate, and that the subscriber component doesn't have to be running for the publisher to generate an event. Also, neither component needs to run for the subscription to be made. This is in contrast to connection points, where both sink component (the subscriber) and event source (the publisher) must be running for subscriptions to be made (IConnectionPoint::Advise()) or events generated.

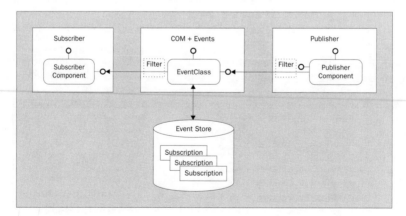

Furthermore, when the publisher generates an event, it doesn't know about the number or location of subscribers – the event system manages that through subscriptions. The event system knows about the events that can be generated through EventClasses described by a type library. This component is implemented by the COM+ Events System, based on the description in the type library. However, since these have to be added to the catalog, you need to create a dummy component and add it to an Application. The reason is that in addition to the type library, EventClasses need to have self- registration code to register the `ThreadingModel` and ProgID for the class. However, let me stress this again: *no instances of the EventClass component are ever created* – the COM+ event system will create its own version of the class.

The interfaces implemented by the EventClass are the event interfaces that the subscriber should implement to receive the events. In this way, the EventClass is an intermediate store of events once a publisher has generated them. Once the EventClass is registered with the system, a publisher can create an instance using the usual COM API and obtain its event interfaces – the COM+ Events System will create an instance of the EventClass. When the publisher calls methods on the interfaces, it generates an event. At this point the publisher knows that the event has been generated and it's no longer involved.

The EventClass will propagate this to all subscribers by looking into the subscription database maintained by the catalog to find the subscribers that have been registered. The EventClass can make the call to the subscribers serially (that is, one thread to make all calls), or in parallel (one thread per subscriber). With the second option, if one subscriber takes a long time handling the event, then this won't delay the event being sent to other subscribers.

If you want to write a publisher, you need to create a dummy component for the EventClass. This component should be similar to other COM+ components, in that it should be described by a type library, be housed in a self-registering DLL, and have a ProgID. However, because it's a dummy component, its methods should do nothing. In addition, since events are effectively made asynchronously, the event methods must only have [in] parameters. The EventClass can be added to an application either through the Component Services snap-in or through the catalog API.

Subscriptions can either be made through the MMC snap-in or by a subscriber at runtime. In the first case, you use the context menu of the Subscriptions node underneath the component node. This gives you a Wizard to allow you to enter details. Such a subscription will be persistent, which means that it remains in the catalog even when the system restarts. When the publisher generates an event, the classes indicated by persistent subscriptions are created and the appropriate event method is called. Once the event has been generated the subscriber component is released, so the subscriber component should record the event in some way.

This means that subscriber components exist specifically to handle an event and then go away. This is in contrast to the connection point model, where an application runs waiting for events to occur. COM+ events have such a facility called transient subscriptions. Information for transient subscriptions also resides in the catalog, but this isn't administered using the Component Services snap-in. This information is stored in a transient area of the catalog, so that when the system reboots it will be cleared. The most important difference between the properties of persistent and transient subscriptions is that while the former has a CLSID of the subscriber class which will be created, the latter leaves this `NULL` and provides the `IUnknown` of an existing (already running) subscriber component.

The lifetime of this subscriber is not determined by the event system, as it will have been created by another process. This type of event subscription is similar to connection points, since the client code needs to create the subscriber component and make the subscription to the event, passing the reference to the subscriber component.

> *It is interesting to take this comparison further. The often quoted problem with connection points is that they take many round trips to make and break connections (5 and 4 respectively), and that this is unacceptable (even though they are a once-only hit, which is often negligible compared to the round trips caused by many events being generated). COM+ transient subscriptions require more round trips to make a connection, because they're made by accessing properties in the catalog, and, as you know, property access is very inefficient. However, bear in mind that making subscriptions only involves calls to the local catalog – in future, you will be able to make subscriptions to publishers on other machines.*

A transient subscription will remain active until either:

❑ the system reboots

❑ the item in the `TransientSubscriptions` collection is removed

If the subscriber component is released before either of these two circumstances arise, and an event is generated, then the system will log this in the event log as a warning.

Note that subscriptions can be based on an event interface or on a particular method. In the second case, if you have many subscriptions based on each method, then these should be added individually to the catalog. Usually, all subscribers to an event will be sent the event when it occurs. However, you can specify filters.

Filters

Another problem with connection points is that when an event is sent to a client, the client *must* handle that event, because the client sink object is tightly coupled to the event source component. Because COM+ events are loosely coupled, code can get in between the publisher and subscriber to determine if the event should be propagated, and, if so, to which subscriber. There are two ways to do this: **subscriber filters** and **publisher filters**.

The subscriber filters are applied through the Component Services snap-in. To do this, you select the properties of the subscription (details will be given in the next section) and type in the criteria that will allow the event to be generated. The criteria should include the parameters of the event according to the type information of the EventClass. For example, if the event interface has a method:

```
void OnCreatedPatient([in] BSTR bstrName, [in] short sAge);
```

you could create a subscription called `NewChild` that's only generated when the age is less than 16, the criterion being:

```
sAge < 16
```

When the publisher generates the OnCreatedPatient event, it will go through to the event system, which will read all the subscriptions. The event system then sees that the NewChild subscription has a criterion, and from the type information of the EventClass, it will be able to extract the correct parameter from the event and compare it with the filter criterion. If this is met, the event system will create the handler component and pass it the event.

You can see that with subscriber filters the event is still generated – it's the event system that determines whether a particular subscription will get the event. With publisher filters, the check is performed earlier on in the event generation, and to do this you need to build a filter component and place its CLSID in the PublisherFilterCLSID property of the EventClass's catalog entry. Note that there's no way to do this using the Component Services snap-in, so if you want to use publisher filters you have to make the changes yourself using the catalog API (explained in a later section).

The filter component implements either the IPublisherFilter or the IMultiInterfacePublisherFilter interface. The former is used if the EventClass has just a single interface, and the latter if the EventClass has more than one event interface. Both of these have an Initialize() method, which is called by the events system to inform the filter component of the event subscriptions. In the case of IPublisherFilter, this method is passed an IEventSystem or IEventControl interface, which the filter can use to determine the subscribers of the event. Because IMultiInterfacePublisherFilter is used when the EventClass supports more than one event interface, the Initialize() method is passed an IMultiInterfaceEventControl pointer, through which it can call GetSubscriptions() to get the subscriptions for *all* event interfaces.

The IEventControl interface looks like this:

Method	Description
SetPublisherFilter()	Assigns a publisher filter to a particular event method. This method has the event method name as a BSTR parameter.
GetSubscriptions()	Obtains the collection of subscriptions associated with the event method passed as a BSTR parameter.
SetDefaultQuery()	Sets a filter criterion that will be used if a filter component isn't set for a specified method.

It also has a property called AllowInprocActivation (with get_ and put_ methods) that determines whether subscribers can be activated inproc to the publisher, or whether they should be activated in a separate process. The SetDefaultQuery() looks odd because you wouldn't expect it to be called (because you *have* defined a publisher filter, right?). However, the IEventControl interface is a general interface which is implemented by the event object instance of the EventClass, regardless of whether a publisher filter has been defined.

IPublisherFilter looks like this:

```
interface IPublisherFilter : IUnknown
{
   HRESULT Initialize([in] BSTR methodName,
                      [in, unique] IDispatch* dispUserDefined);
   HRESULT PrepareToFire([in] BSTR methodName,
                      [in] IFiringControl* firingControl);
};
```

When the publisher generates an event, the EventClass will call `PrepareToFire()` on the filter component, passing the event method name and a reference to `IFiringControl` (For EventClasses that have multiple interfaces, the IID of the particular event interface is also passed to `IMultiInterfacePublisherFilter::PrepareToFire()`.) The `IFiringControl` has a single method called `FireSubscription()`, which has a single `IEventSubscription` parameter. The filter should call this method as many times as required, using the parameter to indicate which subscription the event should be sent to, based on the list offered to it via the call to `Initialize()`.

As you can see, the choice of whether the event is generated for a particular event is made in the publisher process. This will become important in the future, when the COM+ event system will allow subscriptions to be made for remote publishers.

System Events

As you've seen in earlier chapters, MTS generates connection point events when particular events occur in a package. Does COM+ have similar events? Indeed it does, but you must be aware that it *only* has COM+ events for Applications – it no longer generates connection point-based MTS events (so tools like the performance monitor DLL described in the last chapter won't work on Windows 2000).

For example, the system generates events on the `IComAppEvents` interface when Application events occur – that is, when they start, stop, or are forced to shut down. This has a filter that will pass all Application events to a subscriber unless a publisher filter property is set. In this case, the filter will check the property against the event and current running Applications, and use this to determine if the event should be sent to that subscriber.

> At the time of writing, the Platform SDK didn't list the filter properties for this event source. However, from the `COMSpy` example (the updated version of `MtsSpy`) it's apparent that you can specify an Application ID or process ID. A subscriber can therefore specify that it wants to get Application events from a specific Application.

Queued Components

COM+ supports the concept of disconnected components. This represents something of an integration of MSMQ (Microsoft Message Queue Server) and COM. However, there's more to this than appears on the surface. 'Queued components on COM+' means that the reams of code you need to write on NT4 with MSMQ are no longer needed, because the COM+ runtime (in response to the queuing attribute) will ensure that method calls are sent via MSMQ messages, and that the server process will pick up these messages accordingly. Queuing is applied to COM+ Applications via COM+ attributes, so no additional code needs to be written. Client code to activate a queued component requires the use of a moniker, but doesn't need any specific queuing code.

There are essentially three main entities used with queued components: a **recorder**, which takes queued component requests and puts them into a message; a **listener**, which polls the queue for a message; and a **player**, which 'plays' the message to create and use a component. The system provides the recorder and the player, and your COM+ Application is the listener:

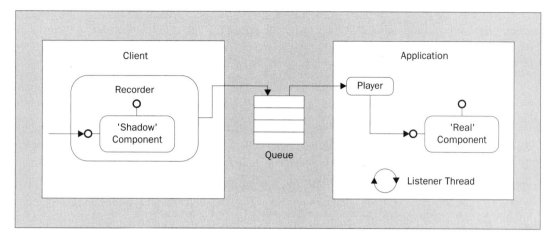

When the client creates a queued component the system creates a 'shadow' component that looks like the queued one. All client calls to this 'shadow' component are recorded (by the recorder) and put into a message, which is sent to the Application's MSMQ queue. The player in the listener reads messages in the queue and 'plays' the messages. This involves creating instances of the requested (queued) component and calling its methods.

Messaging is regarded as *reliable*, so once a message is put into a queue, the client can assume the message will be delivered and therefore that the call will be made. Queued components can be used in a disconnected case, where the transaction on the client side is not distributed across to the server side. Indeed, the message is only sent once the client transaction is committed.

If the message can't be sent for some reason (the queuing system fails, or a server is down) the system tries to re-send the message. COM+ generates a Loosely Coupled Event (LCE) to indicate that there is a problem and to allow the message to be modified. On the third re-try, the message is moved to a dead letter queue where it will sit until the system administrator decides what to do with it.

Although COM+ implements a lot to allow you to use queued components, the client code must also be written to use them, so that the recorder will be used. This occurs through new system moniker called queue, which creates the recorder based on the component's CLSID or ProgID. For example:

```
CoGetObject(L"queue:/new:MyServer.MyObject", NULL, IID_IMyObject,
            (void**)&pObj);
```

Now, whenever the client makes calls to the component, these are recorded in the message. There may be more than one method call to the component, perhaps representing several property set calls, followed by some method call to process those properties. Since the recorder is in-proc there are no performance penalties, even though the actual queued component exists on another machine.

To process the message, the server needs to be run, and needs a listener thread. This is applied by checking the **Listener** check box on the Application's properties, which ensures that it polls its message queue. Any messages in the queue are read and then passed to the player, which creates the component. It then makes the property and method calls (in the order in which they were recorded by the recorder).

On the server side there are a few considerations that you need to take into account, other than specifying that the Application uses queued components. The interface methods must *only* use [in] parameters (reflecting the fact that the methods are called asynchronously, so the client can't expect a response, except to know if the initial queue request worked) and can't use interface pointers. In addition, you should use IDispatch-based interfaces and, in general, only the interface marked as [default], which are restrictions of the recorder.

Unlike many of the other COM+ attributes, a queued component can be identified as using queued component-friendly interfaces in IDL. This is done by applying the QUEUEABLE attribute (actually a macro that applies a [custom()] attribute) to these interfaces.

Compensating Resource Managers

COM+ allows an Application to use a **Compensating Resource Manager** (CRM) This allows the Application to have a say in how MS DTC manages the transaction, and also gives the facility of compensating for failed transactions. To use a CRM you must write various CRM components and write your components to use them – the CRM isn't a transactional component itself. A CRM is made up of three parts: the **clerk**, the **worker**, and the **compensator**. The clerk is implemented by the system and used by the other two CRM components, which you have to implement.

The CRM Worker does most of the CRM work – basically, when you perform some transactional activity you should get the worker to do it. The worker needs to record the actions it's about to perform and inform the clerk of the name of the compensator (either a ProgID or a stringified CLSID) that will be created when the transaction is completed. The worker uses the clerk to record its work, and the clerk ensures that the log is made durable. These logged messages should be carried out *before* the worker actually makes any changes, so that if the transaction fails (or the Application dies) during the work, the compensator will know what the last action was.

The compensator has two purposes. Firstly, it can view the transactional work that the Worker indicates needs to be done, and based on this, decide whether the transaction should succeed. Its other purpose is to *compensate* for a transaction that wasn't completed (perhaps due to a machine crash) using data in the log. The compensator makes these choices by being passed information during the 2-phase commit used by COM+ transactions.

When the transaction is about to be committed, the CRM framework creates the compensator during the first phase, and gives it access to the records that the worker wrote for this transaction. The prepare phase (as you are aware from Chapter 5) exists to allow resource managers to make the transaction log durable, to prepare it before the transaction should be committed. The compensator gets each record that was written by the worker, so when it's informed that the prepare phase is about to end, it can decide (based on these records) whether the prepare should succeed or fail.

If all the resource managers enlisted in the transaction indicate that the prepare phase has succeeded, the final phase starts. As before, the compensator is advised that records are about to be sent. It is then sent all the records for the transaction, and advised that they have been sent. If the first phase indicates that the transaction should succeed, the compensator can commit the transaction by performing the transactional work. The compensator will have appropriate Commit() methods that will be called by the CRM framework. The same process occurs if the transaction aborts, except that the records will be sent to Abort() methods implemented by the compensator.

Now comes the clever bit. If the machine crashes during the second phase, the sequence of actions required by the transaction will be held in durable store. This is so that when the compensator is activated again, it can be fed the logged records and thus complete the transaction. Note that this is not fault tolerance, as the CRM log is saved on the machine where the Application runs (and is therefore not sent to another 'live' machine), and the compensator is not automatically run after an Application crash (the Application will have to be run again to allow the compensator to complete its work).

COM+ and Administration

The first point to make here is that COM and MTS components will work with COM+ – COM+ is COM after all. However, non-COM+ components will not have the benefit of COM+ services. To turn a COM component into one that can use COM+ services, you must configure it with the Component Services snap-in. This allows you to specify the component attributes and henceforth treat it as a configured component.

When you add a component to a COM+ Application, `DllRegisterServer()` is called, and the snap-in will extract the values that it needs for the catalog. With MTS, the catalog was part of the registry held in `HKEY_LOCAL_MACHINE`, but COM registry values put in `HKEY_CLASSES_ROOT` were still used.

With COM+, the values written to `HKEY_CLASSES_ROOT` are not as important as in plain COM. COM+ will look to the catalog first on an activation request, and will use its values to activate the component. If the component isn't configured then the values in `HKEY_CLASSES_ROOT` will be used, as in plain COM.

What about those values `DllRegisterServer()` adds to the registry that are important to COM+? Most of a component's context is determined by the COM+ Component Services snap-in, but there's one value from the component registration that's important: `ThreadingModel`. This is read from the component's `CLSID` entry when you add it to an Application, and stored in the catalog. You can't change this with the snap-in, because clearly it's closely tied to the actual component implementation (although you can change it via the catalog administration API as I'll explain later).

If, during component development, you decide to change the component's threading model, the catalog will be out of sync with `HKEY_CLASSES_ROOT`, so you still have to update the catalog as you did with MTS. This can be done using the context menu of the computer in the Component Services snap-in. However, although `MtxRereg.exe` is no longer provided, it's relatively easy to write a similar tool using the catalog administration API.

> I find it strange that the Component Services snap-in only allows you to refresh *all* components. When you develop an application you typically make small changes, perhaps making these on one component at a time. It would have been nice if the snap-in allowed you to refresh only the components within a single COM+ Application.

Administrative Roles

Before I cover administration of applications and components, it is worth listing the roles of the System Application. Recall that MTS defines two roles for the System package: Administrator and Reader. These determine which accounts can change or read packages on a computer. COM+ defines five roles in Release Candidate 2:

Role	Description
Administrator	Members can modify the configuration of COM applications and components on this system
Reader	Members can read Application configurations and view active component information
Any Application	Members are the *identities* of any COM+ Application that can run on this computer
Server Application	Members are the *identities* of any server Application that can run on this computer
QC Trusted User	Accounts that can transmit messages for queued components

It is interesting to note that only accounts mentioned in the Reader role are able to view performance statistics for COM+ Applications. Since Reader (by default) includes Everyone, this is equivalent to the situation on NT4.

In fact, Release Candidate 2 defined an additional role called IMDB Trusted User, but since the In Memory Database won't make the final release, I have left it out of this table.

Applications

Let's take a look at what configuring means. Like MTS Explorer on NT4, the Component Services snap-in has Wizards, which allow you to install new 'packages' and components. However, as I have already mentioned, a 'package' on Windows 2000 is called a COM+ Application. As with MTS, there is an option allowing you to specify library components that will be loaded into the client process, which are called library Applications.

Earlier in this book, you will have read that when you create a new, empty MTS package, the Explorer will always assume that it is a server Package. This is not so with the COM+ Component Services snap-in:

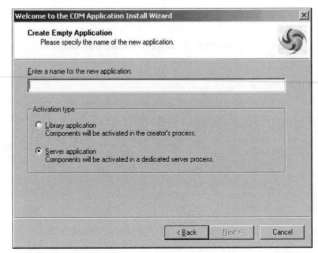

The lower frame determines the Application type. If you choose a Server Application, you will be given the option of determining the Application identity. If you choose a Library Application, this wizard page won't be provided (as it is irrelevant).

Applications have the General, Identity, Activation, Security and Advanced property pages in common with MTS packages. These are essentially the same as for MTS packages, except that there are some additional options on the latter three. In addition, because MSMQ is better integrated with COM, there is also a Queuing page that allows you to specify whether the Application serves queued components.

Activation

The Activation page is similar to its equivalent in MTS 2.0, but has the addition of an edit box in which to specify the host machine name (in the event that the component runs on another machine). This is in contrast with the MTS 2.0 Explorer, which did not associate remote components with a package. (You could use remote components in a package, but the administration tools didn't recognize them when defining it). COM+ treats remote components the same as locally installed components, reinforcing COM's location transparency at an installation level.

Security

Remember that under MTS 2.0 you could apply security to packages (to specify the authentication level and whether role based authorization was used) and components (to indicate if role based authorization was used). Under COM+ you'll find security tabs on the properties of not only Applications and components, but also on the properties of interfaces and methods. As with MTS 2.0, the authorization checks are made against Roles defined in the Application.

Security Tab for:	Description
Application	Specifies the authentication and impersonation levels that will be used, specifies if authorization checks are made and the granularity of those checks (either at the process level, or both at the process and component level).
Component	Specifies if access checks are made at the component level and the roles that can access the component.
Interface	Determines the roles that can access the methods on this interface. The tab lists the roles that have permission to access the component, and allows you to give permission to other roles defined for the Application.
Method	Determines the roles that can access the particular method. The tab lists the roles with permission to access the component and interface. It also allows you to give permission to other roles defined for the Application.

As the previous table implies, you define roles for the Application, then progressively add roles that can access a specified component, specified interfaces on the component, and specified methods on the interfaces. As for MTS roles, you can't indicate that particular accounts are *denied* permissions, so you should make careful choices about adding groups to roles, because if an account is a member of a group it will also be a member of a role it's added to, and the only way to deny that account access is to remove it from the group (you can't indicate that you don't want an account in a role).

The Application Security page looks like this:

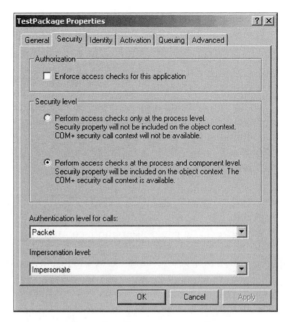

In addition to the general Application-wide authorization switch, and authentication and impersonation levels that were present for MTS Packages, you also have the option of turning off access checks made at component level and interface level.

Windows 2000 adds an additional level of impersonation called delegation. When this is used, it means that if a component in the Application makes a call to a component in another Application, the caller component is happy for the called component to impersonate it for out-of-process calls. LAN Manager security (the default on NT4) did not allow this to happen, but Kerberos (the default on Windows 2000) does allow this, as long as the delegation impersonation level is specified and that two other criteria are met:

❑ The account used by the calling component is set to be 'safe' for delegation in the Active Directory. This means that the administrator has checked the privileges assigned to this account, and has verified that they are not too privileged for such a 'risky' action as allowing the account to be delegated.

❑ The account used by the called component (the one that will impersonate the calling account) is 'trusted' for delegation in the Active Directory. In other words, the administrator is happy that this account is *bone fide* and will use the privilege of delegation with due respect.

Clearly delegation is a powerful facility, so you must use it with caution. It allows a server's account to be 'cloaked', as illustrated in the following diagram:

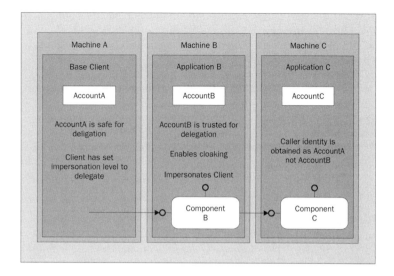

Advanced

The Application Advanced page looks like this:

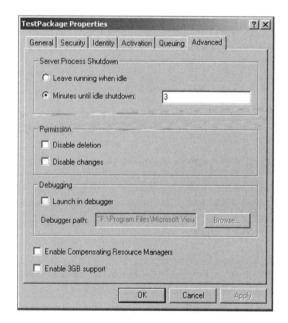

The top two frames are the same as for MTS Packages, but there are some new options at the bottom of the page. The first is Launch in debugger, which allows you to indicate that the Application should be launched under the watchful gaze of a debugger. The tab allows you to specify which debugger you will use. For example, on my machine, I have Visual C++ 6 registered as the default debugger (it is mentioned in the Debugger value under AeDebug in the registry), so the tab uses that as the debugger and gives the following path:

```
msdev.exe dllhost.exe /ProcessID:{8F033820-FF36-11D2-8828-0060973044A8}
```

The GUID is the Application identifier given on the General page. As mentioned before, COM+ assumes that the Application is launched with DllHost as the surrogate. Now stop and think. This is fine if your Application is throwing exceptions and you want to find out what is causing them, but what if you want to set breakpoints?

Well, when you use this option, it means that COM+ won't actually start the Application (despite the inclusion of a ProcessID, this doesn't refer to a running instance of DllHost). Instead, it starts the debugger, instructs it to load DllHost, and says that when the debugger runs the process it should use the specified command line options. You have two options here. In the first you must be quick and use Developer Studio's Project, Settings dialog, selecting the Debug tab, then the Additional DLLs from the Category box to specify the server that you are interested in. Then you can load the source and header files that have the code and set the breakpoints, after which you can start the process and wait for the breakpoints to be hit.

I say that you have to be fast, because the COM+ runtime will give you 90 seconds between trying to access components in the Application and actually starting DllHost, which is a rather short time to search for DLLs and source files. It makes better sense to set up Developer Studio before trying to debug the Application. To do this, load DllHost into Developer Studio yourself, setting the command line options and additional DLLs. You can then load the source files and set the breakpoints without using the COM+ runtime. Once the workspace is set up, you can save it (Developer Studio saves dllhost.opt with the settings you have made), check Launch in debugger in the Component Services Explorer, and run your client. When Developer Studio starts this time, you can just press F5 to run the process and wait for the breakpoints to be hit.

> This may sound like a lot of effort to you, and I agree. I can't see why you would want to use this option when it is clearly simpler to run DllHost.exe under Developer Studio yourself.

Of the other two settings, the second one (Enable 3GB support) is only applicable to the versions of Win2000 (Advanced Server and Data Center) that support it. It specifies that the Application needs 3Gb of virtual memory. Of course, this doesn't necessarily mean that the Application needs 3Gb of physical memory! Microsoft have found that for large users of virtual memory there is a performance boost if the application has 3Gb rather then the default 2Gb.

The other setting (Enable Compensating Resource Managers) indicates that the Application uses a CRM. As mentioned earlier, the CRM allows the Application to have a say in how MS DTC manages the transaction, and also gives the facility of compensating for failed transactions.

Queuing

The Queuing tab is new to COM+
Applications:

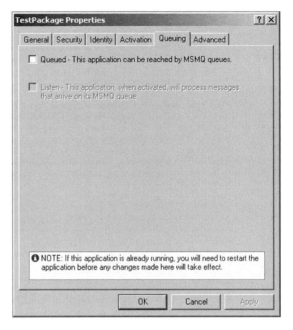

On this page there are two check box options. The first specifies whether the Application will use
queued components, and if you select this then the second option will also be enabled. This second
option indicates that the Application is a **listener**, that is, it will respond to component requests via
messages.

When you do this, COM+ will create a queue for the Application (using the Application name). Now,
when a client makes a request to a queued component, it's made via a message in this queue. The
client is fully aware that the Application may not exist, but this doesn't matter because the queue will
record all method calls made to the component. The component and client, of course, will have to be
written in such a way to take this into account – in particular, methods should only have [in]
parameters.

Configuring Components

Components are added to Applications through a Component Services snap-in wizard. This behaves
in a similar fashion to the corresponding wizard in the MTS Explorer, in that it allows you to add
components directly from a DLL, as well as plain COM components that have already been
registered in HKEY_CLASSES_ROOT, as shown in the screenshot overleaf.

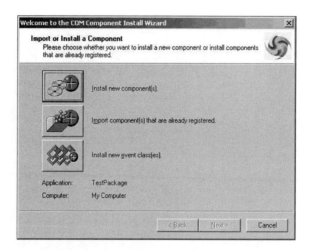

Notice the third button. This is how you add the 'dummy' components that represent the EventClass for COM+ events.

Here are the properties of a configured component within a COM+ Application:

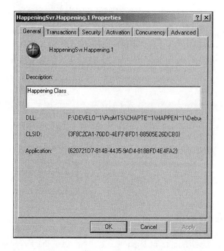

The first thing you'll notice is that there are three additional pages: Activation, Concurrency and Advanced. I will explain these in a moment, but for now let's concentrate on the first page, General. This is similar to the MTS Explorer General tab for a component, but now there's an additional GUID called `Application`. Although it has a similar meaning, this isn't an `AppID` but another GUID, defined by COM+ to uniquely identify the COM+ Application. To illustrate this, try searching the registry for the `Application` GUID. You won't find it, the reason being that since it isn't a plain COM concept, it has no place in the COM registry.

If you click on the other tabs, you'll see that although some of the COM+ attributes correspond to MTS 2.0 attributes, the majority of them are new. The Transaction tab, for example, has the options that you are familiar with from the MTS Explorer, but the Security tab has changed, and there are also those new tabs.

Security

When you open a component's node in the snap-in, you'll see two child nodes: Interfaces and Subscriptions. The former is familiar from MTS – it lists the interfaces that the component implements, as gleaned from a type library. The second node is used by subscriber components to contain its persistent subscriptions. There is something missing though – where is the list of roles that can access the component? This administration is now performed through the Security property page for a component:

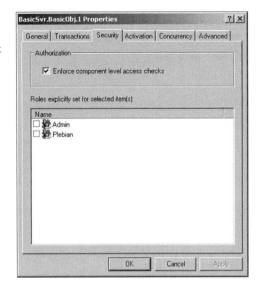

The list box at the bottom of the page gives all the roles that have been defined for the Application, and you can select those that are allowed to access this component. This is a distinct improvement over the MTS Explorer, where package roles and the roles that could access components and interfaces were presented in a similar way. This could therefore lead to confusion for the novice user.

When you check a role on this page, it means that users in that role will be able to access all interfaces on the component.

Activation

The Activation tab on a component looks like this:

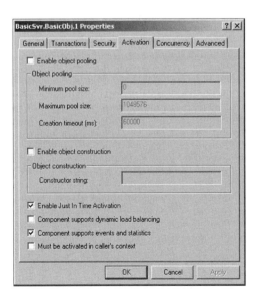

This doesn't exist with MTS 2.0, and requires deeper investigation.

COM+ supports the concept of object pooling (note that `IObjectControl::CanBePooled()` isn't used to determine if the component in general supports pooling, but whether it is returned to the pool after deactivation). Once you've specified that a component can be pooled, you can determine the pooling attributes: the maximum and minimum size of the pool, and how long can be taken to create each component. When the Application starts, COM+ will create the specified minimum number of components, and when the Application is under stress from client connections, COM+ will create components up to the maximum limit.

Object pooling helps in making Applications more scaleable and components more available, because it allows a pool of components to be created (and initialized) when the Application starts, rather than when the component is actually requested. However, there is a downside to this. If the construction time of a component is long (and the minimum number of components in the pool is high) then the start-up time of the application will be long. To prevent this delay from being excessive, you can set a construction timeout value.

If the time taken to construct a component exceeds this value then an error will be generated. Just-in-time activation is implied in object pooling. However, you can also apply it for non-pooled components, which is the reason for the check box on the **Activation** tab. The component should also indicate whether it can generate COM+ events using the **Component supports events and statistics** check box.

The final option on this page determines whether the component should be activated in the same context as the client or not. Note that you should think carefully about using this option. When you say that the component *must* be activated in the client's context, it implies that activation will fail if the client's context doesn't support the facilities used by the component. You would want to check this box if you don't want marshaling to occur (which is how COM+ handles context boundaries crossings), or if the interface is [local] (or you feel that you cannot bear the small amount of time that marshaling involves). In most cases, it is best to leave this option unchecked.

> *This screenshots in this section come from Windows 2000 Release Candidate 2, which had dynamic load balancing. However, the release version of Windows 2000 won't have this facility.*

Concurrency

MTS uses activities to manage concurrency. Components are activated in a new activity when they are created with `CoCreateInstanceEx()` – or if `IObjectContext::CreateInstance()` is used, the component will be created in the same activity as its creator. It works this way because `CoCreateInstanceEx()` doesn't understand MTS, so it doesn't know what the activity of the creator is. Because of this, when it asks `mtx.exe` to create a component, it can't pass on this information, so `mtx.exe` must create a new activity. `CoCreateInstanceEx()` on Windows 2000 *does* understand COM+, so it's able to obtain the activity of the creator. This means that the option of whether the component is created in its creator's activity or in a new activity doesn't have to depend on how the component is created. Instead, COM+ provides the **Synchronization** attribute to indicate this.

The association between activities and synchronization comes from the fact that each activity has a lock, ensuring that all code in an activity is treated as single threaded (that is, concurrent access into an activity isn't allowed). However, note that this lock is only applicable to a single process – an activity can extend across processes and machines, so this guarantee against concurrent access only applies to a single process.

You specify the synchronization attribute for components on their **Concurrency** tab. The following shows the possible values for the synchronization attribute – the threading model is a COM attribute, applied through the `ThreadingModel` value in the registry (in this case `Both`).

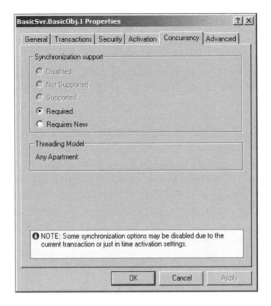

Notice the comment at the bottom of the page – the snap-in has disabled the first three options because this particular component has the **Enable Just In Time Activation** check box checked on the **Activation** page. In general, if a component has transaction support or supports JIT activation then it will need an activity. In both these cases, you'll find that only the last two options will be enabled, indicating that the component must run in a context with an activity. The full set of options is described in the table below:

Synchronization Attribute	Description
Disabled	Synchronization is disabled.
Not Supported	The component is created without an activity.
Supported	If the creator is in an activity then the component will be created in that, otherwise it will be created without an activity.
Requires	If the creator is in an activity then the component will be created in that, otherwise a new activity will be created.
Requires New	A new activity is always created.

Advanced

The Advanced page will look something like this:

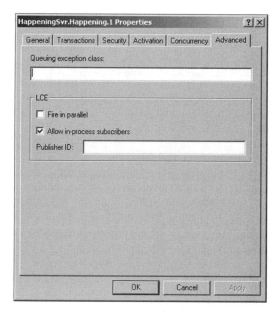

The top edit box will appear for all components, but the LCE frame will only be present for EventClasses.

The Queuing Exception Class is the ProgID of a class that is activated by the queuing player before sending a message to the dead letter queue. This is used to play back the message, so that the exception component can perform some handling based on the message. This exception class should implement the IPlaybackControl interface.

In the LCE frame, the first check box is used to specify that if there is more than one subscriber, events will be generated in parallel and the event system will create several threads to do this. The edit box gives the identifier of the publisher for which it will handle events. If in-process subscribers are allowed then no security checks are made when events are generated – if you are concerned about security checks then you should uncheck this box.

Configuring Subscriptions

Subscriptions are 'properties' of subscriber components that can receive events. Persistent subscriptions can be added to the catalog using the Component Services snap-in. To do this you use the context menu of the Subscriptions node (underneath the subscriber component node), which gives you a Wizard allowing you to enter details. The subscriber component will catch events generated by a publisher, which means that the subscriber component must implement one of the event interfaces indicated by the EventClass that you have already added.

The first page of the Wizard gives the interfaces and methods implemented on a subscriber component:

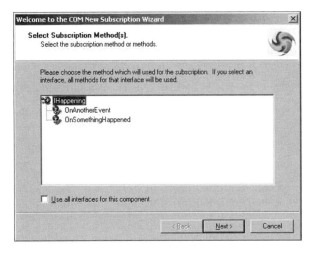

For this subscription you can say that the subscriber will respond to events corresponding to a single method, to all methods on an interface, or all the methods on all its interfaces. This is very flexible, and allows you to design interfaces that group together many different events. If the subscriber is only interested in a few events, all it need do is provide the appropriate methods. Contrast this to connection points, where if your sink component supports a custom sink interface then it must implement all methods.

Once you have selected an event interface, the Wizard will scan the catalog for all the EventClasses that implement it. You then have the option to select one or more EventClasses, or all classes that implement the event interface. Finally, you can give the subscription a name:

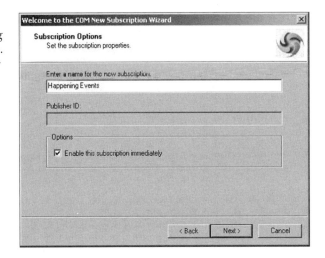

Once you have done this, you will find that the new subscription has been added to the node, and you can then configure its properties. These allow you to specify how the event is generated along with filter criteria. There are other subscription properties (`PerUser` and `Username` for example, where the former specifies that the subscription only applies to the user mentioned in the latter), but to access these you must use the catalog API.

The first page looks like this:

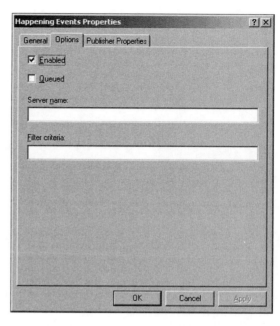

Notice how the subscription can be queued, that is, it can be generated by MSMQ. By default the subscription will be disabled (although you can specify when you create one that it should be enabled), this page gives you the facility to enable it.

The filter criteria are held in a string, containing values that the subscriber filter uses to determine whether the subscriber can receive the event. They can use relational operators like ==, =, <, >, and operators like AND, OR, and NOT. You can also use the CLSID of a filter component.

For each subscription you can also specify properties of the publisher:

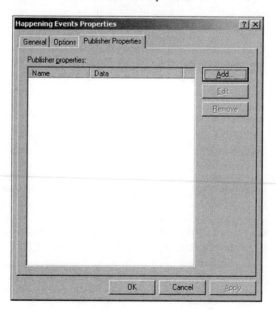

These are string-string pairs. Publishers are associated with a property bag, and can access these pairs through the `IEventPublisher` interface on the system-supplied `CLSID_CEventPublisher` component. The publisher passes this component its ID and then calls `GetDefaultPropertyCollection()` to get the property bag containing them.

Configuring Interfaces

Interfaces have three property pages: General, Queuing and Security. They no longer have the Proxy page that was present for MTS 2.0, regardless of whether the interface is marshaled with a type library or a proxy-stub DLL. The Queuing page has a single check box: Queued, which specifies whether calls to this interface can be called on a queued component – this is disabled if the interface is custom. The Security Page looks like this:

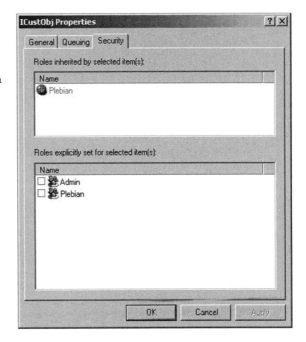

The top box indicates the roles that have been given access to the component that implements this interface (in this case the `Plebian` role). The lower box has the roles defined for the Application, which you can select to give access to the interface. It is interesting to note that inherited roles aren't removed from the lower box, implying that you can explicitly add the role to the interface and to the component. This means that if, at a later stage, you remove the role from the component (indicating that you no longer want the role to have access to *all* interfaces on the component), it will still have access to the interface.

Again, unlike the MTS Explorer there is no Role Membership node under the interface node, because access is given to roles via this property page.

Configuring Methods

The Component Services snap-in no longer lists the `IUnknown` and `IDispatch` interface methods. For the other methods it gives two property pages: General and Security. The first is similar to MTS in that it allows you to give a description for the method. However, it has a new check box, marked Automatically deactivate the object when this method returns. This is disabled if the component doesn't support JIT activation, and you can use it to selectively determine JIT on a method-by-method basis.

The Security page is new to COM+. In MTS, you couldn't specify role-based access checks on methods through the MTS Explorer. This page is similar to the interface security page, in that it lists both the roles that have access to the component and interface, as well as listing the roles defined for the package, so you can give a finer-grained access control policy.

Configuration Summary

Configuration appeared on NT4, with MTS components for which the catalog administrator was able to indicate security and transaction attributes. On Windows 2000, configuration has taken on a far greater role (no pun intended), because the COM runtime libraries have taken on more responsibility for the environment (the context under which a component will run).

This 'catalog administrator' can be either the component developer or someone else with administrative access to the deployment machine (by this I mean someone mentioned in the Administrator role of the System Application). This is both a good thing and a potential problem for the COM+ developer.

By implementing all these facilities into the runtime, the developer is released from having to initialize and use them. Transaction enlistment is therefore automatic, as are access checks, synchronization, and recording of queued component method accesses. However, context is applied to a COM+ component based on its configuration in the catalog. A developer can specify the preferred context by exporting a package, or by using the catalog API in an installation program. However, the catalog administrator is able to alter this context, potentially changing the way that the component behaves.

COM+ Applications (like MTS packages) have a Disable changes option, which will prevent the catalog administrator from changing the configuration – clearly, though, this itself can be changed. Preserving the component configuration of MTS packages has always been important, and with the increased number of attributes and system reliance on COM+ Applications, preservation of their configuration becomes even more important.

The COM+ Catalog

Yes, MTS has administrative components to allow you to access the MTS catalog (as was explained in Chapter 3), but this was essentially just an abstraction of the Transaction Server key in the HKEY_LOCAL_MACHINE hive of the registry. You could always use the registry API to make changes to this key if you chose to. The COM+ catalog is a different entity. For a start, the only way you can programmatically access the COM+ catalog is through the admin components (on Windows 2000 these are the COMAdmin components). The second significant difference is that potentially *all* components running on a Windows 2000 machine will be COM+, and hence included in the catalog – under NT4 the MTS catalog appeared as an interesting admin tool for MTS components, where by and large they were the minority components on a system. The catalog is now an important part of the data needed to create and use COM+ components.

The Platform SDK says that if your component is written as a COM+ component (and is therefore designed to take advantage of COM+ services), then it should *not* be registered in the registry, but only in the catalog. This sounds like the death knell of HKEY_CLASSES_ROOT, but it isn't, at least not quite. For a start there are some values that *must* be put into the registry because they can't be put in type libraries – the ProgID and ThreadingModel for a component in particular. There will always be 'legacy' applications and tools that expect information in HKEY_CLASSES_ROOT, so whenever you register a component with the catalog, the COMAdmin components will add the relevant information to the registry to keep your old programs happy.

> *In fact, in an attempt to try and reinforce the multi-user aspects of NT, developers are recommended not to access data in* HKEY_CLASSES_ROOT, *but are instead directed to use the keys under* HKEY_CURRENT_USER\Software\Classes. *My experience of the Release Candidate 2 build of Windows 2000 is that very few developers have taken this advice (though perhaps this merely reflects the fact that most of the applications I have installed know nothing about Windows 2000, and therefore still use the old registry hives). However, as a developer you should be aware that there will be* three *places for COM information in the foreseeable future:* HKEY_CLASSES_ROOT, HKEY_CURRENT_USER, *and the COM+ catalog.*

Almost all of the COM+ attributes can be changed with the Component Services snap-in. However, there are a few that you can't manipulate in this way. ThreadingModel is an obvious example, as it requires privileged knowledge of how the component is implemented. When you add a component to an Application, the Component Services snap-in will call DllRegisterServer(), read the CLSID, ProgID, ThreadingModel, and DLL name registered, and add these as attributes to the component in the catalog.

You can still use the MTS admin components (Catalog, CatalogCollection, and CatalogObject) to get information about a COM+ configured component, but these will only give access to the MTS 2.0 properties (although clearly properties like PackageName and PackageID are no longer relevant). The same components could have been used to return COM+ attributes, because their programming model gives access to these as named properties. However, Microsoft decided to make the assertive statement that these older components aren't used to administer COM+ components, but are instead used to administer plain COM components. To administer COM+ components, you should use the new components, whose names (and those of their interfaces) are prefixed with COMAdmin as shown in the following table:

MTS 2.0 Component	COM+ Equivalent Component
Catalog	COMAdminCatalog
CatalogCollection	COMAdminCatalogCollection
CatalogObject	COMAdminCatalogObject

You can use these in just the same way as you use the MTS catalog components (see Chapter 4). Significantly though, there are no longer any Util components, and the collection components don't provide the GetUtilInterface() method. The reason for this is that the methods of the Util components are now implemented directly by the COMAdminCatalog component.

In contrast to MTS, the COM+ Admin components are transactional, so whenever you add or change items in the catalog (whether using the MMC snap-in or the components themselves), a transaction will be used.

Catalog Collections

The COM+ admin components support more collections than the MTS 2.0 components. These are shown in the following table, where they are compared with the old MTS components.

MTS 2.0 Collections	COM+ Equivalent Collections
ComponentsInPackage	Components
ComputerList	ComputerList
ErrorInfo	ErrorInfo
InterfacesForComponent	InterfacesForComponent
InterfacesForRemoteComponent	
LocalComputer	LocalComputer
MethodsForInterface	MethodsForInterface
Packages	Applications
PropertyInfo	PropertyInfo
RelatedCollectionInfo	RelatedCollectionInfo
RemoteComponents	
RolesForPackageComponent	RolesForComponent
RolesForPackageComponentInterface	RolesForInterface
RolesInPackage	Roles
UsersInRole	UsersInRole
	ApplicationCluster
	DCOMProtocols
	InprocServers
	RolesForMethod
	Root
	PublisherProperties
	SubscriberProperties
	Subscriptions
	TransientSubscriptions

The following figure shows the relationship between the various collections. The arrows show which ones you can access with a call to `ICatalogCollection::GetCollection()`. Note that most of them have access to `RelatedCollectionInfo`, `PropertyInfo`, and `ErrorInfo`, which I have missed out for clarity.

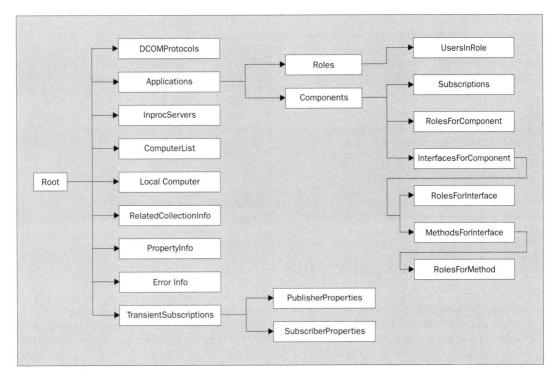

As the name suggests, `Root` is the root of all other collections, only contains collections, and is used to give access to the other top level collections used by the `COMAdmin` components.

Some of the MTS collections have been renamed (`Packages`, for example, becomes `Applications`), but others are more interesting. There is no distinction between interfaces on remote components and those on local components (indeed there is no longer a `RemoteComponents` collection). This reflects that, once installed, the Component Services snap-in treats all COM+ components the same, whether they are installed on different machines or not. This fixes a curious anomaly in the administration components on MTS.

The `InprocServers` collection is a front end to the plain COM registry, and doesn't allow you to add or remove servers. Instead, it merely exists to give you information about those servers that are installed on the system and implemented in DLLs. In effect, this iterates through `HKEY_CLASSES_ROOT\CLSID`, and lists all the items with an `InprocServer32` key. (Since the `COMAdmin` components will add this information for COM+ components, these are also added to the `InprocServers` collection).

The `DCOMProtocols` collection lists the protocols installed on the system. It supports both read and write actions, though I should advise you against adding or removing protocols. It's more useful in allowing you to change the order that DCOM uses (by default) on this machine – remember, DCOM uses lazy protocol loading and will only load a protocol when it detects that it is actually being used. If DCOM packets come in on another protocol, DCOM uses the order in the protocol list to determine which protocol driver to load next. It will clearly take time if your client makes a DCOM request on the protocol at the bottom of the list (since DCOM will first load and try the protocols higher in the list). So, if your network runs on a different protocol to the TCP/IP default, it makes sense to change the order of the protocols using this collection.

> *Note that unlike NT4, Windows 2000 uses TCP/IP as the default protocol. Indeed, Windows 2000 no longer supports the connectionless protocol UDP/IP. This is not a problem, since if you have a TCP network it will support both TCP and UDP packets. Presumably though, this does mean that calls from Windows 2000 to NT4 hosts will experience the old problem (suffered by Win9x clients) of a delay while NT4 lazily loads the TCP protocol – however, this only occurs on the first call made.*

The `TransientSubscriptions` collection contains current transient subscriptions to COM+ events. In addition to the subscription properties, the collection gives access to subscriber and publisher properties (through the `SubscriberProperties` and `PublisherProperties` collections).

The final new collection is `RolesForMethod`. As the name suggests, the administrator can now specify role membership down to the method granularity, thus preventing the developer having to make calls to `IObjectContext::IsCallerInRole()`.

Where Does This Leave You?

If your objects will only be used as COM+ components, you should register them as such and make your installer use the `COMAdmin` components. Indeed, Windows 2000 now features the Windows Installer as a separate facility, as part of the operating system. MTS 2.0, as you know, allows you to export MTS packages to a collection of files that the MTS Explorer can use to import the package (a `.pak` file and the separate server DLLs). The Component Services snap-in will export an Application to a single `.msi` file, and, reflecting the fact that 'MTS' is part of the operating system, the `.msi` file format is used by the entire operating system as part of the zero administration initiative.

The `.msi` file is an OLE compound file that contains all the information needed to install a COM+ Application within OLE streams: catalog information (`.clb` file), type information (`.tlb`) and the actual server DLLs and proxy-stub DLLs (stored as `.cab` files). This means that any Win2000 machine will be able to import the single `.msi` file that has all the information to install the Application. (Windows Installer also allows the `.msi` file of larger applications to point to external `.cab` files for additional information.) Furthermore, the Windows Installer is smart, in that if an Application becomes damaged it can repair the damage using data in the `.msi` file. (For 'damaged' read 'if you delete some of the DLLs or their registration information during an aggressive clean up of your hard disk or your catalog'!)

The preferred way to prepare an Application for deployment to use the Component Services snap-in to configure the Application and its components, then to export them as an `.msi` file. Since all new COM components developed for Windows 2000 should be COM+ components, this means that *any* development you carry out on Win2000 should be done this way, regardless of whether you use transactions. Contrast this with COM development on NT4, where packages were the domain of MTS-based applications.

The information stored in the `.msi` files needs further explanation. Firstly, it contains the component library for your Application (`.clb`). What this actually means is that it contains all the extra configuration information (which you added using the Component Services snap-in) in an undocumented binary file. There is presently no API to load or manipulate `.clb` files (unlike `.tlbs`) – the only way you can access them is through the `COMAdmin` components, and this will only manipulate `.clbs` that have been installed on the system.

On the build of Win2000 that I am using, `.clbs` *are written to the*
`%systemroot%\Registration` *directory, and appear to be used to hold information for
many COM+ components. Hopefully this will change in the future, to allow you to associate a*
`.clb` *with a single component and give developers more control.*

Next, the `.msi` file contains the type information (`.tlb`) and proxy-stub DLLs. Since the proxy-stubs
must be created with fast format string information (`/Oicf`), the combination of these two file types
gives the Component Services snap-in (and COM+) enough information to know the classes,
interfaces, and methods that your components use. This certainly has a feeling of a Version 1.0 of
COM+, being a mixture of the old (`.tlb`, proxy-stubs) and the new (`.clb`). One can only hope that
as the tools get more COM+ aware, the need for the older type information will be reduced, and that
Version 2.0 will give us a richer component library, giving complete component descriptions.

Windows 2000 Transactions

In Windows 2000, the MS DTC has been extended to allow it to use Transaction Internet Protocol
(TIP) transactions and XA transactions, as well as OLE transactions. To accommodate these, the
interfaces available from the DTC proxy have been extended, as have object contexts. Furthermore,
since COM+ Applications have automatic transaction enlistment (which will by default use OLE
transactions) COM+ provides a mechanism called **Bring Your Own Transaction** (**BYOT**), which
allows you to create an external transaction and enlist your COM+ component into it.

Bring Your Own Transaction

COM+, like MTS, will create transactions automatically. The problem with this (as you have seen
previously in this book) is that the transaction will be created with a default timeout. This timeout is
machine-wide, so if a particular component will require a timeout longer than the default 60 seconds,
it means that the machine administrator needs to increase the transaction timeout value for *all*
components on the machine. This is a problem, and there's no way to fix it with MTS.

COM+ introduces BYOT, which allows an application to be associated with, or inherit, an external
transaction (rather then one that COM+ thinks the component should use). You can therefore create
your own transaction and then associate it with a component.

COM+ provides a component called `Byot.ByotServerEx` that will do the association for you,
implementing `ICreateWithTransactionEx` and `ICreateWithTIPTransactionEx`. These
allow you to associate a component with an instance of the MS DTC (or some other OLE transaction
compliant transaction object) or a TIP transaction (see next section). `ICreateWithTransactionEx`
looks like this:

```
interface ICreateWithTransactionEx : IUnknown
{
    HRESULT CreateInstance([in] ITransaction *pTransaction,
        [in] REFCLSID rclsid, [in] REFIID riid,
        [out, iid_is(riid)] void** pObject);
};
```

You should create your own transaction (perhaps by calling
`ITransactionDispenser::BeginTransaction()`) and pass this with the CLSID of the
component you want to create and the IID of the interface that you want to access. The
`Byot.ByotServerEx` object will create the new component and associate it with the specified
transaction. Note that this component must run under COM+ (with at least **Supports transactions**
set) and the object that it creates should run under COM+ and marked as supporting transactions (at
least).

The transaction is a *manual* transaction – that is, when the object is released it isn't automatically
committed, so your code will have to do this explicitly. If you don't do this then the transaction will
remain active, even though the component doesn't exist. The transaction will, of course, end when
the timeout period has run out.

COM+ transactions aren't the same as MTS transactions. You can't propagate a COM+ created
transaction to MTS machines. Indeed, you won't even be able to add MTS 2.0 machines to the
COM+ Component Services snap-in, or add Windows 2000 machines to the MTS Explorer. COM+
does have the facility of converting a COM+ transaction object to an MTS transaction object. COM+
transaction objects implement `ITransaction2` as well as `ITransaction`:

```
interface ITransactionCloner : IUnknown
{
    HRESULT CloneWithCommitDisabled([out] ITransaction ** ppITransaction);
};

interface ITransaction2 : ITransactionCloner
{
    HRESULT GetTransactionInfo2([out] XACTTRANSINFO *pinfo);
};
```

As you can see, the MTS transaction is created with commit disabled – only the COM+ transaction
can be committed, but the transaction can be aborted.

Transaction Internet Protocols Extensions

Transaction Internet Protocol (TIP) is a protocol allowing transactions to be used on the internet
between heterogeneous machines. It has been designed with the web in mind, so it runs over TCP
(port 3372 by default), and may use Transport Layer Security to authenticate transaction managers
and encrypt messages. In this scheme, transaction managers are identified with URLs, as are the
transactions they create. TIP supports exporting and importing (pushing and pulling in TIP parlance)
transactions between transaction managers, which means that a transaction could be active across
several machines on the internet.

COM+ allows you to use TIP transactions with COM+ transactions through the BYOT object. This
object supports the `ICreateWithTipTransactionEx` interface, which allows you to create an
object with the separate TIP transaction:

```
interface ICreateWithTipTransactionEx : IUnknown
{
    HRESULT CreateInstance([in] BSTR bstrTipUrl,
                           [in] REFCLSID rclsid,
                           [in] REFIID riid,
                           [iid_is(riid), out] void** pObject);
};
```

As with `ICreateWithTransactionEx`, this has the CLSID of the object that the BYOT object will create and enlist in the external transaction. The transaction is represented by the URL passed in the `BSTR` first parameter.

To import TIP transactions as OLE transactions you can use `ITipHelper`, which allows you to import either synchronously (`Pull()`) or asynchronously (`PullAsync()`). Since a TIP transaction could be created on a remote server across the internet, it may take a long time to get access to the transaction. (If the same transaction has already been 'pulled', the cached value will be used.) The asynchronous version allows you to pass a reference to the `ITipPullSink` on a client-implemented sink object. Thus the client thread will not be blocked while the transaction is pulled. The OLE transaction object that is created will have both the `ITransaction` and `ITipTransaction` interfaces:

```
interface ITipTransaction : public IUnknown
{
    HRESULT Push([in, string] char* i_pszRemoteTmUrl,
                 [out, string] char** o_ppszRemoteTxUrl);
    HRESULT GetTransactionUrl([out, string] char** o_ppszLocalTxUrl);
};
```

This allows you to export a transaction ('push' it) to a TIP transaction manager.

Furthermore, the component context object also supports `IObjectContextTip`:

```
interface IObjectContextTip : public IUnknown
{
    HRESULT GetTipUrl([retval, out] BSTR* pTipUrl);
};
```

Phase 0 Enlistment Objects

In Chapter 5 I explained how an application (but not an MTS application) can use a voter object to participate in the first phase of the 2-phase commit. Windows 2000 introduces Phase 0 enlistment objects, which allow client code to be informed before the 2-phase commit is just about to start.

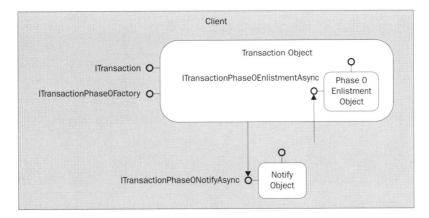

As with the other asynchronous notification mechanisms, the client first obtains the factory interface. However, in this case the factory interface is on the transaction object that you wish to receive the notifications for, rather than the DTC proxy. The client then calls the `Create()` method to obtain the Phase 0 enlistment object. This method also takes a reference to the notify object implemented by the client code.

Note that this is a one shot process, so once notifications are sent the client code needs to call `Create()` again to get further notifications. The enlistment interface looks like this:

```
interface ITransactionPhase0EnlistmentAsync : IUnknown
{
    HRESULT Enable(void);
    HRESULT WaitForEnlistment(void);
    HRESULT Phase0Done(void);
    HRESULT Unenlist(void);
    HRESULT GetTransaction([out] ITransaction** ppITransaction);
};
```

`GetTransaction()` just returns a reference to the associated transaction. The enlistment object itself is created in a disabled state, so the client code must first call `Enable()` or `WaitForEnlistment()` to indicate that it is ready to accept notifications. When it no longer wants the notifications it calls `Unenlist()`. Most of the methods in this interface are handled asynchronously (hence the names of the interfaces) – for example, when the client calls `Enable()` to enlist in notifications, the calling thread will continue while the actual enlistment is carried out. Since this is asynchronous, `Enable()` doesn't return a value to indicate if the enlistment was completed. Instead, this status is passed to the notify object through the `EnlistCompleted()` method of `ITransactionPhase0NotifyAsync`.

If the client wishes synchronous enlistment, that is, it wishes to block until the enlistment is completed, it should call `WaitForEnlistment()`, the return value indicating whether the enlistment was successful.

When the MS DTC wants to indicate that the 2-phase commit is about to start, the proxy calls `Phase0Request()` on the client's notify object. The client can then perform its preparation for 2-phase commit. Once this is done, it calls `Phase0Done()` on the enlistment object. At this point, the enlistment object is in a 'done' state, which means that when it's released, the client doesn't want the associated transaction to abort. However, if the client didn't call `Phase0Done()` or `Unenlist()`, then when the enlistment object is released it will abort the transaction.

Summary

The title of this chapter says it all – COM+ is the way forward for COM development. COM+ attributes mark a shift in the way that you should develop your code. To get services in the old days (for example to use the NT Event Log) you had to explicitly call API methods to initialize those services and use their facilities. COM+ represents a change in programming, in that you don't request the use of services in your code. Instead, an administrator marks the component with an attribute, to indicate that it will use the service, and the facilities are added at runtime using interception. The current release of COM+ is the first wave of such services (sadly, these don't include the services of the Event Log, so you still have to use the arcane API). We can only hope that in the future Microsoft will allow developers to add their own services to COM+, also applied through attributes.

Microsoft has decided that the registry is no longer the best place for COM information (a tradition that goes back to the days of OLE2 on Windows 3.1). Instead, the COM+ catalog is used, which as a technology appears to be in its infancy. You can view and manipulate attributes through the COMAdmin components, but there's no support for .clb files in the current tools (to allow you to deploy your components with a 'preferred' configuration). Also, installation of components is applied using a mixed model, with the older information in type libraries and proxy-stubs, and registration information from DllRegisterServer(), as well as attributes from the catalog. However, the good news is that COM+ Applications are exported using the Windows Installer, which makes deployment of complete COM+ Applications far simpler and far more robust than before.

MTS Events

MTS 2.0 runs as part of the operating system, and it can run on NT when there is no user logged on. This means that when an error occurs it can't present a dialog on screen like most user applications. For a start, there may not be a user actually looking at the screen, or the error could occur in a Windows Station that isn't associated with the interactive user. Even if MTS did do this it wouldn't be desirable, since while a modal dialog is on screen it's blocking a thread, and unnecessarily blocked threads aren't good when it comes to scaleable applications.

When an error does occur, MTS will record the error in the NT Event Log. This is an NT service that has been built to be scaleable and reliable – many clients can report messages to the event log at the same time. NT provides the Event Viewer application to show the events that have been reported, and you can filter or sort these events depending on what sort of bug you are trying to trace. It's actually quite useful *not* to filter events, as you can compare events from various sources to trace a bug as it cascades from one application to another.

Furthermore, the Event Log can be accessed over RPC, so you can access the event logs on several machines, which is very useful for distributed applications.

MTS events are logged under the source of Transaction Server, and will be reported using one of seven categories:

Category ID	Category
1	SVC
2	Executive
3	Context Wrapper

Category ID	Category
4	Class Factory Wrapper
5	Executive Process
6	Catalog
7	Catalog

The events that can be reported are shown in the next table. I have given the event ID as shown in the event viewer – this is the low WORD of the actual event ID. The upper WORD gives the facility and the severity of the event. For all events except 4097 and 4098 the facility is FACILITY_DISPATCH (the other two are FACILITY_NULL).

The table gives the **format string** for the message – when the event is reported, the source can pass parameter strings which can be inserted into the format string (the API FormatMessage() is used to do this). In the table, the placeholders for these insert strings are indicated by %1, %2, etc.

Event ID	Severity	Event Format String
4097	Informational	Microsoft Transaction Server has started.
4098	Informational	Unexpected object reference count. The object still had references after the run-time environment released its last reference. %1
4097	Warning	An error occurred in your Microsoft Transaction Server component. %1
4098	Warning	Client is not authorized to make the call. %1
4100	Warning	DCOM was unable to provide a logical thread ID. Entering activity without acquiring a lock.
4101	Warning	An attempt was made to launch a server process for a package that was already actively supported by another server process on this computer. %1
4102	Warning	The version of MS DTC installed on this machine is incompatible with Microsoft Transaction Server. Please re-install MTS to upgrade to a compatible version of MS DTC. %1
4103	Warning	The run-time environment was unable to obtain the identity of the caller. An access error may be returned to the caller. %1
4097	Error	The run-time environment has detected an inconsistency in its internal state and has terminated the process. Please contact Microsoft Product Support Services to report this error. %1

Event ID	Severity	Event Format String
4098	Error	The run-time environment has detected the absence of a critical resource and has caused the process that hosted it to terminate. %1
4099	Error	The run-time environment was unable to initialize for transactions required to support transactional components. Make sure that MS DTC is running.%1
4100	Error	An attempt to access the registry failed. You might not have the necessary permissions, or the registry is corrupted. %1
4101	Error	The interface is too large. The limit on the number of methods for this interface has been exceeded. %1
4102	Error	Failed to initialize AspExec RESOURCE MANAGER. %1
4103	Error	Microsoft Transaction Server does not support this interface because it is a custom interface built with MIDL and has not been linked with the type info helper library. %1
4104	Error	An object call caused an exception. %1
4105	Error	Could not obtain a proxy/stub class factory for given interface. Proxy/stub is not registered correctly. %1
4106	Error	Failed to create a stub object for given interface. %1
4107	Error	No registry entry exists for given interface. %1
4108	Error	No type library registry entry exists for given interface. %1
4109	Error	Could not load the proxy/stub DLL for given interface. One possible cause is that the DLL does not exist. %1
4110	Error	QueryInterface failed during object activation due to an error in your component. This error caused the process to terminate. %1
4111	Error	Failed to allocate thread state. %1
4112	Error	Failed to write thread state. A possible cause is that your system might be low in resources. %1
4113	Error	IUnknown::QueryInterface failed on given object. %1
4114	Error	Failed to unbind on given interface. %1
4115	Error	Invalid stack size for given method. A possible cause is that the method has parameters of data types not supported by Microsoft Transaction Server. %1
4116	Error	Out of stack space for given method. %1

Event ID	Severity	Event Format String
4117	Error	Failed to clear out parameters for given method. There was a failure before or after the call was made to this object. A possible cause is that this method has parameters of data types not supported by Microsoft Transaction Server. %1
4118	Error	Call to invalid method. A component is trying to call a method that does not exist on this interface. %1
4119	Error	Failed to walk given interface. %1
4120	Error	The type library is registered, but could not be loaded. %1
4121	Error	No type information for this interface exists in the associated type library. A possible cause is that the type library is corrupted or out of date. %1
4122	Error	Invalid type library for this interface. A possible cause is that the type library is corrupted. %1
4123	Error	Invalid function description in the type library for this interface. A possible cause is that the type library is corrupted. %1
4124	Error	Invalid function parameter description in the type library for this interface. A possible cause is that the type library is corrupted. %1
4125	Error	Invalid parameter size in the type library for this interface. Possible causes are that the type library is corrupted or that your interface has methods that use parameters with data types not supported by Microsoft Transaction Server. %1
4126	Error	Invalid type library registry value for this interface. A possible cause is that the registry is corrupted. %1
4127	Error	A method on this interface has an unsupported data type. %1
4128	Error	The run-time environment was unable to load an application component due to either an error obtaining its properties from the catalog, loading the DLL, or getting the procedure address of DllGetClassObject. This error caused the process to terminate. %1
4129	Error	The run-time environment caught an exception during a call into your component. This error caused the process to terminate. %1
4130	Error	An error occurred during a run-time environment call to a COM API. This error caused the process to terminate. %1
4131	Error	A server process failed during initialization. The most common cause is an invalid command line, which may indicate an inconsistent or corrupted catalog. This error caused the process to terminate. %1

Event ID	Severity	Event Format String
4132	Error	Replication: Invalid machine name supplied for %1.
4133	Error	Interface is not supported by Microsoft Transaction Server. It does not have either a type library or a proxy stub. The object that implements it does not support IDispatch::GetTypeInfo, ITypeLib, or ITypeInfo: %1
4134	Error	Failed on creation from object context: %1
4135	Error	Failed on creation within a server process. %1
4136	Error	An application used an object context that is not currently active. %1
4137	Error	The run-time environment was unable to create a new UUID. This error caused the process to terminate. %1
4138	Error	An error occurred when starting a transaction for an object. References to that object and other related objects in its activity become obsolete. %1
4139	Error	An error occurred when communicating with the root of a transaction. References to the associated objects become obsolete. %1
4140	Error	A call that required the transaction to be imported failed because an error occurred when the run-time environment attempted to import a transaction into the process. %1
4141	Error	A call failed because of a transaction export error. %1
4142	Error	Your license to use Microsoft Transaction Server has expired. %
4143	Error	An attempt was made to create an object that would have resulted in components with different threading models running in the same activity within the same process. %1
4144	Error	A time-out occurred while waiting for a client's call to get exclusive access to an activity that was already in a call from another client. The call fails with CONTEXT_E_ACTIVITYTIMEOUT. %1
4145	Error	A call failed due to an activation error returned by the component. %1
4146	Error	Invalid component configuration. %1
4147	Error	Invalid component configuration. The transaction support for this component is invalid. %1
4148	Error	An object released more references to its object context than it had acquired. The extra release is ignored. %1

Event ID	Severity	Event Format String
4149	Error	The Shared Property Manager (SPM) requires a context for method level locking. Make sure that the component using SPM is a Transaction Server component. %1
4150	Error	Unable to obtain extended information about this interface. The interface may not have been generated using the -Oicf options in MIDL or the interface has methods with types (float or double) that are not currently supported for custom interfaces. %1
4151	Error	Your evaluation copy has expired. %1
4152	Error	The following registry path was expected to exist but is missing: %1
4153	Error	An exception occurred within a Resource Dispenser: %1
4154	Error	License Service failed or is unavailable, status code returned: %1
4155	Error	The package could not be started under the debugger because it is configured to run as a different identity. %1
4156	Error	Replication: Invalid datastore version on %1
4157	Error	Replication: Could not start administration SDK server
4158	Error	Replication: One or more remote components on source are set to run on destination
4159	Error	Replication: An error occurred while removing remote computers on destination
4160	Error	Replication: An error occurred while removing packages on destination
4161	Error	Replication: An error occurred while removing remote components on destination
4162	Error	Replication: An error occurred while replicating packages
4163	Error	Replication: An error occurred while replicating remote components
4164	Error	Replication: An error occurred while replicating local computer properties
4165	Error	Replication: Replication Share property not properly set on source machine
4166	Error	Replication: An error occured determining if Internet Information Server is installed on computer %1

Event ID	Severity	Event Format String
4167	Error	Replication: Internet Information Server Version 4.0 or greater is installed on computer %1. You must use the Internet Information Server replication utility to replicate catalogs to or from this computer.
4168	Error	Replication: Error %1 occured while installing a package on the destination computer.
4169	Error	Replication: Error %1 occured while exporting a package on the source computer.
4170	Error	Replication: Errors occured reading properties for computer %1
4171	Error	Replication: Both source and destination computers must be running Windows NT.
4172	Error	Replication: Internet Information Server Version 4.0 or greater is not installed on computer %1. Both computers must have Internet Information Server 4.0 or greater installed.
4173	Error	Replication: Destination machine name is the same as the source machine name!

Index

Symbols

.msi file
  COM+ Applications, 294
  COM+ catalog, 294
  Component Services, 294
  description, 294

.pak file
  packages, exporting, 139

/Oicf switch
  MIDL, 22
  MTS components, 47

[custom] attribute, 136

[dual] attribute, 17

[hidden] attribute
  ODL, 18

[oleautomation] attribute, 17

__MIDL_ProcFormatString table, 27
  FormatStringOffset() function, 27

__uuidof() function, 212

_Close() function
  performance monitor, 232, 246

_Collect() function
  performance monitor, 232, 242

_Open() function
  performance monitor, 232, 242

2-phase commit
  commit message, 178, 179
  distributed transactions, 176
  MS DTC, 164, 179
  Phase 0 enlistment objects, 297
  prepare message, 178, 179
  reasons for using, 178

A

Abort() method
  ITransaction interface, 175
  Session object, 118

Abort() methods
  CRM compensator, 274

Aborted() method
  ITransactionVoterNotifyAsync interface, 176

AbortRequest() method
  ITransactionResourceAsync interface, 179

AbortRequestDone() method
  ITransactionEnlistmentAsync interface, 179

access checks
  components, creating, 198
    CheckClient() method, 199
    QueryBlanket() method, 199
  interface level, 199
    ItfCheckAccess() method, 200
    ItfCheckClient() method, 200
    QueryInterface() method, 200
  method level, 200
    MethodCheckClient() method, 201

Access Control Lists
  see ACLs

access tokens
  CreateProcess() method, 207
  security, 207

accessor binding map
  accessor class, 115

accessor class
  accessor binding map, 115
  ATL OLE DB Consumer classes, 115
  Open() method, 117
  OpenDataSource() method, 117
  OpenRowset() method, 117

AccessPermissions
  AppIDs, 195
  component AppIDs lack these values, 217

AccountName property
  ISecurityIdentityColl interface, 265

ACID properties
  Atomicity, 53
  Consistency, 53
  Durability, 53
  Isolation, 53
  transactions, 53

ACLs
  AccessPermissions, 195
  LaunchPermissions, 195
  roles, 216

Activate() method
  initialization in, care with, 77
  IObjectControl interface, 51, 60, 76, 266

Index

Index

Index